PATERNOSTER BIBLICA

Living the Word, Resisting the World

The Life and Thought of Jacques Ellul

PATERNOSTER BIBLICAL AND THEOLOGICAL MONOGRAPHS

A full listing of all titles in this series appears at the close of this book.

Living the Word, Resisting the World

The Life and Thought of Jacques Ellul

Andrew Goddard

PASTERNOSTER PRESS

First published 2002 by Paternoster Press

Paternoster Press is an imprint of Authentic Media,
P.O. Box 300, Carlisle, Cumbria, CA3 0QS, U.K.
and
P.O. Box 1047, Waynesboro, GA 30830-2047 U.S.A.

08 07 06 05 04 03 02   7 6 5 4 3 2 1

British Library Cataloguing in Publication Data
A catalogue record for this book is available from the British Library

ISBN 1-84227-053-2

Typeset by the author
and printed and bound in Great Britain by
Nottingham Alpha Graphics

SERIES PREFACE

At the present time we are experiencing a veritable explosion in the field of biblical and theological research with more and more academic theses of high quality being produced by younger scholars from all over the world. One of the considerations taken into account by the examiners of doctoral theses is that, if they are to be worthy of the award of a degree, then they should contain material that needs to be read by other scholars; if so, it follows that the facilities must exist for them to be made accessible. In some cases (perhaps more often than is always realised) it will be most appropriate for the distinctive contribution of the thesis to be harvested in journal articles; in others there may be the possibility of a revision that will produce a book of wider appeal than simply to professional scholars. But many theses of outstanding quality can and should be published more or less as they stand for the benefit of other scholars and interested persons.

Hitherto it has not been easy for authors to find publishers willing to publish works that, while highly significant as works of scholarship, cannot be expected to become 'best-sellers' with a large circulation. Fortunately the development of printing technology now makes it relatively easy for publishers to produce specialist works without the commercial risks that would have prevented them doing so in the past.

The Paternoster Press is one of the first publishers to make use of this new technology. Its aim is quite simply to assist biblical and theological scholarship by the publication of theses and other monographs of high quality at affordable prices.

Different publishers serve different constituencies. The Paternoster Press stands in the tradition of evangelical Christianity and exists to serve that constituency, though not in any narrow way. What is offered, therefore, in this series, is the best of scholarship by evangelical Christians.

Since the inception of this series in 1997 the scope of the works published has broadened considerably. The opportunity is now being taken to initiate parallel series which will cater in a more focussed way for the history and theology of the evangelical movement and for other interests. Alongside this series we now have *Studies in Evangelical History and Thought* and *Studies in Baptist History and Thought*. This development will leave the present series with a sufficiently wide field in biblical studies and theology.

For Elisabeth,
Jonathan
and
Alianore

CONTENTS

CONCLUSION

Acknowledgments

This book originated over ten years ago when I started work on Jacques Ellul for my doctoral thesis. Since submission of that thesis to Oxford University in 1995 other responsibilities have prevented me fulfilling my wish to prepare it for publication and even now I have been unable to make as many revisions and improvements as I had hoped. Apart from supplying all quotations and references in English rather than the original French and updating some of the material, what follows is therefore not significantly different from the original thesis.

Through the years spent researching Ellul's life and thought, innumerable people have provided loving support, encouragement, guidance, and stimulation. The one person who has constantly and consistently provided all four has been my wife Elisabeth and so this volume is dedicated with love to her and to our two children, Jonathan and Alianore, who have lived with Ellul as part of our family all their lives. My wider family, especially my parents and parents-in-law, have also given me much, both materially and spiritually.

The original thesis was supervised by Professor Oliver O'Donovan. He was not only a prudent supervisor, stimulating tutor, and example of careful, Christian scholarship but assisted me greatly in beginning theological research after my initial PPE degree and has regularly provided wise advice, encouragement, inspiration and practical assistance in both personal and academic matters. My thanks go also to my examiners, Gabriel Vahanian and Tim Gorringe.

Extensive financial assistance enabled our family to survive during the research and helped fund my visit to the Ellul Archive at Wheaton College, Illinois. Support was provided by the Scottish Education Department, the Whitefield Institute, the Squire and Marriott Bursary Fund, the Harnborough Trust of St. John's College, Oxford, the Community of the Word of God, and Dr. Tony Spackman. The Whitefield Institute provided academic as well as financial support.

A graduate theologians' support group involving Sabina Alkire, Tony Cummins, Paula Gooder, Kendall Harmon, Bruce Hindmarsh, Moyer Hubbard, Sylvia Keesmaat, Rick Simpson and Nick Townsend – gave everything one could want from good academic friendships both individually and collectively: invigorating and informed discussion, entertainment, relaxation, and prayerful support and advice. The friendship of Brendan George and Sam Whittaker also sustained Elisabeth and me throughout the period of research as they regularly provided us with discussion/argument, humour, food, and drink.

As is obvious from the book's content, many people provided me with source materials and answered questions about Ellul. David Malone and others at Wheaton College's Special Collections were immensely helpful when I visited its Ellul Archive in late 1992. Christian Roy, Vernard Eller and Patrick Chastenet have also been most helpful correspondents. At an early stage in my research Sze Chi Chan kindly gave me access to material he had already collected in the course of his research and shared with me some of his own thinking and initial writing on Ellul. Dr. Herminio Martins of St. Antony's College, Oxford helped in a number of ways, not least by drawing my attention to Christian Roy's article on Ellul, Charbonneau, and French personalism which proved so valuable to my research. The staff at *Foi et Vie* kindly supplied me with all the back editions of the journal which contained articles by Ellul. Most of all, Joyce Hanks, the creator of the Wheaton Archive and author of the Ellul bibliographies has been of immeasurable assistance in my research, providing copies of articles, answering my numerous questions in frequent correspondence, and encouraging my work.

Since completion of the thesis the parishes of Cogges & South Leigh and the staff and students at Wycliffe Hall have provided stimulating contexts in which to continue learning and teaching. I am grateful to Paternoster for including this study in their excellent series and especially Jeremy Mudditt and Anthony Cross who have shown great patience and provided practical assistance as the thesis was prepared for publication.

Finally, I must thank Jacques Ellul himself. His life and thought have never been far from me for the last decade and will, I hope, continue to challenge and instruct me for many years to come. My sole personal contact with him, although it contributed little to the substance of the thesis, was one of the highlights of my research. I had written to him in early 1993 hoping to arrange a visit to Bordeaux but, presumably due to his regular ill health, I failed to get any reply. Then, in February 1994, I wrote to the Law Faculty at Bordeaux. Three weeks later, a *Faculté de Droit* envelope arrived containing a hand-written response. The letter began, 'La Faculté m'a transmis votre lettre...' and, to my amazement, my first question was answered with, '(1) les noms des Professeurs quand j'étais étudiant...' ! In that short letter, written just two months before his death, Ellul revealed that gracious, caring, humble, encouraging character about which those who knew him well often wrote. I thank God that, albeit so briefly, I too was able to encounter personally that Jacques Ellul and hope and pray that this study may in some way encourage more people to discover his work.

Preface

Sixty years ago, during the Second World War, Jacques Ellul, a young French Protestant academic forced by Nazi occupation to flee his home town of Bordeaux, set out for himself a plan of study and writing that was to occupy him for almost half a century. The life-work he there sketched in outline comprised a detailed analysis of the structure and novelty of the modern Western world and a corresponding series of biblical, theological, and ethical reflections on the Christian's calling. Passionate in his fulfilment of this dual quest to understand the world and to live out God's Word in resistance to it, Ellul became a prolific writer who, by the time of his death in May 1994, had written over fifty published volumes and around one thousand newspaper and journal articles.

Sadly, despite the breadth and depth of his work Ellul's writing has received little serious attention in the world of Christian theology. A number of features of his writing - its scope and frequently polemical style, its complexity, and its origins in the theological backwater of modern French Reformed theology - may shed some light (but cannot justify) such neglect. Ellul's work remains, in its scope and content, unique within modern Christian social and political thought and, as the Christian church enters a new century, his is a significant and prophetic twentieth century voice that needs to be heard.[1]

Part of Ellul's distinctive contribution lies in the fact that he produced both sociological and theological studies. Although in both spheres he clearly had his mentors (primarily Marx and Weber in sociology and Kierkegaard and Barth in theology) he also had an extensive and detailed knowledge in a wide range of scholarly disciplines and his appropriation of the work of these intellectual giants shows him to have been a highly original, insightful and controversial thinker. His theology and ethics are concrete and contextual as they dialogue with his distinctive sociological reflections on modern Western civilization. Long before Latin American liberation theologians sought to understand their socio-political world and how the revolutionary Christian gospel was to be expressed within it, Ellul was undertaking a comparable enterprise for the Christian church in the West and his work remains of great value today.

It would of course be false to suggest Ellul has been totally ignored and forgotten. Despite the failure of the wider Christian community to engage with

---

[1] The recent formation of the International Jacques Ellul Association (IJEA) may encourage much wider interest in Ellul and his work – www.ellul.org.

Ellul's thought, Joyce Main Hanks' invaluable bibliographical research has shown that a wider secondary literature discussing Ellul is already in existence.[2] This literature falls into two broad categories.

In a number of academic fields there exist scholars who are aware of Ellul's contributions to their speciality and who, to varying degrees, enter into fruitful dialogue with his work. These studies usually relate to his sociological rather than theological and ethical writings. The overwhelming majority are discussions in the growing literature on technology that focus quite narrowly on Ellul's study of Technique.[3] Such studies, by concentrating on particular aspects of Ellul's analysis and placing his work in dialogue with wider academic discourse on the subjects he addresses, often prove of great value in evaluating and developing features of Ellul's thought. Often, however, the authors have not read widely in Ellul's corpus and can misrepresent or misinterpret either that part of Ellul's thought which is their particular concern or his motivation and work as a whole. In particular, many writers appear to be acquainted with only one of the two strands of his work and to know little or nothing of the other strand or the relationship between them.

In addition to these works, there are also articles, unpublished theses, and a small number of books devoted to Ellul's work. Reflecting the scope of that work, these authors come from a range of academic disciplines - theologians, philosophers, and social scientists. Although this second category of writing tends to demonstrate a much better knowledge of Ellul than the first category of works, a number of weaknesses remain in much of this strand of the secondary literature. Many authors still appear to know only a relatively small fraction of Ellul's work which, given the interrelatedness of all his writing, can lead to minor or, on occasion, serious distortions in the presentation of his arguments.[4] In addition, even the most comprehensive study was usually rendered incomplete shortly after (if not before) its publication due to Ellul's extensive output.[5] A further problem is that Ellul always wrote in French.

---

[2] Hanks 1984a, 1991 & 1995. A single-volume bibliography of secondary material which unites these in a single volume to complement her comprehensive bibliography of Ellul's works (Hanks 2000) is forthcoming.

[3] Some of these studies are noted in chapter three while some of the works engaging with his writing on law, violence, the state, and politics are cited in chapters five to seven. One other area where Ellul's work has been significant in subsequent discussion is that of communication theory, especially through the writings of Clifford Christians.

[4] Bauman 1992a is a classic illustration of this as it critiques Ellul's political theology while seemingly unaware of his major sociological study of modern politics.

[5] Temple's excellent 1976 thesis notes the lack of discussion of *Ethique de la Liberté* and *Trahison de l'Occident*; Fasching's 'systematic exposition' adds a postscript recognising this difficulty (Fasching 1981, x). As yet, no major studies from Ellul have appeared posthumously although the manuscripts of both his *Ethics of Holiness* and his work on

Writers who rely on the English editions of his works are handicapped both by
the large number (and highly variable quality) of different translators and by
the fact that a significant amount of important material remains untranslated.
Much of that untranslated material is found in articles most of which were
unknown and not easily available until Joyce Hanks' investigations led to the
publication of her Ellul bibliographies and the creation of the Ellul Archive at
Wheaton College, Illinois.[6] Finally, nearly all these earlier studies treat Ellul's
thought largely abstracted from his life as a whole.

This study seeks to overcome some of these weaknesses and make a
contribution to this latter category of Ellul-specific studies. It will be able to
introduce some to Ellul for the first time while also offering a sympathetic
reading and new interpretation of his life and thought to those who already
know something about him. Its goal is to comprehend, expound and interpret
Ellul's work and show him to be someone who sought faithfully to live God's
word and to resist the powers of this world both through what he wrote and
what he did. Like Fasching, therefore, 'I do not so much attempt to stand
outside of Ellul's work and judge it as to get inside it and clarify it'.[7] In order
to achieve this end, I have drawn extensively on three main primary sources
and try in what follows to give a flavour of what is found in them through
letting Ellul speak for himself by regularly quoting his work, particularly
where it is not translated or hard to obtain. First and foremost, of course, there
are all Ellul's published books, especially the original French editions.[8] These
have then been supplemented by the mass of material found in articles by
Ellul and now referenced in Hanks' bibliography[9] and also by several

---

Theology and Technology may be published in the future.

[6] Only a very small fraction of Ellul's articles are listed in the bibliographies of even the
best and most recent studies e.g. Clendenin 1987 lists 34 (over half in English), Lovekin
1991 has 44, Dawn 1992 gives 48, and Chastenet 1992 includes only 19.

[7] Fasching 1981, ix. Although the pages which follow contain some dialogue with others
who have sought to understand and comment on Ellul, interaction with wider theological
and ethical discourse and with the scholarly discussions surrounding many of the issues
treated is minimal due to this focus on getting to grips with Ellul's own life and thought.

[8] For ease of reference all citations here are from English translations where they exist. All
quotations also appear in English (usually the published translation, occasionally a
corrected translation and, where no translation exists, my own translation) although
sometimes key French words and phrases in the original are noted. All books are
referenced in the texts and footnotes by means of a single word from (or an acronym of)
their title. A complete list of these abbreviations appears before (and refers the reader to)
the bibliography's fully cross-referenced listing of all Ellul's published books in French
and English.

[9] Due to the limits of space and the availability of Hanks' definitive and comprehensive
work (Hanks 2000), the bibliography here only includes those articles (about 350 in

significant unpublished pieces of writing by Ellul in the Wheaton Archive, particularly a number from the 1930s personalist movement.[10]

The book falls into two parts: a 'macro-analysis' of Ellul's life and work (Part One) followed by more specific 'micro-analyses' of subjects central to his social and political thought (Part Two). It takes this particular form because Ellul's writing on any specific subject, perhaps especially within his social and political thinking, can only be properly understood in the light of his life and thought as a whole while any global interpretation of Ellul must, in turn, be substantiated by more detailed analysis of his studies in particular areas.

Part One opens with a foundational first chapter that sets all Ellul's work in the context of his life. It shows his *oeuvre* was conceived, and must be read, as a whole with two distinct strands: an historical/sociological set of works and his various theological/ethical studies. In the most detailed account of Ellul's life yet available the great significance of the years of his further education (1928-38) are particularly highlighted. These are marked by his discovery of the major intellectual influences upon his later thought (Marx, Kierkegaard, and Barth), the beginnings of his Christian faith, the establishment of his life-long friendships with Jean Bosc and Bernard Charbonneau, and his legal training. In addition it is shown that the personalist groups of South-West France were decisive as they provided the original context for both Ellul's sociological analysis of the modern world and his life-long work for revolutionary change. Following an account of the war years and the political disillusionment engendered by his own brief political career in the immediate post-war period, the lengthy teaching and retirement years (1947-94) are examined thematically. Accounts of his academic career, church life, political and social activity, and work with young delinquents show Ellul to have been a critical Christian voice who, from the margins, was constantly and actively engaged in resisting many of the trends of the modern world and working for radical change.

This biography not only introduces Ellul as a person but enables later chapters, especially in Part Two, to demonstrate the close relation between Ellul's life and his thought and how an understanding of his life activities facilitates a clearer and more sympathetic interpretation of his writing.

The chapter's concluding section explains the origin and purpose of Ellul's corpus. Its important dialectical structure comprises historical/sociological

---

number) explicitly cited in the book, under half the total used in the research. All articles are referenced in the text and footnotes by the year of their publication and an identifying letter e.g. 1956a with full details in the bibliography of Articles by Jacques Ellul.

[10] An annotated bibliography of these unpublished works also appears at the end of the book.

studies of the world he sought to resist and theological/ethical works which explored how that resistance took shape in the form of living in obedience to God's Word. These two strands of Ellul's thought structure the remainder of Part One and each of the chapters in Part Two.

Chapter two presents an original interpretation of Ellul's theology and ethics in the face of both the difficulties in constructing an ordered account of Ellul's theology and the various 'interpretive keys' already offered in the literature. It presents a reading focused on the relationship between God and the world in terms of communion and rupture, opening with Ellul's doctrine of God in terms of four central affirmations: God is living, Wholly Other, love, and free. Ellul's doctrine of creation is expressed in terms of the world's communion with God as humans reflect God's four characteristics. This communion is, however, now ruptured (by 'the Fall') and the effects of this are expounded in a description of the world of ruptured communion which comprises three main elements (humans, their works, and the powers). This world, symbolised by the city, is characterised by four features that are the polar opposites of those displayed by God and the world in communion with him (i.e. death, unity/closure, Eros/power, and necessity). In response to this situation, God's eschatological goal for the world centres on a final judgment (viewed as a divine rupture of the world) and a new creation that is the recapitulation of human history and the renewal of communion between God and the world.

Within this wider theology, God's present historical relationship with the world of ruptured communion is viewed in terms of a dialectic of rupture and communion: man's rupture from God and God's quest for communion by means of his living, holy, and free Word of love. Man's rupture is fully overcome only by the incarnation of God's Word in Jesus Christ. Christ both reveals communion with God and assumes all the consequences of man's rupture from God thereby securing the ultimate triumph of God's quest for communion over man's rupture of that communion. Humans must now either re-enter communion with God through union with Christ or continue to ally themselves with the ruptured world and the rebellious powers in their continued opposition to God's goal of renewed communion. This theology shapes Ellul's account of the Christian's calling in the world (which takes the form of resistance to the fallen world because God's Word leads the believer to live a life of freedom, holiness, and love in communion with God) and determines his conception of the task and structure of any ethic for Christians.

Throughout the chapter, significant changes in Ellul's theology are noted, especially the shift away from the belief in his early writing in a divine order of preservation to guide social and political structures in the fallen world and his views of the powers. These, as Part Two shows, have important consequences for his theologies of law and the state.

Chapter Three turns to the other strand of Ellul's work and demonstrates the origins of Ellul's sociology in the personalist movement. A brief introduction to Ellul's sociological method stresses the importance of his training as an historian, his focus on the underlying forces that shape any society, and the centrality of dialectical process in his view of history. It shows that Ellul offers a 'global sociology' derived from reflection on his own lived experience (another sign of the importance of his biography) and a critical analysis of commonplaces and the sacred in our society.

The heart of the chapter is a new interpretation of Ellul's sociology which sets what is usually seen as its centre – his analysis of Technique - in the wider context of the development of his thought from the 1930s onwards. Through examining his early personalist manifesto and various post-war articles - all written prior to *La Technique* in 1954 - it is shown that Ellul's central and over-arching thesis is that the modern world is radically new and represents a crisis of civilization in which the dialectical forces necessary to create history are blocked by the dominance of Technique. By bringing these much neglected themes in Ellul's writing to the fore the proper context is set for an account of his conception of Technique, his claim that Technique is man's new milieu, and his emphasis on the fundamental incompatibility of Technique and civilization. As the more detailed case studies in Part Two subsequently demonstrate, the novelty of the modern world and the civilizational crisis this has provoked are foundational to Ellul's more specific sociological studies.

A short conclusion to Part One is provided by chapter four's discussion of the dialectical relationship between Ellul's sociology and his theology. Although Ellul's allegiance to revelation makes his theological account of the world of ruptured communion the overall context for his sociology, his theology does not determine his sociological conclusions about the modern world. These originate instead in the personalist movement and are the fruit of 'natural' and not 'revealed' knowledge. Ellul does, however, offer theological reflections upon his sociological conclusions as he interprets the modern world in terms of man's subjection to the powers and the predominance of the marks of the world of ruptured communion: death, integration/exclusion, Eros, and necessity. His theology of God's Word then leads him to interpret the late twentieth century as a time of God's silence while his emphasis on the importance of the Christian calling to live the Word means Christians bear a particular responsibility for the contemporary crisis of civilization because they have subverted God's revelation. The chapter also shows that a distinction is to be drawn between Ellul's permanent revolutionary ethic based on the Christian's unique calling to resist the world of ruptured communion on the basis of God's Word and his specific contemporary revolutionary goals which (as Part Two demonstrates more fully) take concrete shape largely from his sociological analysis and personalist beliefs.

Part One therefore concludes that in order to understand Ellul, each strand of his writing must be understood as having its own method, consistency, and integrity and that, although they are in dialogue with and influence each other, neither dominates the other nor determines the other's conclusions.

In Part Two, each chapter looks at a specific area of Ellul's thought, focussing on themes of importance in his juridical and political writings: violence (chapter five), law (chapter six), the state and politics (chapter seven). Reflecting the two strands of his work described in Part One, each chapter opens with an account of his sociological thinking before turning to examine his theological and ethical writings on the subject. The primary purpose remains an exposition and interpretation of Ellul's life and thought in these areas but three concerns predominate within this over-riding goal and explain the selection of these specific case-studies and their relationship to each other and the 'macro-analysis' of the preceding chapters.

First, in relation to Part One, these micro-readings test the macro-reading offered in the opening four chapters. They seek to show how an understanding of Ellul's life and the larger picture of his sociological and theological thought provided in the initial chapters sheds light on his treatment of specific subjects. A similar exercise could be undertaken on a wide range of issues within the Ellul corpus but these three studies are of particular importance and form a coherent whole. The subject of violence is an interesting test case because Ellul's book on this subject is one of his best-known works and yet it initially appears that it is not integrated into his writing or thought as a whole. The subject of law is, of course, Ellul's area of primary academic expertise but his significant writing on this subject has received little serious attention until now. The twin subjects of the state and political activity are another area where Ellul's stance – advocacy of a form of anarchism – is well known but often misunderstood because his writing in this area is divorced from his life and work as a whole.

Second, in relation to Ellul's sociology, these three subjects are of great importance. Given his analysis of the crisis of civilisation in the modern Western world, the central political question we face is one of whether and how the structure and direction of society can be changed. Two standard lines of response are common when faced with this question. One is to seek a violent overthrow of the current system, the other is to seek to use the existing system of law and the established political institutions and processes to effect change. The sociological sections of each chapter in this second part will therefore seek to offer an account of Ellul's analysis of each phenomenon in the contemporary world and its place in his wider assessment of the crisis of civilisation and the proper revolutionary response to this crisis.

Third, in relation to Ellul's theology, in each of these three areas Ellul stands as a critic of the mainstream Western Christian tradition of legal and political thought. That tradition has privileged law and established political authority as divinely established means for the ordering of society and the pursuit of the common good. It has further argued that certain forms of coercion are legitimate in relation to these institutions and these ends. Part of these chapters is therefore an attempt to understand the structure of Ellul's theological and ethical writings on these subjects in order that a constructive dialogue (here more implicit than explicit) may occur between Ellul and this strand of the Christian tradition of political thought. In addition, in relation to both law and the state, significant developments can be traced in Ellul's own thinking. These are given particular attention as they both reflect some of the tensions and changes in his wider theology and highlight important theological issues in the construction of a contemporary Christian response to legal and political institutions and processes.

Turning to each chapter individually, the account of Ellul's thought on violence offered in chapter five demonstrates its coherence with the interpretation of his thought as a whole while explaining why his sociological work on violence is less integrated into his overall thought than his sociological writing on other subjects. It shows that his 'laws of violence' are a sociological and not a theological account and that, although less prominent, Ellul does offer reflections upon the distinctive features of violence in the modern world. Turning to his theological writing, after outlining Ellul's account and critique of traditional theological approaches to violence it is shown that, in the light of his wider theology (and contrary to the claims of some critics) there is coherence within his own distinctive theology and ethics of violence whose 'dualist' structure and recognition that Christians will use violence also both arise from the basic structure of his theology and ethics.

Chapter six turns to the area of Ellul's academic expertise to examine his much neglected (but extensive and largely untranslated) writing on law. It does so in the light of his admission that he frequently changed his views on this subject. Setting his sociology of law within the context of the jurisprudential school of sociological positivism it proposes two distinct periods in this strand of his writing. The first (1935-60) focuses on the evolution of human law and the effect of juridical technique. Here Ellul's primary concern is that technique and the state need to be restrained so that law is firmly rooted within social life and is truly a 'living law'. The second period (1960-94) develops an elaborate sociology of law comprising an account of law's creation and evolution, applicability, and specificity. It also presents an analysis of the novelty of law in the modern world in which he argues that law has been transformed into administration and regulation by the state and that this is central to the wider crisis of civilization the world is now facing.

Ellul's developing theology of law and his juridical ethic proves even more complex despite the basic continuities of a consistent contrast between divine and human justice and a rejection of natural law. By focussing on Ellul's changing view of law's theological foundation and his different assessments of the significance of Old Testament Law, four phases in his theology of law are distinguished. Initially, human law is founded on conscience and the Torah understood as a juridical phenomenon (1939). Then, in his book on the subject (1946), an elaborate Christological foundation is proposed and the Law is viewed as non-juridical. For two decades following this book (1947-67) much of its argument is maintained although the Old Testament is now viewed as offering a juridical system valuable to Christian reflection on law. Then, in the final phase of writing (1971-94), Ellul refuses a theological foundation for human law and reverts to a non-juridical interpretation of Torah, stressing the opposition between law and grace. The chapter concludes by suggesting possible reasons for these significant changes in Ellul's theological thinking about law.

In the light of all that has gone before, the final study turns to Ellul's thinking on the state and politics and his advocacy of anarchy in the modern world. Clarifying Ellul's distinction between 'state' and 'politics', his sociology of the state is analysed to show that, although the rise of the state is seen as a long-standing historical phenomenon, its modern technological, bureaucratic, and totalitarian form is qualitatively different from the state in the past. Following a survey of his remarkably insightful writings on modern politics as autonomous, impotent, and ultimately a demonic illusion, the development of Ellul's anarchist beliefs are sketched from their origins in the 1930s and the characteristic features of the 'anarchy' he proposes for the contemporary world are examined.

Ellul's theology of the state is shown to develop from early and more positive accounts (which view the state primarily as part of the divine order of preservation for the world) through a period of greater ambivalence until, finally, he proposes a strong correlation between the state and the rebellious powers. By relating this increasingly negative account of the state to his unpublished theology of authority, the implications for the Christian's relationship to political power and the structure of political authority are discussed, leading into a study of Ellul's conception of the Christian's distinctive role in political life. Finally, the relationship Ellul envisages between anarchy and Christianity is elucidated.

In conclusion, a brief assessment is offered of the significance of Ellul's life and thought for the church at the start of a new century as it seeks to understand and often resist a complex and confusing world and to discern what it means to faithfully live God's Word.

PART ONE

A GLOBAL READING OF

ELLUL'S LIFE AND THOUGHT

CHAPTER 1

Introduction to Jacques Ellul's Life and Work

In order to understand either Ellul's thought as a whole or his thinking on any specific subject it is first necessary to step back from isolated comments or particular publications and gain a clearer and wider perspective on the man and his work as a whole. His thought must, in other words, be set in the context of a panoramic view of his life and his complete corpus. This opening chapter therefore seeks to provide such an overview by presenting a detailed biography and then a briefer account of the origins, structure, content, and purposes of his literary *oeuvre*.

Biography of Jacques Ellul (1912-94)

The casual reader of Jacques Ellul's books will, unfortunately, find out little about his life from his writing. Of even greater concern is that publishers' information about their author often makes wide-ranging and disturbing errors. [1] Fortunately, considerable biographical detail is now available from a number of sources. There are now three books based on interviews with Ellul that contain much information about his life. His friend William Vanderburg published *Perspectives on our Age* in 1981 based on a number of interviews for the Canadian Broadcasting Corporation and in the same year a series of

---

[1] A selection of English and French editions misinform readers concerning his education (he was not professor of History and Contemporary Sociology at Bordeaux from 1938 as claimed in the Vintage paperback edition of his best-selling work, *The Technological Society*), his Christian faith (he is not a Catholic layman although described as such on the back of the same book), his family (he has not, despite the claim of *L'Illusion Politique*, fathered seven children), his home (he has not lived in Bordeaux since 1941), his political career (he did not 'serve with distinction as Mayor of Bordeaux', *Apocalypse*), and the nature of his work (he frequently disclaims being a philosopher although several books describe him as one).

interviews given to Madeleine Garrigou-Lagrange appeared as *A temps et à contretemps* (ET 1982 *In Season, Out of Season*). Shortly after his death in 1994 his Bordeaux colleague Patrick Chastenet published *Entretiens avec Jacques Ellul* (ET 1998 *Jacques Ellul on Religion, Technology and Politics*) that contains even more biographical detail and a short biographical introduction by Chastenet. These, in addition to occasional comments in Ellul's other books, some articles and newspaper interviews, enable a reasonably accurate account to be given of his life although, as will become clear, Ellul's memory is not always consistent or accurate. Ellul himself completed a two-volume memoir that may yet be published.

Any significant thinker is understood better when their thought is set in the context of their life but with Ellul it could be said that his writing will never be properly understood unless one knows something of his life story. Ellul's life and his thought are intricately interwoven. He wrote out of what he lived and he lived out what he wrote. In the terms of his own theology, it is his life as a whole that constitutes his true oeuvre and his words can take their true value and be properly understood only when they are read as *his* words in unity with *his* person.[2] It is, therefore, essential to understand the man himself before one begins to try to understand his thought.

Many writers on Ellul acknowledge the importance of his biography but few give more than the sketchiest account of his life.[3] In particular, little attention has been paid to the crucial formative years prior to Ellul's publications, especially the 1930s and his participation in the personalist movement.[4]

This chapter attempts to fill this major gap in the literature on Ellul by offering the most comprehensive account to date of his life. The important years preceding Ellul's full-time teaching at Bordeaux University are divided chronologically into four periods: his childhood and early education (1912-29), his further education (1929-38), the war years (1939-44) and the political years (1944-47). After this, chronological division is of little value and so his

---

[2] On these themes in his writing see *Ethique* II, 56-70; *Faith*, 167ff; *Humiliation*.

[3] Exceptions are Holland 1986; Lovekin 1991; Wennemann 1991b. The best short account is Hanks 2000:xi-xiii. Wren 1977:31-57 attempts to set Ellul's life in the context of twentieth century France but, despite recognising the significance of the 1930s, gives little detail about Ellul himself and attempts to use his general history to produce an astonishingly inaccurate picture of Ellul's motivations in writing. For a recent scholarly study of this period of French history see Agulhon 1993.

[4] Wren 1977, Holland 1986 & Wennemann 1991b:49-51 note the importance of this period but it is only the recent work of Chastenet 1992, 1994b, 1999 & 2000 which comes close to seeing its true significance. Dawn 1992 recognises the importance of the early Ellul but only examines a few of his immediate post-war writings.

teaching and retirement years (1947-94) are treated thematically.

Childhood and Early Education (1912-29)

Jacques César Ellul was born in Bordeaux on January 6, 1912 to Joseph and Martha Ellul. Both of his parents were comparatively old (his mother thirty-three and his father around forty) and Jacques was to be their only child.

The family experiences of both his parents were of initial wealth followed by poverty. Joseph was an Austrian subject whose father (an Italian ship owner based in Trieste) had such a strong sense of honour that, when faced with the shame of going bankrupt in the late 1890s, he committed suicide. He left his widow, a descendant of the Serbian Obrenoviche dynasty, to live the rest of her life as a mourning recluse. On his arrival in Bordeaux in 1902, Joseph, although 'he always felt more Italian than anything else' (*Conversations*, 37), registered as British as he could claim British nationality because his father had been born in Malta. In Bordeaux Joseph Ellul met Martha Mendès, daughter of a French Protestant mother and a Portuguese Catholic father, probably of Jewish descent. Despite her family's earlier wealth, she was at the time struggling to provide for her widowed mother and two sick sisters by giving drawing and painting lessons. They married in 1907.

Ellul could therefore say, 'I owe my existence to an encounter between a Portuguese woman and an Austrian which took place in Bordeaux' (*Conversations*, 35) and this unusual hybrid heritage was to be of significance. Whether in attempting to understand his dislike of nationalism or his constant involvement on the margins of society it is important to recall that

> Through my parents, I am a specimen of what people call a *métèque* [a derogatory term for a dark-skinned foreigner akin to 'wog'], a product of the melting pot (*un cosmopolite*) (*Season*, 4-5).

Inevitably, both parents shaped the character of their son. Ellul's father was quite distant, reflecting in part his aristocratic background and values. A fluent speaker of five languages, he placed great emphasis on honour even though it cost him and his family dearly. He had come to Bordeaux through his work with Louis Eschenauer, the wine merchant, but lost his position after demanding a public apology from his employer after being insulted by him. This pattern was then repeated in Ellul's infancy when he was again made redundant during the war after he publicly denounced the firm where he was working as chief accountant for sending rotten food to soldiers. The bankruptcy of another employer in 1922 and a year's unemployment after the 1929 crash meant that 'little by little he slipped down the social ladder' (*Conversations*, 37) and that throughout Ellul's childhood 'poverty was a part of everyday life' (*Season*, 8).

In later life, Ellul often emphasized his father's importance in shaping his life and character, even speaking of him as 'my role model' (*Conversations*, 92). In one of his final public addresses, at the end of a 1993 conference in his honour, Ellul explained the imperatives that drove him and in so doing paid public tribute to his father.

> There was the value derived from my father and realized through a rigorous education: that is, honour. For him, an agnostic, honour was the code of his whole life. But does one still know what that is? Honour, this passé aspiration I was raised with, included four rules: never lie to others, never lie to yourself, be merciful toward the weak, and never yield to the mighty (*être inflexible devant les puissants*) (1994b).[5]

Ellul's mother was much closer to her son than his sometimes distant father. She earned essential extra income for the family through painting portraits and teaching art. In addition to engendering Ellul's own passion for art[6] she also passed on her love of poetry to her young son.

> Mother, who adored poetry, always guided me towards the better poets. From the age of six or seven I have had a taste for poetry. Poetry is the art form which pleases me the most and in which I find deep meaning (*Conversations*, 49).[7]

Reflecting on these features of his parents and his childhood home, Ellul recalled, 'I lived in this universe of honour and art that today would be labelled a fantasy world' (*Season*, 8).

Only towards the end of his life did Ellul speak or write much about his childhood, which, in the light of conversations with him, Chastenet sums up as 'studious, poor, but happy' (*Conversations*, 2). The importance of the period is clear, however, from an illuminating passage in his last sociological study. There Ellul describes the world of his childhood in some detail concluding,

> In writing these memories…I want to say one very simple thing which is that in the harshness of those times (which I knew better than most of those who

---

[5] The original French is found in 1994a and Chastenet 1994d: 357-9.

[6] Although not obvious from his translated works (apart from *Conversations*, chapter fifteen) Ellul wrote a considerable amount on the subject of art. In addition to his book *L'Empire* see especially 1966a; 1979l; 1980i & 1980l.

[7] Two volumes of Ellul's poetry (*Silences, Oratorio*) have been published posthumously.

paint a bleak picture), there was more individual independence, less marginalisation, less deviance (not less delinquency), less administrative policing, less social control than today...We were at the turning point between traditional society and modern society (*Déviances*, 67).[8]

Ellul's first memory is, given his later thinking on violence and war, an intriguing one.

It must have been in 1914 when I was two and a half. I was playing in the park, the Jardin Public, and I remember being drawn towards the sound of music, military music, when I saw some soldiers coming towards us carrying rifles and my mother saying to me: 'Look at them they are soldiers going off to the war'. Then I don't really know what got hold of me but I went over to a flower-bed, picked a small bunch of flowers, and took it over to one of the soldiers and said: 'Here soldier this is for you'. I remember that he then took me in his arms and kissed me. I was extremely moved by that procession. Naturally at that age I had no idea what war was but I did understand that something extremely serious was going on (*Conversations*, 43).[9]

Soldiers and fighting continued to be important to the young Ellul as he made and painted lead soldiers in uniform (a collection he kept throughout his life, according to *Conversations*, 48), formed a self-defence pact with two other small boys who were also bullied in school, and later engaged in inter-school battles in the Jardin Public. The Jardin Public near his home was one of his favourite haunts along with the Bordeaux quays and the marshland north-east of Bordeaux where he used to roam with his closest friend, Pierre Farbos.

His enjoyment of such freedom even within a city such as Bordeaux did not, however, distract him from his studies where in his early schooling he was regularly top of his class. Later, the disappointing experience of a new class in which he was no longer the brightest student combined with being an only child and his parents' poverty to make him become more of a loner devoted to his study. By his mid-teens he was 'a typical good student, a real intellectual machine' (*Season*, 23) and 'at sixteen I was a little brute interested in absolutely no-one except my friend Farbos and I was an absolute glutton for work. Work and books were my passion' (*Conversations*, 48). His particular passion was history but his favourite subjects also included French, Latin, Greek and recitation and he excelled also in German. Mathematics was one of his few weaknesses.

---

[8] Further details of this pattern of life are also now given in *Conversations*, chapter four.

[9] See also *Conversations*, 93.

Among another of Ellul's early interests was the Bible, one of relatively few books in the house – 'I began reading the Bible at the age of seven or eight. It was a book that I found fascinating' (*Conversations*, 51). This interest was not, however, something actively encouraged by his parents and his childhood was generally marked by a lack of any religious formation – 'there was not a Christian atmosphere, a Christian upbringing, nor even reference to Christian morality in my home' (*Season*, 13).

This was because his father, although Greek Orthodox by upbringing, was in practice a Voltarian sceptic and critical of all religion. His mother, in contrast, was a Protestant and 'a deeply religious Christian' (*Perspectives*, 2) but she refrained from sharing her faith in any active way with her son.

> My mother...held her husband in enormous esteem. She never taught me how to pray, she never tried to influence me in religious matters because she had promised her husband that she wouldn't. Simply I would see her kneeling down to pray each evening. I used to ask her what she was doing and she would reply that she was praying. Nothing more. She had made my father a promise and she was sufficiently honest to keep it...This is most extraordinary when you consider that she was a woman driven by such faith and yet she had managed to keep her word, without flinching for so long. She never attended services, she never went to see the minister. She conducted her faith alone (*Conversations*, 40-1).

In reading the Bible Ellul found that 'many things interested me - even, I would say, seduced me' (*Perspectives*, 13) and, although attracted more by the Old Testament stories and prophets than the New Testament, it was from the gospels that, aged about ten, he had the memorable experience of a sentence ('I will make you fishers of men') which leaped out at him and continued to haunt him for years (*Season*, 3-4). This private interest in the Bible, although it received little encouragement from others and was partly motivated by his historical interest, was clearly of great significance as 'whenever I had got my work out of the way before dinner I would sit down and read a passage of the Bible for the sheer pleasure of it' (*Conversations*, 52). Unsurprisingly, Ellul's reading produced many questions in his young mind but he found neither his mother nor her pastor were able to provide him with answers and a period of catechism around 1926/7 was totally uninteresting apart from a text in Pascal's *Pensées*.[10] Faced with this inability

---

[10] Here, as elsewhere, there are disparities in Ellul's accounts. At *Season*, 13 he speaks of a year of catechism aged fourteen but he later refers to a three-month period when he was fifteen (1984a, 16). On the failure to receive answers see 1980l, 11 (aged fifteen or sixteen) and *Conversations*, 51-2.

of others to explain or to encourage his interest, a pattern was set for his later theological writing in which his own often highly original and illuminating reading of the Bible would be so central.

> I said to myself: 'You're going to have to manage on your own. Grown-ups simply don't understand anything'. This episode pretty well illustrates how I would read the Bible later on (*Conversations*, 51).

At this stage, however, Ellul would not have described himself as a Christian. His personal faith, which was to become so central to who he was, finds its origins, like so much of significance in his life, in his experiences after he left school. On receiving his baccalaureate and leaving Bordeaux's Lycée Michel-Montaigne Ellul's future was set more by his parents than his own choice.[11] Ellul had hoped that on leaving school he would begin a career at sea and become a naval officer but about the age of fifteen his father had informed him that he would study law and 'when my father said something there was no arguing. I was pretty furious but there was nothing I could do' (*Conversations*, 45). He was then offered a well-paid job in a family firm by a member of Bordeaux high society but, despite their difficult financial circumstances, his mother emphatically rejected the offer, insisting that 'my son is far too gifted to go into trade' (*Conversations*, 47). Ellul therefore began as a student in the law faculty at Bordeaux University and his life-forming experiences in this next decade of his life were to shape him decisively as a person and set him on his life's work of writing and activity.

The Years of Further Education (1929-38)

STUDENT OF LAW

Although Ellul was originally forced by his father to abandon his naval ambitions and instead to study law he not only complied but immediately determined to take his legal training seriously and pursue it to 'the bitter end' (*Conversations*, 46). It was, however, unclear what this would mean in practice. Although he passed exams easily he had no desire to become a judge, was a poor speaker, and lacked the money to start a private legal practice. Through his training his primary passion remained historical.

> I liked history. Even in high school, nothing excited me so much as history. I was a historian because I liked it, because I was impassioned by it (*Season*,

---

[11] It remains unclear whether Ellul left for university in 1928 (the date Ellul gave) or 1929 (as Chastenet now believes, *Conversations*, 2 cf. *Entretiens*, 10).

20-1).

As a result, although he found many subjects of little interest, there was one exception and this led him down an academic path rather than into the legal profession.

> I had always had a passion for History. I was good at Latin. I was bored stiff by Civil Law. I wasn't interested in Constitutional law and I didn't find Political Economics very exciting at least the way it was taught to us then. So this left me with Roman law. One advantage was that it plunged me back into Antiquity, into the atmosphere of Rome that I'd always liked and the other advantage was that I completely fell for the logical rigour of the construction of Roman law...Roman law was a core subject which was taught from first year and I managed to win the first prize in the end of year competition. In second year I did the same thing...(*Conversations*, 71, 72).

Ellul's academic success led him, after gaining a number of qualifications,[12] to complete his doctorate in 1936 after a short break for obligatory military service (in 1934-5) from which Ellul was eventually released on health grounds.[13] His doctoral thesis studied the origins and development of the ancient Roman legal institution of mancipium, which (ironically given Ellul's personal history) permitted a father to sell his son.[14]

The final hurdle Ellul then faced to reach 'the bitter end' in his legal studies was the *agrégation*, a national bi-annual academic competitive exam to gain access to the top university teaching posts in a discipline. Ellul entered this in 1937 but, like most candidates, failed to be awarded it on the first attempt. Following this near miss he left Bordeaux, being appointed for a year as senior lecturer in Montpellier and then, in 1938, he took a post as assistant lecturer and director of studies at Strasbourg University.

For some university students such a simple academic curriculum vitae is all that need be said of their years of further education in order to understand their later career. With Ellul, almost the opposite is the case. Compared with other events in his life during these years, his formal academic study was of little significance in the shaping of this young scholar.

---

[12] Ellul obtained his *licence en droit* in 1931 and his *licence libre en lettres* in 1932 (*Temps*, 207 cf. *Season*, 234) and proceeded to gain post-graduate diplomas in political economy and in public law (*Conversations*, 72).

[13] For Ellul's account of this experience see *Conversations*, 48.

[14] The thesis was entitled 'Etude sur l'évolution et la nature juridique du Mancipium'. On this institution see brief summary at *Conversations*, 72 and fuller account in *Institutions* 2:252f, 384f.

THE BIRTH AND GROWTH OF CHRISTIAN FAITH

Toward the end of his life, when asked about the most significant experience in his life, Ellul gave priority to 'when God came to me' (*Conversations*, 93). There is no doubt that, after years of reading the Bible, his first real encounter with God was to change his life totally. Ellul himself was always highly critical of those who publicized their own conversion accounts and in interviews he preferred to keep details of his conversion to a minimum, simply describing it as a violent experience and one which led to a long period of struggling with God (*Season*, 14). Towards the end of his life, however, he spoke more fully about what happened to Patrick Chastenet.

> It was overwhelming I would even say violent. It happened during the summer holidays. I was staying with friends in Blanquefort not far from Bordeaux. I must have been seventeen at the time as I had just taken my final exams at school. I was alone in the house busy translating Faust when suddenly, and I have not doubts on this at all, I knew myself to be in the presence of a something so astounding, so overwhelming that entered me to the very centre of my being. That's all I can tell you. I was so moved that I left the room in a stunned state. In the courtyard there was a bicycle lying around. I jumped on it and fled. I have no idea whatsoever how many dozens of kilometers I must have covered. Afterwards I thought to myself 'You have been in the presence of God'. And there you are (*Conversations*, 52).

The immediate effect of this conversion was not to lead Ellul into being a positive, faithful and uncritical Christian disciple. On the contrary,

> I very quickly realized that I was experiencing a conversion and that indeed I should put it to the test to see if it held strong or not. So I set about reading antichristian writers. By the time I was eighteen I had read Celsus, Holbach and also Marx whom I'd come across earlier. My faith did not budge. It was for real (*Conversations*, 52).[15]

Although Ellul's faith was for real it was also a struggling faith and Ellul even spoke of himself as fleeing from God in the years following this existential encounter. Ellul's conversion was then in one sense sudden but it was not short and simple. It was a lengthy and painful process. In 1972 Ellul wrote to Ronald Ray that the struggle lasted five or six years and that after he first experienced the presence of God he did not truly believe in Christ and

---

[15] A similar account appears in 1982c, 15 and *L'Homme*, 87n.

continued to doubt and to refuse God's will.[16] Later he expressed it even more
strongly.

> And then [after the catechism] there was an event in my life that could be
> called a conversion and that I don't wish to relate...I will mention just two
> things on this subject. First, it was as violent as the most violent conversion
> you have heard of; second, I started to run for my life from the One who had
> revealed himself to me. It wasn't the kind of positive conversion that pushes
> you to read the Bible or go to church. It was the opposite. No, not exactly
> the opposite; I realized God had spoken, but I didn't want him to have me. I
> fled. This struggle lasted for ten years...An issue between God and me. I
> didn't talk about it with anyone. You might say I wanted to remain master of
> my life, and I had the impression that in giving in to this pressure from God
> I would no longer be the boss (*Season*, 14).[17]

Highlighting a concern which remained central throughout his life, Ellul
explained that this 'negative' effect after his initial violent conversion was in
part because 'I hadn't understood...that faith can bring extraordinary freedom.
For me Christianity was a sort of orthodoxy, a moral constraint and not at all a
sort of liberation' (*Conversations*, 53). Nevertheless, he continued to keep
reading the Bible - 'I reread some things in the Bible, especially the beginning
of John. I was very impressed, and continued to look in the Bible over the
next few years' (1984a, 17). His direct sense of God's presence in his
conversion experience and the failure of other influences such as Karl Marx to
address existential questions continued to be significant and then 'through the
Bible I was led to receive a word which was not invented or created by my
intelligence and yet which I recognized as being the truth. From that, my
conception of the world and of humanity was totally different' (1980l, 11).

In particular, in what he described as 'a second stage in my conversion...an
awesome experience for me' (*Season*, 15), God spoke to him through the
eighth chapter of Paul's letter to the Romans. In 1980, in a short meditation
reflecting on this chapter and entitled 'How I Discovered Hope' Ellul
described this experience and its impact.

> I realize now that Romans 8, without my knowing it, has inspired all the

---

[16] Ray 1973:iv, n2.

[17] The powerful 1938 article 'Amour de soi' (1938a) is often highly personal and may well
reflect the recent resolution of Ellul's long period of spiritual wrestling. Gill says that by
1938 Ellul 'chose decisively for Christianity' (Gill 1984b:19, the source of this quotation
from Ellul is not given). The fact Ellul's first biblical study was on Jonah arises out of his
own long struggle with God (*Season*, 216).

research I've done for the last fifty years. Reading the eighth chapter of Paul's Letter to the Romans was a watershed in my life. In fact, it was such a totally decisive experience that it became one of the steps in my conversion. And for the first time in my life, a biblical text really became God's Word to me. I had often read the Bible. I had found it to be of great religious and intellectual interest. I had discovered admirable poetic texts. I'd found historical knowledge – and subjects worthy of reflection. I'd even found – in the Gospels, for example – some elements to nourish my young faith. But until that decisive, watershed experience I'd never been seized by a written text. Never before had a text so suddenly transformed itself into Absolute Truth, truth beyond debate, truth like a blinding light. I can't even describe what happened then. Nor do I think it could possibly be explained psychologically. But this eighth chapter of Romans, which I'd already read many times, suddenly became many things for me. It became the answer to so many of the questions I'd been asking. It became the place where I simultaneously encountered the Absolute and Eternity. It became a living contemporary Word, which I could no longer question, which was beyond all discussion. And that Word then became the point of departure for all my reflections in the faith (1980e, 28).[18]

Much of this struggle appears to have been kept private and personal but, in a moving account, Ellul describes how he broke the news to his mother who had faithfully kept her promise to her husband not to teach her faith to their son.

> One day, I must have been eighteen or nineteen, I had been reading the Bible quite a lot, had become passionate about it and believed in Jesus Christ, I went to find her in the kitchen and said to her: 'Do you know something, Mother? I believe in Jesus Christ and I have converted'. She replied without even turning round that she was not at all surprised and that she had been praying each night for that to happen ever since I was born (*Conversations*, 40-1).

Although the main elements of Ellul's coming to faith in Christ – a sudden conversion, a period of struggle, and the centrality of the Bible – are now fairly well established its time frame remains rather uncertain. Ellul's memory concerning dates is not always accurate and this has caused much confusion. In one of his earliest statements about this decisive event he implied a date of

---

[18] Reference is also made to this significant experience in 1984a, 17 and probably the account in 1980l, 11 ('One day, in a very explosive manner, it was revealed to me, very simply, through a text of the Bible, that if God is not then nothing is. I received it as a certainty which has never been moved') refers to this as well.

1934 by claiming that 'around twenty-two years of age, I was also reading the Bible, and it happened that I was converted – with a certain "brutality" !' (1970c). Later, however, he explained that 'I became a Christian and I was obliged to profess myself a Christian in 1932' (*Perspectives*, 14). In fact, it would now appear that his initial encounter with God described above in conversation with Chastenet happened on August 10th 1930 and that throughout the 1930s Ellul, even as he continued to experience a strong sense of personal struggle with God, grew in faith and become a publicly professing disciple of Christ.[19]

Following Ellul's public profession, it soon became clear that his spiritual home would be among the minority Protestant community although he apparently showed a brief interest in the Roman Catholic Church in 1932-3 (*Perspectives*, 16).[20] This was because, like Calvin's *Institutes* which he read at this time, the Protestants seemed most faithful to Scripture.[21] Of particular importance to him was the Protestant student body, *La Fédération française des associations chrétiennes d'étudiants* and a group of students who regularly went camping in what Ellul mischievously described as a 'Protestant anti-scout movement' (*Conversations*, 62). Speaking in the 1980s at a conference of the more evangelical GBU student Christian group, Ellul spoke of the importance of this group.

> I think that groups of schoolchildren or students in a Faculty who witness to their faith in small meetings are something fundamental. I think this way because it was in one such group of students – the Fédé – that I truly

---

[19] See *Conversations*, 59n1. Early discussions of Ellul's conversion tended to give dates of either 1932 (e.g. Hanks, T. 1985:26) or 1934 (e.g. Mitcham & Mackey 1971:104). Lovekin gives 1934 as the date of a second conversion, while Gill safely asserts that Ellul was converted 'by 1934' (Gill 1984c:19). The first sign these dates were inaccurate came when Ellul placed his conversion between his catechism class (c.1926) and his discovery of Karl Marx (c.1930) and dated the 'second stage' experience through Romans 8 to 'around age twenty-two' (c. 1934) (*Season*, 13-4). In his 1972 letter to Ray, Ellul claimed he first experienced the presence of God when he was approximately twenty years old (Ray 1973:iv, n2) while Roy 1992:70 claims, without citing his source, that Ellul became a Christian aged sixteen (i.e. 1928). Charbonneau's comments that 'in our youth, the essential thing for him was his conversion to the Christian faith about which he remained reserved' (Charbonneau 1994:19) also supports a date earlier than 1932 or 1934 given their close friendship from early in their student days.

[20] Larkin 1997:19 claims there were less than one million baptized Protestants in France in the 1930s, about 2.5% of the population.

[21] *Season*, 16; *Conversations*, 41; 1980l, 11. For a brief history of French Protestantism see Encrevé 1993b.

grasped (*j'ai pris conscience*) what faith was all about.[22]

Around 1935, Ellul met the National Secretary of the Fédé, Jean Bosc. Bosc was to become a great life-long friend and his theological mentor. In his 1993 address in which he acknowledged the importance of his father, Ellul also spoke of Bosc's friendship and witness to the Christian faith.

> Not that I was converted to Christian faith by his testimony, but after my conversion, he showed me what the Christian intellectual can be and taught me the meaning of theology (1994b).[23]

Even before meeting Bosc, Ellul was already well versed in theology, having read widely among both Protestant and Catholic theologians. He found himself in sympathy with Augustine and Calvin but although he read Aquinas, Duns Scotus and other medieval theologians, he found little to attract him to their more philosophical theology. In addition, initiating a policy he continued in all his academic work, he also read the most stringent critics of his new-found faith in order to test its credibility.[24]

Of all the Christian writers Ellul read in his student days, two were to prove life-long companions and guides. Early in the 1930s he discovered and fell in love with the work of the nineteenth century Danish Lutheran Søren Kierkegaard.

> I was captivated by Kierkegaard because what he said went straight to my soul. Quite abruptly I realized that reasoning with the intellect alone and reasoning based on living experience are simply worlds apart. My passion for Kierkegaard began at that time and has remained with me through the rest of my life (*Conversations*, 54).

In the course of his life, Ellul read all Kierkegaard's work (*L'Homme*, 23) and claimed to have found little with which he disagreed (*Si*, 13).[25]

---

[22] Unpublished GBU Conference. See also 1984a, 17.

[23] Note that inexplicably the name given here is Jacques Boso. The original French (1994a) clearly refers to Jean Bosc.

[24] *Conversations*, 52. The seeds of Ellul's later interest in Islam (cf. 1985a) also stem from this period when he read the Koran (1980l). He worked on a major book on Islam that was advertised as 'Propos sur l'Islam' in *Genèse*.

[25] This re-discovery of Kierkegaard was a common feature of the French intellectual world of the 1930s (Loubet del Bayle 1969:25). Ellul's own views of Kierkegaard are most fully discussed in 1963c; 1979j; 1984a, 17-8 and *L'Homme*, 24-6. The major discussions of Kierkegaard's influence on Ellul's own thinking are Eller 1971 & 1981 and Blanc 1990. Villaneix 1974 represents an interpretation of Kierkegaard with which Ellul would be

Subsequently, after discovering Kierkegaard, Ellul was introduced by Jean Bosc to Karl Barth, himself much influenced by Kierkegaard. Bosc, who was to be a leading figure in the Barthian challenge which revived French Protestantism from the 1930s onwards, suggested Ellul read Barth's *The Word of God and the Word of Man*.[26] On discovering Barth's dialectical theology, Ellul's initial attraction to Calvin diminished.

> Barth...became the second great element in my intellectual life, completely effacing Calvin. Obviously, once I began reading Karl Barth, I stopped being a Calvinist...(*Perspectives*, 17).[27]

Although Ellul took care to say 'I have never been an unconditional "Barthian"' (*Freedom*, 8) he was quite clear that Barth was 'the greatest theologian of the twentieth century' (*Conférence*, 23) and it appears that he read *Church Dogmatics* in German prior to its French translation.[28] Barth himself would later show an interest in Ellul's early writings, holding a discussion on his book on law[29] and apparently a query from Barth about what Ellul meant by 'la technique' in *Presence*, encouraged him to write his most famous work, *La Technique*.[30]

From early days, Ellul's Christian faith and theological studies bore fruit in social and political engagements. In 1984 he was adamant that 'since 1935 I have stated incessantly that the church should express itself politically' (*Subversion*, 127) and in his 1960s study critiquing much contemporary Christian political activity he recalled

> A certain Protestant intellectual, today one of the staunch supporters of the

---

sympathetic.

[26] On Bosc see Fouilloux 1993 and for Ellul's relationship with him *Season*, chapter two; *Déviances*, 156-7; 1969f & g; 1971c; 1979e and 1984a, 17. Ellul writes of 'le choc barthien' (1979m, 117) in a stagnant church and refers to 'le règne barthien' in the Fédé from 1930 to 1960 (1981d). On Barth's influence on the French church, especially through Maury (who edited *Foi et Vie* throughout the 1930s), see 1978d; Bolle 1982; Reymond 1985.

[27] This apparent acceptance that he was once a Calvinist is contradicted by his later emphatic assertion that he was never a Calvinist but always more influenced by Luther and Kierkegaard (*Conversations*, 49).

[28] Footnote references at *Vouloir*, 173 are to the German edition. Ellul writes concerning the translation of Church Dogmatics into French at 1952b and discusses his debt to Barth in 1978d. The best discussions of their relationship are Bromiley 1981 and Holland 1986 (who shows Ellul's closer affinity to the earlier, more Kierkegaardian, Barth).

[29] Busch 1976:388.

[30] Mitcham 1985b:1, n2.

Church's political involvement, said to me in April, 1938: 'I don't understand your interest in politics. How can that possibly change the essential human situation? God's action is independent of the political contingencies...' (*False*, 165).[31]

KARL MARX AND RADICAL POLITICAL ACTIVISM

In order to understand Ellul's political commitments in this period it is necessary to return to the context in which he began his university studies and to his relationship with two more great thinkers who would shape his later sociological analyses as much as Barth and Kierkegaard moulded his theology – Karl Marx and Bernard Charbonneau.

Ellul was, in reality, not a full-time university student in the early years of his study because his parents' financial situation required him to work. From the age of about fifteen, he had been teaching Latin, Greek, German and French to ten year olds for three or four hours daily. Ellul's need to combine this work with his own academic study.[32] This forced him into a careful regulation of his time which was the source of his own personal drive for efficiency, the quest he so roundly condemns in his later works but which in part enabled him to become so prolific a writer and active in so many different walks of life.[33]

These financial pressures on Ellul increased significantly when, in 1929, his father again lost his job and the family had to rely for their income solely on Ellul's teaching and his mother's drawing lessons. This had an enormous impact on Ellul both personally and politically.

> I learned what unemployment is with no assistance, with no hope whatsoever, with no help from anywhere. I learned what it is to be sick with no government medical care and no money to pay the doctor or the druggist. I remember my father spending his days looking for work. Given his abilities, I felt that it was an absolutely stupefying, incredible injustice that a man like him was unemployed; that he had to go from company to company, and factory to factory, looking for any job at all and getting turned down everywhere. And it was an injustice that I did not understand (*Perspectives*, 5).

---

[31] Ellul claimed that a 1936 article 'Christianisme et Révolution' already contained the seeds of his later writing in *Presence* (*Ethique* III, 175).

[32] Explaining his activities during his student days, Ellul explained, 'I divided my time between attending classes, reading and working to keep myself. I used to give private classes every evening for a couple of hours' (*Conversations*, 56).

[33] On Ellul's efficiency and commitment to writing see Joyce Hanks' preface in *Marx*, xi and his own remarks in *Conversations*, 29-30, 87.

Contemporaneous with this experience, during his second year at university, Ellul was introduced to the writing of Karl Marx by his political economy professor, Joseph Benzacar. As a result, he borrowed the first French edition of *Le Capital* from the library. Even half a century later, Ellul vividly portrayed the powerful revelation experienced when reading this work.[34]

> When I came by chance upon *Das Kapital*, I had the sudden impression of a connection...I discovered a global interpretation of the world, the explanation for this drama of misery and decadence that we had experienced. The excellence of Marx's thinking, in the domain of economic theory, convinced me (*Season*, 4, 11).

> All at once I felt as if I had discovered something totally unexpected and totally stupefying, precisely because it related directly to my practical experience...I felt I understood everything. I felt that at last I knew why my father was out of work, at last I knew why we were destitute...Marx was an astonishing discovery of the reality of this world...I plunged into Marx's thinking with an incredible joy: I had finally found *the* explanation...I discovered in Marx the possibility of understanding what was going on. I felt I had a deeper insight into the things I was being taught at the Faculty of Law...(*Perspectives*, 4-6).

Marx was to prove a life-long influence on Ellul who confessed, 'I owe much of my intellectual development to him' (*Conversations*, 26). He was the only author other than Kierkegaard of whom Ellul would claim that he had read all his works (*Conversations*, 55) and from the immediate post-war period he regularly taught courses (among the first in French universities) on Marx and later Marxist thought.[35] His own sociological writings are strongly influenced by Marx's method making it is no co-incidence that what he called for in his important 1947 article was a new Karl Marx (*Sources*, chapter two) while his theological writings regularly discuss, often quite polemically, Christian responses to Marx and Marxism.[36] Even at this early stage Ellul

---

[34] The vivid excitement represented here needs to be placed alongside the frank confession, 'I tried reading *Capital* first and of course I had to give up. But then I read *German Ideology* and that really got to me' (*Conversations*, 55).

[35] See section three of the bibliography of unpublished works for further details.

[36] References to Marx and interaction with him are found in numerous works but see especially *Autopsy, Marx, Révolution, Changer, Institutions* 5; 1981b & r. The fullest and best account of the relationship between Ellul's thought and that of Marx is Menninger 1981a. Much less sympathetic and at times seriously inaccurate are Berthoud 1982 and

realized that although Marx provided him with great assistance in his quest for insight concerning economic, social and political matters he 'didn't answer the questions of my life' (1984a, 17) as there were existential questions of life and death and love where Marx did not help (*Perspectives*, 14).

As throughout his life, Ellul's intellectual discoveries did not remain theoretical but were put into practice in his life. Partly because he was convinced by much of Marx's analysis and partly out of his tendency to side with the minority,[37] Ellul became involved with the radical political left in the turbulent French and international politics of the 1930s.[38] However, he never became an unconditional Marxist. This was partly because of his Christian faith, partly due to his sympathy with writers such as Proudhon whom he first read about this time but particularly because of the influence of Charbonneau and the personalist movement.[39]

His initial contacts with the socialist *Section Française de l'Internationale Ouvrière* (SFIO) proved a disappointment to Ellul as did those with the communists he met (*Anarchy*, 2). His initial attraction to communism because of its cynicism and its refusal of justification led him, at one time, to place great hopes in it (1958c) but he found party members were only interested in party dogma and conflict and not Marx's thought.

When I made contact with communists in the Party – in 1932…I found people totally preoccupied with petty tactical thingamabobs, the infiltration of this or that union etc. When I tried to discuss with them, in depth, the thought of Marx, I realized that that didn't interest them much (1982c, 14).[40]

Ellul therefore remained on the fringes of the communist party and wider movement, never becoming a member himself (despite the claims by some)

Bauman 1992a. Bauman's review of Jesus and Marx (Bauman 1988) provoked one of Ellul's most scathing and vitriolic pieces in response (1989b).

[37] Ellul claimed to have been one of only three students in the Law Faculty who were on the left (1966c, 94). See *Conversations*, 55, 57.

[38] On France in the 1930s see Berstein 1988, Agulhon 1993:214-61 and Weber 1995. Recent wider histories shedding light on this period and providing illuminating accounts of the context of Ellul's thought are Mazower 1999 and Brendon 2000.

[39] Ellul appears to have become well versed in anarchist writers such as Bakunin, Proudhon and Kropotkin towards the end of the decade although he confessed, 'intellectually, the anarchists have not impressed me' (*Conversations*, 87).

[40] That Ellul's strong anti-capitalist views were not limited to academic discussions of Marx is shown by the fact that around this time he apparently considered the impact of bombing the Paris Bourse (*Anarchie*, 15). Note the ET (*Anarchy*, 11) mistranslates 'vers vingt ans' as 'about twenty years ago' thus dating the event to the late 1960s rather than the early 1930s.

and becoming increasingly disillusioned. From his early contacts he was concerned by and opposed the hostile attitude of German communists to the Social Democrats in the face of rising popular support for the Nazis.[41] He completely broke with the communists during the Moscow Show Trials by which time he was already widely read in Marx and Marxist writers and an admirer of Bukharin who was condemned as a traitor by the Soviet regime. This split proved decisive in his attitude to communism and explains Ellul's common polemic against French intellectuals who continued to support the Communist Party until the 1950s and 1960s. He was convinced that, 'anyone who was willing could see already in 1935 and 1936 what would be denounced twenty years later' (*Anarchy*, 2).

Ellul was passionately involved in the anti-Fascist movement (*L'Homme*, 116-7), claiming 'I did belong to every single antifascist movement I could find' (*Conversations*, 107). This commitment was particularly galvanized by the right-wing riots of February 6, 1934 that helped bring down the elected government. Through opposition to groups such as the *Croix de Feu* Ellul became involved in conflicts with the police and 'came to abhor not so much the capitalist system as the state' (*Anarchy*, 1-2). In 'a period of very intense political involvement' (*Perspectives*, 18) he was no stranger to political violence, being grateful that his best friend among the student lawyers 'was an extremely good boxer, so after 1934 when the serious fighting began he became my bodyguard' (*Conversations*, 57).[42]

Having resisted the far right Ellul had great hopes for the Popular Front that united communists, socialists, and radicals and took power in 1936. He was, however, soon disillusioned.[43] His later writing often refers to the hope of real revolution at this time. In 1953, for example, writing on the strikes of August of that year, he commented

> It is probable that we have never been so close to a revolutionary current of opinion since 1936. But this current of opinion seems very different from that at the start of 1936. Then it was full of hope, we were moving towards solutions, and proletarian opinion was 'positive'. Today it is rather a reaction of despair...(1953g).

---

[41] Ellul himself visited Germany during this period in 1934 and 1935 and even attended a Nazi rally out of curiosity (*Conversations*, 63).

[42] Ellul often refers to Feb 6, 1934 (e.g. *Hope*, 279-80). On this period and these events see Weber 1995, chapter five who notes that thirty seven died on February 6, 9, and 12 and that between mid Feb 1934 and early May 1936 there were 1,063 riotous assemblies, processions or demonstrations, most organised by the Left.

[43] Chastenet 1999:65 claims Ellul voted for the Popular Front in the elections of 1936 although he notes that Ellul also claimed never to have voted (*Conversations*, 82).

In 1981, in contrast, he used the experience of 1936 to challenge those who were hailing the election of a socialist government under Mitterand as a fundamental change in French politics and society (1981l).[44]

France's political struggles in this decade were always set within and influenced by the wider international context and Ellul's political concerns therefore inevitably spread beyond France. As early as 1934 Ellul was among the first to discern the potential conflict brewing in Algeria and became actively involved in attempts to raise public awareness of the need for a negotiated settlement (1970j, 201). He also viewed the lack of international response to Italy's invasion of Ethiopia in 1935 as highly significant (*Violence*, 7). This, like the February riots of the previous year, was an incident to which he returned in later life when commenting on international events whether in Poland in relation to Solidarity (1982e) or even more starkly in his strong response to the overthrow of Allende in Chile.

> I have often written during the cold war era that one need not fear a generalized conflict. I now say, very simply, for the first time, and without being able to offer proofs or demonstrations, that now with the Chilean coup, the developing process of world war has begun. When I head the news I was seized with the same fear which I remember perfectly well having at the moment of the Ethiopian war in 1935. That seemed to me to be exceptionally serious. It could appear simply a colonial war or a war to enhance Italian prestige but for me it was the start of escalation and I believe I was right. The Ethiopian war was much more important on the stage of world politics than the Spanish War. It was the first true victory of fascism not only over a small country but over world opinion which simply let it be and did not react. The Ethiopian war was the test of the passivity which from them on would leave fascist policies alone and let them develop (1973b).

An important domestic repercussion of the Ethiopian conflict was the widespread right-wing popular student demonstrations against Professor Gaston Jèze who defended Ethiopia in The Hague. Here, as so often in his life, Ellul found himself in a small minority but stood his ground.

> Jèze...provoked an incredible mobilization of extreme right-wing students in all the law schools throughout France...In the turmoil I can still see myself grabbing demonstrators by their jacket lapels out of the fray and asking them 'But do you have the faintest idea who Jèze is?'. They had no idea but kept on shouting 'Jèze must go!'. For me that was quite a revelation

---

[44] For brief accounts of The Popular Front see Berstein 1988:103-54 and Larkin 1997.

into the base mentality of the masses. In the end there were only three of us left standing against these baying hounds…(*Conversations*, 58).

One of the others left standing was 'a girl who looked as if she may be Dutch and who was trying to curb the demonstrators' (*Conversations*, 58). She was Yvette Lensvelt, a former nurse turned law student and Ellul invited her to join one of their camping expeditions. There, despite her earlier rejection of her Catholic upbringing and embracing of Nietzsche's thought, she began reading the Bible with him and 'thanks to the Bible we became close' (*Conversations*, 59). On July 31st 1937, they married and, until she died of cancer of the pancreas on April 16th 1991, she would be a major but highly private influence on Ellul's life and thought. By drawing Ellul out from his books she 'helped me learn to live'…She also taught me to listen…' (*Conversations*, 93) and was particularly important in the preparation of his biblical studies and his attitude to politics and power.[45]

Among Yvette's earliest influences was her involvement in leading Ellul to play a brief part (until late 1937) in a final significant political event of the 1930s, the Spanish Civil War. Through her, Ellul had contact with Spanish anarchists and he sought to supply them with arms for their struggle. Although he himself did not go and fight in Spain (largely because of his relationship with Yvette) he later confessed that 'I think it was the one time in my life that I was sufficiently motivated to commit an act of violence' (*Conversations*, 68). Through his links with anarchists, and particularly his knowledge of their massacre by the communists, Ellul's political outlook moved still further from any sympathy with Soviet communism to a more anarchist-inclined Proudhonian socialism (*Anarchy*, 2).[46]

As Europe drifted into war, Ellul's stance led to much confusion and criticism. Despite his vehement anti-fascist views he was a pacifist in the 1930s who favoured disarmament (*False*, 173-4). On the grounds of a politically realist stance that it was either too late or too soon to enter into war with Germany he also supported the Munich agreement (*Conversations*, 39). However, in 1937 he denounced the film 'All Quiet on the Western Front' because he believed its pacifist message would actually deter people from the necessary struggle to prevent war and so lead them to accept it when it came (*Humiliation*, 129).

---

[45] In interviews, particularly later in life and after her death, Ellul would place great emphasis on Yvette's influence on him (*Season*, 31-2, 189, 193, 216-7, 226; *Conversations*, 1, 80ff, 93ff). See also 1988a and his dedication of *Reason*.

[46] Ellul often refers to his experience with the Spanish anarchists (e.g. 1981c, 166; 1983i, 194) and his comment that 'the Spanish are the most courageous and least realist people that I know…' (1950h) perhaps reflects his experience of this time.

Even more controversially, Ellul often highlighted the continuity between developments in capitalist, liberal democratic states and those in Fascist and Nazi regimes. His stance and its rationale would recur throughout his later life. In 1939 he wrote, 'I do not enjoy playing the role of the perpetual protestor or little prophet tucked away in his corner' and over fifty years later he was reminded of these words and recalled his approach

> Within the Protestant community I was classified exactly like that. Even at that stage they saw that I had a protestant side – in the worst sense of the word: the perpetual protestor – on the other hand they were also beginning to refer to me as a 'prophet', I refused to be considered as such…What I wanted to fight against was that good conscience which enabled democracies to state: 'We are right'. I believed that we should indeed fight dictatorships but also always be mindful that our very own democracies contain their own dose of dictatorship …It is a fact that I am unable to say that on one side there is Good and the other Evil. I simply can't do that (*Conversations*, 107, 108).

CHARBONNEAU AND THE PERSONALIST MOVEMENT

To understand why Ellul was so critical of Western democracies and to set these political stances in their proper context and show how wrong it would be to portray him as simply a left-wing Marxist or communist, it is necessary to return to the beginning of the decade and another great influence on his life - his relationship with Bernard Charbonneau.[47] This led to the most significant of all Ellul's theological and political commitments in these years of further education, his involvement in the personalist movement.

According to Ellul, it was at school that he first met Bernard Charbonneau although it was after they met again in their first year at university (apparently through a meeting of the Fédé) that their friendship was cemented when Charbonneau invited Ellul to camp with him in the Pyrenees.[48] Charbonneau

---

[47] Charbonneau (b. November 28, 1910 in Bordeaux, d. April 28, 1996) would in later life work alongside Ellul in many enterprises. His own studies of the modern world have much in common with Ellul's work and merit much higher regard in the wider academic community. His writing on theological and ethical matters, such as his critiques of de Chardin and *Je Fus* (his important study on freedom) also show the closeness of their thinking. He never became as well known as Ellul, many of his writings even failing to gain a publisher until recent years. For an introduction to his thought see Ellul's own assessment (1985c), Cérézuelle 1994 and especially Prades 1997, proceedings of a 1996 conference held in Charbonneau's honour.

[48] As with other events in this period, there remains confusion about the origins and dates of their friendship. Ellul claims that they met when at *lycée* (*Season*, 25; *Conversations*, 55), apparently when Ellul was around 14 (1984a, 17) and Cérézuelle 1994 dates their first

was studying history not law (he went on to pass his *agrégation* in history and geography) and was an agnostic rather than a Christian but Ellul was captivated by him, his knowledge of political and social structures, and his critical and original thinking.

> I was bedazzled to find myself with someone who was ten times more cultivated than myself, who could talk about loads of writers I'd never even heard of...Charbonneau taught me how to think and how to be a free spirit...Among other things he taught me, a confirmed city-dweller, to love nature and the countryside...For years he was my intellectual master. He was the one who told me what to read and influenced my views on society. Make no mistake about it he was the captain and I was an excellent first-mate (*Conversations*, 56).[49]

In particular, Charbonneau was already developing Marx's thought into what Ellul viewed as an even deeper critique of society and so, around 1934, Ellul became convinced that Technique and not capital was the dominant factor in the modern world.

> I was strongly influenced by Marx when I was young and the question for me was 'if Marx was writing now (that it to say, at the moment when I was asking that question, about 1934) would he bring all his analysis to bear on the problem of capital and its accumulation? Would there not be another more important question in his eyes?'. Together with one or two friends, we thought that the central question was the development of *la technique* and that it was necessary to undertake an analysis of the technical phenomenon (*phénomène technicien*) as Marx had attempted to analyse capital (1981g).

Charbonneau was undoubtedly the most important of these 'one or two friends' but both he and Ellul were part of a wider Bordeaux-based group that formed a distinctive element within the nascent French personalist movement. This was the primary context in which Ellul's social and political views

---

meeting to 1927. However, other evidence (*Season*, 29; Roy 1992:72) suggests they perhaps did not become close until around 1930, which appears to be Charbonneau's own recollection of when they first met (Chastenet 1999:60).

[49] Ellul discusses his relationship with Charbonneau in *Season*, chapter two, *Conversations*, chapters five and six, and 1994b. Charbonneau's own reflections after Ellul's death (Charbonneau 1994) offer a fuller and fascinating account of their friendship. Ellul reviewed a number of Charbonneau's books (1952c; 1974m; 1980b) and offers one of relatively few accounts of Charbonneau's thought in 1985c. Their relationship is most fully discussed in Hanks 2001 (part of an edition of The Ellul Forum on the two men), Roy 1992, Cérézuelle 1994 & 1996 and various writings of Chastenet.

developed in this period and where he began his lifelong work of drawing on both his Christian faith and anarcho-socialist beliefs to attempt to bring about a fundamental personal, social, economic, political, and spiritual revolution in the modern world.

Until Christian Roy's groundbreaking 1992 study,[50] Ellul's claims to have been, along with Charbonneau, a leader among the original founders of the French personalist movement seemed greatly exaggerated.[51] Now, however, it is clear that Ellul and Charbonneau were leaders of a personalist movement in South-western France which, though related to the national groups of *Esprit* and (less directly) *Ordre Nouveau (ON)*, was distinct in both its organisation and its outlook.[52]

From about 1930, Ellul and Charbonneau had begun to form small groups with other students in the southwest of France. Their groups sought (often in the context of austere hiking and camping trips) to examine how, by focussing on the idea of the human person, it might be possible to draw on central ideas of Western civilization (nature, freedom, democracy, etc.) to understand and respond to the fundamental changes that they perceived were occurring.

Ellul and Charbonneau heard of Mounier's plans for *Esprit* (the movement was set up in August 1932 and the journal of that name first appeared in October 1932) from one of his friends at Bordeaux. In the first half of 1933 they visited Paris and met with *Esprit* members. They found *Esprit* shared many of the concerns and criticisms of the modern world which had been expressed in their own groups in the Southwest and that, faced with the choice between whether to follow Hitler, Stalin or America, they too wished to find another way.[53] After the February 1934 riots, Ellul attended his first public *Esprit* meeting and around the same time Charbonneau helped to found an official Bordeaux *Esprit* group in which Ellul played an active role.

---

[50] Roy 1992. I am grateful to Dr. Christian Roy for his assistance in providing me with further details and material and to Dr Herminio Martins of St Antony's College, Oxford who first drew my attention to this article.

[51] Despite Ellul's strong claims (e.g. *Perspectives*, 18-9, *Season*, chapter three, 1970c) to have helped found Esprit alongside Mounier, almost all the major studies of Mounier, Esprit and the 1930s personalists (e.g. Guissard 1962; Loubet del Bayle 1969; Domenach 1972; de Senarclens 1974; Kelly 1979; Collot-Guyer 1983) contain no mention of either Ellul or Charbonneau. Winock 1975:169 simply notes their presence as delegates at an Esprit conference.

[52] Charbonneau offers his own brief account of this in Charbonneau 1994:19-21 and Ellul gives much more detail in *Conversations*, especially chapter six. In addition to Roy 1992 (and his wider 'revisionist' reading of French personalism in Roy 1995), this movement and Ellul's role in it is now most fully acknowledged and documented in Chastenet's work and Loubet del Bayle 1994 & 2001.

[53] *L'Homme*, 80; 1982c, 12.

Despite their common sympathies, Ellul and Charbonneau both had doubts about *Esprit*. Ellul was tempted to keep a critical distance because of his contacts with *Ordre Nouveau*, a separate personalist grouping under the leadership of men like Alexandre Marc, Denis de Rougemont, Robert Aron and Arnaud Dandieu.[54] The differences between *ON* and *Esprit* were not insignificant. Although neither was explicitly confessional, *Esprit* was more Catholic and *ON* more Protestant in its constituency.[55] In addition, *ON* attracted Ellul because of its greater interest in the impact of Technique on the individual and society, its anti-statist political outlook, and its obvious desire for concrete revolutionary action. Ellul, who claimed to have been a federalist since 1930 (1949c), was inevitably attracted by the fact that 'Ordre Nouveau showed itself resolute in the dismantling of the nation-state, a fatal melting-pot of massification, in order to replace it by a federal network of local communities inspired by Proudhon and syndicalism'.[56]

Nevertheless, Ellul and Charbonneau were ultimately drawn more towards *Esprit* because of its greater emphasis upon the communal nature of the personalist movement. Their own experience had convinced them that all existing models of political movements had to be rejected and new forms of small, local communities created.

> To carry out revolutionary activities, we must leave behind all the existing models…We thought it was necessary to carry out both a personal and a collective transformation and that this could only take place in a community setting, that of small groups capable of locally inventing their organization and tactics (*Season*, 38).

Based around the journals of the two organisations, the writings of their leaders, and their own locally produced journal, Ellul and Charbonneau continued to encourage such small groups throughout the southwest of France.[57] It was in this context that Ellul began to study and write on many of

---

[54] *Ordre Nouveau*'s ideas appear in Aron & Dandieu 1993. First published in 1933 this work is listed in the bibliography of *TS* and cited often in *Autopsy*. Loubet del Bayle 1969 offers the fullest study of these and other groups of the period.

[55] Ellul mentions this confessional difference as perhaps significant at *Conversations*, 66. De Rougement had also founded *Hic et Nunc* in November 1932, a Barthian journal which encouraged the re-discovery of Luther and Kierkegaard (Bolle 1982).

[56] Roy 1992:75. On the inter-relation of federalism and personalism see Kinsky 1979.

[57] There were about eighty members in the southwest including Bordeaux (about twenty members), Pau (for an account of this group see Eggly n.d.) and Bayonne (where Charbonneau was based from 1936). As *Esprit* itself never had more than one thousand subscribers they were, in Chastenet's phrase with which Ellul concurred and which sums up much of Ellul's life, 'in a minority in a minority movement' (*Conversations*, 65).

the themes that dominate his later work - law, federalism, anarchism, the city, the press, money, progress, totalitarianism, commonplaces and Technique. The central beliefs of these groups were that all the varied social, economic and political structures of the modern world (whether of right or left) marked a radical break with the past and were totalitarian and destructive of the human person. A purely political revolution could, they held, not alter this. A more radical revolution, both personal and collective, was required. Beginning in their personalist groups this required the creation of new social forms and institutions based on the freedom of the human person and genuine spiritual rather than purely materialist values.[58]

Ellul and Charbonneau hoped to encourage *Esprit* to create revolutionary personalist groups similar to their own across France. These groups (*Amis d'Esprit*) had their own separate monthly internal bulletin and reports from them appeared on a regular basis in editions of the main *Esprit* journal.[59] The lack of support from the Paris-based leadership for their vision of how this project should develop produced tensions that contributed to their final break with the movement during 1937-8. These strains were present since at least Mounier's February 1935 visit to the Bordeaux group after which he wrote in his notebook,

---

[58] For more details see Roy 1992 and chapter three below.

[59] The Bordeaux group appears first in the June 1934 edition of the journal (*Esprit* Year 2, No 21, pp518-9). In September 1934 the Bordeaux Correspondant is named as Jean Imberti (for Ellul's dismissive views on his role see *Conversations*, 64) and in their December report Charbonneau is named as link (3/27, p535) with a full report of the group appearing in January 1935 (3/28, p700). After a brief mention in March (3/30, p1020), the group's 28 Feb meeting with Mounier and their future plans are reported in April (3/31, p158) and another edition of their local bulletin announced in July (3/34, p661). At the close of 1935 Charbonneau's departure for Bayonne is announced and Jean Gouin replaces him as Bordeaux link (for Ellul's comments see *Conversations*, 66). Charbonneau's mark on the group is clear in the plans for a three day Christmas camp in the Pyrenees (3/35, p502) ! A paper entitled 'Le personnalisme révolution immédiate' is announced in Feb 1936 (4/41, p846, the paper was by Ellul although this is not noted, see part 1 of the bibliography of unpublished material). No more appears until the announcement in Feb 1937 that the group is going to press with a public manifesto and action plan (5/53, p860). Around this time Ellul takes over as official Esprit Correspondant and his one and only publication in the journal appeared in February (1937). In April 1937 (5/5, p216) in a general report on the groups around France the 'extraordinary vitality' of the groups in the South-West is highlighted and a Bordeaux member's account of their experience of community at one of the camps in the Pyrenees is quoted. Mounier's report on the 1937 congress (5/60, pp689-96) refers both to the Bordeaux group's analytic work (694) and Charbonneau's work on education (published in November 1937, 6/62, pp198-228). Ellul is still listed as Bordeaux link in early 1938 but by the middle of the year there is no longer a Bordeaux group listed.

This little handful of Protestants round Charbonneau who share visions of
revolution and disorder in the language of small town gossip and parochial
ideas. Somewhat Jansenist, though solid, peasant-like, hard-working (they
pass around a journal that they have cyclo-styled themselves). They have
more or less sworn themselves to celibacy to be better able to carry out the
spiritual revolution: all rather boyish but very ardent.[60]

This clear divergence in views increased with time and by the first annual
congress of *Amis d'Esprit* (26-27 September 1936), Ellul and Charbonneau
were clearly fairly isolated within the movement. Reflecting the tone of his
notebook entry, in 1937 Mounier called Charbonneau (in a letter he destroyed
in anger) 'a bad-tempered little schoolboy' (*Conversations*, 13). The second
Esprit Congress (28 July-1 August 1937), confirmed their limited following.[61]
At around this time, Ellul and Charbonneau realised their vision was now too
divergent from that of *Esprit* as a whole and they submitted their resignations
from the group.[62] The official announcement of their departure appeared in
the March 1938 internal bulletin of the Friends of Esprit.

This clear-thinking act undoubtedly honours both them and us. It proves, at
the very least, that even in our pluralism (and to the displeasure of those
who constantly reproach us concerning the vagueness of our formulae) we
have some doctrinal and historic positions which are consistent enough that
one is able to know whether someone accepts or rejects them. We do not
doubt that outside Esprit our two former comrades will continue to work,
with less discomfort for both them and for us, towards the future of the
personalist city.[63]

Ellul's reasons for this final break with *Esprit* can be broadly classed under
two headings: the more theoretical or theological and then the practical or

[60] *Conversations*, 10 taken from Mounier's unpublished Notebook of 9th March 1935 and
originally quoted in Roy 1992:86.
[61] Roy 1992:86-7. Mounier was under constant pressure from more conservative Roman
Catholics (notably Jacques Maritain) to restrain the radical and revolutionary tendencies
within *Esprit* (Hellman 1980).
[62] Once again there is some confusion over dates. Hanks 2001:4 cites early 1937 which fits
with Ellul's claim that 'Charbonneau and I had sent in our resignations to Mounier some
time before the Esprit congress which took place at the end of July 1937' (*Conversations*,
67) but Charbonneau's widow corrects this claiming that the rift took place after the
congress, a claim supported by Roy 1992:87f and the fact that the group (with Ellul as
correspondent) continues to be listed in the journal in early 1938.
[63] Quoted in Roy 1992:89.

organisational.[64] His Protestantism and particularly the influence of the early Barth inevitably produced tensions with the Thomistic thought of the Catholic Mounier.[65] In his important 1950 article for the Protestant newspaper *Réforme* explaining (on Mounier's death) his break with Mounier and Esprit ('Pourquoi je me suis séparé de Mounier'), Ellul highlights these theological differences. From the start, Ellul had disliked the name of the group with its ambiguity and dubious overtones. Unlike many of its leaders, he did not believe in 'spiritual values common to all people and valid in and of themselves' (1950f, 6). In addition, he could not agree with Mounier that 'human perversion is not radical' and found unacceptable Mounier's rejection of the idea that 'humans are really able to be put in danger by the powers of the world (*les puissances du monde*)' (1950f, 7). At heart, Ellul sympathised with de Rougemont's view that the proper Christian political attitude was one of *pessimisme actif* and not Mounier's *optimisme tragique*.[66] Mounier in turn rejected Ellul's theological outlook and the political attitude it engendered.

> Mounier could not come to terms with what he called my 'prophetism' or my 'catastrophism'. By that he meant this double attitude: on the one hand, all Christian social or political action has no meaning in itself, but only as prophecy of the very action of God; on the other hand, it is God's act which really changes society, just as grace changes humans and, definitively, political or economic reforms are not preparing the kingdom of God which will come about by a brutal change, 'through fire' and 'like a thief'...(1950f, 7).[67]

Ellul saw these theological differences also reflected in their different sociological analyses. Mounier thought the problem lay primarily with human use of the state, technique, money etc. Ellul saw the problem lying in the absolutely novel contemporary forms of the phenomena themselves. Dating this significant difference to as far back as 1933, Ellul remarks that it was Mounier's different theology which meant that 'he was unable to give up that

---

[64] In relation to Charbonneau there also appears to have been a major personality clash evident not only in Mounier's insulting letter quoted above but also Ellul's comments at *Conversations*, 68.

[65] The strength of the young Ellul's rejection of Thomism is most evident in 1948e, 1 where it is called a heresy as serious as that of modern materialism !

[66] This contrast of active pessimism and tragic optimism reappears often in Ellul's books e.g. *City*, 181; *Hope*, 225.

[67] Mounier apparently held that Ellul's thought was marked by 'déviation eschatologique' (Zorn 1971:251) and Ellul returns to this difference in *Apocalypse*, 62, 276n2 where he links Mounier's view to that of de Chardin.

conception of a human being deciding almost totally freely, choosing the use and as demiurge, at each instant capable of dominating the powers (*dominer les puissances*)' (1950f, 7). Mounier was also never convinced that Technique was as central a phenomenon within the modern world as Ellul and Charbonneau claimed and his strong patriotism did not fit with Ellul's antinationalism and desire for small-scale political units within a federal structure.

As Mounier increasingly dominated *Esprit* both organizationally and intellectually (the number of his articles in the journal far outnumbered those of any other contributor), it was inevitable that these fundamental theoretical differences would lead to practical difficulties in working together. Ellul sums up his account of their disagreements with the comment that 'these divergences did not prevent conversation, but they ruled out common action…' (1950f, 7).

Ellul and Charbonneau had initially joined *Esprit* primarily to extend their local movement into a national network of small revolutionary groups (*Conversations*, 10-11). Despite repeated encouragements for others to follow their example in their short news bulletins in the *Amis d'Esprit* columns, the response to this from the *Esprit* leadership and wider movement varied from apathy to outright hostility. This was partly due to the desire of the Paris-based organisers to keep a strong grip on the national organization (1982i) but it also arose from their quite different conception of *Esprit*'s task which concentrated on dissemination of the journal aimed at the intellectual elite. Local groups were encouraged but their primary task was seen as discussion of issues raised in the review. Ellul and Charbonneau, in contrast, wanted a much broader-based movement incorporating followers of *ON* and fully committed to concrete action to transform society.

> The rupture was consummated over this dilemma: whether to establish a movement having a revolutionary impact or to be nothing but a journal read by intellectuals (*Season*, 37).[68]

These quite different visions had led to great debate throughout 1934-7 and the failure of Ellul and Charbonneau to win this debate was clear and central in their decision to leave.

> We had failed to make anything out of Esprit other than simply a review for intellectuals. We wanted to create a real revolutionary movement, made up of small groups of fifteen persons or so. The groups would be federated

---

[68] Unsurprisingly, after being disbanded in 1939, the *Esprit* movement was not revived after the war when only the journal continued.

together and would be able to act locally in a concrete fashion according to the slogan 'Think globally act locally' (*Conversations*, 67).

Related to this divergence of view there were implicit disagreements over the possible recourse to violence. Although the groups Ellul and Charbonneau formed were never engaged in violence, they recognised any revolution would necessarily involve shedding blood and that, given their own lack of organisational skills, they could not control a truly revolutionary movement. Ellul, as a conscientious objector, rejected military and nationalistic violence but accepted the necessity of revolutionary violence. Mounier, however, totally rejected this. Although never explicit in their dispute, Ellul acknowledged that in the attempts to persuade the leadership to follow their course of action it probably played a part in Mounier's refusal and thus was another factor in the decision to go their separate ways (*Season*, 41-2).

Overall, Ellul's experience with the personalist movement proved a disappointment and failure. Not only did *Esprit* fail to take the revolutionary path he wished, but specific proposals (e.g. the 1936 attempt to persuade the government to recognise civil rather than military service for conscientious objectors and the plans, around the time of the break with *Esprit* in 1937/8, to set up an alternative university) also came to nothing.[69] Even more fundamentally, society continued on the same path and the radical social transformation Ellul sought throughout the 1930s failed to materialise, as he himself bitterly acknowledged in 1980 in a passage which vividly sums up this decisive decade in Ellul's early life.

I am sick over the world I shall leave behind, sick at heart, physically and intellectually sick. I had been so hopeful when at the age of twenty I first committed myself to action, when we hoped to change the course of the world. In 1930 we could already see the oppression and disorder of that world taking shape. And we had the absurd hope of turning it away, however slightly, in a different direction, toward humanity and freedom, toward justice, toward a true democracy. I tried everything. I seized all the opportunities that seemed favourable. I thought and thought, but managed only to understand what was going on…I saw correctly, I spoke, I gave warning – it all went for nothing. When the time was ripe no one listened, and when my message gradually found an audience, it was too late. We had started down a slope that we couldn't climb back up; we had accumulated powers that were indestructible; we couldn't get back to our origins anymore from which to strike out on a new path. It all went for nothing. Inexorably it has become the worst of all possible worlds. We never wanted *that* (*Faith*,

---

[69] Roy 1992:77-8, 99.

211-2).

The War Years (1939-45)

REFUGE AND RESISTANCE

When war with Germany broke out, Ellul was still teaching law at Strasbourg University. The conflict forced the university to move to Clermont-Ferrand some months into the conflict and there, on or around 20 June, 1940, Ellul made remarks which would have a determinative effect on the next four years of his life.

After a faculty meeting, Ellul was confronted by a crowd of fifty to sixty Alsatian students anxious about the incorporation of their home region into Germany and uncertain as to what to do when the Germans arrived. In a short speech Ellul advised them not to bow to German pressure to return to Alsace as they would then be drafted into the German army, and warned them that Pétain and his new government were not to be trusted. A student reported Ellul to the police and, two days later, he had to give a statement to the commissioner who filed a report to the Vichy regime. Their investigations uncovered the fact that Ellul's father was registered as a British citizen and had never become a French citizen. This gave further grounds for action against Ellul. On about 10 July the Vichy government fired him from his teaching post. Shortly afterwards he was forced to flee back to Bordeaux with Yvette and their new-born son, Jean when a group trying to re-form the French army and resist German advances requisitioned the property in which they had been living.

Shortly after Ellul's return, his father was ordered to appear before the German military police and, believing he was protected by international law, he ignored his son's advice and answered the summons only to be imprisoned immediately. He died in detention in 1942. Some time later, Ellul was warned that Yvette (born in Holland and with a British passport) was also under investigation and liable to be arrested so the family fled to a small property in Martres (a hamlet of about five hundred residents approximately thirty miles east of Bordeaux in the Entre-deux-Mers region).

The change in life this necessitated is summed up in Ellul's comment that 'throughout that period, I lived almost totally isolated from my former interests and activities' (*Perspectives*, 22). His primary source of income had to be farming which, as a total novice, he was instructed in by the locals. This, along with financial assistance from his wife's mother and money earned by preparing reports for a specialist in the commercial law court, supported not only Ellul, his wife and children (their second son, Simon, was born in 1941), but also Ellul's widowed mother. They were also helped when, in October

1941, Ellul won the prize offered by the French Academy (*Prix d'histoire de l'académie française*) in a competition for work on recruitment in the French army in the sixteenth and seventeenth centuries.

Despite the enforced detachment from his former academic environment, Ellul also took a correspondence course in theology through Strasbourg University during these years and only failed to obtain the degree because he never wrote the necessary thesis.[70] Of even longer-lasting significance, he used his time to plan out (around 1942/3) the course of writing which he would pursue in the following decades.

Due to his dismissal from his teaching post, Ellul was disqualified from attempting the 1941 *agrégation* but he appealed against this ruling and in 1943 (on his second attempt but six years after his first near-miss) he was successful in the competition.[71] This, despite the strongly right-wing composition of the examination board and the opposition of President Laval to his being given any university position, was a scenario the anarchistic supporter of the Resistance understandably relished.

> In other words the examination board, for all it was presided by a monarchist and made up of right-wingers, had awarded a place to a candidate who had been removed from his post by Vichy and who anyway was banned from teaching were he to succeed. You must admit this is a fine example of the independence of the university body, when it exists! (*Conversations*, 75).

Despite the ban on his appointment to a university teaching position, and a Pétainist dean, the law faculty at Bordeaux (with the support of the vice-Dean Henri Vizioz) unofficially and anonymously employed Ellul from 1943 to 1945 to teach the basic legal studies course.

FROM RESISTANCE TO....

During his four years of enforced exile from his home city Ellul became involved in the Resistance, taking advantage of his strategic position on the border between the occupied and free zones of France to provide false papers, hideouts, and safe passage to those (particularly Jews) seeking to escape arrest. He also housed resistance workers and refugees, acted as link and lookout between neighbouring groups of guerrilla soldiers (*maquis*), and used

---

[70] It was during this course that he apparently spent a whole year devoted to reading Calvin (1984a, 18 cf. *Conversations*, 49).

[71] Ellul's book-length manuscript for his agrégation is usually entitled 'Introduction à l'histoire de la discipline des Eglises réformées de France' although the Wheaton Archive manuscript is headed, 'Introduction au Droit Canon des Eglises réformées de France'.

his legal training when locals turned to him, rather than the official authorities, for resolution of their various disputes (*Anarchy*, 18). He never personally participated in violent action and his one attempt to secure weapons was unsuccessful. His later reflections on the period reflect his developed thinking about violence explored in chapter five.

> I was never involved in any fighting…I didn't have a theoretical position on the subject [of non-violence]…Had we been able to lay hands on some revolvers or tommy-guns no doubt we would have joined the maquis in Sauveterre. I was perfectly well aware that if I got involved in the fighting I would be crossing over into the realm of necessity but if I had to I was quite prepared to give up my liberty (*Conversations*, 76, 77).

Through his links with the *maquis* Ellul also discovered a small local Protestant community and, following visits to a number of farmers, in 1943 he began to pastor them and to lead regular worship in an abandoned local church.

By May 1943, Ellul, unlike Charbonneau, was convinced that the revolution he had so long sought would take place after the war. In the words of the *Combat* slogan, the French would move from resistance to revolution ('*de la Résistance à la Révolution*'). The vision at this time was similar to that of the earlier personalist groups.

> We did not mean a Communist, Stalinist, Soviet revolution. We meant a fundamental revolution of society, and we made great plans for transforming the press, the media, and the economic structures. They all had elements of socialism, to be sure; but I would say it was more of a Proudhonian socialism, going back to grassroots by means of a federative and cooperative approach. (*Perspectives*, 22).[72]

In seeking to achieve this Ellul became regional secretary of the *Mouvement de Libération Nationale* and sent some of his and Charbonneau's pre-war personalist writings to its leader, Henri Frenay. However, he soon began to realise that others had quite different visions for post-war France. In particular, de Gaulle had widespread support for his goal of restoring traditional republican government and many with whom Ellul had sympathies were determined to revive the old left-wing parties and past political debates.[73]

---

[72] The comparison with the 1930s personalist groups is acknowledged at *Conversations*, 82.

[73] De Gaulle preferred to speak of moving to renovation rather than revolution (Larkin

By the Liberation of Paris in August 1944, Ellul had spent almost four years enjoying farming and rural life while also, in the last few years, being able to continue with part-time academic teaching and research. His wife was eager to keep their new way of life and it appears to have been a difficult decision to return to Bordeaux. One factor, above all others, swayed Ellul

What made up my mind to come back was the political element. I believed it was going to be possible to carry out a large-scale political effort (*Season*, 50).

Ellul's motivation in this was clear.

I first became involved in politics at the Liberation when I heard the slogan 'Forward from the Resistance to the Revolution'. We were convinced that we would be able to bring about a deep change in society through politics because society was in a very malleable state straight after the war... (*Conversations*, 39).

Ellul continues with words repeating his assessment of the personalist movement and which ring through much of his life – 'our hopes were to be thwarted'. This was to prove decisive for his later political thought. Although many of the details remain vague, the effect of his political experience in the immediate aftermath of the war is evident -

Basically, this experience determined many of my later political and administrative analyses (*Season*, 53).

The first confusing detail concerning Ellul's active political role is its length. Once again Ellul himself is to blame for much of this confusion. He spoke variously of it lasting a year and half (*Season*, 53 which would bring it to a close in 1946), ending in 1947 (1982c, 15), and of 'my political experience (as deputy mayor of Bordeaux) in 1944-48' (1970j, 203). However, in a short piece in *Réforme* in January 1950 he wrote of 'my brief political experience of ten months, following the Liberation' (1950a, 3) and this, rather than the later and more exaggerated claims, proves to be accurate.

Following the removal of the collaborationist council and prior to new municipal elections the *commissaire de la République*, Gaston Cusin, selected a new council and, as a member of the Gironde resistance, Ellul was invited to

---

1997:124) which explains why Ellul says, 'I must point out that I never liked de Gaulle and never included myself among his followers, although I would have been able to do so in 1944' (1981l,note). Cf. *Conversations*, 38.

join as a delegated council member serving as deputy to the socialist mayor, Fernand Audeguil. The council sat from October 31st 1944 to April 25th 1945.[74] On the council Ellul had special responsibilities in the areas of commerce and public works but quickly became disillusioned with the system and a rather irregular attender of council meetings who felt he was being made an acceptable front-man for decisions made by party cabals in smoke-filled rooms (*Conversations*, chapter eight).

Two central features of Ellul's experience made it a frustrating and disappointing one and would shape his later political reflections. First, the size and complexity of the tasks he was to perform and the number of important technical decisions he was called upon to make required him to attend to thirty or forty issues daily. Unable to master everything, he inevitably had to rely upon departmental heads and wider administrative networks. As a result, he found himself signing studies, reports and decisions he did not understand or with which he disagreed. The troubled context of reconstruction after Nazi occupation undoubtedly increased Ellul's workload, but it also increased his sense of failure and disappointment because 'from all appearances we were starting almost from scratch and the old structures were open to question' (*Season*, 53). In reality, he was able to secure no significant changes to the system. This was due in large part to the second central feature of his experience: the power of established political parties. His vision of a new political map proved hopelessly naïve as the old loyalties reasserted themselves:

> There were several of us who went into politics in 1944 with really new ideas, ready for a socio-economic transformation. And we ran into such things as the territorial divisions (*le quadrillage*) of the traditional political parties: they remained exactly the same as before the war…The political networks (*les réseaux politiques*) were immediately reformed. Dating from this defeat and these manipulations, I developed a mistrust and even a hatred for political circles… (*Season*, 55-6).

In the aftermath of the experience of collaboration and resistance, feelings inevitably ran high. A foretaste of the revival of old political enmities had already occurred when, in March 1944, the local Communist underground group killed all the members of a Gaullist group simply because of their

---

[74] Chastenet gives these dates in *Conversations*, 13 but his question to Ellul on the subject gives the dates as August 1944 to April 1945 (*Conversations*, 79), presumably beginning with the liberation of Paris and bringing the figure closer to the ten months Ellul refers to in his 1950 article.

political beliefs.[75] As a respected lawyer Ellul played an important role in the official coming-to-terms with the past, especially in the university system (*Conversations*, 77). In the following months and years, Ellul served on a number of juries judging collaborators and regularly protested against actions taken by the successful Resistance against former collaborators, Vichy sympathisers, and German soldiers.[76] His rationale was simple and powerful.

> As long as the enemy was active and strong, we had to do everything to defeat them. Once we had defeated the enemy we had to be as liberal as possible. We must pardon, not seek revenge or punish after the event when we had the upper hand (*Conversations*, 92, revised).

By the time of the spring 1945 elections to replace the liberation council, Ellul was already disillusioned after his short experience of political office and so he rejected the opportunity of standing as a socialist candidate and participating in the new council. Other political opportunities arose, however, and at the instigation of Eugène Claudius-Petit and Gabriel Delauney he was offered the powerful post of *préfet* in the *Nord departement*. The hostility of both Charbonneau (Charbonneau 1994: 22) and Yvette were decisive in preventing him from becoming a national political figure.

> My wife was ABSOLUTELY against my holding any position of authority and power…My wife would say to me: 'As a Christian, you cannot hold such a post. It's completely incompatible. Christian teaching is about serving, not at all about dominating or controlling'. These moral arguments were quite hard for me because it goes without saying that I was sorely tempted to take up the post of *préfet*…I think that I would…have accepted had it not been for my wife…(*Conversations*, 80).[77]

The temptation to continue in politics was however strong as is evident from Ellul's involvement during the general election of October 21st 1945. Although he never highlighted this fact, Ellul was a candidate (third on the party list) of the UDSR (*Union démocratique et socialiste de la Résistance*), a group derived from the *Mouvement de Libération Nationale*.[78] Despite active

---

[75] See 1975c and 1981c, 167.

[76] *Season*, 2; *Violence*, 96, 138-9; 1949a&b; 1978f, 110.

[77] Another factor in this decision is revealed by his comment that, 'It is this inevitability of war and of violence in politics which has led me personally to refuse a political career' (1982l). For Ellul's hostility to the powers of the French prefect see 1953f, 1958b, and the unpublished 'Exposé de M. le Professeur Ellul'.

[78] The group gets little attention in the histories of the period except for the fact that the

campaigning by Ellul the grouping gained less than 5% in his Gironde region and so had no deputies elected.[79]

Political temptations continued to come Ellul's way. In 1947, Jacques Chaban-Delmas (who was to serve as Bordeaux Mayor from 1947 to 1995 as well as French Prime Minister and Presidential candidate in the late 1960s and early 1970) invited Ellul to be on his list. Ellul had, however, rapidly become disillusioned with the prospect of securing the revolutionary change he sought through seeking and gaining political power. Already in early 1946 in a piece on the current political situation in France his disappointment was clear.

> That this revolution is necessary does not need to be shown. But are we in the process of accomplishing it? Without doubt there is the 'shift to the left', elections which are more and more 'red'. But does this mean that the revolution is advancing? What does this shift mean in reality? In fact, it is distressing to see that nothing, whether near at hand or at a distance, is revolutionary (1946h, 287).[80]

Clearly, Ellul was now convinced that his revolutionary ideals, developed through the personalist movement in the 1930s, could not be achieved through the usual political means. His hope and faith in political revolution was now fully shattered.

> Try to understand me. I had seen the failure of the Popular Front in 1936; the failure of the personalist movement, which we intended to be revolutionary and which we tried to start on a modest scale; the failure of the Spanish revolution, which had great importance for Charbonneau and me; and the failure of the liberation. All of this formed an accumulation of ruined revolutionary possibilities. After this, I never believed anything could be changed by this route (*Season*, 56).[81]

The Teaching and Retirement Years (1944-94)

In contrast to his earlier life, no useful chronological division can be devised for Ellul's life from his appointment as Professor of Law at Bordeaux

---

later socialist president François Mitterand was a leading member. Larkin 1997:133 describes it as 'a forlorn attempt to keep alive the solidarity of the Resistance years; but without the unifying factor of German oppression, it retained only a handful of supporters'.

[79] This part of Ellul's life has come to light through the work of Patrick Chastenet who outlines some of Ellul's policies at this time at *Conversations*, 14.

[80] This short article not only expresses Ellul's disillusion with the political world but also contains the central argument of his much later *Autopsy*.

[81] For a similar statement see *Conversations*, 23.

University in 1944 to his death from cancer of the lymphatic system, after several years of ill health, on May 19, 1994. Instead, the central concerns of his life during these fifty years (with the notable exception of his family life[82]) can be categorized and examined in some detail under the four broad headings of academic life, church life, political activity, and work with young delinquents. [83] The other major activity of this period –the extensive writing he had planned during the war - is discussed in the following section of the chapter.

ACADEMIC LIFE

Throughout his academic career Ellul held the posts of Professor of the History and Sociology of Institutions in the Law Faculty of Bordeaux University and Professor in the Institute of Political Studies founded in 1946.[84] Until his retirement in 1980, Ellul regularly added new lecture courses and annually revised the content of his standard lectures. Some of these are the origin of later published works but many lectures such as those on Roman law, philosophy of law, *Droit d'information*, and his annual Institute courses on Marx and Marxism have never had a wider audience than his Bordeaux students.[85]

Despite the size of the Festschrift produced in his honour,[86] Ellul's principled decision to remain in Bordeaux (arising from his insistence on the importance in the modern world of being rooted in a particular community) diminished his influence in French academia by detaching him from the intellectual milieu focussed on Paris.[87] Internationally, his academic involvement was also limited although he often participated in conferences outside France, taught regularly in Morocco, and was awarded honorary doctorates by the Free University of Amsterdam (1970) and Aberdeen

[82] Ellul's third son (Yves) was born in 1945 and their daughter (Dominique) in 1949, two years after the death of their second son (Simon) at the age of six.

[83] In addition it should be noted that Ellul was director (1945-55) of a Bordeaux film club analysing modern cinema. Although he wrote little about this, his interest in modern cinema and his use of it in his sociological analysis is illustrated in *Hope*, 57f; *Betrayal*, 24-7; *Reason*, 286-7; 1960j; 1953a; 1974f.

[84] Lavroff 1983. Lacoue-Labarthe 1994 offers a student's tribute to Ellul.

[85] Ellul believes that his course on Marxist thought, taught every year from 1947 to 1979, was the first such university course in France (*Anarchy*, 43-4; 1981r, 70ff; 1984a, 18). It is hoped that some of these courses may now be published from student notes. The course on social class has already been published and work is underway on lectures on Marx and his successors. See further details in part 3 of the bibliography of unpublished material.

[86] Dravasa *et.al.* 1983b is nearly 900 pages long, contains 66 articles and an eight-page list of subscribers.

[87] See 1981k; 1982i and Berthomeau 1981. On *l'enracinement* see e.g. *Déviances*, 152-4.

University (1980).

His lack of significant professional advancement in Bordeaux ('my university career was pretty abysmal', *Conversations*, 31) was due to a number of factors. In part, as Joyce Hanks' extensive bibliography demonstrates it was due to his near total disregard for established disciplinary boundaries and refusal to specialize in a particular field. Within the law faculty his main interest remained Roman law (although he wrote little on the subject) but he also specialised in the institutions of the fourteenth and fifteenth centuries which he saw as so significant for Western history.[88]

> That organization [of medieval society] will be turned upside down in the fourteenth and fifteenth centuries by a series of crises and conflicts...And it will be through these crises and conflicts that the society called 'modern' is born...(*Institutions* 4:8).

Ellul's research interests and writing energies were, however, never concentrated in any of these areas and his activity in other spheres often made him unpopular. As one colleague informed him when he was again passed over for promotion in preference for a non-productive colleague, 'You are being penalized not for not doing what you are paid to do, but for what you are doing in fields in which you are not paid' (*Conversations*, 31).

In addition, Ellul (again with strong encouragement from Yvette) resisted opportunities for prestige and power when they arose. In the 1950s, on the death of Poplawski, the Dean (*doyen*) of the Law School who had taught him back in the 1930s when he was a student, Ellul would, given his position, normally have succeeded and had much support among the faculty. Aware, however, of the nasty political atmosphere and that support for him did not extend to support for his views on how to run the faculty, Ellul 'asked them to vote on a little programme rather than on my name and they didn't accept that' (*Conversations*, 81).

Throughout his teaching career, university reform was a significant and constant concern for Ellul. In the immediate post-war period, from about 1947, he revived the idea of the late 1930s and again considered founding an alternative parallel university. These ideas were initially given concrete expression when he and Charbonneau ran outdoor camps where their best students went into the mountains for a period of weeks or months in order to pursue a course of both practical work and critical reflection on society.[89] It

---

[88] *Anarchy*, 29, n12. For Ellul's more detailed description of this period see *Institutions* 3: 295-390. One of his earliest articles and probably the most narrowly specialist was a paper on municipal taxes in Montpellier in the thirteenth and fourteenth centuries (1938b) !

[89] See 1946f; 1967k; Roy 1992:95-6; Charbonneau 1994:22-4.

was in these that Charbonneau developed the ideas for his significant study of the state and Ellul researched the nature of modern society and the Christian's role in it.[90]

According to Christian Roy, after a few years, Charbonneau hoped to transform these camps into communities of action and to distribute a set of theses to the established universities which would oppose their complicity in the 'scientification' and unlimited development of the world. This plan was, however, opposed by many involved and, in the mid 1950s, these camps came to an end.[91]

From the mid 1960s, Ellul's responsibilities in the law faculty were concentrated on teaching doctoral courses but he continued to form personal contacts with his students and to share their interests.[92] In the 1968 student revolts he was able to play an important mediating role between the university authorities and the protestors.[93] Although not uncritical of the 1968 protestors, Ellul had great sympathy with some of their demands due to his own long-standing desire for radical institutional reform of universities.

His vision of the task of a university and his opposition to the series of post-war government education reforms demonstrate the correlation between the concerns of his concrete daily life and his general analysis of the modern world.[94] He lamented the university becoming a mere technical school, mass-producing technicians and executives with diplomas and professional qualifications for our technological society. His alternative vision was of 'a truly interdisciplinary *universitas*' (*Season*, 166) that would be independent and free from state interference, enabling its students and staff to undertake a serious study of the world and to act as a critical voice within it. In the early 1970s Ellul and Charbonneau once again seriously considered putting such ideas into practice and creating some sort of college devoted to the critique of scientific and industrial development but as they were both by then in their

---

[90] Ellul's studies were synthesised for the 1946 lectures at the WCC Ecumenical Institute of Bossey and published in a revised form as *Presence* (*Presence*, x). Charbonneau's work (*L'Etat*) was completed in 1949, published personally in 1951 (see 1952c for Ellul's review), and finally gained a wider audience when republished as Charbonneau 1987. *Conversations*, 88 shows Ellul's high regard for this study and also speaks of Ellul and Charbonneau dividing their labour so that Ellul (at first unwillingly) focussed on Technique and Charbonneau on the state.

[91] Roy 1992:96-7. See also Charbonneau 1994:23-4.

[92] 1966e & 1984a.

[93] 1968:a, b & d; 1969:b & d; 1983i, 199.

[94] Details are found in *Season*, chapter eleven; *Révolution*, 57-61; 1968e; 1969b; 1973f; 1980:j, k, o, p & v; 1981n; 1983:g, h & i; Unpublished "Exposé"; Spirlet 1976.

sixties, they decided they were too old to attempt such a large-scale project.[95] Ellul remained teaching at Bordeaux University, continuing to direct theses in his capacity as Professor Emeritus after his official retirement from teaching in 1980.

CHURCH LIFE

When, in the late 1940s, Ellul gave up his faith in the potential of politically organised revolutionary activity, he did not renounce his radical zeal. He redirected his 1930s personalist vision into the church.

> I said to myself that if there are any people capable of changing the society they live in, then it would be the Christians. I had my Christian reasons for transforming this society - why not work with other Christians? Why could I not get the church to change and become the salt of the earth, a leaven, a force that would change society? (*Perspectives*, 24).

The full extent of the continuity between the aims of his 1930s personalist movement and his early vision of the church's task is made clear by comparing extracts from the personalist manifesto *Directives* and his post-war talks to the World Council of Churches published as *Presence of the Kingdom*. In that book, particularly the closing sections of his second chapter on revolutionary Christianity, there is exactly the same emphasis on the need to understand a complex world which we currently do not understand, to develop a different lifestyle, and to sow the seeds of a new civilization.[96]

This decision to devote himself to church life rather than political life bore fruit not only in Ellul's writings but also in his active church life internationally, nationally, and locally.

From 1945 Ellul was involved in the formation of the World Council of Churches (WCC).[97] In 1946 he lectured at its Bossey Institute and began to serve on its committee on work. In preparation for the 1948 First Assembly of the WCC held in Amsterdam on the theme 'Man's Disorder and God's Design' he was appointed to the commission that examined 'The Church and the Disorder of Society'. This included such theological giants as Reinhold Niebuhr (Chairman),[98] Nicolas Berdyaev,[99] and Emil Brunner,[100] with Ellul

---

[95] Roy 1992:99.

[96] The key points in the manifesto here are §1 & 40, 45 & 46, 36-38 all of which are echoed at Presence, 46-7.

[97] On the WCC see Duff 1956 & van Elderen 1990. 1948c reveals Ellul's early optimistic vision and 1988c his later less enthusiastic assessment.

[98] Fox 1985:235 laments Niebuhr's failure to engage Ellul's analysis more seriously.

[99] Berdyaev, one of the first contributors to *Esprit*, influenced French personalist thought

writing on 'The Situation in Europe' (1948f).

Ellul's active participation in the WCC ceased in the early 1950s but he remained a supporter albeit one increasingly unhappy with what he viewed as its uncritical embrace of a radical leftist political agenda. At the 1966 Geneva Conference on Church and Society he was highly critical and publicly broke with the movement.[101] Despite his continued criticism of the organisation,[102] in 1988 Ellul was invited to reflect on the impact of the 1948 Amsterdam Conference and his article offers insight into both his initial sympathies and his subsequent distancing from the WCC (1988c).

Domestically, Ellul's spiritual home was always the French Reformed Church.[103] From 1947 he was a member of its National Synod and in 1951 began nearly twenty years of service on its National Council. Together with Jean Bosc, his friend from 1930s student days, he worked on the Council with a radical programme:

> It was another great undertaking, trying in a way to transform the Reformed Church into an active movement within society. This was my goal, but to begin with, the church had to be transformed (*Season*, 85).

Ellul served on the special committee on strategy set up in the late 1950s which discovered there were only about 300,000 active church members and set about discussing reforms in the church's structures which resulted in rather episcopalian proposals.[104] After six years of work, the plan of gradual reforms failed due to the ignorance and traditionalism of rank-and-file Protestants.

Through the 1960s Ellul's stance on a number of matters such as the new

---

(Baird 1992) and was also a Christian anarchist (Nicholls 1989:118ff) whose anarchism Ellul later praised (*Marx*, 171f). Cf. Chastenet 1992:77.

[100] Brunner's 1948 Gifford Lectures on Christianity and Civilization includes a treatment of Technics that perhaps demonstrate some influence from Ellul. He comments that 'Technology has become the dominating factor of modern civilization. The changes which technology has wrought in the last two centuries are beyond all comparison with those in previous ages' (Brunner 1949:2) and concludes, 'As long as technics is subordinate to human will, and human will is obedient to the divine will, technics is neutral, and as a means of goodwill is itself good...But we can hardly avoid the question whether technical evolution has not already passed the limits within which it is controllable by feeble, mortal man' (Brunner 1949:15). For Ellul's similar analysis at this time see chapter three below.

[101] 1966b & d and 1970j, 202. A 1967 WCC paper on the church and the world (quoted in Hoekstra 1979:75-6) vividly demonstrates its distance from Ellul's own theology as outlined in chapter two below.

[102] See, for example, *Violence*, 70; *Season*, 67; *Subversion*, 207n9.

[103] Maillot 1994 offers a brief account of Ellul's contribution to the church.

[104] For Ellul's thinking on church structure see 1951d; 1955c; 1968f; 1972c.

hermeneutics and demythologisation, the church leadership's political pronouncements (including those on Algeria), and the popularity of 'service theology' (which he critiqued due to his own personal emphasis on the word) left him increasingly marginalized on the Council.[105]

Ellul left the National Council in 1970 but remained active on a national level with a project started in 1968 with Jean Bosc. Drawing on many earlier proposals for the reform of theological teaching, the committee on theological studies drew up a radical programme for change based on three principles.[106] First, theological study should be open to those who did not wish to be ordained while those who did seek ordination should be encouraged to test their calling by studying theology before starting their ministerial training. Second, a strong social science education (in psychology, sociology, economic and political science) was deemed to be essential alongside theological training. Third, theology and ministerial training had to be related to life in the modern world. Following Bosc's death, Ellul became the main force behind these reforms and in 1972 presented them to the National Synod where they were accepted. He then served on a committee that visited the training schools, adapted the proposals, and produced annual reports. After several major alterations, the proposals appeared a success and, although some of the changes were gradually undone, Ellul continued to view this as one of his few real achievements in the church.

> I felt that the study of theology would have to be changed. And in this, I succeeded (*Perspectives*, 24).[107]

In the mid 1980s, Ellul's quest for institutional change in the Reformed church took on new life culminating in the presentation of his 'Propositions pour des Etats Généraux du protestantisme français' at the October 1985 meeting for the 300th anniversary of the Revocation of the Edict of Nantes.[108] This drew on Ellul's life-long experience of small-scale organisations seeking reform and sought to revitalise French Protestantism through by-passing the established institutions and initiating a consultation at the base with all those actively involved in any Protestant church or organisation. The aim was to move from each small group's own reports through a synthesis of these to an *Etats Généraux* which could reform and set new directions for the church. As

---

[105] 1970j, 201-3; 1972e. The best illustration is *False*, a book that apparently put an end to Ellul's influence in ecumenical Protestant circles (Hanks, T. 1985:24).

[106] 1969f; 1972c; 1974j; 1977a; Fesquet 1971 & 1972.

[107] This success did not, however, prevent him proclaiming French Protestantism in need of resurrection from the dead (Fesquet 1975).

[108] Bizeul 1991.

so often before, this time in part due to his ill health, Ellul's vision failed to be realised.

Among Ellul's many other campaigns in the Reformed Church one of particular relevance to the case studies in this book is his belief that the church's stance encouraging conscientious objection was hypocritical. This came to a head at the 1973 National Synod where Ellul again failed to get the church to provide more concrete support to its young members who refused military service. He wanted the church to widen its protest and attack other areas of military power. He also demanded that the government, if it continued to take action against conscientious objectors, should enforce comparable legal sanctions against those who supported and encouraged objectors and not just those who refused service.[109]

In addition to his activities within the leadership of the national church, Ellul often acted as pastor to the congregation within his home parish of Pessac.[110] When Ellul's family settled in Pessac in 1953 only about ten residents were active in the larger parish of Talence of which it was a part. Ellul and his wife began to hold two services a month in their own dining room and a Bible school for children. The church very rapidly grew and within a few years they had a weekly children's meeting with up to 60 children. Services attracted a similar number and became weekly and a women's group was started by Yvette. In Ellul's words, 'in coming here to settle down, my wife and I were in a way the "Christianizers" of this parish' (*Season*, 98).[111] The church was remarkable in several ways: almost all those on the church roll were regular attenders, they were predominantly working class, and a real community was created. This all changed, however, around 1960 when the congregation ceased to meet in Ellul's family home and transformed the adjacent building into a church sanctuary. From that time, the working men ceased to be active church members and pastors were assigned to the church, reducing Ellul's involvement.

The working class and non-intellectual composition of the church made this constituency different from that of Ellul's writing but there were significant overlaps. All of Ellul's biblical studies have their origins in his experience of preaching and leading bible studies within the parish.[112] Within

---

[109] 1973j; Auber 1973.

[110] For details of Pessac see *Jeunesse*, 48-68.

[111] When, in 1987, Ellul was asked what he considered most important to him as he looked back over the years he responded that his leadership and creation of the French Reformed parish in Pessac 'gave me the most joy because I did it with my wife' (1988a, 26).

[112] *Dieu*, 24n. For an example of a sermon see 1994c. Ellul continued to lead regular local Bible studies in the 1980s and came to view the best arrangement as a group composed equally of Protestants, Catholics, Jews, and non-believers (1984a, 20; Hanks, T. 1985:27;

the congregation, Ellul also found it possible to encourage Christians to be more responsible in their professions and he provided a forum for dialogue between violently opposed political viewpoints, especially during the Algerian War. In addition, this experience of a thriving home-based ministry among working people lies behind both his criticism of radical Marxist-inspired Christians who claim to speak for the poor and his anti-institutional attitude to the church.

Three other important church-related activities should be noted. After the war, Ellul and Jean Bosc started groups to assist Protestants working in various professions. The *Associations Professionnelles Protestantes* (A.P.P.) had a clear aim and one familiar to any who knew Ellul's past.[113]

> They were not intended to defend professional interests but to present people who practiced a profession with an ethical imperative that the Bible can provide for any job or profession. We thought that if we managed to revolutionise professional practices, change would begin there and would probably spread in a decisive manner to entire segments of society (*Season*, 63-4).

A number of small groups were created and studied their professional situation, placing it in dialectical tension with biblical teaching. Their success varied but most were disbanded in the early 1950s as, once again, Ellul 'realized that we were not yet approaching a fundamental transformation of society' (*Season*, 65).[114]

Ellul was also an early and then regular contributor (over two hundred articles) to *Réforme*, the weekly Protestant newspaper which Bosc helped start after the war.[115] Finally, he was actively involved with *Foi et Vie*, the bi-monthly Protestant journal which has represented the Barthian wing of French Protestantism.[116] At the end of 1950 he joined the editorial board and, at Bosc's own request, succeeded him as editor in 1969 on his death (1969g).[117]

Dawn 1988b).

[113] On this organisation see *Season*, 63-6, 84-5; *False*, 47; *Ethique* III, 10; 1947f, 10; 1984a, 20f. An outline of some of their material appears in part 2 of the bibliography of unpublished materials.

[114] The Centre de Villemétrie was founded to carry on similar work. See 1988d.

[115] Finet 1982; Bolle 1993.

[116] For Ellul's own statement of its publishing policy during the time of his involvement see 1977g.

[117] Ellul also served on the editorial board of a number of other journals both Christian (Katallagete: Be Reconciled; Christianisme au XXe siècle and Réforme) and secular (Mendès-France's Cahiers de la République).

He held this post until the end of 1985 when he became honorary editor on the editorial board. In addition to editorial responsibilities, Ellul contributed over seventy articles to the journal between 1939 and 1994.[118]

POLITICAL AND SOCIAL ACTIVITIES

Despite Ellul's disenchantment with mainstream politics, he never withdrew from commenting or acting upon matters of interest in the political and social realm. Never a member of any political party he was, nevertheless, seen as a potentially significant political figure by many on the left who knew him. In the late 1950s he was approached by a delegation of socialists and communists and asked to consider standing for mayor of Pessac. His response was typical and unsurprising given his earlier political experience.

> I accepted on one condition that I would be free to fill a third of the list with independent personalities. They didn't like that. They wanted me to preside over a list made up solely of socialists and communists. I wouldn't back down. And neither would they (*Conversations*, 84).

As his choice of the UDSR after the war showed, however, he was never in the mainstream of left-wing politics. His sympathies with anarchistic forms of socialism were sufficiently obvious to be noted in the late 1940s.[119] His personal voting strategy was to spoil his ballot paper and he often called on others to follow his example.[120] Around 1964 it was only the unacceptability of his Christian faith that apparently prevented him joining the Situationists with which he had contact through Guy Debord.[121] His distrust of mainstream left-wing politics was always evident[122] and his form of socialism meant that he was increasingly on the political margins.[123]

---

[118] The December 1994 tribute issue of *Foi et Vie* contains many important articles on Ellul and his work and a bibliography of his contributions to *Foi et Vie* (pp173-4).

[119] *Marx*, 156, n2.

[120] 1973g; 1974e. Although this is a policy with very few Christian advocates, O'Donovan notes, 'the Gospel may raise serious difficulties for an order that conceives itself as democratic...the Christian population may need to send a message of disapproval not to the governing party but to the political classes at large...Jacques Ellul waged periodic campaigns against voting; they deserve at least a respectful mention in the annals of Christian political witness' (O'Donovan 1996:225).

[121] *Anarchy*, 2-3. Several of Ellul's books refer to this movement or Debord - *Autopsy*, especially pp291ff; *Révolution*, 254; *Hope*, 59; *Humiliation*, 114-5; *Ethique* III, 171. See also 1967j,note; 1969e; Zorn 1971:138-9 & Chastenet 1992:75-6. On the Situationists see Marshall 1993:546-53 and on Debord see Hussey 2001.

[122] See, for example, 1967j & 1981a.

[123] Because Ellul fails to fit neatly into any traditional mainstream political categories, he

The main source for details of Ellul's political and social activity is his numerous newspaper articles. In addition to being a regular contributor to *Réforme*, he often wrote for *Le Monde* and, after several years of occasional writing, became a columnist for his regional newspaper *Sud-Ouest*. From these pieces a fascinating and detailed account can be constructed of Ellul's commentary upon and involvement in current affairs throughout the post-war years. Amongst the many different subjects on which he commented and often aroused controversy, four in particular should be noted as of most importance in understanding Ellul's political thinking.[124]

First, the Algerian question.[125] Ellul began to campaign on Algeria as far back as 1934 when it was of little or no interest to either the French public or political elite. He continued to call for a swift resolution of the colonisation problem, drawing on his knowledge of Roman law to advocate the institution of a form of dual nationality. When the rebellion began, he urged the government to stop the repression and accept the demands of the FLN (*Front de Libération Nationale*) but was ignored. Algeria became an issue of major national political controversy from the mid 1950s (eventually bringing about the collapse of the Fourth Republic in 1958) and at this stage Ellul withdrew from all public debate on the issue believing the matter now beyond peaceful, political settlement and the French government embroiled in a war it could not win. This experience strengthened his conviction that the church has to foresee and warn of looming conflicts but, if they then erupt, must avoid taking sides and instead pray and prepare for reconciliation and reconstruction when some resolution to the conflict has been found.

Second, Ellul's other major international concern has been the state of Israel and the politics of the Middle East. Living as a Christian with Jewish ancestry in pro-Arab France, Ellul became extremely unpopular for his strong pro-Israeli writings. His first significant involvement came at the time of the third Arab-Israeli war when he insisted on the need to support Israel against the Arabs (1967b). He then consistently defended Israel in all military conflicts and was highly critical of those, especially Christians, who supported the PLO and called for a Palestinian state.[126]

---

has often, despite his protestations, been placed on the right politically (1957a & c; Schram 1954). Even De Jouvenel took this view (Wilkinson 1970:164). His political stance, discussed further in chapter seven below, is closest to early anti-statist revolutionary forms of socialism (*Anarchy*, 1ff; *Changer*).

[124] In addition to these Ellul also commented controversially on South Africa in the late 1980s (see *Conversations*, 98f).

[125] For more on this see *Season*, 102ff; *Conversations*, 33; *False*; *FLN*; *Betrayal*, 110-1; 1955a; 1956b; 1970j, 201; 1973h, 53; 1976b, 188; 1984c, 60.

[126] Even at the time of Israel's invasion of Lebanon and the Sabra and Chatila massacres

Third, From 1976 Ellul served on the Alain Peyrefitte national commission on violence, crime and delinquency set up by the government. In 1978 this published a study of violence, policing and crime in France which made 106 recommendations, most of which were not implemented.[127]

Finally, perhaps the most important activity was Ellul's involvement in the ecology movement. Ellul and Charbonneau can, in many ways, legitimately claim to be the originators of the French ecological movement in the pre-war personalist movement and the source of many contemporary environmentalist ideas.[128] In line with the dictum, 'Think globally, act locally',[129] his primary concern was his own Aquitaine region. From 1968, Ellul was involved in the formation of environmentalist groups to counter the work of MIACA [*La Mission Interministérielle d'Aménagement de la côte Aquitaine*] as it proposed and implemented plans for the 'development' of the Aquitaine region. As in the 1930s, these were small, locally based and organised groups and were co-ordinated by Ellul, Charbonneau and the Committee for the Defence of the Aquitaine Region.[130]

Although they succeeded in raising awareness of MIACA's projects and unscrupulous activities, the campaign failed to halt plans due to the total mismatch of financial and political resources and the excessive secrecy of MIACA. All legal actions against MIACA were lost and the conduct of the administrative courts confirmed to Ellul that the law was now subordinate to the totalitarian power of state administration. Technical studies of proposed projects were undertaken and revealed serious flaws but although this led to some being abandoned, others were simply revised and reappeared in new forms or continued unamended, resulting in enormous waste.[131]

This campaign struck at the heart of many of Ellul's concerns and there is little doubt that it hardened his view of the modern world.

I committed myself totally because M.I.A.C.A. embodies in an overt and

---

Ellul wrote in support of Begin (1982:d & l). See also 1970:d, i & m; 1974b; 1977b & c; 1978e; 1980f; 1981o; 1982j; 1990b and Maillot 1994:45. The fullest treatment is the untranslated *Israël* and on the theology of Israel in Romans 9-11 his (also untranslated) *Dieu*.

[127] *Foi*, 277n [deleted from ET]; 1978c; 1980w; 1989c, 86.

[128] 1983i, 203; *Conversations*, 64-5, 119-21; Roy 1990 & 1992; Cans 1992; Charbonneau 1994.

[129] 1982i; Vanderburg 1987 & 1994. Ellul's comment at *Conversations*, 67 imply this now-famous slogan originated with their 1930s personalist groups.

[130] For details of this see *Season*, chapter ten; *Déviances*, 101-4; 1974:h, k & l; 1975b & g; l; 1978:a & g; 1980a; 1981s; 1982i; 1983c; RJ 1977; Charbonneau 1991b & 1994 and Cérézuelle 1996.

[131] Many examples cited by Ellul in *Bluff* arise from this campaign.

monstrous way three elements I detest: technocracy, the bureaucratic
attitude and capitalist power (*Season*, 154).

WORK AMONG DELINQUENT YOUTH

Ellul combined his academic work among students with a calling to assist
young delinquents.[132] This originated when, in the late 1950s, a Protestant girl
came to Ellul on behalf of Yves Charrier who was working with street gangs
and wished legal advice about his position in cases where he knew of a crime
but did not report the offender.[133] Thus began over a decade of collaboration
between Charrier and Ellul.

Charrier worked mainly among 'blousons noirs' (Teddy Boys) and this
inevitably involved the use of violence and brushes with the authorities. Ellul
acted as his counsellor (including over his use of violence[134]) and an advocate
when he ran into trouble with the police. In 1958, with government money,
Charrier could be paid a salary and subsequently a Prevention Club was
established to provide a centre offering activities for both boys and girls.[135]
The club, only the second in France, had a professional technical staff and
began to discern previously unnoticed problems, notably drug abuse.
Inevitably, given their work, the club authorities were in conflict with the
police but this was reduced when Ellul acted as a buffer between Charrier and
the authorities and established a positive relationship with two successive
police commissioners. Ellul regularly attended the club and for a short time in
the late 1960s he also ran a Bible study among the hippies. This attracted
about thirty young people and had a significant impact on his theology.

> It was out of the question to speak in religious language to them and bring
> them into a closed world; I had to create good, biblically authentic theology
> that could be immediately understood…These groups made me work hard
> and had a great influence on me (*Season*, 132).[136]

---

[132] The fullest account is *Jeunesse*, the more accessible are *Season*, chapter nine,
Conversations, 89-90, and 1989c. See also *Déviances*; 1967a & h; 1969e & h; 1970:a, f &
h; 1980m; 1982a; 1983d; 1988a; Briselet 1967; Meury 1975.

[133] Again there is confusion about timing. The year of meeting is regularly given as 1958
(1989c, 75; *Conversations*, 89) but Ellul's comment at *Jeunesse*, 5 (published in 1971) that
they met 15 years earlier suggests they may have met at the earlier date of 1956.

[134] Ellul accepted the need for Charrier to use violence against some of the Teddy Boys in
order to establish a positive relationship and break their hold over others (*Season*, 119). A
graphic example of this is given at *Jeunesse*, 121ff.

[135] The club (Action Jeunesse Pessac) still exists. Its website dates its birth to December
12th 1962 and includes a profile of Ellul (http://wwwusers.imaginet.fr/~ajp33/index.htm).

[136] See also 1989c, 81-2; *Conversations*, 89.

The club's philosophy was not to view the youngsters as maladjusted.

> It is not young people who are maladjusted to society but our society which is maladjusted to human beings (*Déviances*, 140).

Its aim therefore was emphatically not to bring about their conformity to society. It sought instead to help them develop their personality and to enable them to become, in Ellul's phrase, 'positively maladjusted'.

> We consider that the end of preventing maladjustment is not to adjust the young person to society but to help them to develop for themselves a strong enough personality to be able to find or give a meaning to their life so that they are also able to overcome their maladjustment. That option is radical, decisive and serious. We consider that prevention work which has adaptation as its end is a *total* error (*Jeunesse*, 163).

Following Charrier's death in 1970,[137] Ellul took over as team leader and, recognising the changing patterns of youth culture, reorganised the club and the model of prevention. Then, in 1972/3, Luc Fauconnet took over and the club closed as new teams of counsellors worked in the streets developing one-to-one relations with the young people, especially those who were already extreme dropouts.

Aware of increasing popular hostility to their work and unhappy with trends in the training of those in prevention work, Ellul also created a federation of prevention clubs in the Gironde. This soon expanded to become the National Committee for Unity between Clubs and Teams of Prevention that he headed until 1977 when he retired from both the national and local work.[138]

Although this work did not change Ellul's fundamental sociological analysis, it provided concrete evidence of the negative effects of the technological and bureaucratic society on young people. In relation to the concerns of later chapters, it had two important effects. Firstly, it confirmed his scepticism about the ability of the state and politicians to address serious social problems. His 1989 article reports on aspects of this concluding,

> An action close to the 'marginalized' can itself only be marginal and as a result incomprehensible to any Power (*Pouvoir*), whatever it be (1989c, 86).

---

[137] *Jeunesse*, 5 gives the date of Charrier's death as December 2, 1970 at the age of thirty-nine although again Ellul often gives a different date, referring to it as occurring in 1969 (*Season*, 126; *Conversations*, 89).

[138] 1989c, 86 dates the origin of this national committee to 1968.

Secondly, the work forced him to alter his conception of violence.

> I became much more sensitive to social violence than to the individual
> violence of young people. The phenomenon of social violence –
> administrative violence, violence of the judicial system, and so on – has
> been for me the frightening discovery of something against which we are
> totally helpless...(*Season*, 132-3).

Overall, Ellul reckons that he devoted more time to this work than to his
long struggles in the Reformed church (1976a). However, in the midst of so
many failed projects, the concrete personal successes and radically changed
lives that were achieved made it, along with his parish experience, among the
most fulfilling of the many activities in his life (1988a, 26-7).

Conclusion

This biography has demonstrated that although Ellul is best known for his
extensive literary output, this was only one element of an incredibly diverse
and active life. As is already becoming clear, Ellul's life and thought are
closely inter-related and knowledge of Ellul's life illuminates his writing.
Although he acknowledged his personal failings, Ellul's goal was simple:

> I have always tried to write exactly as I live and to live as I have written
> (*Season*, 225-6). [139]

The portrait offered here has highlighted the importance of the years prior
to his publications, especially the 1930s and his involvement in the personalist
movement. It has also shown Ellul to be an activist whose personalist
convictions and faith in Jesus Christ made him a revolutionary dissenter and
true 'protest-ant' who in living out the Word of God radically critiqued and
resisted established institutions and the direction of the modern world. It is
this that explains the life-pattern of intense and lengthy involvements in
causes that were then often suddenly brought to an end when Ellul felt himself
being forced to conform to certain patterns of engagement.

> The number of radical breaks (*ruptures radicales*) I have made is
> significant, I think...These breaks did not result from a change of mind or
> from instability, but from a sort of judgment that was both realistic and

---

[139] The close correlation of his life and thought is perhaps clearest (although never
explicit) in much of the discussion in the untranslated *Ethique* II.

spiritual…I decided on these breaks whenever I had the impression that I was being conditioned by the group or by the milieu…(*Season*, 2).

Ellul's biography also shows that, throughout his life, he was constantly to be found on the margins rather than the mainstream. Ecclesiologically, he was not only in the minority Reformed church but a minority within that. Politically, he was on the left but never close to either the Communist or Socialist parties, preferring the 'fringe' groups. Academically, his refusal to leave Bordeaux or to make a name in a narrow speciality led to a general lack of recognition in France.[140] It is also clear that the majority of his activities - from the personalist movement through to his post-war political engagement, his work in the French Reformed church, and his attempted university reforms - appeared to him to end in failure with his revolutionary hopes and goals unfulfilled. One of the permanent legacies he left, however, was his writing and, before a detailed account of his thought, the structure and purpose of his writing needs to be clarified.

Ellul's Corpus: A Brief Overview of his Writing

The major feature of Ellul's life omitted from the biographical account offered above is his writing. This makes explicit the convictions which, originating in the 1930s, underlay and motivated Ellul's activities in so many different areas of life. Although he wrote over a thousand articles for journals and newspapers, it is his many books published since 1946 that form the heart of his writing.[141]

Any reader of Ellul's books faces a number of major difficulties. Most obvious is Ellul's distinctive style characterised not only by the seemingly unsystematic nature of his thought and his broad brush accounts and sweeping statements but also by an often frustrating enthusiasm for dialectic and contradiction combined with a desire to shock, challenge, and even offend his readers.[142] There is also the sheer mass of material, its enormous diversity, and the fact that much material is not translated. Even in translation, problems

---

[140] For discussion of this lack of recognition see now Chastenet 1994e:39-43.

[141] For accounts of his writing pattern see *Conversations*, 29-30, 87, 100 and *Season*, 187ff.

[142] Comments on Ellul's style are found throughout the secondary literature e.g. Vahanian 1970:52 writes, 'were it not for his most distinctive style and its caustic effects, one could hardly believe it is the same man who has written all the books he has published to date…' while Christians 1974:10,n26 refers to a reviewer who commented that reading Ellul's writings was like 'wading through thick mud' yet 'surprisingly well worthwhile'.

arise from having to rely on an assortment of translators whose knowledge of Ellul's thought varies enormously. Finally, there are the problems of how his works relate to one another, whether there is any coherence to his thought, and the difficult question of the inter-relationship of his theological and non-theological writings.

The remainder of Part One addresses some of these difficulties but the following section sketches the origins and overall structure of his corpus. It is followed by a brief statement of the purpose of both his sociological and his theological works. Chapter two then presents an account of the fundamental structure of his theology and ethics while chapter three explains what lies at the heart of his sociological studies. In the light of the interpretation of Ellul's thought offered in these chapters, the question of the relationship between the two strands of his work is finally examined in chapter four which functions as a brief conclusion to Part One.

The Structure of the Corpus

> In fact...I have not actually written a wide variety of books but rather one long book in which each 'individual book' constitutes a chapter. It's a gamble and a little insane to believe that there will be some readers patient enough to see how my thirty-six works actually belong together (*Conversations*, 22).[143]

In this brief statement, Ellul encapsulates the difficulty faced by those who wish to understand his thought. Although perhaps a little extreme to claim that 'as demanding a task as it may be, his work really must be read in its entirety or not at all',[144] it is the case that if any aspect of Ellul's thought is to be seriously examined and properly interpreted, it must be set within the context of the whole Ellul corpus. This is essential not only because the works themselves form a whole but also because Ellul, from the start, planned them as such and claimed that 'it is certain that I have conceived my books as a whole' (*L'Homme*, 26).

As already noted in his biography, it was at least as early as 1942-3 that Ellul outlined the basic structure and themes of his subsequent writing.[145] In fact some evidence suggests that the writing project originated even earlier in 1936-7. Certainly, as chapter three shows, the seeds of Ellul's thinking were

---

[143] This statement was made in 1981, by his death there were a dozen more 'chapters'.

[144] Boli-Bennett 1980:197. In addition to this article, other good brief accounts of the structure and purpose of Ellul's corpus are found in Sturm 1984; Temple 1985; Clendenin 1989.

[145] *Season*, 174; 1982c, 12.

planted when he was in his twenties.[146] Although this plan was not exactly followed, Ellul adhered to its main lines and its structure of two distinct paths of study (historical/sociological and theological/ethical) was consistently maintained. This dual element in Ellul's writing is the fruit of his youthful encounters with Marx and, more important, Jesus Christ.

> I thus remained unable to eliminate Marx, unable to eliminate the biblical revelation, and unable to merge the two. For me, it was impossible to put them together. So I began to be torn between the two, and I have remained so all my life. The development of my thinking can be explained starting with this contradiction (*Season*, 16).

Ellul could not see Christianity as able to explain his social world or offer an economic or political system but Marx could not answer the existential questions of his human condition. Each therefore made their own specific contribution:

> The economic and political facets of Marx's thinking (I knew nothing then of his philosophical thought) became for me a good framework for comprehending the society in which I lived. But the revelation…allowed me to live in society, to be alive in it (*Season*, 19).

This contrast is the underlying basis of Ellul's two sets of works and his corpus is dialectically constructed around his understanding of the modern world under the influence of Marx and his theological reflection upon Christian faith and practice under the witness of revelation.[147] Focussed on two central questions – 'What theology, what ethic, what biblical knowledge, in *this* particular world? And reciprocally, *what* is this particular world?'[148] - Ellul's work as a whole forms 'a composition in counterpoint' (1970j, 201). Any attempt to understand his thought that concentrates excessively on one of the two strands or ignores the relation between them is therefore liable to

---

[146] In support of an earlier date for the basic structure of his work and at least the planning of some of his later works there is Ellul's claim in 1987 to have planned to write on Ecclesiastes for over 50 years (*Reason*, 2), his tracing of the origins of *Presence* to a 1936 article (*Ethique* III, 175), and his 1972 claim that, 'Thirty five years ago I set myself as a line of work the question of Christian faith and Power…' (1972f, 4n). Zorn claims, on the basis of private correspondence with Ellul, that 'the author himself has conceived his work since 1936' (Zorn 1971:251).

[147] On this dialectic see the self-critical interlude at *Hope*, 156-66; *Season*, 172ff and discussion of dialectic in his works at *WIB*, 43-6; *L'Homme*, 26 and 1970j, 200f.

[148] Personal letter cited in Metzger 1992:40.

distort his thinking.[149] As Ellul told Chastenet when he enquired how, if he had written 'one book', the sociological works and theological writings were interconnected.

> The interplay between the two is very important for me as I have always thought that there should be a dialectical relation between a sociological and theological writing. It is not possible to read one without the other...They do belong to two different registers. They are inter-related if you like. In much the same way as a negative pole and a positive pole interact and then sparks fly between them...(*Conversations*, 90-1).

The Purpose of the Two Strands[150]

THE SOCIOLOGICAL STUDIES[151]

The motivation for Ellul's sociological studies was personal and simple: 'I was living in a terrible world...*I needed to understand*' (*L'Homme*, 79). Two phrases which recur constantly throughout his writing reveal Ellul's response to this need and sum up the heart of his sociological studies: *prendre conscience de* and *(re)mettre en question*.[152]

One of the central problems Ellul sees in the contemporary world is people's refusal to become aware of the complex reality in which they live and the nature of their own alienation.[153] His sociological studies therefore attempt to provide readers with his own interpretive key to (and analysis of) the structure of the modern world with the aim of encouraging them to pursue

---

[149] This is the limitation of the excellent Ray 1973 which only examines his ethics and, on the other side, the problems with Lovekin 1991 and Wennemann 1991b arise from their explicit refusal to take his theology seriously as theology.

[150] A good number of Ellul's published books do not easily fit into the two strands. These are the books based on interviews (*Season, Perspectives, Conversations*), more general writings (*WIB, L'Homme*), historical studies (*Institutions* 1-5, *Histoire*), studies of contemporary political situations (*FLN, Israël*), and the posthumously published poetry (*Silences, Oratorio*), volume of early articles (*Sources*) and notes on his lectures (*Classes*).

[151] The best short accounts of Ellul's sociological work and its purpose are Cérézuelle 1979; Temple 1980 & 1985; Sturm 1984; Wennemann 1991b. The best book-length study is Chastenet 1992.

[152] Unfortunately, these terms and their cognates are variously translated e.g. 'become aware of', 'recognise', 'discover' and 'question' or 'challenge'. Menninger 1974:12-4, 217ff discusses these aspects of Ellul's work.

[153] *Presence*, 81-2; *Freedom*, 44-5. The fullest discussions of what is involved in the necessary *prise de conscience* are *Presence*, 98-112; *Freedom*, 226-35.

their own critical reflection upon it.[154] These studies are not, however, simply academic. Ever since the 1930s, Ellul subscribed to Marx's famous 11th Thesis on Feuerbach.

> Very early on I wanted to understand what was happening. And the more I read in order to understand, the more at the same time I noticed in my experience. The more I learned to generalise from these local experiences and to find deeper roots, the more I grew in discovery of a terrible world. My friend Charbonneau helped me greatly in this understanding and awareness (*prise de conscience*). I also had the sense that if people gained the same awareness as I had of this fact they would be able to change this world. A year or two later I was struck by Marx's famous aphorism: 'it is not enough to understand the world, it is necessary to change it'...So then what was one to do?...The only way which was open to us was to address the individual... And it was in this way that I was led to write these books on our society (*L'Homme*, 79, 80, 81).[155]

From early on Ellul described this sociological task as a work of realism and, demonstrating that these sociological studies were not divorced from his Christian faith, he insisted that this goal was also a Christian calling before it was a Marxist one. Thus in 1947 he wrote,

> Christian realism is essentially active. It will never be a matter of mere talk, but rather of an effort to penetrate into reality and to transform, modify the course of this reality...The task is not to understand, but to change the world. This idea, which was developed by Karl Marx, was essentially, and well before Marx, a Christian idea...But because Christians had relinquished it, others took possession of it (*Sources*, 77).

Ellul's sociological studies therefore seek to enable individual readers to separate themselves from the mass, examine and question themselves and their world, and then to say 'no' and act with understanding in order to resist the world and bring about change. Although often bleak in their description of the world and their prognosis, these works are fundamentally misunderstood if they are dismissed as pessimistic or fatalistic.[156] In fact, the central purpose

---

[154] The stress on the need for consciousness of the situation is, of course, indebted to Marx ('*for Marx* the way of Revolution inevitably *begins* by *la prise de conscience*', *Ethique* III, 155; cf. *Changer*, 218) and this is a central theme of Charbonneau's studies (*Reason*, 177-8).

[155] See also discussion in *Révolution*, 324-8.

[156] Ellul acknowledges he is widely viewed as a pessimist (e.g. *Hope*, 167) but defends himself by comparing his task as equivalent to that of a doctor facing a patient with cancer

of these books is quite the opposite.

> They are written in order to call the reader to a recognition (*une prise de conscience*) of the world in which they are living and to take decisions about the way in which to engage with this world in order to change it. As a result, I have in no way sought to make people more pessimistic, more hopeless, more powerless (*L'Homme*, 28).[157]

The sociological works as a whole were also, from the beginning, structured around a central goal: 'All the work I conceived during that period was intended to be, with a few exceptions, part of the detailed analysis of this technical society' (*Season*, 176). Therefore, each book - whether focussing on Technique, propaganda and the mass media, politics, revolution, religion and Christianity, social fragmentation, art, or language - is primarily a study of a feature within the multi-faceted modern technical world.[158]

THE THEOLOGICAL STUDIES

Ellul's theological works encompass studies of biblical books, biblical studies of social phenomena, theological ethics, and more general studies relating to the Christian life. They have in common a desire to enable Christians to hear and in obedience live out the Word of God in the modern world.

> I planned, on the theological side, a series of exegetical and theological Bible studies (*théologie biblique*), and on the other side, given the great deficiency of Protestantism in this area, a search for ethics from a political perspective, in which I would find out how the Christian life can be expressed collectively, under the conditions of *this* society (which must consequently be understood). That was the task (*Season*, 174).

As with the sociological studies, if this general orientation is forgotten then

---

(*Conversations*, 28) or living through an epidemic (*TS*, xxvii). Chastenet 1992 studies Ellul's thought in relation to this question of his pessimism which is raised particularly by Christians 1974:276ff.

[157] Baker 1991 defends this method and Skillen 1982 critiques it. In the foreword to *TS* Ellul says his predictions would be falsified by an awareness of the situation and a change of behaviour (*TS*, xxx) thus demonstrating that his sociological works can be seen to have a quasi-prophetic function in that he writes to warn society where it is heading and to call for people to change course.

[158] The seventeen works generally listed as Ellul's sociological studies are, in chronological order of first publication, *TS*, *Propaganda*, *Illusion*, *Critique*, *Métamorphose*, *Autopsy*, *Jeunesse*, *Révolution*, *Demons*, *Betrayal*, *TSys*, *Marx*, *L'Empire*, *Humiliation*, *Changer*, *Bluff* and *Déviances*.

Ellul's theological and ethical writings are easily misinterpreted. First, these works, especially the ethics, are addressed primarily to Christians and cannot be universalised and applied to those without faith. They are grossly distorted if they are made to offer a Christian solution to the world's problems. Second, although as the next chapter shows, there is an underlying coherent structure to Ellul's theology, the books are not an attempt to offer a comprehensive theological or ethical system. They are a means of enabling people to hear the call of God and to make a personal response to it

> Christianity does not offer (and is not made to offer!) a solution for social, political, economic problems (or even for moral or spiritual problems!). God in Jesus Christ puts questions to us – questions about ourselves, our politics, our economy – and does not supply the answers; it is the Christian himself who must make answer (1970j, 201).[159]

Finally, the studies must be understood in relation to Ellul's sociological analysis of the modern world. They are written for Christians here and now (Ellul frequently emphasizes this aspect of *hic et nunc*) and are liable to be misunderstood if their specific proposals are treated as expressions of timeless truths applicable to any situation.

> In taking my studies in themselves one loses their reference to our times and to the person in our society in relation to which they were written. One is therefore tempted to give an everlasting value in themselves to what are ad hoc translations of revealed Truth (*L'Homme*, 30).[160]

Conclusion

This introductory overview of Ellul's corpus shows that his extensive writing was clearly conceived as a single project with a dialectical structure comprising two different strands of work: history/sociology and theology/ethics. The sociological strand aims to enable readers to become aware of the reality of the modern technical world and then to put that world into question, to resist it, and to work for change. The various theological writings seek to enable Christians to hear the Word of God today and to live in obedience to that Word within the world studied in Ellul's sociology. With

---

[159] See also the explanation at *L'Homme*, 28-30.

[160] The works generally viewed as theological/ethical works are *Law, Presence, Jonah, Money, False, TWTD, Politics, Violence, Prayer, City, Hope, Freedom/Ethique I-III, Apocalypse, Faith, Subversion, Conférence, Genèse, Reason, Anarchy, Dieu, Si.*

this big picture in place, a more detailed study of the basic structure of each of these strands and an introduction to their central themes is offered in the following two chapters before returning to the dialectical relationship between them in the fourth chapter.

CHAPTER 2

Ellul's Theology: Rupture and Communion

Interpreting Ellul's Theology

The task of interpreting Ellul's theology is a challenging one. In addition to the problems already noted due to the style and structure of his writing, there are a number of problems specific to his theological work.

Ellul, despite his theological training, does not consider himself a professional theologian and he is particularly wary about constructing a theological system that could prevent us from hearing God speak his Word to us.[1] None of his books therefore present a clear statement of his theology and so it is necessary to piece this together from comments and discussions scattered across his writing. This task is made more complex by two further features of his work. On the one hand, the dialectical structure of his theology leads him to embrace contradictory elements within his thought that must be held together in tension in any faithful account.[2] On the other hand, although he himself never explicitly acknowledged them as such, other contradictions within his corpus are not due to the dialectical 'both-and' structure of his thought but to changes and developments within his theological position.

In the light of these problems, it is unsurprising that although Ellul's affinity with Kierkegaard and Barth has been widely acknowledged, the content and structure of his own theology have been largely neglected outside the narrow confines of Ellul scholarship and there is some confusion about how to classify his theological work.[3] Within the secondary literature devoted to Ellul, three different approaches to his theology can be found. A number of authors ignore this aspect of his work altogether or pay little attention to it.[4]

---

[1] *TWTD*, 2; *Money* 31-2; 1969f relates this theological self-understanding to Jean Bosc and his theology.

[2] *Subversion*, 43-6 discusses this ('there is no logic in the biblical revelation') while one of Ellul's main criticisms of Barth's interpreters is their failure to be faithful to his dialectic (*False*, 9).

[3] Clendenin 1987, ch. 1 offers a survey of the literature in terms of Ellul as a theological positivist, as existentialist, as prophet, and as dialectician before calling him 'eclectic'.

[4] Mitcham 1969; Christians 1974; Wren 1977. Chastenet's otherwise excellent 1992 study is weakest in his brief discussions of Ellul's theology.

This runs the risk of producing a distorted picture of Ellul.[5] Others have contributed studies of specific areas within Ellul's theology and ethics and chapters five to seven in Part Two fall within this category.[6] Inevitably, such studies often overlap with the final category that provides a more comprehensive account of Ellul's theology and ethics and suggests their controlling elements and foci. The goal of this chapter is to propose a new interpretive key to Ellul's theological work - the relationship between God and the world expressed in terms of communion and rupture - and to demonstrate that making this feature structurally central enables a coherent account to be given of Ellul's wider theology and ethics. This then sets the wider context for the more focused studies of Part Two. Before developing this account of Ellul's theology in detail, however, other major proposals offered as keys to understanding Ellul's theology should be noted.

Matheke's thesis presents Ellul's 'theological presuppositions' in some detail. Many of his claims are valid and reveal Ellul's essential Protestantism but he distorts Ellul by structuring his argument too closely around the loci of classic Reformed theology and giving the impression that Ellul remains essentially a Calvinist.[7] Burke, in contrast, finds the heart of Ellul's theology in his Christocentricism and even writes that for Ellul the teaching of the Bible can be reduced to the person of Christ.[8] Miller is similar but less reductionist, arguing that 'the Word of God is the central idea of Jacques Ellul's thought'.[9]

Other studies have integrated Ellul's theology much more with his ethics and sought to understand the relationship between the theological and sociological strands of his writing. In one of the most thorough studies of Ellul's work, Katharine Temple's unpublished thesis seeks to show that Ellul's interpretation of the traditional Christian framework of the two realms/kingdoms/cities 'forms the cornerstone of his thought'.[10] Two major Ellul scholars have, in different ways, sharpened this insight and suggested

---

[5] Wilson 1975 and Ihara 1975 both view him as a Calvinist, and Lovekin 1991 is flawed because of his philosophical rather than theological interest – 'It is not my concern to treat Ellul's theological thought theologically. It is beyond the scope and interest of this study to trace Ellul's theology...' (p54).

[6] See e.g. Gill 1984b; Clark 1981; Holland 1986; Dawn 1992.

[7] Matheke 1972:6-40.

[8] 'Ellul's christocentric emphasis forms the cornerstone of his entire theology' (Burke 1980:57).

[9] Miller 1970:124. Although Gill 1984b and Holland 1986 focus on Ellul's doctrine of the Word of God neither propose it as central and Gill's categorisation of Ellul as a prophet effectively refuses to search for coherence or a central structuring theme.

[10] Temple 1976:20. The importance of this theme for Ellul is further shown in the choice of *Les Deux Cités* as the title for the A.P.P. journal.

their own interpretive keys to unlock Ellul's work. Darrell Fasching, in a number of important studies originating with his two-volume 1978 thesis under Gabriel Vahanian on Ellul's social ethics, has argued that at the heart of Ellul's thought is the distinction and contrast between the sacred (which performs the sociological functions of integration and legitimation in the world) and the holy (which demands separation and openness to transformation).[11] Finally, Daniel Clendenin, in a thesis devoted to Ellul's theological method, places himself within the overall context of Temple's proposal but argues for a more specific focus.

> The dialectic between freedom and necessity is the central and controlling idea in all of Ellul's work...This freedom/necessity dialectic is, I propose, the golden thread running throughout his corpus, the kernel, or the 'essential inspiration' which governs his entire theology.[12]

All these proposals draw attention to important Ellulian themes and enable a clearer understanding of elements within his theology or ethics. None of them, however, produce a convincing and comprehensive account of the whole and so they must be taken as providing only secondary or penultimate structures for Ellul's work. This is true even for the most wide-ranging of the suggestions, Temple's focus on the relationship between the church and the world. Ellul's distinctive conclusions about the exact nature of the Christian presence in the world (elements of which Fasching and Clendenin highlight) arise from his belief that the Christian is only different from the world on account of the word and work of God. The distinction between the two realms lies in the fact that the Christian 'derives his thought from another source. He has another master...He stands up for the interests of his Master, as an ambassador champions the interests of his country' (*Presence*, 33,34). In other words, the relationship between the church and the world is undergirded by the more fundamental relationship between God and the world.

This centrality of the relationship between God and the world in Ellul's thought is noted by other writers but usually left undeveloped and limited to the opposition between God and the fallen world as in Douglas Sturm's excellent short introduction to Ellul's thought.[13] Probably the clearest

---

[11] Fasching 1978; 1981:104-5,162ff & 1992:154ff.

[12] Clendenin 1987:59 (apparently unaware of this view in Ray 1973:10). Wennemann 1991b follows Clendenin.

[13] Sturm 1984. Others noting this theme include Miller 1970:124,126; Mulkey 1973:93,167; Gill 1984b:46; Temple 1985:35; Holland 1986:173.

recognition of this theme as central in Ellul's thought is found in the writings of Vernard Eller who sees Ellul's 'most notable doctrine' as 'his insistence on maintaining an absolute distinction between who God is on the one hand and what the world is on the other'.[14]

The central thesis of this chapter is that the relationship between God and the world, viewed in the terms of communion and rupture, lies at the heart of Ellul's theology, gives shape to his understanding of the Christian life, structures his ethic for Christians, and embraces all the other proposals outlined above as possible keys to Ellul's thought.[15] The following part of this chapter presents the case for this framework by giving an account of Ellul's theology structured around God's relationship with the world in terms of communion and rupture. A brief treatment of Ellul's doctrine of God provides the necessary introduction, followed by an analysis of Ellul's conception of creation in terms of unbroken communion between God and the world. After studying how this relationship is ruptured by 'the Fall', the characteristics and central elements of the fallen world are described. Then, contrasting with this world of ruptured communion, Ellul's understanding of God's *eschatological* goal of renewed communion with the world in his new creation (following the rupture of his final judgment) is examined. Finally, in the light of these accounts of 'full' communion and 'full' rupture within the God-world relationship, God's *historical* relationship with the world by means of his spoken and incarnate Word can be elaborated in terms of the dialectic between communion and rupture. The chapter's final part shows how this theology then shapes both Ellul's view of the Christian's proper relationship with the world and the task and structure of Christian ethics.

Ellul's Theology: God and The World in Communion and Rupture

God

Ellul's doctrine of God is perhaps the most difficult aspect of his theology to understand because he believes that it is impossible to present a logically coherent discourse about God. He confesses

---

[14] Eller 1985:75. Eller relates this to Barth who learned from Blumhardt that 'World is world; but God is God' (cf. Busch 1976:87).

[15] I use 'God' and 'the world' here because they are traditional theological terms. They are effectively synonymous with Ellul's other regularly used terms, 'truth' and 'reality' (see 1959e; 1960l, and *Humiliation* (especially pp252ff) for these as parallel contrasts). Kristensen 1976:109 and Dujancourt 1989 use these alternative categories.

My first reflections revolve around the central conviction that I cannot have a single coherent image of God. I cannot say at a given moment that God is simply this or that for me. He is, but he is also other things at the same time which may finally be the opposite. I cannot attempt a synthesis or reconciliation between the different elements in what I believe I can understand about God. *I thus renounce here any attempt at intellectual coherence.* (*WIB*, 169. Italics added)

Ellul is adamant that we can only speak about God on the basis of his self-revelation. However, one result of this for him is that we can only know God in terms of his relationship to us and never God in himself (*Faith*, 190-1). This perhaps explains why, despite claiming that the Trinity is central to Christian faith and praising both Barth and Moltmann in relation to this insight,[16] Ellul's theology is not structured around the doctrine of the Trinity. Indeed he even states,

We can affirm neither that the ultimate being of God is Trinity nor that this teaching exhausts the fullness of God...we must...refrain from speculation concerning the identity of God with his revelation (1987, 218).[17]

Despite these problems, Ellul's understanding of God is clearly focussed on four central affirmations: God is the living God, God is Wholly Other, God is love and God is free.[18] These characteristics recur throughout his writing. They undergird his emphasis on man's inability to know God fully and play a central role in determining the character of man and the world, both in communion with God and broken from him. A brief comment on each is therefore necessary before examining God's creation of a world in communion with him.

LIVING GOD

'Le Dieu vivant' appears as a description of God in one of Ellul's first

---

[16] In answering a question in relation to Islam Ellul comments, 'What is fundamental in Christianity is that it is not a closed monotheism...the keystone is the Trinity' (*Conférence*, 110-1). On Barth see 1975e, 174 and on Moltmann, *WIB*, 177.

[17] This contrasts with Barth's method at Church Dogmatics I/1:479. Ellul's brief note at *Subversion*, 11 shows his understanding of the Trinity could fall into modalism (I am grateful to Sze Chi Chan for first drawing my attention to this) perhaps because he interprets *persona* through its usage in Roman law, an important theme for Ellul e.g. *Institutions* 2, 480-1.

[18] Scott 1989:21-5 claims to find twelve characteristics of God in Ellul's work but incredibly manages to miss these four except God's freedom. In contrast to his account, that offered here is based on those designations of God central in Ellul's own writing.

published pieces of theological writing (1938a, 421). It recurs constantly throughout his later books.[19] It is an understanding of God that he believes Barth re-established but whose first great modern defender was Kierkegaard.[20] Ellul argues that, biblically, to speak of God as the Eternal is to speak of the Living One (*'le Vivant'*) and that God is 'the only living one and the only one who can say "I am" ' (1986, 67). It is this that distinguishes the true God from fixed and distant idols and the God of the philosophers. Because he is the living God there can be a living, dynamic historical relationship between God and his world.[21]

WHOLLY OTHER GOD

By far the most regular designation for God in Ellul's corpus is Wholly Other ['le Tout Autre'].[22] He can even define true Christianity as 'the revelation of the Wholly Other' (*Violence*, 148) and 'faith in the revelation of the Wholly Other' (*Demons*, 64). This emphasis on God's transcendence is, of course, a prominent element throughout the Reformed tradition. Ellul views it as central to Calvin and includes among Barth's contributions to contemporary theology his stress on 'The Wholly Other God...radical transcendence' (1977g, 3).[23]

God's radical transcendence is the primary cause of Ellul's reticence to develop a more comprehensive doctrine of God and his advocacy of the *via negativa*

> Only a negative theology is possible. We can only know what God is not. Nothing more. He is the Wholly Other whom we cannot know. There is nothing in common between him and his creation (*Subversion*, 44).

Truth is lost, however, if emphasis is placed solely on God's Wholly Otherness. This is because God rarely acts in a transcendent manner but rather uses a human instrument (*Presence*, 73-4).[24] It must never be forgotten that

---

[19] As with all these characteristics and designations, I will list only a small selection of illustrative examples from Ellul's earliest to latest works often selecting those where more than one of the four is mentioned. On the living God see *Presence*, 40; *Jonah*, 28; *TWTD*, 204; *Hope*, 129; *Subversion*, 24; *Si*, 74.

[20] 1950g, 14; 1979j,vii; 1981b, 18.

[21] Ellul claims that Scripture shows us 'the History of "God-with-men"...a living, that is to say, historical, God' (1981b, 18).

[22] *False*, 40; *Politics*, 151; *Prayer*, 148; *Hope*, viii; *Humiliation*, 110. See Gill 1984b:160 and Zorn 1971:183-204.

[23] See further Ray 1973:61ff. Ellul uses God's transcendence to extend Weber's analysis of Calvinism and capitalism (1964,13).

[24] *False* warns against dangers in a theology of transcendence (pp9-10, 79-81).

the fundamental contradiction of Christianity is the confession that

> God the Wholly Other is incarnate in a man. He is still the Wholly Other...If I say that God is transcendent and stop there, this is not the biblical God. If I say only that Jesus Christ is God, this is not the gospel (*Subversion*, 44-5).

Thus, on the basis that God would actually be the source of man's alienation were he only Wholly Other, Ellul appeals to the third characteristic when he writes that because we are speaking of the Transcendent who reveals himself in Jesus Christ, 'since he is love, he is himself the guarantee of the nonalienation of the person to whom he reveals himself' (*Hope*, 246).

GOD IS LOVE

Ellul insists that 'the center of the revelation which God has given of himself is that he is love' (*TWTD*, 263) and that 'the true face of the biblical God is love' (*Anarchy*, 35).[25] Indeed, it is only because God is love that he reveals himself so we can know him and it is because he is love that his revelation is by his Word.[26] In a vitally important move, Ellul insists that this divine self-giving *agape* love is the polar opposite of *eros*. In his fullest discussion of this in his *Foi et Vie* article on Agape and Eros he writes that

> if Paul (and others !) felt the need to use another word in order to designate love, and supremely the love of God for humans in Jesus Christ...this is precisely in order to testify that the love of God and the love among the brethren which flows from this, has absolutely nothing to do with Eros and that it is its very opposite (1976d, 62).[27]

GOD IS FREE[28]

Here again Ellul places himself fully within the Reformed tradition and the

---

[25] See also *Jonah*, 96; *Politics*, 46 ('the living and loving God'); *Hope*, 104 ('has chosen to be totally and uniquely love'); *Reason*, 249; *Si*, 62; *Dieu*, 58 and *Conversations*, 105 on defining the specificity of the God he believes in. Scott's comment, that 'it is of interest to note the relative scarcity in Ellul's thought of an element central to most discussion of God: love' (Scott 1989:26) is blatantly false.

[26] *Humiliation*, 59ff; 1983k,87.

[27] In his books this is discussed at *Money*, 88 and *Betrayal*, 71ff both of which refer favourably although not uncritically to the classic exposition of this polarity in Nygren 1932-9.

[28] Although Ellul occasionally speaks of God as 'freedom' (*la liberté*) (e.g. *Humiliation*, 63) he usually avoids this even writing that 'We cannot say that God is freedom, since this would be pure speculation' (*Freedom*, 51). He prefers to speak of God as 'free' (*libre*) and of 'the freedom of God' (*la liberté de Dieu*).

thought of Kierkegaard and Barth.[29] His central concern is to emphasise that God is bound by nothing and that we cannot seek an explanation for his actions other than his freedom to do as he wills.[30] Thus, in describing God's presence in history he writes of the total freedom of God's decision and claims we can find no reason behind it because God's free will lacks any cause.[31]

> God is free. God is sovereign. But above all he is, in the words of Kierkegaard, the *Inconditionné* – with no conditions (*Conversations*, 115).

This emphasis on God's sovereign freedom obviously correlates with the affirmations of God as the living God who is Wholly Other and could lead to a conception of God as totally arbitrary and utterly beyond any human comprehension. It is, therefore, once again vital that God's freedom is never separated from his love. In his study of the book of Revelation Ellul writes of the Apocalypse as 'the great book of the constant affirmation of the liberty of God' but adds that God 'is sovereignly free, conditioned in his liberty only by his love' (*Apocalypse*, 63). This dialectic of freedom and love is illustrated in Ellul's discussion of our next subject – God's creation of a world to be in communion with him. Here he refuses to accept that creation is *either* an arbitrary act of God *or* a necessity for God and instead holds both together in dialectical tension (1983k, 81).

These four affirmations about God – that he is the Living God, the Wholly Other God, the God who is Love and the God who is Free – are central to Ellul's theology. They have significant implications for the character of the world God made both when it is in a relationship of communion with God and when it has ruptured that communion and also for the pattern of the Christian life.[32]

---

[29] *Anarchy*, 37; 1972d, 48; 1978d, 24. Ellul's major book reflecting on the freedom of God does so in Barth's framework of 'the free determination of man in the free decision of God' (*Politics*, 15).

[30] *Money*, 86-7; *Jonah*, 76; *TWTD*, 59ff ; *Humiliation*, 110-11; *Subversion*, 169ff; *Si*, 65-6; *Dieu*, 39-40. In Ellul studies, God's freedom has not received as much attention as Christian freedom but see Minnema 1973:19-20; Van Hook 1981:134ff; and Clendenin 1987:105ff.

[31] *Politics*, 57ff. Reference is here made to Job who appears regularly as an example in Ellul's books. A hand-written, unpublished series of studies on Job by Ellul is in the Wheaton Archive.

[32] Although Ellul nowhere explicitly expresses his doctrine of God in terms of these four affirmations, the trilogy of Freedom, Life and Love appear at the end of his ethics of freedom (*Ethique* III, 333) and he speaks of Jesus Christ as 'a peremptory historical

Creation as Communion with God

Ellul is often criticised for having a weak or non-existent doctrine of creation with one writer even commenting that 'in vain I search for any indications of a doctrine of creation'.[33] This is due to a number of factors. Creation does not have a significant place in any of his translated works (although there is the untranslated *Genèse*, some important articles, and discussions in, for example, *Humiliation*). Furthermore his prominent and strong doctrine of the Fall (discussed in the next section) combines with his insistence that grace is opposed to nature and that Christians are to be 'anti-nature' in such a way that he can easily be misconstrued.[34] When, in addition, he explicitly downplays the significance of God as Creator by claiming that 'this concept occupies a lesser place in the Bible than later theology claimed for it' (*Faith*, 96) and emphasizing that it was as Liberator in the Exodus that Israel first came to know God and only subsequently as the universal creator (*Anarchy*, 39), the common negative conclusion is perhaps understandable. It is, however, false. Ellul developed an elaborate doctrine of creation, the heart of which is expressed in terms of a relationship of communion between God and the world.[35]

Ellul's doctrine of creation begins, as in the Genesis account, with the Word of God for 'the first act of God is to speak: God says. It is through **his Word** that God brings things to be' (*Genèse*, 30, emphasis original). As with the reference to the Spirit of God in Genesis 1.2, this speaks of God entering into relationship with something other than himself.

> The God who speaks through the Word ('God says…') is neither far off nor abstract. Rather, he is the creator by means of something that is primarily a means of relationship. The Word is the essential relationship (*Humiliation*, 50-1).

In establishing this relation with creation by his Word, God reveals himself as both freedom and love (*Humiliation*, 58-60) and so, despite his strong Barthian rejection of natural theology, Ellul, following Calvin, allows that 'the Bible teaches us to read creation as a mirror of God, but it sends us to Him through it' (1980q, 272).[36]

---

affirmation that uniquely combines life, love, and freedom' (*Subversion*, 187).

[33] Logan 1977:15. See also Holmes 1981; Skillen 1982; Gill 1984b:120, 176.

[34] On creation, nature and grace see most fully 1975f.

[35] For other accounts of Ellul's doctrine of creation see Miller 1970:126-31; Blocher 1972:121-3; Kemp 1976; Temple 1976:315-29.

[36] *Institutes*, 1.14.21.

Ellul argues that the Genesis account does not teach creation from nothing as prior to God's creative word there is *Tohu wa bohu* which Ellul interprets as showing that what there was is indescribable.

> We must remember that the act of creation does not graft itself onto an absence, a nothing, a nonbeing. It is not a matter of a creation ex nihilo. It is the affirmation of the hope of God against the aggressive power of nonbeing…against the aggression of the negative (*Hope*, 229).[37]

God acts on this nothingness by his word in order to give it form, establish separations within it, and put it in order. The result is a work of God which is totally other than God and related to him only by his word (*Genèse*, 34-6). He sums up his view of creation as 'the institution of the relation between the Created and the Creator, the setting in place of the Created through relation to the Creator' (1975f, 40).

Within Ellul's doctrine of creation his primary concern is with humanity.[38] Although man remains a creature wholly dependent on God, his significance within creation is highlighted in the Genesis narratives by such means as the reference to the divine deliberation at the start of the sixth day (*Genèse*, 68) and the account of man naming the animals (*Humiliation*, 52). Ellul sees the human creature as the crowning achievement (*le couronnement*), head (*le chef*), and keeper (*le gardien*) who is at the summit and centre of God's creative work (*Genèse*, 74). His special position is not, however, based on some essential human nature but on his unique relationship with God because 'biblically, there is not a human nature but a certain relationship between man and God' (1975f, 43). This relationship is based on God's Word that humans are to hear and to which they are to respond and thereby enter into dialogue with God.[39] In God's creative purpose we were made to live in existential

---

[37] Here 'nonbeing' is *Le Néant* and Ellul appears to draw on Barth's discussion of Nothingness (CD III/3, §50). This is explicitly linked to *Tohu wa bohu* (on which see *Genèse*, 29) at a number of places in Ellul's study of Revelation (*L'Apocalypse*, 75, 221) although this is less obvious in ET where Néant is 'nothingness' but 'Tohou Bohou' is 'chaos' (74) and 'confusion' (211).

[38] Despite this focus on humanity, Ellul cannot be accused of ignoring non-human creation. Among other matters, he discusses the evolution of the animal creation, emphasises God's blessing establishes animals within a loving relationship (*Genèse*, 40-1; *Jonah*, 94-5), and views time and space as creatures (1960i). For these reasons, together with the fact that Ellul also places great emphasis on man's works and the powers as part of the world ruptured from God, 'the world' rather than 'humanity' is used in this account of Ellul's theology.

[39] *Humiliation*, 63ff. Ellul's *Ethique* II, 180ff contains an important discussion of his understanding of 'responsibility' in this sense of response to God's word.

communion with God and obey his Word by living in the freedom of love. This is central to Ellul's understanding.

> In the divine fellowship of an as yet unshattered creation...all that counted was the relation to God and its expression in action. Adam...had fellowship with God. That was all (*Freedom*, 51).[40]

On this basis, the unique calling of men and women is to act as mediator between God and the rest of the world, representing the creation before God and representing God in creation as his steward and *lieu-tenant* (1974g, 138). As God's representative within the world, humans, when in communion with God, reflect the four characteristics of God discussed above.

First, God makes man a living being. In discussing Ecclesiastes 12 and Genesis 2 Ellul comments on the breath/spirit

> This breath is the very breath of the Creator, since it makes a person a living being. And God the Creator is himself called the Living One (*le Vivant*). How could this life that he transmits to humanity be anything but the life that comes from him...the life that comes from the Living One (*Reason*, 289).

This is, in part, what it means to be set apart within creation as the image of God because 'the only possible image of God, is man...It is the living man (*l'homme vivant*) who is that image' (1977e, 145). Indeed, one element of Ellul's iconoclastic theology of the image is that 'if humanity was created as the image of God, and if the only perfect image is Jesus Christ, this means that the living God (*le Dieu vivant*) cannot tolerate sterile material images. He requires living images; this is the basis of the Incarnation' (*Humiliation*, 85).

Second, God's Wholly Otherness is reflected in two ways within human creation. Humanity's role vis-à-vis the rest of creation has parallels with God's relationship to the whole world. We are called to have 'a wholly other (*tout autre*) role than all other elements of creation' (*Genèse*, 68). Central to this is our power of speech.

> God creates human beings as speaking beings. Perhaps this is one of the meanings of the image of God...The human being is the only one, out of the entire creation, who is capable of language...Speech constitutes human specificity, just as it constitutes the specificity of God as compared with all other gods (*Humiliation*, 63).

---

[40] On this centrality of Adam's *communion* with God in creation 1960e is the fullest discussion but see passing comments at *Violence*, 128 and *Reason*, 254.

In addition to this, humanity is differentiated into male and female. Discussing this bipolarity of humanity and the significance of the discovery of the other who is similar and yet different, Ellul draws a startling parallel with God's Otherness – 'the question is that of the relation between the Creator and his Creation. The other in relation is truly other' (1976d, 72).[41]

Third, in relation to man in the image of God, Ellul follows Barth and sees 'image of God' in Genesis 1.26 given its meaning in what follows: 'male and female he created them'.[42] On the basis that the relation of man and woman is one of love the conclusion is then drawn that the image of God is love. This love shapes humanity's mediating function in the world: humans are to love God, to bring to God the love of his creation, and to be the bearer of God's love in their relationship of dominion over the rest of creation.

> Human beings are the stewards of the world out of love, for the sake of love. If God tells them to 'rule over' it...this comes *immediately* after the proclamation that man and woman together are the image of God. The image of God is Love; there is no other. And that means that people ought to rule over creation in exactly the same way that God himself does, that is, not by violence or constraint or technology but by love (*Faith*, 57).

Fourth, Ellul stresses the freedom of created human beings.[43] God who is free and out of love creates something other than himself to respond to his love, must include in his creation a free agent: humans (1974g, 138). The relation of human freedom to divine freedom is even stronger because, in communion with God, Adam can even be said to share in God's own freedom.

> The original creation expresses the freedom of God and it lives in and by this freedom. If there is no choice, this is not as in a machine in which calculation rules out choice. It is in the harmony of fellowship [*l'harmonie d'une communion*]. Adam, living in fellowship with God, is free...Freedom is living in God's own freedom through this fellowship and in the unbroken unity of all creation in which there are no separate and incoherent bits and pieces between which to choose [*la liberté pour lui, c'est par cette communion...vivre de la liberté même de Dieu*] (*Freedom*, 114; *Ethique* I,

---

[41] Ellul does not here say that man represents God and woman represents creation. For his novel interpretations of the role of women in Scripture see *Subversion*, 73ff; *Ethique* III, 324ff; 1950d; 1985b, 7-8. Hanks 1988a provides the fullest discussion.

[42] *Ethique* III, 304. For Barth's discussion see CD III/1:183ff.

[43] *Genèse*, 73-4; *Humiliation*, 66.

130).

In Adam's original communion with God, humans in creation are given a number of commands and Ellul's understanding of three of these is of particular significance in his theology and ethics. Firstly, as already noted, the task of ruling over the rest of creation must, Ellul insists, take the form of God's own rule and so be a rule of love and freedom by the word

> Since God creates and governs through his Word, and the human being is the image of God, called by God to subdue (govern) and have dominion (command), he can only do it *by the same means*; that is, the *word* (*Humiliation*, 67).

In addition, humans are called to bear fruit. Here, in an important elaboration of the traditional interpretation, Ellul extends this commandment beyond procreation to include all human works: 'you are called to bring forth all sorts of fruits, moral, spiritual, artistic etc' (*Genèse*, 75). Thirdly, Ellul provides a distinctive emphasis in his understanding of the command to work. This is not a vocation to co-creation with God. Nor is it work as we now know it. In fact, Adam's work in Eden is marked by freedom and inutility because God himself has already made a perfect, finished creation in which the whole is in fruitful communion.[44]

This last claim about creation as a whole requires brief elaboration through a sketch of Ellul's vision of the Edenic state of the created world. The different and distinct elements of the creation constitute a unity, a whole filled with God, in which each of the parts is in living communion with all the others. Apart from man's special role of mediation between the rest of creation and the creator, there is no mediation, but only an immediate relation of mutual knowledge and love.[45] This unity in communion of all the diverse creation, crowned by man's own special living relationship of love and freedom in dialogue and communion with God, is shattered by an event which fundamentally transforms the relationship between God and the world: The Fall.

---

[44] The most powerful discussion of this theme is Ellul's concluding meditation on inutility at *Politics*, 190ff. More fully on work and creation see *Ethique* III, 258ff (shorter discussion in ET at *Freedom*, 495ff); 1972i and 1980u.

[45] This vision of creation is alluded to in a number of his books (*Politics*, 191; *Freedom*, 114-5; *Season*, 140-2; *Genèse*, 77,111; *Déviances*, 46-8) and discussed most fully in a number of articles (1960e, 102-3; 1974g, 144; 1974n, 18).

The Fall: Rupture of Communion with God[46]

Ellul is highly critical of modern theologians who downplay or dismiss the traditional Christian doctrine of the Fall (*Critique*, 253). He sees this as part of an overly optimistic, progressivist ideology and, in sharp contrast, insists that the Fall ('*la rupture de l'homme avec Dieu*') is among the fundamental themes in Scripture to which we must adhere (1973e, 73). In some of his earlier work Ellul was happy to speak of the Fall by its traditional designation as *la chute* without critical comment,[47] and translators nearly always make him speak of 'the Fall'. It is, however, significant that he came to prefer the terminology of *la rupture*, writing of 'the break (*la rupture*) between man and God known as the fall (*le chute*)' (*Hope*, 235/*L'Espérance*, 225; cf. *Humiliation*, 229). Indeed, at times he claims that *la chute* is a misnomer and a theological error.

> That idea of 'Fall' is found in many myths, particularly Greco-Roman myths, but emphatically not in Genesis. It is by a deplorable laxity that Christian theologians have adopted this vocabulary which does not fit with biblical thought (1980x, 77n3).[48]

This matter of nomenclature is of great importance because Ellul sees the root of all the world's problems lying in the rupture of man's original, personal communion with his maker. It is this rejection of the heart of God's creative purpose that fundamentally alters the world and its relationship with God.

The creation of humans as free beings in communion with God carried the risk they would break that relationship. Ellul's understanding of the form and cause of that break is based on the narrative of Genesis 3. He sees the seeds of the rupture in Eve's separation of the visible created world (reality) from the Word of God (truth), the disregard for God's word, and particularly in human covetousness (*la convoitise*).[49] As a result, humans disobey the divine commandment not to eat of the tree of the knowledge of good and evil.

Ellul's theology and ethics are built upon a quite specific understanding of the knowledge of good and evil in Genesis.[50] As he argues most fully in the

---

[46] For other accounts of Ellul's theology of the Fall and its effects see Miller 1970:131-4; Zorn 1971:141-60; Mulkey 1973:96-101; Ray 1973:10-41; Ihara 1975:97-139; Temple 1976:330-54.

[47] *L'Argent*, 55; *Jonas*, 129.

[48] A similar statement a year later refers to the error of calling man's rupture with God 'the fall' (1981j, 3). In his books see especially *TWTD*, 39 and *Season*, 140.

[49] *Humiliation*, 96ff (note *Parole*,107 has 'la rupture'); *Ethique* II, 121ff; *Si*, 19.

[50] On different views of the phrase's meaning see Westermann 1984:240-8. Ellul's

opening two chapters of *TWTD*, the good is the will of God and no good exists outside of God's decision. Humans in creation did not choose between good and evil but lived in communion with God whose will is the Good. In disobeying this command of God, we break communion with God and seek to become like God by securing 'the power to *decide* on one's own *what is good and what is evil*' (*Humiliation*, 96n; cf. *Jonah*, 94). This declaration of autonomy and refusal to be a dependent creature in communion with God has a permanent and radical effect on humans and the rest of the created world. The reason for this is found in Ellul's relational conception of man's distinctive position in creation that leaves no room for compromise in the effect of Adam's disobedience

> It is not our intention to enter into a discussion of the hundreds of doctrines put forth as interpretations of what the Bible describes for us as an event. We adhere to the most traditional one, which seems to us best to fit the biblical account and the indisputable certainty that the broken communion with God totally changes the life of the creature (*La rupture de la communion avec Dieu change la totalité de la vie et de l'être*). Either the communion with God is the very ground of one's being, of life and of good, in which case the rupture of that communion changes the whole, or else the change is only partial, which implies that the communion with God was only secondary and not decisive. We cannot agree with those who try to minimize the importance of this event (*TWTD*, 39; *Vouloir*, 36).

The problem of original sin is thus not the transmission to all humanity of Adam's corruption of human nature or some human faculty. It is rather 'a generalized condition that is found to be in place by every child who is born...He lives from his first minute in this universe of *la rupture*' (1986, 67-8). The problem of sin is that of humanity's separation from God and Ellul writes that 'sin is exclusively separation from God' (*False*, 29).[51] To focus on particular 'sins' or personal guilt is misplaced because sin is primarily man's situation, state and condition. This is central to the whole of Ellul's theological and ethical thought and leads to the important conclusion that *every single human act now bears the mark of man's sin and rupture from God*. Indeed

> The main keys in the gospel – the proclamation of grace, the declaration of pardon, and the opening up of life to freedom – imply that *all* conduct,

---

interpretation is clearly indebted to Bonhoeffer 1955.

[51] For fuller discussion see 1986. Ellul follows Kierkegaard and views faith (not virtue) as the opposite of sin (*Money*, 126; 1946e, 23).

including that of the devout, or the most moral, is wholly engulfed in sin. Roman Catholicism…lessened the gravity of sin…but radical Christianity and the Reformation have always stressed this human condition. Whatever we do comes under its law. We can accomplish nothing on our own. We can achieve nothing good or beautiful or true. Everything is rotted and falsified from the intention on. All acts and decisions and projects express the basic state of sin. We are set in unceasing evil, and from the very moment that we separate ourselves from God, whatever we do leads to it. We *are* effectively separated from God… (*Subversion*, 70, 142-3).

Because human beings are the crown of creation acting as mediator between the whole of creation and its Creator, our rupture with God ruptured the unity in communion of all creation. In this new situation 'the mirror of creation is shattered. The *universum* is broken…There is no more immediate contact. Everything has become mediated' (1960e, 132). In a use of terms that has caused much confusion, Ellul expresses this change as creation becoming Nature as a result of the rupture with God.[52] 'Nature' therefore functions for Ellul as the opposite of creation, a shorthand term for a world that, due to the rupture, has lost its open, living gracious relationship of communion with God. It has become instead a closed, self-sufficient world with its own laws and marked by aggression. Humanity's whole relation with the world is therefore now different. Humans seek to define the world in relation to themselves broken from God rather than in communion with the creator. This is the deepest root of our present ecological crisis and so Ellul argues that a right relationship with the non-human creation can only be fully restored as a result of a right relationship with the creator.[53]

Ellul's beliefs about how Christians should view the world and understand their response to it are significantly shaped by this account of The Rupture and its place in his theology and ethics. He regularly writes that a basic Christian truth is that our world is that of the fall. Our world is no longer that of creation which is now totally unknowable to us:

That world has been shattered, it has been subjected to a transformation so radical and so total that we are not able to discern from our world, even by analogy, what creation was (1954d, 164-5).

---

[52] The fullest discussion of this is in 1975f. Its discussion of the contrast between creation and nature shapes the account here and clarifies what Ellul means by speaking of Christians needing to be anti-nature and insisting that grace is against nature rather than perfecting (Thomist) or restoring (classic Reformed) it.

[53] Ellul cites the example of Saint Francis at 1981j, 3.

From his earliest writings, Ellul therefore refuses to accept any appeal in our present situation to the pre-Fall accounts of Genesis, often drawing attention to the covenant with Noah and contrasting it with God's Word to Adam.[54] So, in critiquing the concept of stewardship in relation to possessions he writes,

> We forget too easily that if man is God's steward according to the texts in Genesis, this is true primarily in the order of creation – and we abuse the text by extending that which belongs to the order of creation to the order in which we now live, the order of the Fall. We forget too easily that a rather important event lies between these two orders (*Money*, 30).

In order to understand our present world our primary task is therefore not to study the world that God created in communion with him, but the world which resulted from man's rupture with God and God's new relationship with that world. The following section examines both the character and the elements of our world broken from God.

The World of Ruptured Communion

Although the rupture occurs with Adam and Eve and its immediate consequences are evident in the total disruption of all their relationships, Ellul sees the full import of our loss of communion with God progressively revealed in the remainder of the primeval history in Genesis 1-11, particularly the stories of Cain and Babel.[55] The rest of Scripture, and supremely Jesus Christ, reveal the reality of what John's gospel calls 'the *kosmos*', man's world apart from God (1974n).

In Ellul's work there are three central elements to be considered in the world that has broken its communion with God: humans, human works, and the powers.[56] This world is symbolised by the city and it is therefore unsurprising that one of his earliest works and what he considered 'his most

---

[54] *False*, 27-8; *Season*, 141; 1974g, 142-3.

[55] In addition to *City*, see 1969a on Cain and 1970n on Babel both of which use the language of *la rupture*.

[56] In addition to these three elements the following must also be included in a full account of Ellul's understanding of the historical world: the rest of the non-human creation, the presence of God by his Word, those restored to communion in Christ who live that Word in the world, and (in his early work) a divine order of preservation. This section only studies the character and elements of the world apart from God and (as with so many areas of his theology) it would seriously misrepresent Ellul if, in describing his outlook on our contemporary world, these three elements were not put into relationship with the others discussed below.

important theological book'[57] is a theology of the city.[58] This work should therefore be read not only as an early and powerful piece of what is now classed as urban theology but also as Ellul's theology of the world which has broken communion with God and its relationship with God and the Christian. This wider significance is clear from descriptions of the city scattered throughout the work such as 'the city is the symbol of the world' (*City*, 72). One of the strongest statements is found in a wider discussion of necessity:

> In the Bible the city is depicted as the world which man makes for himself in rejection of what God has created for man and consequently in rejection of God himself. The city is the world in which man wants to be without God. It expresses the attempt to exclude God, to shut oneself off from him, to fabricate a world which is purely and exclusively human (*Freedom*, 39).[59]

Drawing on Ellul's study of the city but also much more widely, it becomes clear that four inter-related characteristics of our fallen world appear repeatedly throughout his writing. Furthermore, because this world is defined by its declaration of autonomy and the rupture of its communion with God, these four features are the polar opposites of the four characteristics of God (and humans and creation in communion). Before examining each of the world's three constituent elements (humans, human works, and the powers) these four global characteristics of the world as a whole need to be outlined.

THE FOUR CHARACTERISTICS OF THE WORLD OF RUPTURED COMMUNION.

First, death rather than life is the result of the rupture with God and the

---

[57] Quoted in Lee 1985:92.

[58] Although it did not appear until 1970, (the French edition following in 1975 with new introductory material and a few new paragraphs in the text) *City* is one of Ellul's earliest manuscripts dating from the late 1940s and early 1950s as shown by: *(1)* The French edition concludes with two dates, 'Noël 1947. Pâques 1951' (*Feu*, 297) suggesting the period of writing; *(2)* The ET dedication ('In memory of my son Simon, who passed away as this book was being born') dates the book's 'birth' to 1947. *(3)* Bosc introduces Ellul's 1950 *Foi et Vie* piece on the city as extracts from his next book which will appear under the title 'Sans feu ni lieu' (1950c, 2). In fact, pp5-7 of the article appear as *Feu*, 246-8 and pp7-19 as *Feu*, 249-261 and there are also overlaps between *Feu* and sections of 1950j; *(4)* In the note on Comblin's book (*Feu*, 19), Ellul writes, 'this book was written long before Comblin's Theology of the City appeared in 1968'; *(5)* Elements of the book's theology - the acceptance of divinely ordained institutions (*Feu*, 224, omitted from *City*, 154) and the apparent rejection of universalism in the language of 'eternal reprobation' (*Feu*, 134; *City*, 85) - are closer to the early thought of Ellul; (6) An early dating makes the writing of *Feu* contemporaneous with its theological counterpart, *Technique* (1970j,201).

[59] Similar comments are made about the city generally (*Freedom*, 275), Nineveh (*Jonah*, 26-7, 95) and Jericho (*Apocalypse*, 70).

Suicide is at the heart of the world

hallmark of the world.[60] This is, of course, quite logical:

> By the break with God, the living God, man is thrown onto the side of nothingness. He is cut off from life. He dies inevitably (*TWTD*, 276n1).[61]

> Death is the final, inescapable reality of human life. And death is tied to sin, in that sin is a break with God. Since God is the Living One, a break with God inevitably leads to death (1980e, 29).

In this break with God, humanity sides with *le Néant* opposed to God's creative purpose and so alters the whole world (*Ethique* III, 198-9). Humans have become by nature alienated, 'booked to die/*un être pour la mort*' (*Freedom*, 69/*Ethique* I, 79) and possessed by 'the death wish/*la volonté de mort*' (*Faith*, 50/*Foi*, 79). This sorry state extends further in the fallen world as, without the action of God, every human work 'is dead; it fades into nothingness' (*Presence*, 97). Nature as a whole is now characterised by murder and headed to death and even God's gifts are now deadly (e.g. 1976d, 78 on sexuality).

As the pale horseman of the Apocalypse, death is also one of the powers at work in the world and so, in the classic statement of *Presence*, 'if we let ourselves drift along the stream of history, without knowing it, we shall have chosen the power of suicide, which is at the heart of the world' (*Presence*, 31).

In the light of this it is unsurprising that Ellul particularly identifies man's greatest work - the city - with death. The city is, of course, originally built by the murderer Cain (Genesis 4) and, after opening his study with the implications of this, Ellul proceeds to speak of the city as 'death's domain/*monde de la mort*', 'condemned to death because of everything she represents' and itself 'dead, made of dead things for dead people…Anything living must come from outside' (*City*, 162, 45, 150).

Second, as a result of the rupture the world is fragmented and divided rather than forming the unity in diversity and communion present in creation through man's communion with God. The human response to this new situation is two-fold: human beings seek to exclude the Wholly Other by creating their own world closed off from God *and* also to re-create a unified world of their own which now entails exclusion of the other.

---

[60] As earlier, only select citations from across the corpus will be given: *Presence*, 23 ("If we take the Fall seriously, the expulsion from Eden, which implies the constant presence of death…"); *City*, 6 (which should read 'death which results *from* the fall'); *Apocalypse*, 229; *Dieu*, 176.

[61] For Ellul's important detailed theological reflections on death see 1974c & 1981q.

This conception of the world spans the whole of Ellul's writing. It appears in his final sociological study where he studies society's response to social deviance (*Déviances*, 46-8) and yet can be traced back to his earliest unpublished writings in the 1930s where he claims that

> A society can only be oriented to the end of excluding God from the life of man – an orientation that may be conscious or unconscious – the perfection of society represents the apotheosis of sin (*Les Forces Morales*, p3).

The world of the rupture is now characterised not by communion with the Wholly Other and that which is other within itself but its polar opposite: a quest for closure from God and for internal unity.

> The world, ever since it has been the world, seeks to close itself up (*se fermer*), to shut itself in (*se clore*), to exclude God (*exclure Dieu*), to make itself one and complete (*se faire unitaire et complet*) (*False*, 208).

The essence of the four phrases Ellul here uses to describe the world is the attempt to eliminate true dialogue and dialectic. This is evident in both our intellectual and social worlds and Ellul believes it to be particularly prominent in modern times.[62] Numerous aspects of the world which are subjected to regular criticism in Ellul's thought are correlated with these characteristics: our constant self-justification (*Ethique* II, 192), development of beliefs and religions (*Faith*, 142ff; *Subversion*, 29), and concern with the sacred and images in contrast to the word (*Humiliation*, 94) are all signs of a desire to shut ourselves off from God's questioning and to affirm our unity and that of our world apart from God.

The work of the city once again symbolises this dual aspect of the world as is made most explicit in Ellul's exposition of the Genesis story of Babel

> The people wanted to be definitively separated from God (*se séparer définitivement de Dieu*)...It is the desire to exclude God (*la volonté d'exclure Dieu*) from his creation...It is this solidarity in a name, this unity in separation from God (*unité de séparation d'avec Dieu*) which was to keep men from ever again being separated on earth. And the sign and symbol of this enterprise is the city they wanted to build together (*City*, 16).[63]

---

[62] *Ethique* II, 163; *Subversion*, 46ff offers an historical account while *Ethique* III, 97 describes the frantic will for Unity as an expression of the absolute evil of our time.

[63] This feature is confirmed in Rev 18 where the city 'excludes all that which is not herself, all that which does not enter directly into her activity, all that which does not reinforce her;

Third, the world of ruptured communion is no longer characterised by God's self-giving love which humanity was created to image in creation. Instead it is characterised by Eros. Here Ellul, in contrast to many contemporary writers, accepts Nygren's account

> The opposition established by Nygren is basically correct: there is a love which possesses, takes, captures, dominates, uses and enslaves the other, and a love which gives itself, leads to self-sacrifice for the other, considers the other's interest above its own. These are two antithetical and irreconcilable orientations (1976d, 62).

Although Ellul refers to the former of these loves as Eros (*l'Eros*) he also and more often uses the language of covetousness (*la convoitise*) and the will to power or the spirit of power (*la volonté/l'esprit de puissance*).[64]

Covetousness is universal and lies at the heart of man in rebellion against God (*Subversion*, 166). It is defined by Ellul as

> Man's desire to take (*s'emparer*) what belongs to others, to master (*s'assimiler*) others, to destroy (*détruire*) them both in what they have and in what they are. It is the source of the desire above all things to take possession (*s'emparer*) of God' (*Freedom*, 134).[65]

The origins of covetousness lie in 'the flesh' which is that which distinguishes man from God. This covetousness is the source of the rupture and all sin (*Subversion*, 13) and so the commandment against it is the climax and summing up of the Decalogue.[66] This characteristic is not only seen in fallen man but mars the whole world apart from God, most obviously through the powers discussed below. As with the other characteristics of the fallen world, the city is again paradigmatic for Ellul as she is 'expression of the spirit of power, herself a material and spiritual power' (*City*, 118).

The significance of this feature of our world in Ellul's outlook on society is clear from the following passage in his last theological work

---

she kills all that which comes for the sake of God' (*Apocalypse*, 195-6).

[64] 'Covetousness is equivalent to the spirit of power or domination' (*Humiliation*, 101 cf. *Si*, 19). That these are synonymous with Eros is clear from both Ellul's explicit statements (*Ethique* II, 119ff) and comparison of his definitions of the terms.

[65] Unfortunately, the fullest discussions of *la convoitise* are in two untranslated works, *Ethique* II, 118-47 and *Si*, 19-22.

[66] In his discussion of Paul's use of the tenth commandment in Romans 7:7, Ziesler comments, 'in Jewish tradition coveting could be identified as the sin of Adam, and could also be regarded as the essence and origin of all sin' (Ziesler 1989:185).

What are the keys of *our* society (but also of *all* societies known to history)? They are covetousness and the spirit of power. The truth is that every society expresses itself and founds itself on this will to power…and this covetousness…(*Dieu*, 176).

Fourth, the Ellulian designation of the world that has received most attention in discussion of his work is his claim that it is a place of necessity (*nécessité*) rather than freedom (*liberté*).[67] In communion with God, Adam and the creation were free and knew no necessity. Necessity arose only with the rupture (*Violence*, 128) and, as with the move from life to death, necessity is the logical consequence of breaking away from God who alone is free.

> In breaking with God we acquire independence or autonomy but never freedom, for God alone is free and a relationship with him grants the only possibility of becoming free…the break with God has brought bondage and subjection to the determinisms and necessities that progressively change into destiny (*Subversion*, 169).

Unfortunately, Ellul never offers a detailed explanation of this important term. As Marva Dawn comments, 'the concept of necessity will be encountered throughout Ellul's work, though he must be criticized for never clearly defining it'.[68] There would appear to be at least three strands in his understanding. Firstly, necessity embraces that which humans both individually and collectively have to do in order to continue to live. This aspect of necessity appears in relation to morality (*TWTD*, 61ff) but is most prominent in Ellul's discussion of work before and after the rupture. In Eden, Adam will not die if he does not work and so there is work without necessity but now one must work in order to live.[69]

Necessity is, secondly, evident in the world whenever humans are unable to fulfil their calling of ruling the world and find themselves enslaved in some way. Thus, in relation to violence, Ellul explains that

> Violence is of the *order* of *Necessity*…The man or group who conforms to it

---

[67] Ellul's fullest account is *Freedom* (especially pp 37-50) but see also *TWTD*, ch. 4 and *Violence* (discussed in ch. 5 below). An important early statement of his position is 1950i. For discussion of Ellul on necessity see Temple 1976:337-40; Fasching 1978:347ff; Clendenin 1987 (especially pp57-87).

[68] Dawn 1992:173. Ellul only gives a very general definition – 'Necessity is definable as what man does because he cannot do otherwise' (*Violence*, 128). For attempts to expand Ellul's definition see Konyndyk 1981:260ff; Clendenin 1987:66ff.

[69] See 1960e, 101 and 1980c, 3.

enters into an order which is that of necessity, an order where one follows the necessary downward pull of one's passions and of sociological or economic trends. One ceases to be an independent, innovative agent (*Violents*, 119 own translation cf. *Violence*, 91).

Related to this second strand, and found in both his sociological and theological studies, is Ellul's third use of the term *nécessité*. This is to describe the experience that all forces, structures, and institutions within society have tendencies to extend themselves, to dominate over other societal elements, to develop their own laws, and to take on a spiritual value (1980n). Interestingly, the city as necessity is not particularly emphasised by Ellul although it is present in his study (e.g. *City*, 40-1) and he later wrote of 'the necessity expressed in and by the city' (*Freedom*, 38-9).

These four characteristics mark humanity and the world when their created communion with God has been ruptured. As with the four characteristics of God and creation they mirror, they cannot be taken in isolation from one another. They must be viewed as inter-related features of the world of ruptured communion. This becomes clear from the connections and correlations Ellul himself often makes between the different characteristics. To give a few examples, necessity arises because of the need to avoid death and yet Ellul also speaks of death itself as the supreme necessity of the fallen world (*TWTD*, 60-61). Similarly, the city achieves its closure through killing that which is other (*Apocalypse*, 195-6) and yet any community needs challenge, refusal and non-conformity within it if it is to live (*Ethique* II, 89) and so when a society achieves closure and unity it inevitably dies. Finally, Ellul explicitly states that conformity to the will to power and human covetousness are inevitably associated with the quest for unity (*Déviances*, 48) and the end of these for any society is death (*Dieu*, 176). It is, therefore, unsurprising that Ellul relates not only the city but also Technique, religion, and other social phenomena to more than one of the four characteristics.

Death, Unity and Closure, Eros (as Power/Covetousness) and Necessity are inextricably bound together as the distinctive and inevitable marks of a world which has ruptured its communion with the living, Wholly Other God who loves in freedom.[70]

---

[70] The problem with Clendenin's study which isolates the contrast of necessity and freedom is perhaps clearest in his statement, 'Loss of communion with God was *one result* of the Fall, but, *more broadly*, Ellul describes the Fall as bringing about a transition from an order of freedom to an order of necessity' (Clendenin 1987:67-8, italics added). For Ellul the rupture of communion with God is not just one, rather narrow, result of the Fall but the essence of the Fall from which every other result of the Fall, including necessity,

THE WORLD OF RUPTURED COMMUNION: HUMANS, HUMAN WORKS, THE POWERS

The world of ruptured communion with these four characteristic features comprises three central elements in Ellul's thought – humans, their works, and the powers. Each merits brief discussion.[71]

The focus of the break in human communion with God was the desire of human beings to gain for themselves the knowledge of good and evil. This ability to declare what is good was bought at the cost of disobeying the Creator and breaking our communion with the Good that is the will of God. As a result, humans find themselves driven by a need to justify themselves.

> It is because man has become the master for declaring good and evil that at the same time and by the same action he claims to give himself his own justification. Man's thirst for justification rests on his capacity to settle the good for himself. But just as this thirst for justification is nothing, other than the desire to flee the judgment of God, so also the settling of the good by man is nothing other than his refusal to be in communion with God. Those are the two aspects of the same revolt…(*TWTD*, 19).[72]

This self-justification is immediately revealed in Genesis 3 when, after their disobedience, Adam and Eve each accuse others in order to justify themselves. Ellul understands Satan in terms of such accusation (*Subversion*, 182ff) and views our accusatory self-justifications as not only an expression of covetousness but also the opposite of freedom and evidence of the lack of love.[73]

Humans will now attempt to use the Word of God, the church, and theology to justify themselves in the state of their rupture from God.[74] The list of other means of self-justification that humans have developed is almost endless: myths (*False*, 31), ideologies (*False*, 81), a morality of necessity

---

follows.

[71] It is impossible to do justice here to Ellul's treatment of any of these subjects and what follows is an attempt to state succinctly the heart of these areas in Ellul's theology, show their inter-relatedness, provide links with his overall theology and set the context for the more detailed studies of Part Two.

[72] This classic Reformation theme of justification and human self-justification is central in Ellul's theology (e.g. *False*, 30-1; *Freedom*, 243ff; *Subversion*, 159f). Self-justification is evident in Jonah (*Jonah*, 73) and was one of the temptations of Christ (*Si*, 95-7). The theme is also in his sociological study of the bourgeoisie, *Métamorphose* (e.g. 39ff, 93-7, 284-8).

[73] *TWTD*, 13; *Faith*, 64; *Ethique* II, 190ff. *Métamorphose*, 96 suggests self-justification can also be correlated with unity/closure and denial of the other.

[74] *Jonah*, 73-5; *False*, ch. one; *Violence*, 27-8.

(*TWTD*, 68ff), the transfer of facts into values (*TWTD*, 157-8), the absolutisation of the relative (*Ethique* II, 39). Ellul particularly highlights the self-justificatory function of propaganda and states that it was this aspect of the phenomenon that led him to view it as amoral (1981c, 173).

As a good Protestant, Ellul incorporates all such humanly devised means of self-justification under the rubric of 'works', a distinctive category in Ellul because he insists that human works cannot be viewed only in terms of religious or moral works but must embrace all human activity (*Freedom*, 142ff).[75] Human works are significant because humans in God's creation were created and commanded to bear such fruit (*Genèse*, 75 offers this wider reading of Gen 1.27). However, all these works also now express our loss of communion with God and as such they are described by Ellul as vanity (*Reason*, 51ff) and works of darkness (*False*, 22) so that 'every work of a human separated from God is necessarily and without any qualification declared bad (*mauvaise*) and sinful (*pécheresse*) throughout the whole of Scripture' (*Ethique* II, 68). Because of the rupturing of human communion with God Ellul insists we cannot accept that our works are simply neutral or to be morally distinguished on the basis of how we use them.

> The tragedy of the whole thing is that we already know exactly how man will use his work – created by a radically evil man, itself radically evil. We already know that the evil (*mauvais*) work will be utilized by evil man…So we are not trying to come up with a moral classification, but rather to consider how man's work fits in with condemnation and redemption (*City*, 178).

The insatiable desire of fallen humans to justify themselves by their works makes this situation even worse. This is because, by the logic of justification, that which a person views as justifying them becomes greater than them and is viewed as a superior power (*Money*, 48). Once, therefore, any human works are the means of human justification our attitude to them changes. They cease to be relative and penultimate and become a value in themselves, the objects of human love, belief and devotion. Even more seriously they become the origin of human slavery and alienation because when the work of man is glorified 'this always entails the sacrifice of the human' (*Freedom*, 251). In his discussion of freedom Ellul therefore emphasizes this point.

> The final aspect of liberation from self is liberation with regard to 'the work of my hands'. Now obviously when the Bible speaks of the work of man's hands this is to be taken very concretely…the reference is to a total reality

---

[75] Ellul's fullest discussion of human works is in the untranslated Ethique II, 56-70.

of life and not just to moral works…In reality the works of man's hands in their social context and their concrete signification may have positive value but they may also be destructive. They are this when man submerges himself completely in his work, when he exalts it above himself, when he falls down before it and worships it (*Freedom*, 142).

When this transformation in the relationship between humans and their works takes place we find our attention drawn to the third element of the fallen world, the powers.

Ellul's theology of the powers is of particular significance within his political theology and one of the most important but also most difficult areas of his thought. Any attempt to understand it is complicated by his shifting position in the course of his writing and the different terms he uses (*forces, puissances, pouvoirs, exousiai*).[76] His earliest work appears to hold a much more positive view of the powers which are described as created institutions (*Law*, 76-9).[77] This attitude changes from his 1954 study of money when he becomes wholly negative towards the powers, viewing them as in permanent rebellion against God. A similar attitude is found in his contemporaneous study of the city.[78]

In relation to the being of the powers, Ellul's position can be best understood by ruling out two common views at either end of the theological discussion and placing Ellul between two more central positions.[79] At no point does Ellul view the powers as demons in the traditional sense and nowhere does he deny their reality or follow a Bultmannian dismissal of the biblical language as irrelevant mythology. At times, particularly in his earlier work, he sees the powers having an existence of their own.

---

[76] The most important work on this subject is that of Marva Dawn. The fullest discussion (her unpublished thesis, Dawn 1992) shows Ellul's understanding of the powers links his sociology and theology and many of her other writings discuss the subject, especially Dawn 1999 & 2001. She refers to Ellul's changing position and corresponded with him concerning it but does not focus on this aspect in her work.

[77] Both here and in his early more positive account of the sacred (*Presence*, 109ff) Ellul does not explicitly refer to the powers. See further Fasching 1978:179ff & Dawn 1992:93,n7.

[78] In his introductions to the 1975 French publication Ellul states his negative stance towards the powers, writing in response to Cox's claim that in Christ the powers can be made to serve in a positive sense, 'I do not see any texts which allow us to affirm this: they always remain harmful (*nocives*), rebellious (*rebelles*), defeated (*vaincues*), bound (*enchaînées*), but never positive' (*Feu*, 20).

[79] This categorization is used at *Freedom*, 151f. Ellul here and elsewhere acknowledges his debt to Barth and Cullmann on this subject. The fullest systematic study of the powers is Wink's trilogy (Wink 1984,1986 & 1992).

Power is something that acts by itself, is capable of moving other things, is autonomous (or claims to be), is a law unto itself, and presents itself as an active agent...Power has a spiritual value...Power is more or less personal...Money is not a power because man uses it, because it is the means of wealth or because accumulating money makes things possible. It is a power before all that, and those exterior signs are only the manifestations of this power which has, or claims to have, a reality of its own (*Money*, 76-7).

At other points, particularly in his later writing, Ellul views the powers instead as human dispositions which 'exist' only by human determination and are present in interpersonal relationships in the forms of accusation/Satan and division/devil (*Subversion*, ch. 9; *Si*, 16-24).

The tensions Ellul struggles with as he seeks to understand the powers and their relation to human beings and their works are vividly portrayed in his discussion of the four horsemen of the Apocalypse.

I certainly do not mean that these four horsemen exist in reality, that they take the form of horsemen. But...do they exist as concentrated power in a sort of being that acts with a kind of will?...I do not mean to say that war has a kind of entity, is an 'essence', like Bellona...We admit that everything happens on the human plane. If war breaks out, it is man who unleashes it. Human, nothing except human, too human...We can affirm that certainly all is of man; but finally we know well that no man ever decides...All is of man but in this domain all escapes him. To take refuge in the unconscious, the subconscious, or collective psychology does not resolve anything either...I do not say that there is a Mars and Bellona who use men as pawns upon a chess board and manipulate them without the will of these men having any part in the action. But everything happens as if in fact we found ourselves in the presence of a superior determination, an irresistible force, and ultimately a kind of polarization or inciting intention. Everything happens 'as if'. Whatever the advancement of knowledge might be...there remains an incommensurable, inexplicable part...a margin in which the intervention of something else is registered, something that we discern very quickly as independent of man. Everything happens as if...There are all the human motivations and a strange kind of transhuman which is disclosed...Men are the agents as well as the inventors. But there is more than men alone (*Apocalypse*, 152-3).

Whatever their origin and ontology, whatever the exact relationship between human will and the powers, the powers are important to Ellul not in themselves but only as they relate to the human world and human works. The fixed point in Ellul's understanding is that the powers are present wherever and whenever any human work ceases to be a relative work under human control. Ellul describes such relative works as secular (*laïque*) and contrasts them with works which have become autonomous, absolute, or sacred, exerting a power or authority over human beings which is inexplicable in purely rational terms.[80] Even when he views the powers as having a real existence apart from human beings, however, they only have power in the world due to human initiative. So 'money would be nothing, materially speaking, without human consent' (*Money*, 81) and in relation to the city it is when 'man puts all his power into it' that 'other powers come backing up man's efforts' (*City*, 9). In his later writings the universal phenomenon of human covetousness and the spirit of power are sufficient for the production of the super-human powers at work in the world (*Si*, 20).

The powers are, therefore, central in Ellul's understanding of the world not in themselves but because, after the rupture, humans are in relationship with them. This theme is strongest in his study of Revelation where language used in relation to the God-human relationship in creation is extended to speak of communion and even covenant between humans and the powers (*Apocalypse*, 186). As a result of this bond that exists between humans and the powers, human works in the world can even be described as the incarnation of these powers opposed to God.

> The historic incarnations of the powers (state, city, money, etc)…were the *works*, and the *works* of *man*…the work of the power of man is a complexity, a mixture, a point of encounter between man and the powers… (*Apocalypse*, 201-2).

CONCLUSION

The world today, the world according to Scripture, is not God's good creation of life, love and freedom in which humans in communion with God mediate his presence in the world. It is the counter-creation of rebellious human beings and the powers bearing the marks of its rejection of the Creator in death, closure/unity, Eros and necessity. It is the lost world of defiance and opposition to God.

> The world of which John, Paul, James or Peter speaks is, in spite of the distortions to which many of the passages are subjected, the world in which we are living: the political, economic and social world; the scientific, artistic and technological world in which man lives. It is partly the work of man and partly the work of demons, or of the powers…(*False*, 38).

---

[80] See, for example, *Violence*, 162fff; *Faith*, 243ff; *Si*, 18.

Although many readers of Ellul quickly discern his bleak outlook on the fallen world and reject him as an extreme pessimist, this cannot be all that is said about the present world for 'the world is, at once, *lost* and *loved*' (1974n, 17). The very fact of its continued existence witnesses to the fact that the living, Wholly Other God who loves in freedom maintains a relationship with the world even though it has broken its communion with him. However, because Ellul is an eschatological thinker, the nature of God's present historical relationship with the fallen world can only be properly understood in the light of his promise, purpose, and goal for it.

God's Final Judgment and New Creation

God, because he is love, acknowledges man's break with him and preserves and works within the lost world which man creates for himself outside of communion with God. But God, because he is love, cannot accept this rupture of communion as final. His goal is to overcome the world's break with him and to re-establish the world in full communion with himself in the Kingdom of God.

> This relates to the New Creation…In the Kingdom of God, there is no more separation. The rupture brought about by the Fall of Adam is obliterated (*Humiliation*, 252).

In overcoming our rupture of communion, God does not, however, deal only with human beings and ignore their works. In love, he also takes human works into consideration:

> God takes man's labour into account even though it is labour in sin and it participates in evil. God takes seriously what man does, for he loves man totally, and hence with his work too (*Jonah*, 95).

The great human work of the city again acts a paradigm for the world in relationship to God. It is of the greatest significance that at the end of history God does not restore his own original creation and place human beings back in a garden. Instead he promises us that communion with him will, in the end, be re-established within that which symbolises our rebellion against him, the city (*Conversations*, 104-5).[81]

On this basis Ellul develops a doctrine of the eschatological recapitulation of human history and human works. Human works of the post-rupture world are taken up by God to contribute to the new creation and so they can truly be said to serve the work of God. It is fitting that, at the end of his book delineating what he believes, Ellul shows he is far from the pessimist many allege him to be.

> God has granted us independence to lead our own lives, to undertake our own works, to build up our own histories…God issues directives, gives signs, makes appeals, and sometimes intervenes, for he always expects us to do *his* work. We finally cooperate with God in erecting this perfect Jerusalem, for if it is exclusively God's work, he builds it with the materials that we bring, materials of all kinds which, when approved by God, reveal a certain human greatness which is our glory (*WIB*, 223).[82]

Although Ellul says relatively little in concrete terms about this new creation, at its heart lies the re-establishing of that relationship of communion between God and the world which marked creation and has been lost with the fall: 'In Christ, God is with us. In the new city, his presence will be constant. Our communion with him will be without interruption (*sans rupture*)' (*City*, 189).

It is even possible to discern in Ellul's limited writing on the new creation, the four characteristics of the world in communion with God that we have contrasted with those of the world of ruptured communion. *First*, death is destroyed so that only Life and the Living remain (*Apocalypse*, 210f). *Second*, God remains transcendent over his new creation and in making it an open city he takes possession of and overturns that very human creation which sought to close itself off and exclude him. Here, with peoples gathered from every nation, the world finds true unity in diversity with communion replacing the division and quest for false unity found in the post-rupture world (*City*, 189-95). *Third*, the whole of the new creation is a work of God's love for his world and within it Eros and power are replaced by agape love. Indeed, 'the communion with God is more complete than it was at the beginning…the city of God is the place where we shall know by love. The holy city bespeaks of the triumph of love' (*City*, 207). *Fourth*, God's freedom is manifest in his selection of man's works to incorporate within his new creation while man is

---

[81] The fullest discussion of this point is in the untranslated *Conférence*, 88-93.

[82] These themes are also central to *City*, chapters five and six and *Apocalypse*, chapter seven.

no longer subject to any necessity but rather lives in full freedom and in full communion with God (*City*, 195).

By encompassing human works, this new creation embraces the history of the fallen world. Its exact relationship to that history is a crucial element of Ellul's theology. Despite his emphasis on the integration of human works in God's new creation, Ellul, from his earliest writing, is highly critical of those who stress continuity between the present world and the new creation (*Presence*, 36).[83] Instead, he emphasises discontinuity, writing of another radical break, another rupture. This must occur before the world produced within man's rupture of communion with God can become again the world of communion with God. 'Instead of being the continuation of history, the crowning act of history is a break (*une rupture*) with history' (*City*, 163).[84]

This 'rupture' is that of God's final judgment:

> It is impossible that there be continuity between our history and the world of God, the kingdom of God...There is a rupture (*une rupture*), there is a radical breakage (*une cassure*), the breakage of Judgment, the breakage of the destruction of Babylon the Great (*Conférence*, 24,25).

For Ellul, this final divine judgment is not a weighing of good and bad or a separation of what is judged good and so saved from that which is judged to be evil and so damned (*Money*, 89). It is the subjection of the entire world to the discriminating word of God whose 'No' in judgment leads to destruction and annihilation (*l'anéantissement*) but whose 'Yes' recreates.

> Let us avoid such a terribly simplistic notion as a clear separation between good men and evil men, right and wrong. The judgment of God is not separation of good and evil, but annihilation and re-creation (*City*, 73).

By such final judgment God effects a separation within the three elements of the fallen world. There is separation of humans from their works and of human works from the powers that, together with humans, produced those works in history. The divine judgment on each of these three elements of the world is important.[85]

The powers are, Ellul insists, strictly damned. God speaks only his 'No' to them and they have no place in God's new creation. This is not true of their

---

[83] See also *Marx*, 46ff.

[84] Similar terminology is used at *Apocalypse*, 46 and 1980x, 81.

[85] For what follows see especially *Apocalypse*, chapter six; *Conférence*, 81-8; *WIB*, 188-223.

historical incarnations because they are also the works of humans and God in his love accepts these into his new creation. These works are, however, unable to be accepted as they stand because they are inextricably bound to the powers and humans have utilized them as means of self-justification and worshipped them as idols which then enslave them. Human works are therefore also condemned and destroyed by God's 'No' as symbolised by the fall of Babylon in Revelation 18. However, unlike the powers, God's re-creative 'Yes' returns human works to humanity purged of the marks of human rebellion and communion with the powers. This is symbolised by the New Jerusalem coming down from heaven in Revelation 21.

This 'No' of God spoken to the powers and to human works is also a judgment suffered by humans. In the annihilation of the powers and their incarnations humans 'see disappear all that in which they have believed, that which they have created, which they have loved, that with which they have communed' (*Apocalypse*, 199). Furthermore, this judgment on human works is a judgment on humans according to their works for, as we have seen, each person's works are the fruit of their life (*Ethique* II, 56ff).[86] There is, therefore, a negative and painful divine judgment experienced by human beings who, in rebellion against God, declared themselves autonomous.

In his early writing Ellul also clearly spoke of the damnation of some men in God's final judgment, most starkly in relation to the rich.

> We are thus in the presence of a final, eternal condemnation…this power of fire is more often mentioned for the rich than for anyone else…If the rich do not need God's love on earth, they will not find it in heaven either…With death, the situation that people want becomes definitive. This is how it is a devouring fire: people stay eternally, with no possibility of change, with the comforter they have chosen… (*Money*, 140-1).

In the 1960s, however, as a result of his reading of Barth and his study of Revelation, Ellul became a convinced universalist. He first affirmed this position in his 1966 study of 2 Kings and did so frequently in later works.[87] From then on, Ellul still insisted on the destroying and recreating judgment of

---

[86] Ellul here universalises Paul's imagery in 1 Cor. 3:12-15 (*WIB*, 210ff).

[87] The first evidence of Ellul's change is found in *Politics*, 54ff, 109f. If his comments at *False*, 40ff are not purely rhetorical, his conversion to universalism can thus be dated between 1963 and 1966 (implied also by Chastenet 1992:151). Ellul's reasons for his change are given in *Apocalypse*, 275-6n1 and *Season*, 58, 75-6, 211-2. His fullest account is *WIB*, chapter fourteen. For discussion of Ellul's universalism see Bromiley 1981:40f; Clendenin 1987:135-41; Fasching 1988a&b; Morris 1988; Dawn 1988a and Chastenet 1992:151-4.

God upon human beings and all their works but refused to accept that this judgment entailed any discrimination between saved and damned people. His final eschatological vision is therefore clear and far from pessimistic.

> I am not pessimistic because I am convinced that the history of the human race, no matter how tragic, will ultimately lead to the Kingdom of God. I am convinced that all the works of humankind will be reintegrated in the work of God, and that each one of us, no matter how sinful, will ultimately be saved. In other words, the situation may be historically dreadful; but it is never desperate on any level. Consequently I can take the reality we live in very seriously, but see it in relation to salvation and God's love, which leaves no room for pessimism (*Perspectives*, 104).

Given that this is the end of the history of the world of ruptured communion and the goal of God's continued relationship with our world, it is now possible to understand the historical relationship between God and the fallen world and see how this eschatological renewal of communion with God is related to the historical world of man's rupture from God.

History as a Dialectic of Communion and Rupture

Man's communion with God is ruptured and he is part of a ruptured world characterised by death, closure/unity, eros, and necessity. To say only this about our world is, however, to forget that this lost world is still loved by God who will judge and re-create it in communion with him and who continues to be in relationship with it prior to that final judgment and recapitulation. Instead of abandoning humans in their disobedience, God acknowledges their choice for autonomy, reaffirms his own creational choice of human beings as his covenantal partner called to represent him in the world, and acts within this new situation to preserve and redeem his world. How God does this is the concern of this section.

THE WORD OF GOD

Ellul is insistent that God's action in the world by which he seeks to restore communion is of the same form as his action by which created the world and by which he will finally judge and re-create it: 'God expresses himself, acts, and is found only in his Word' (*Humiliation*, 50).[88] The Word of God spoken in the world makes the end of God's Kingdom present. It thus takes the form of a rupture in which the fallen world is addressed by God's 'No' of judgment together with his 'Yes' of grace, pardon, and restored communion.

Ellul acknowledges that, in emphasising God relates to his world by speaking his Word, he and Scripture are using analogy to describe the characteristic form of God's revelatory action (*Humiliation*, 48ff).[89] Although never explicit (the nearest is the distinction between the individual and the collective experience of God's silence at *Hope*, 125-6), Ellul appears to distinguish two aspects of God's Word in his discussion: the more general working of God's Word as a power within human history and the specific and personal address of God to an individual.

The Word of God as an active power in human history is symbolised in Revelation 6 by the white horse among the four horsemen that make history (*Apocalypse*, 147ff).[90] Ellul's argument for this interpretation makes clear that the dialectic between a world broken from God and the Word of God acting to restore the world to communion with God is central to his understanding of our historical world. It also shows that it is only the presence of the Word of God in the world that preserves it and limits the effects of our ruptured communion with God.

> It is also because all biblical thought…is dialectic that we are assured that the white horseman is certainly the Word of God…In order that there be history, dialectic process is necessary…But our dialectic, that of the Bible, operates between the historical powers and the metahistorical power that is historicized. It is the only true dialectic possible. The final dialectic…The scourge is always accompanied by the Word of God, who at the same time brings the expression of the judgment of God and his pardon…the scourge…proceeds always accompanied by grace, the promise, and the awakening of hope (*Apocalypse*, 155-6).

Alongside this collective action of God's Word in history there is also God's Word addressed to an individual. This personalises her and seeks to re-engage her in that inter-personal dialogue and communion with God which

---

[88] For discussions of Ellul's theology of the Word of God see Miller 1970:120-63; Fasching 1978:369ff; Bromiley 1981:34ff; Gill 1984b:59-88; Holland 1986.

[89] Here and elsewhere Ellul refers to the fact that the Hebrew *davar* signifies 'action' as well as word. The characteristics of the word are discussed most fully in *Humiliation*'s opening chapter.

[90] For a critique of this positive interpretation and an alternative see Caird 1966:80-1. Beale 1999:375ff summarises the case for and against different views.

characterised Adam but was lost with the rupture (*Jonah*, 22-3). Ellul regularly describes three common forms of this personal Word: commandment, question and warning.

As in Eden, God's Word comes to us as commandment. Ellul here follows Barth and understands this not as a juridical injunction but a personal address laying before someone the boundary between life and death and enabling them to choose life and so resist the world's tendency to death.[91]

As with Adam in the garden after the rupture and Cain after the murder of Abel, God's Word also puts us and our world into question and makes us responsible (i.e. able to give an answer). This questioning divine Word opens a breach in a person's self-justification because, by their answer, they must condemn themselves before God.[92]

As with the Old Testament prophets (and clearest in Ellul's studies of Jonah and 2 Kings), God's Word also comes as a warning that reveals the dangerous consequences of human choices and calls for a true repentance and a change in the world's direction.

Whatever its form, God's Word, like every true word, is intrinsically related to the person who speaks it. It follows that God's four characteristics are also characteristics of his Word which, when present in the fallen world, reproduces those features which define a relationship of communion with God.

First, as the Word of the living God it is itself a living Word (*Freedom*, 145) and a Word which gives life to those who, knowing they cannot live by bread alone, receive it from God (*Si*, 74).[93]

Second, the Word of God reveals that he is incommensurable with all other gods and expresses the presence of the Wholly Other in the world. (*False*, 183). God's Word is therefore characterised by its holiness (being other than the world) and its effect is to set apart those who receive it so that they can be witnesses of the Word, bringing into the world that which is other and external to it.

> The witness to the Word of God produces the greatest change, innovation, and rupture that can be imagined. He testifies to the Wholly Other...The witness introduces this Wholly Other into our visible, concrete, measurable and analysable reality. The Wholly Other takes this reality upon himself, limits it, measures it, and gives it another dimension...This presence of the

---

[91] *Prayer*, 102ff; *Freedom*, 145ff; *Reason*, 295ff. For Barth see CD II/2:552ff.

[92] *Ethique* II, 164f, 180ff; *Faith*, 101ff; 1952d.

[93] 'Living word' (*parole vivante*) and similar designations recur throughout Ellul's writing and it this that changes law into commandment and distinguishes the word from images (*Humiliation*, 111).

Wholly Other is one of the most basic necessities of our society and our time (*Humiliation*, 110).[94]

Third, because the Word is the Word of the God who is love, it is always a Word of love. Indeed, it is a characteristic of the word that it is a means of love for it shows the desire on the part of the speaker to call others to respond and enter into dialogue and relationship, a relationship which, with God, is always positive and expressive of God's love for man (*Humiliation*, 59ff).

Fourth, God's Word is, like God himself, totally free and unbounded (*Jonah*, 76).[95] When this free Word is present in our world it 'is always liberating in and of itself' (*Prayer*, 121). Those who hear and obey the Word of God do so freely and for anyone who bears witness to the Word, 'the Word of God is the source, guarantee, and thrust of the freedom of its witness' (*Freedom*, 124).

In the light of these four characteristics it is important briefly to clarify Ellul's understanding of Scripture vis-à-vis the Word of God.[96] Despite the high place Ellul accords Scripture in his theology and ethics, it has, as a permanent written record, the ambiguity of all written words (*Humiliation*, 42-7). Ellul stresses that the Bible 'in its materiality is not the Word of God made visible through reading' (*Humiliation*, 63) and that it 'is never automatically and in itself the Word of God, but is always capable of becoming that Word' (*Faith*, 128). He is therefore strongly critical of the Reformers for developing an ethic that identified Scripture as itself the Word of God (*TWTD*, 245f). As is clear, his position is again close to Barth, viewing Scripture as a witness to God's revealed Word through history which can once again *become* God's living, holy, loving and liberating Word by God's action in the present.

> God has laid down the first word of this dialogue...It is because he began to speak that what follows is possible. Yet the first act is objective. The word is spoken, but has become Scripture...The God who spoke must speak again (*Prayer*, 155-6).[97]

---

[94] Cf. *Faith*, 105 and *Apocalypse*, 156ff. The importance of this today is discussed in 1972h.

[95] *Freedom*, 130ff has a discussion of this in relation to Scripture drawing on Barth's understanding of the freedom of God's Word (*CD I/2*:661-95).

[96] David Gill has made the major contributions in this area (e.g. 1979b, 1981b, 1982 & 1984b). See also Bromiley 1981:34ff; Metzger 1992. For Ellul's discussion of hermeneutics see *Sources*, 186-99 and Ray 1979.

[97] For Barth on Scripture see CD I/2:457-740 and discussions in Biggar 1993:97ff, Hart 1999:28-47 and Webster 2000:49-73. Ellul's doctrine of Scripture is probably close to that offered in Bloesch 1994.

Despite our rebellion, God perseveres in his relationship with the world and, by his Word resists the consequences of the rupture and re-establishes a relationship of communion. He thereby makes present within the fallen world that life, otherness, love and freedom which is necessary for its preservation and begins to restore humanity as his faithful representative, dialogue partner and bearer of his Word in the world. [98]

THE INCARNATION OF GOD'S WORD: REVELATION

Ellul's theology of the Word is closely related to his theology of the covenant people of God who receive that Word and are called to be its bearers who live it in the world. This gives Israel great importance within Ellul's theology.

> Either Israel is the chosen people and receives a revelation from God, so that what it holds, transcribes, and transmits is a Word of God and not its own ideas, or Israel is not the chosen people and its ideas and myths and writings are of no more interest than those of the Aztecs or the Japanese. We have to make a decision here, a decision of faith. For my part I confess that Israel is the chosen people (*Politics*, 27). [99]

Israel, however, even when reduced to a remnant, proved constantly unfaithful to her divine calling to represent God in the world. This is because whoever receives the Word of God remains someone who has broken from God. The rupture of communion in the relationship between God and the world cannot therefore be annulled from the human side. True reconciliation and communion between God and the world requires nothing less than the incarnation of God's Word in the man Jesus Christ who is 'the bearer of God's Word but to a point so extreme and complete that that Word is incarnated in him' (*Si*, 90).

> In Jesus Christ God has done much more than in anything else before him. In him there is the very presence of God inseparably connected with man (*City*, 136).

The incarnation is therefore the very heart of Christian revelation. For Ellul the incarnation is nothing less than God's rupturing of man's world set apart from God. It is

---

[98] In addition to the presence of God by his Word, Ellul's earliest writing refers to a divine order of preservation as an element in God's relationship with the post-rupture world. This is discussed below and again in chapters six and seven.

[99] The fullest discussions of Israel are in *Chrétien*, 17-78 and *Dieu* (especially, pp45-56).

The momentous event of God on earth...the historical fact of the breaking (*la rupture*) of the barrier between God and man. A bridge has been built between the absolute and the relative, the eternal and the temporal...God in his totality has localized himself in flesh...This fact alone...has cut history in two (*Freedom*, 275 cf. *Apocalypse*, 73).

In Jesus Christ, God fully enters into the world that has broken from him and we witness 'the only moment in world history where truth rejoins reality' (*Humiliation*, 79). God thereby establishes his covenant through an unbreakable union between himself, all people, and the whole world:

The New Covenant cannot be better described than as the heart itself of God; and a covenant which cannot be put in question, since now a true identification of God with man is realized...the Incarnation is the total union of the whole of man with the whole of God...The union is so perfect that it can leave no place for rupture... (*Apocalypse*, 82, 85, 87).

In Jesus Christ, God gives us the fullest revelation of himself and reveals the extent of his love for the world. In him we also discover what it means to be the image of God (*False*, 28-9), the reality and extent of our rupture from God (*Apocalypse*, 83-4), the fulfilment of all God's words to Israel (*Si*, 108-9), the meaning of history (*Apocalypse*, 69-70), the seriousness of God's 'No' in judgment upon the world broken from him (*Apocalypse*, 146-7), and the presence of that new creation which is his 'Yes' to the world (*Humiliation*, 252f).

THE INCARNATION OF GOD'S WORD: REDEMPTION AND RECONCILIATION

The work of God in Christ is not only revelatory it is redemptive and reconciliatory. To understand this work of redemption it is necessary to return to the four characteristics of God and the creation and their opposites within the fallen world. In Christ, God re-establishes true communion between himself and the fallen world by incarnating life, holiness, love, and freedom in contrast to the way of the fallen world. Christ also fully assumes, suffers and overcomes the death, closure, eros, and necessity of that fallen world as is most fully described by Ellul in his sadly untranslated study of Christ's sufferings and temptations (*Si*) and the section of his study of the city which provides the title of the French edition, 'Neither Hearth Nor Home' (*City*, 120-4).

First, as early as *Presence*, Ellul emphasises the link between Jesus and the living God when he writes that 'it is in the living man, Jesus, that the living God (*le Dieu vivant*) has incarnated himself ' (*Presence*, 108). And yet in the fallen world Christ freely gives up his life and endures death. (*Si*, 60f, 100ff). As God incarnate, his death is nothing less than the death of the living God.

> Jesus Christ was condemned and put to death. In itself this amounts to no more than the death of Spartacus. But the miracle is that he who died on the cross is God himself...The miracle is that God enters into the life of man even to the point of death...This is the meaning of the death of Jesus Christ at the intersection of history. It is the incarnation of the Word, and the death of the Incarnate, which interrupts the process of fatality (*Politics*, 186).

From his first published piece of theological writing Ellul saw this as the real stumbling block of Christianity - 'The intolerable intellectual scandal remains of the God who must die in order that his creatures may be saved (1938a, 428).

Second, the incarnation only has meaning because it is an engagement with the world on the part of God who is Wholly Other. Jesus' holy presence reveals the false unity that the fallen world seeks to establish. Jesus provokes ruptures within this world as he calls out disciples from the world and demonstrates that there is 'an absolute choice to made between the will of his Father and the wishes of the world' (*Si*, 33-4). He challenges our self-justifications (*Ethique* II, 192) and even draws people out from the city, the symbol of their rebellion and closure against God in the fallen world (*City*, 131ff). Jesus, in turn, suffers in a two-fold sense. He suffers because he provokes rupture, even with his own family, in a world made for unity and communion with God

> Jesus did not come *in order to* divide the world and provoke these ruptures. But, simply by his presence and his word, division immediately erupts. The simple presence of Jesus inevitably provokes these ruptures and he is the first to suffer from them... (*Si*, 35).

He suffers also as, with all faithful witnesses to God's Word, he faces the world's hostility and exclusion. The world unites (Jews and Romans) in its will to kill him, an act that symbolically takes place outside the city (*City*, 123-4).

Third, Jesus' life is in total contrast to the world's eros, covetousness, and power. Ellul frequently highlights the fact that Jesus' life is one of non-power and speaks of Christ as 'anti-covetousness' (*Humiliation*, 81). He is 'the incarnation of love itself, the love which goes so far as to give itself, to abandon itself' (*Apocalypse*, 121). In him we see the fullness of God's agape love as God 'despoils himself of everything that makes his greatness, his power, his immortality, to enter into the human condition' (*Faith*, 139).

Because he follows this path of non-power, God in Christ then suffers and provokes the world's power against himself.

> This God who has become the weakest of men, has renounced acting by constraint, has witnessed to his absolute love and it is in the face of that that man truly reveals himself, who he is. As long as he revolts against an oppressor, he plays a noble role. But now he responds to love by hate, to non-power by the unleashing of power, to grace by the triumph of money, to the gift by rape, to the covenant by war – then man actually reveals what he is: and there his judgment resides (*Apocalypse*, 84).

Fourth, in Christ God enters the world of necessity and becomes subject to it and to man so that 'captive man takes God captive…His bondage becomes the bondage and death of God' (*Freedom*, 50). Ellul is quite explicit that Jesus endured necessity but within this necessity he is obedient to God and shows himself to be 'the free man par excellence…free in every way' (*Reason*, 298). It is therefore God's Incarnation that is the source of human liberation and true freedom.

In loving and free obedience to God's will, Jesus Christ lived that communion with God which humans otherwise lack. The fundamental problem in the world's relationship with God has thus found its resolution:

> It is a question of sin and, above all, of the rupture with God: in Jesus, alone, the definitive reconciliation has taken place precisely because he is God uniting himself to man in order that from now on there can no longer be rupture. The fundamental word is that of Reconciliation (*Dieu*, 198).

At the heart of this reconciliation is Christ's death. Its meaning and significance is summed up for Ellul supremely by Christ's cry of abandonment from the cross, 'My God, my God, why have you forsaken me?' (Mk. 15:34).[100] Ellul sees God here embracing fully within himself, in his incarnate Son, the world's rupture from him and all that rupture entails.

> But there is this cry. Jesus was not psychologically deluded. God abandoned God. He abandoned himself. He went down into the abyss out of which he had brought the creation. There was a break between Father and Son (*Rupture du Fils et du Père*), and what is more, a splitting apart of God within God – the possible impossibility (*Hope*, 121).

After this experience of God's 'No' against the world broken from him,

---

[100] The most focussed discussion is 1967g (cf. Moltmann 1974).

Jesus then receives God's affirmative word, his 'Yes' of life, which raises him from the dead and makes him Lord over the world and human history.

The question of the historical impact on the fallen world of Christ's incarnation, death, resurrection, and present lordship is important in any attempt to understand Ellul's work. From his early writing he sees his thinking here differentiating him from more positive appraisals of the modern world found in much contemporary theological reflection as he explores most fully in *False*.

Ellul is clear that there are certain eschatological consequences of Christ's incarnation (*TWTD*, 102f) but it is wrong to transfer these into human history as 'an ontological restoration of the world is not brought about by the incarnation and crucifixion of Christ and the redemption thereby effected' (*Freedom*, 15). Rather, in a phrase that recurs throughout Ellul's work, 'the world is still the world' (e.g. *False*, 16). Even after Christ has come the world remains the world of ruptured communion. It is marked by the same characteristics it always had. It has not ceased to be in rebellion against God. It is not restored to a relationship of communion with God. It does not show in reality that Jesus Christ is Lord. Its history is not a progress towards the kingdom of God.[101] Ellul is emphatic,

> It is a mistake – an enormous mistake – to suppose that the Incarnation and Lordship of Jesus Christ have *resolved* the problem. If the Incarnation has a meaning it can only be that God came into the most abominable of places (and he did not, by his coming, either validate or change that place). The 'Lordship of Jesus Christ' does not mean that everything that happens, happens by the decision of that Lord. No, the world remains the world, but whether or not it knows it the world is subject to that Lord (*Violence*, 25).

Despite this fundamental continuity, Ellul also speaks of fundamental change in the world as a result of God entering history in Jesus Christ. He even speaks of the Incarnation as 'the breaking (*la rupture*) of the powers and of history' (*Apocalypse*, 68).

> The incarnation of Christ, his coming to earth, has effectively changed history...Jesus Christ has set up a new relation between man and society and also between man and nature, which has been implanted in the world and cannot be taken out of it, since he was the Son of God (*Freedom*, 274-5).

The nature of this change is best illustrated in relation to the effect upon the

---

[101] Claims such as these can be found throughout Ellul's work (e.g. *City*, 167ff; *False*, chapter one; *Freedom*, 15ff; *Humiliation*, 79ff).

powers of Christ's incarnation and lordship. It here becomes clear that Christ's positive work produces a new historical situation but also opens up the possibility of making the world worse.

On the positive side, Ellul constantly affirms that one of Christ's central achievements is the condemnation, defeat, and despoiling of all the powers opposed to God. Christ is now lord over the world with all authority. The powers are therefore stripped of their authority, separated from human works, and deprived of their decisive power. They cannot ultimately separate the world from God by their rebellion against him. Their final damnation is certain.[102] However, Christ has not destroyed the powers and his victory over them is not automatically visible within the world.[103] Indeed, the powers' defeat produces a yet more violent response on their part as they fight to destroy the reconciliation between God and the world secured in Christ:

> The powers have been defeated and repulsed and deflected. But by the same token they have also been unleashed...They are on the earth with all the forces of powers which know that they have been outclassed and superseded and broken, but which for this reason do not need to observe any rules or limits and can cause every kind of upheaval in expression of their final revolt (*Freedom*, 288).

The implications of this are particularly important for human society and politics. In the past, the powers could grant humans a certain stability and equilibrium in the world apart from God but their defeat and unleashing mean this is no longer possible

> Now it is true that the world as world remains the same, that is to say in its separation from God, in its revolt and refusal...Nevertheless, something changes. This is the totality of collective securities that man has set up in his separation from God. The whole balanced system of powers, cultures, religions, magic, production, cities and commerce, all this, without God, was an order that man had set up...It was a livable order for man...But the incarnation, objectively, destroys it. From now on man can no longer be comfortable in these forms, for no less than God himself has come...(*Freedom*, 277).

As a result, humans are now placed before a new and stark dilemma. *Either*

---

[102] Examples of such claims can be found in *Money*, 85,133; *City*, 132; *Apocalypse*, 86ff; *Subversion*, 60.
[103] This other side of the Christian truth about Christ's victory over the powers is stated e.g. in *City*, 36f; *False*, 16-7; *Subversion*, 177.

through union with Christ a person can be liberated from the powers, share in Christ's victory over them, and make that victory present in the fallen world, *or* she can continue to ally herself with the truly vanquished yet seemingly victorious powers so that they are once more incarnate in humans works which then become weapons of the powers in their historic struggle against the finished work of Christ. 'The issue here is knowing if man is going to follow Jesus, is going to enter into the plan of God, is going to accept this unity with God' (*Apocalypse*, 90).[104]

The consequences of this decision for the world are clear:

> It is Jesus Christ himself who in his incarnation...forces man up against the wall: Either you live by love and freedom, which will make the life of society possible and establish a new civilization, or finally there will be no livable human society or culture (*Freedom*, 281).

The placing before humans of this choice between re-entering the life of communion with God through Christ or persevering in a life broken from him is the primary historic effect, in and for the fallen world, of God's work in Jesus Christ. As a result, the character of the Christian life and the development of an ethic for Christians are central concerns in Ellul's theology. They, by providing an account of life in communion with God within the world of ruptured communion, will give substance to the dialectic of communion and rupture that now characterises the historical relationship between God and the world.

Ellul's Theological Ethic for Christians[105]

The previous section has shown that Ellul's theology is best interpreted through a focus on the relationship between God and the world in terms of communion and rupture. This theological framework also shapes this section on Ellul's ethic and its accounts of the life of the disciple of Christ in the world, Ellul's conception of the task of Christian ethics, the structure of his own theological ethic, and his changing position on whether the Christian has

---

[104] Cf. *Money*, 115; *Faith*, chapter 23; *Subversion*, chapter 9.

[105] For other discussions of these subjects see Zorn 1971:199ff; Ray 1973 (which, though dated, remains the best account of Ellul's ethics); Logan 1977; Fasching 1978,1981,1990,1991; Boli-Bennett 1980:187-91,193-7; Punzo 1980; Outka 1981; Gill 1984c (especially chapter 2); Sturm 1984; Clendenin 1987; Scott 1989; Dawn 1992. Temple 1976 unfortunately only touches briefly on Ellul's ethic.

any ethic to guide the fallen world outside of renewed communion with God.

The Christian's Relationship with God and the World

For Ellul, the Christian life is to be understood primarily as a form of presence in the fallen world. The character of this presence can be summed up in the phrase 'in this world, not of it' (*Faith*, 273). The first chapter of *Presence* is therefore 'The Christian in the world' and (in the 1960s) *False Presence of the Kingdom* is written largely because Ellul fears many Christians, in their desire to be in the world, have also become of the world. In preparing lessons for the Professional Protestant Associations (A.P.P.), Ellul wrote the first on 'The Christian and the world' and this theme appears throughout his writing (most notably the introduction to 1959e) as do such biblical images as the call to be salt, light, sheep among wolves, ambassadors, watchmen.

In the terms of his theology outlined above, the Christian is someone who in Christ is restored to communion with God but who experiences and lives this communion within the world of the rupture. He is therefore properly to be found at the juncture between the world of ruptured communion and the call of God to communion through his Word: 'the Christian ought to place himself at the point of contact between two currents: the will of the Lord, and the will of the world' (*Presence*, 18).

It is within this wider framework that Ellul's thought can be related to the Christian tradition's discussion of the two realms highlighted by Temple in her work on Ellul. Here Ellul's emphasis is that 'the Christian belongs to two Cities...the two Cities to which he belongs can never coincide, and the Christian must not abandon either the one or the other...' (*Presence*, 33, 34). There cannot therefore be a neat separation between the Christian (in communion with God) and the world (broken from God). The Christian remains fully within the ruptured world and shares in its sin (*Presence*, 9-10) while the rupture remains fully within the Christian so that she is never personally in full and perfect communion with God (*TWTD*, 210f). The Christian lives this tension between the two cities within herself (*Ethique* III, 97) and this leads to what Ellul calls an 'agonistic' way of life (*Presence*, 13). From his earliest writings therefore Ellul self-consciously follows Kierkegaard and Luther in the insistence that 'if the Christian is free before God as one justified before God...he is always sinful' (1939b, 178).[106] The believer is truly always both justified and a sinner (*semper peccator et justus*).[107]

The Christian is distinguished from the world in that through ceasing her

---

[106] See also 1979j, vii for discussion of the theological roots of this belief.
[107] This theme runs from one of his first (*Presence*, 9) to his final theological study (*Dieu*, 61).

quest for self-justification and receiving God's Word and God's justification in repentance and faith (*Dieu*, 97), she has entered again into communion with God in Christ. This is what is special, indeed unique, about the Christian and her life and so, to cite one example, 'the freedom to use all things is granted only for the man for whom Christ is the living Son of God...the man who is in communion with Christ' (*Freedom*, 192). The Christian's life can therefore become a vehicle of God's own action with and for people in the fallen world. The basis of the Christian life is therefore a renewed relationship with God through Jesus Christ within which the Christian calling is to live in obedience to the Word by which God relates to his world and reveals his will. It 'is not a life conformed to a morality, but one conformed to a word revealed, present and living' (*TWTD*, 86).

Because God's Word cannot be restricted to only some areas of the world's life and the Christian is called to a life which lives this Word, Ellul (in what may be seen as a precursor to the recent resurgence of interest in the ethics of character through the work of writers such as Stanley Hauerwas) highlights from his early writing (*Presence*, 74ff) that the Christian life is matter of *being* someone who lives the grace of God more than *doing* certain things.

> Revelation tells us that to be in the covenant of God is much less a matter of doing something than of being someone, and in reality of living by the grace of God. Action, the bringing to pass of the good, the carrying out of some moral law...has no value in itself. It is a matter of living, and of pursuing day after day a certain kind of life...The action only has value insofar as it is the expression of a certain life (*TWTD*, 215).

There is therefore nothing which can *a priori* be considered irrelevant to the Christian calling (*TWTD*, 29-30) which is to nothing less than a new style of life within the world (*Presence*, 119ff). Ellul is even willing to speak of this new life-style, rooted in communion with Christ, as a continuation of the incarnation of God's Word in the world that was fully accomplished only in Jesus Christ.

> As Bonhoeffer says, the problem of the life of the Christian is that of incarnating the work of Christ in ourselves. Christ is not a model, nor an ideal, etc. He is the one who comes in us, and who makes us to be crucified and risen again with him. Jesus Christ makes it possible for man to become that man whom God became... (*TWTD*, 302n10).

As with Christ, this pattern of life based on communion with God can be viewed in one of two ways. It can be seen in reference to the original creation such that 'the commandment authorizes man finally to live as he was meant to live in the creation' (*TWTD*, 87). It is, however, better to view the Christian life from an eschatological perspective as the hidden presence within the world of the new creation secured by Christ's work (*TWTD*, 222). This is what (in a novel interpretation which appears in passing in a number of works and is promised fuller treatment in his *Ethics of Holiness*) Ellul refers to as 'the kingdom of heaven' as distinct from 'the kingdom of God'.[108] The characteristics and dynamic of this way of life can thus be expressed in terms of the same four characteristics that structured our earlier accounts: life, otherness, agape love, and freedom.

First, Ellul's concern is with the Christian life as a lived reality and way of being in the world, not with Christian ideas, principles, or codes of conduct (*Presence*, 40). Whenever he writes of any aspect of the Christian life he insists that this cannot remain theoretical. If it is to have any meaning or any effect on the world, it must be lived by Christians as part of that new life they have received in Christ (e.g. in relation to hope see *Hope*, 224). Referring to one of his favourite Scripture passages (Romans 12.1,2), Ellul insists that Christians are to be *living* sacrifices because, 'man can glorify God in manifesting by his life, by his being, who this God is that he adores' (*Apocalypse*, 235).

It is by living the word of God as a result of his relationship with the living God that the Christian also makes life present within the dying world. This resistance to the world of death opens up the possibility that society too can continue to live despite its rupture with God.

> When the Christian…declares the consequences of the lordship of God, then he plays the most fruitful, the most positive, the most original role possible: putting the tension into society and thus keeping it alive (*TWTD*, 107).

The Christian, through expressing his relationship with the living God in the fallen world, can therefore 'lead humans towards life and the maintenance of life…and not towards the destruction and constant triumph of Nothingness which is rejected by God' (*Dieu*, 177).

Second, the Christian is made holy and set apart from the world through receiving and living the Word of God. This Word uproots him and creates a rupture between him and the world broken from God. This is seen dramatically in the biblical call of prophets like Jonah who finds that 'there is a rupture with his daily life, his background, his country' (*Jonah*, 24) but it is true of all Christians who are pilgrims and strangers in their discipleship.

Christians have chosen to be uprooted (*déracinement*). They have been

---

[108] For Ellul on the kingdom of heaven see 1979i and Hanks 1988b.

called by God and this has brought a break (*une rupture*) with all else, a parting from it (*une mise à part*)...They have become strangers...strangers to the world in which they live... (*Freedom*, 302).

The Christian's life is therefore marked by a release (*dégagement*) from the world which arises out of his relationship with the Wholly Other God who demands that the believer be holy and separate from the world just as God himself is holy.

Christian faith places people in an extremely uncomfortable position...the context of God's radical demand that we be holy. 'Be holy because I am holy', the Bible tells us...Holiness means separation: I am a God separated from the world and from other divinities and you too are separated from the normal, habitual course of society and history (*Perspectives*, 96-7).[109]

This release from the world, which can take the form of prayer, is particularly important in relation to the powers and their expression in the world's myths and sacred (*Politics*, 37ff). As a result of effecting this break with the world the Christian can then fulfil their calling to be the 'incarnate presence of the Wholly Other at the heart of the world' (*Politics*, 141-2). Only in this way can he bring something unique and hence revolutionary into the world because 'before the presence in the world can mean anything, it has to be the presence of "that which is not the world"' (*False*, 83).[110] Through bearing witness to the Wholly Other God in this way, he questions, challenges and resists the world, relativising its absolutist pretensions as it seeks to close itself off from God.

We have to make the dimension of the Wholly Other penetrate and make a breach in the closed universe that man constantly wishes to rebuild (1956b, 52).

Third, just as in Ellul's doctrine of God an emphasis on God as Wholly Other needs to be placed in a dialectic with the God who is love and becomes incarnate, so in relation to his theological ethic, the *dégagement* of the Christian life must be related to the Christian's *engagement* with the world out of love.

Scripture's teaching is that the two attitudes of engagement and release in

---

[109] Until *Ethics of Holiness* appears, the fullest discussions of this holiness are in *False*, chapter three and *Ethique* II, 95-111.

[110] The best discussion of the Christian life as revolutionary is *Presence*, chapter two.

relation to the world's affairs are equally valid. But they are only legitimate if they are linked to one another (*Ethique* II, 95).

This reiterates that the Christian life, to be a faithful witness, must be lived out in the world for 'God became incarnate – it is not for us to undo his work' (*Presence*, 7). Those who have received God's grace have done so for the world's benefit and their release from the world can only be in order to be engaged in the world (*Jonah*, 89). In this engagement with the world the Christian is called to make present the agape love of God in the face of the world's eros.

What one might have expected of Christians and the church is that they would have replaced false love with the true love that comes from God, that they would have substituted the *agape* that serves for the conquering *eros* of the Greeks, that they would have put the spirit of service in place of the spirit of domination...(*Subversion*, 92).

Fourth, the Christian has been liberated by Christ and is called to live a life of freedom within the world of necessity.[111] This freedom is not something inherent in man or even in Christians. It arises out of the believer's living communion with Christ and can be described as God's own freedom incarnate in the world.

The freedom thus received through Jesus Christ is God's own freedom...to the degree that we are in fellowship (*communion*) with him, and hence to the degree that this freedom expresses the will of God (*Freedom*, 216).

Because the Christian life is one of freedom and arises from each person's relationship with Christ it is important to recognise that, although it is possible to provide a general sketch of the character of the Christian life, a more detailed or prescriptive account cannot be provided as 'this personalization causes each life to become singular. There is not one Christian life. There are as many Christian lives as there are Christians' (*TWTD*, 219).

In addition to these four characteristics, the final feature of the Christian life is given by the dialectical character of God's Word to the world as both 'No' and 'Yes'. Here Ellul again insists the 'Yes' and 'No' must be kept in relationship with one another (*False*, 23-6). The Christian herself constantly lives under God's 'No' and 'Yes' and so lives a life of ongoing repentance. When she lives God's word in the world she must reflect this dialectic.

---

[111] In addition to *Freedom* there are short earlier treatments in 1950i (now *Sources*, 115-31) and 1951c. See discussions in Ray 1973:42-93; Outka 1981; Clendenin 1987:89-120.

It is a matter of being present with that function of being at the same time the No and the Yes exactly as God pronounces the No and the Yes on the activity of every person, every society, every Church (and every Christian!) (*Ethique* III, 207).

More concrete guidance on the relative weight to be given to affirmation and negation is, however, difficult. This is because, as the world changes, the proper Christian response will change – 'Every moment in history is not the same. One day we must say Yes, the next No, to the very same thing' (*City*, 182).[112] However, Ellul's overall theology shows that the 'No' is most emphatically to be spoken against the defeated powers and all their incarnations in human works. In contrast, God speaks a 'Yes' as well as a 'No' to fallen human beings and their humble, relative works. This is the foundation for Ellul's constant emphasis on desacralisation, his relativisation of all human works, and his attacks on self-justifications.

In Ellul's theological ethic, the Christian is therefore viewed as the meeting point between the Word of God and the will of the world. As such he plays a crucial part in God's present relationship with the world. By living the word and resisting the world, he is vital in maintaining the dialectic of communion and rupture that we have seen is central to human history in the world of ruptured communion.

In addition, Ellul's ethic is a missionary ethic. Perhaps reflecting his own experience, he places great emphasis on personal conversion, writing that 'one becomes a Christian only by conversion...Conversion alone, conscious and recognized...produces the Christian' (*Subversion*, 104). By bearing witness to Jesus Christ, the Christian life, when combined with verbal proclamation of the gospel, can lead others within the world to break with the world and become Christ's disciples.[113] This is also central to Ellul's understanding of the Christian presence in the world.

We must insist rigorously that the preaching of the Gospel has as its sole meaning the hope that a person should come to know the grace available to him in Jesus Christ, that through this he should come to recognise that Jesus is truly the Christ, the Saviour, the Lord, in other words, that this person might be converted to the true God. The presence vis-à-vis the world of Christians and of the Church, the presence in the midst of men, has no meaning, no value, no truth, unless it brings a person to this conversion

---

[112] This theme is discussed at length in relation to Ecclesiastes 3 at *Reason*, 231-48.

[113] For a discussion of evangelism that discusses and develops this feature in Ellul see Tomlin 2002.

(*False*, 105-6).

Failure by Christians to be faithful to their calling to live and preach the Gospel has disastrous consequences which is one reason why Ellul often writes so often and passionately against certain features of the church (e.g. *False*, *Marx*, *Subversion*). These are not understood as ultimately eternal consequences for individuals because of Ellul's universalism but the fact they are historical consequences does not make them unimportant. It is by Christian faithfulness to this calling that God's work in Christ is made present within the fallen world and the world preserved from the full effects of its rupture with God and the unleashing of the powers. Failure here therefore makes Christians culpable for the disasters experienced by the world as Ellul frequently points out.[114] In the light of this pivotal role of the Christian's relationship with God and the world it is important to examine Ellul's understanding of the possibility and function a more definite Christian ethic to give substance to this general theology of the Christian life.

Ellul's Ethic for Christians

If the task of an ethic is to provide an account of the good then Ellul's theology renders this highly problematic because he believes the good is God's will which is only knowable through revelation and in communion with Him. The human quest to define good and evil for themselves lies at the heart of the rupture from God and to produce a Christian ethic threatens to limit the freedom of the living God and to objectify and possess his will.[115]

The Christian calling is to a way of life expressing a living personal relationship with God in Christ, not adherence to a set of injunctions. Ellul believes this fundamental truth is denied by all systems of Christian morality that easily become a protection against God's word and the source of such dangers as moralism and self-justification (*TWTD*, chapter twelve).

> Every honest reflection must absolutely begin by acknowledging that…there cannot be a Christian ethic, that the whole of revelation is against it, and that every attempt to construct such a morality, no matter how faithful, is a betrayal of the revelation of God in Jesus Christ, and in the last analysis an imposture (*TWTD*, 201).

However, in an extreme example of his dialectical thinking, Ellul also

---

[114] In relation to the environment, for example, see 1974g.

[115] *TWTD* is the fullest account of the problem of a Christian ethic but a helpful brief sketch is found in *Subversion*, chapter four.

recognises that in the fallen world an ethic is necessary for Christians if they are to fulfil their calling – 'a Christian ethic is indispensable' (*TWTD*, 245). The church, like all human societies in the world will have to produce some form of morality in order to structure its life. Experience shows that unless the church explicitly formulates a *Christian* ethic it will follow one of two other paths (*TWTD*, chapter thirteen). *Either* it will follow one of the world's moralities and become increasingly detached from a theological basis in God's revelation *or*, like the Reformers, it will fall back onto an absolute, fixed, and literalistic ethic from Scripture which is detached from the reality of the world in which it lives. Furthermore, to leave the Christian only with the general call to incarnate God's word in the world often makes him morally indifferent. A Christian ethic is therefore necessary because the incarnation of faith is central, theology alone cannot ensure good action, and the church must respond to the question of what is signified by the work of Jesus Christ and the Christian's relationship with him.

In this impossibility and yet necessity of an ethic there is a demonstration of the tension within the Christian's life as he finds it impossible to live in full communion with God within the world of ruptured communion. Standing between God and the world, he finds that what the will of God declares unacceptable is necessary for him as a sinner living in the fallen world. Ellul therefore characterises an authentic Christian ethic for the church as one that is 'a conscious morality, aware of its relativity, humble and under condemnation, in the service of the faithful and not imposed upon them' (*TWTD*, 249).

On the basis of his overall theology, Ellul argues that as this ethic is for a world of ruptured communion it cannot be based on either a supposed creation order or as if we were already in God's kingdom. Both creation and kingdom are states of pure communion with God (*Ethique* III, 223-35). In addition, it must be an ethic for here and now and so, like the Christian himself, at the meeting place of the Word of God and the changing world (*TWTD*, 264ff). This relative nature of the Christian ethic means that a proper understanding of the contemporary world becomes vital in the development of an ethic and that this ethic is to be constantly evolving (1960i). Its function as an ethic for Christians cannot be to give an account of the good nor to provide specific solutions for all the problems the Christian faces when seeking to fulfil his calling in the world. Instead, 'Christian morality can only be indicative and not imperative, hortatory and not dogmatic' (*TWTD*, 252).

This ethic is to act as a call and spur to the incarnation of faith in the concrete problems of life in the world. It is to provide an aid to the weakness of faith's initiative and creative imagination and assist the task of remembering the Word of God in times of God's silence. It is to be, in effect, primarily a preparation for the hearing of the Word of God. Here Ellul again turns to Barth, commenting (with reference to *CD III/4*, §52) that,

> The task of ethics cannot be to decide on the content of God's commandment, nor to judge man's action, but to describe the limits of God's commandment and of man's corresponding action (*TWTD*, 248).

These implications of his overall theology for the work of the Christian ethicist are summed up by Ellul in an important contrast between what he calls 'a Christian ethic' and 'an ethic for Christians'

> There can never be any question of a Christian ethic…The only thing we can try to do is to describe an ethic for Christians that will be within all the limits indicated by a servant role, beneath the cross and in the hope of its pardon (*TWTD*, 266).

Although Ellul was much influenced by Barth he believed Barth had failed here and left a task that still needed to be accomplished.

> I also understood that we could receive from him [Barth] a kind of 'mission'…I had the impression that the ethical consequences of Barth's theology had never been elicited. I was not satisfied with his volumes of ethics and politics, which seemed to be based on an insufficient knowledge of the world and of politics (1978d, 24).

This task became a central concern of his own writing and, because it was to be an ethic for the here and now, Ellul's analysis of the modern world (discussed in the following chapter) is a key component in his own contemporary three-fold ethic for Christians. Ellul based this ethic on the traditional theological virtues of faith, hope and love which were expressed in the three characteristics of the Christian life structuring his ethics.[116]

> It seems to me that hope corresponds to an ethics of freedom, faith to an ethics of holiness, and love to an ethics of relationship (*Freedom*, 7).[117]

Unfortunately, Ellul never fully explained the correspondence between each virtue and a certain ethic.[118] The link between hope and freedom is,

---

[116] The New Testament triad of virtues often appears in Ellul's writing (e.g. *Ethique* II, 76ff; 1973c).

[117] This three-fold structure of freedom, holiness and relation is sketched as early as 1950i.

[118] Ellul apparently intended to expound the links between the virtues and his ethic in the

however, clear from both *Hope* and *Freedom* and that between faith and holiness can be seen in *Faith*.[119] His *Ethics of Holiness* is reportedly complete in the form of a 1200 page handwritten manuscript and is being prepared for publication. At present, however, only his *Ethics of Freedom* has been published and this is only partially translated.[120] This easily leads to excessive weight being given to this particular part of his ethics at the expense of the wider ethical project.[121] Although we cannot be certain, it appears that Ellul's intention was, in each part of his ethics, to offer an account of his particular focus (freedom, holiness or relation/love) in the Christian life and to describe the form this can take in relation to the specific areas which traditionally form the subject matter of Christian ethics.

> I also want to make it clear that instead of following the usual course and discussing the Christian and the state, money, and so forth, I shall begin at each point with the ethical situation, e.g., the Christian as free man in politics, the Christian as a saint in politics, the Christian as an agent of love in politics (*Freedom*, 369).[122]

The very structure of this projected ethic, with its focus on freedom, holiness and love, demonstrates that Ellul's ethic derives from the overall theology and character of God described above. It is an ethic for confessing Christians seeking to incarnate their communion with God and not an ethic for the world apart from God. It is therefore necessary, finally, to examine what,

---

second part of the introduction to his ethics, the first part of which appeared as *TWTD*.

[119] See especially *Faith*, 104ff and chapter eighteen.

[120] There is long-standing confusion over the inter-relationship of the French and English editions of *Ethique de la Liberté*. I have concluded that *Ethique* II is untranslated and that much of the material which appears in *Ethique* III (1984) is also lacking from the English translation of 1976. This conclusion is significantly different from the account offered in Fasching 1981:217-8 and cited with approval in Hanks 1984a:56-7 (see now Hanks 2000:57). Contrary to Bromiley (*Freedom*, 5) and Ellul (*Ethique* III, 7), *Freedom* is a translation of *Ethique* I and an original (perhaps 1966) draft of *Ethique* III. It has absolutely no connection with *Ethique* II, which appears to have been unavailable to Bromiley (hence not only the lack of any of its material in the English but also the confused translation of *Ethique* III, 82 at *Freedom*, 352 which only makes sense in the light of the section 'Soyez des hommes' in *Ethique* II). Therefore, although Ellul's comment to Fasching that 'the English edition is the more complete' had an element of truth prior to the publication of *Ethique* III, English readers now lack much material to be found in the three volume French edition.

[121] Clendenin 1987:132 recognises but downplays the wider ethical project in his criticism of Ellul's focus on freedom.

[122] Cf. *Ethique* III, 223. As these passages show, Ellul usually refers to 'love' rather than 'relationship' for the third part of his ethic.

if anything, Ellul's theology can offer as ethical counsel for those who, within the fallen world, are not in communion with God in Christ.

An Ethic for the World ?

> From the Biblical point of view, the world ought to be the world, and society should not play the game of being the Church or a Kingdom of God on earth. Composed as it is of sinful men, it ought to be the manifestation of it. This way things are honest. (1959e, 135).

Ellul here powerfully summarises the permanent historical consequences of the world's ruptured communion and the error of attempting to deny or alter the fallen world's basic characteristics. In one of his earliest articles he argued that the central rediscovery of the Reformers was the necessity of a clear distinction between the church and the world. In his view (not without its difficulties historically), the Reformation 'gives up applying the principles of Christian morality to the world, hands the world over to itself, leaves it to its own initiatives and endeavours' (1945d, 141-2).

Given these views and his overall theology, it is unsurprising that Ellul consistently refused to apply his Christian ethic to non-Christians (*Violence*, 156) and emphatically rejected the project of 'Christianising' society by creating *une chrétienté*, some form of Christian society such as in Christendom (*Money*, 7-8). His concern is that Christians fulfil their calling and live God's word wherever they are placed within the world because God works to preserve and transform the fallen world through this presence of his faithful people (*Presence*, 15ff).[123]

Ellul illustrates his position here by reference to the approach of the first Christians towards slavery in wider society. They did not condemn it, reform it, abolish it, or advocate it. Instead, they accepted it as a possible context for bearing witness to Christ in the world through a Christian way of life and they thus undermined the institution from within.[124]

Any society in the world will always formulate its own morality, social ethic, and institutions. Christians must recognise and accept these as works of fallen humans that enable them to continue to live in harmony in the world. As with all such works, Christians cannot simply affirm and justify these actions of the world but nor can they condemn and reject them as of no value. Instead, they are to view them as under God's 'No' and his 'Yes' and to live

---

[123] Fasching 1990 has an excellent discussion relating this aspect of Ellul's ethics to Lutheran and Anabaptist models of the Christian's relation to the world.

[124] This example appears throughout his work e.g. *Presence*, 69; *Freedom*, 313ff; *Ethique* III, 144-56. *Institutions* 2:539, 570 provides his historical treatment.

out their own obedience to God's Word (*TWTD*, chapter five). This will result in Christians being a disturbing presence as, by requiring society and its morality to live in a process of constant change and development, they will prevent the world from absolutising itself and thereby enable it to fulfil its important but strictly relative function (1972d).

In addition to this constant emphasis there is also, in Ellul's earlier work, a belief that God establishes within the fallen world a clear and apparently quite complex order of preservation. This is related concretely to the communities of family and the nation, the state, law, marriage, social hierarchy, and the economy.[125] The heart of this understanding is that God has established in the world a certain order that can in part be known without reference to revelation. This order delimits what forms of institutions such as the state, marriage and property are able to serve the conservation of the world.

This divinely ordained order of preservation for the fallen world is clearly different from that of the communion found in the kingdom of God (*Presence*, 35ff). Ellul claims that Christians must seek to understand this order from Scripture and social observation and then demand that the world recognise and conform to it because disregard of it leads to ruin for any society.[126] Christians are also to work in the world so that 'the order willed by God may be incarnated in actual institutions and organisms' (*Presence*, 35). This is because, in words written for the first WCC Conference in Amsterdam, 'the church exists in order to insist on constant change in society and civilization, in order to bring them more into conformity with the order of God' (1948f, 59).

In an important 1948 article, Ellul explains that strictly speaking there cannot be a Christian civilization because civilization is necessarily of the fallen world. However, there are important differences between civilizations and in the late 1940s he believed there is a certain sense in which it may be possible to refer to a civilization as 'Christian'. The two necessary requirements for this are shown, by implication, in Ellul's statement of what constitutes a non-Christian civilization:

> To the extent that we find a false relation between the Church and the world and a false conception of the order of the world in relation to God's revelation, we can speak of a non-Christian civilization (1948e, 3).

Ellul always rejected applying the Christian ethic to the world, constructing

---

[125] Numerous articles in the 1940s work with this understanding (e.g. 1942; 1945a; 1946c, d & e; 1947b; 1948:e & f; 1949e) which is further discussed in chapters six and seven below.

[126] *Presence*, 18f, 35; *Law*, 139-40; 1946b, 681; 1946d, 23; 1946e, 23.

a 'Christian' ethic that the world and Christians could have in common, and developing an ethic to enable Christians to 'improve' the world. However, his early writing does not leave him with only a distinctive Christian ethic and little or nothing concrete to say to the world as the world of ruptured communion. There, alongside the unique calling of the Christian in relation to the world, a certain divine order for the preservation of the world can also be found, an order which can be known by both reason and revelation and which should guide the world and not only the Christian.

In one of the most important changes in his theology and ethics, references to this divine order begin to fade from Ellul's work in the early 1950s. No explanation is ever offered for the omission but he did later acknowledge that, 'it is obvious that I no longer analyse the Christian ethic in the same terms I used between 1945 and 1950' (*Season*, 186). Although not specific, given his other comment that 'I no longer think that one can derive from the Bible a political or social doctrine that is more true than others' (*Season*, 91), this admission probably refers, at least in part, to this shift in his thinking. This shift also appears related to the development of his elaborate three-fold ethic for Christians that was discussed above and first appeared in print in 1950 (1950i).

In Ellul's later writing there are occasional references to an order of conservation but this is significantly different from his earlier writing. As will be seen in chapters six and seven, this order is increasingly viewed as a purely pragmatic human construct in order to preserve life. There is no longer any suggestion of a higher, divinely sanctioned preserving order of the world which has broken from God. Although never stated explicitly, it would appear that in most of his work Ellul's earlier, rather complex and comprehensive God-given order for the fallen world has become merely a recognition that man in the fallen world must create for himself patterns of life and social structures which enable him to continue to live in the world. This different understanding is then combined with a belief that if this goal is to be achieved all such attempts must be viewed by the world as not absolute but relative. Social and political structures must be constantly open to criticism and change and truly *laïque*, by which Ellul means not only free from church control but also not the incarnations of the powers (i.e. the locus of the sacred and man's love and worship). The Christian participates in the work of reaching this goal alongside the world and, through being faithful to his own unique calling, is the primary means of ensuring that all the world's works, whatever their form, remain works which conserve rather than destroy human life.

Conclusion

The major difficulties facing any interpreter of Ellul's theology were discussed at the beginning of this chapter It was proposed that the best means of understanding its fundamental dialectical structure was to see its heart as the relationship between God and the world, a relationship best traced in terms of communion and rupture. This, it was claimed, would also create the context for Ellul's understanding of the Christian life and his theological ethics and embrace within it others' insights into his theology and ethics. While there are evidently many important themes in Christian theology and within Ellul's theological writing that have not been discussed in the account offered here and there has not been space to critique his proposals, the most important elements have been briefly expounded within the interpretive framework being proposed. [127]

We have seen that Ellul views creation and new creation in terms of a relationship of pure communion between God and the world. In contrast, he understands our present world in the light of humanity's rupture of that communion with God by 'the Fall' and the development of a world apart from communion with God. In response to this, God's goal is to restore the world to full communion with himself, which he will do by re-creation and recapitulation of human history after a rupture of the present world through his act of final judgment.

Human history between the rupture of creation's communion with God and God's new creation must now be viewed in terms of a dialectical interplay of rupture and communion. Rebellious humans and the powers seek, through their works, to create a world wholly apart from God. God, however, refuses to accept humanity's rupture and seeks to make a break in our counter-world and re-establish communion through his Word and decisively in the incarnation. In Christ, God has fully assumed the ruptured world and ensured the ultimate triumph of his desire for communion over the world's rupture of communion in its quest for self-destructive autonomy.

Within this overall theology, the Christian stands at the crossroads of God and the world and the dialectic between communion and rupture. God has re-

---

[127] The most glaring omission is Ellul's ecclesiology. Although some writers regularly refer to 'the church' when discussing Ellul's theology (e.g. Temple 1976), others are critical of his concentration on the individual Christian at the expense of the church (e.g. Gill 1976a:24; Hendricks 1989:214-5). While a theology of the church could be constructed from Ellul's writings it is not central to his theology or ethics as God's communion is re-established in history with individual persons who become part of the body of Christ in the fallen world.

established communion with any person in Christ but they still remain part of the world of the rupture. Their unique calling is to live out their communion with God in that world. This requires a life that can be described in various terms but perhaps most succinctly as one that lives the Word and in so doing resists the fallen world.

This account of Ellul's theology encompasses many of the alternative proposals for the heart of Ellul's theology sketched in the opening section. Ellul's Christocentric theology (Burke), his emphasis on the Word of God (Miller) and the significance of the Two Realms (Temple) all now take their proper, significant, but secondary place. The two other main suggestions noted (Fasching's dialectic of the holy and the sacred and Clendenin's dialectic of freedom and necessity) have also been incorporated into the account offered here. This was achieved by delineating the central characteristics of God (he is living, Wholly Other, agape love, and free) and showing that these determine the characteristics of both the world in communion with him (thus marked by life, otherness, love, and freedom) and the world of ruptured communion in opposition to God (characterized by the polar opposites of death, closure/unity, eros, and necessity). This wider account also explains Ellul's three-fold ethic for Christians and his emphasis on the Christian life as one of freedom in the face of necessity, holiness in opposition to the closure/unity expressed in the sacred, and agape love and non-power in the face of Eros.

Finally, a number of important developments within Ellul's theology have also been noted. As will become clear in Part Two (where attention is focussed on Ellul's treatment of particular socio-political subjects) some of these changes in his theology (his changing view of the powers, his embracing of universalism, and his significant repudiation of any institutional divine order of preservation for the fallen world) are almost as significant as the wider theological continuity discerned in his work. There is, nevertheless, a fundamental continuity and theological coherence that is centred on the motif of the relationship between God and the world expressed in terms of communion and rupture. In relation to his theological ethics this focuses on the dialectic between the world humans now seek to create having ruptured their communion with God and God's quest to restore that fallen world to communion with himself through his spoken and incarnate Word lived by Christians who resist the world.

CHAPTER 3

Ellul's Sociology: Modernity, Civilization and Technique

The opening chapter has already shown that Ellul's sociological writings aim to encourage and enable his readers to become aware of the nature of the modern world in which they live and then to question it and act to change it. The previous chapter has also made clear that Ellul's theological ethic for Christians, because it is an ethic for here and now, will be shaped by the contemporary situation and the Christian understanding of it. This chapter now focuses on clarifying the central features of the sociological strand of his writing as a whole. A brief introduction outlines the basic elements of Ellul's sociological method. It is then argued that the interpretive key to Ellul's sociological thought originates in the personalist movement of the 1930s long before his first major sociological studies were published. Ellul's writings from that period show that what is usually understood to be the heart of his sociological studies - the centrality and dominance of Technique in the modern world - has to be understood in the wider context of his belief that we have witnessed the creation of a totally unprecedented social situation which is destructive of the human person and amounts to a break with previous civilization.

Introduction to Ellul's Sociological Method[1]

In order to make sense of Ellul's contemporary sociological analyses a number of important and wider issues must be addressed. It is first important to recall that Ellul's academic training is not in sociology. As we have seen, Ellul's expertise is in the history of law and Ellul often referred to himself as an historian.[2] In addition to his detailed unpublished historical studies and the untranslated five volume *Histoire des Institutions*, he wrote a number of articles comprising historical analysis, discussions of methodology in history,

---

[1] The best general discussions of Ellul's sociological method are Temple 1976 & 1980 and Boli-Bennett 1980. See also 1988e for a helpful interview with Ellul on this by David Gill.

[2] *Freedom*, 194; *Betrayal*, 12; *Season*, 160; *Conversations*, 25.

and reflections upon the philosophy of history.[3] Ellul's sociological studies of the contemporary world must be viewed from this wider historical perspective and are therefore misunderstood if not properly set in relation both to Ellul's radical programme for the future, and his historian's perspective on the past and the historical process.[4]

Once his sociological studies are set in this wider historical context it is then essential to grasp that Ellul follows Hegel and particularly Marx in viewing dialectical process as fundamental to life and history (*WIB*, 32f). He claims that 'in order that there be history, dialectic process is necessary' (*Apocalypse*, 156) and so history is to be understood in terms of conflicts and tensions. Understanding any particular society or processes of historical change therefore requires a person to discern the contradictory forces that drive it.

With this emphasis on the centrality of conflict, tensions and dialectic in historical and social change in place, these beliefs must be related to Ellul's conception of different levels within the structure of society. His seminal 1947 *Foi et Vie* article, 'On demande un nouveau Karl Marx', only recently made available in English by Marva Dawn, effectively outlined his own sociological programme. There Ellul first sketched his conception of society's three-fold structure. Having spoken often in the article about *les structures* and *les données fondamentales* he then clarifies these in the following terms:

> Thus far I have repeatedly used the terms structures or fundamental givens. The meaning should be clarified, since the search for these structures will be the object of these articles. Underneath the phenomena that we are able to see in the social, political, economic realms, there are some permanent forces of which the tracks are found in each of the phenomena considered, and which ensure its unity...Exactly as in a tapestry, there is an unseen warp that ensures the unity of the fabric (*Sources*, 42).

These 'forces' and 'structures' are then distinguished from the 'permanent, eternal elements of the world' studied by philosophers. This is because Ellul 'will regard as a structure in the question of civilization that which is specific to modern times, and not at all what is common to every civilization, to every society' (*Sources*, 43). He then makes clear where his concern lies in his sociological writings.

---

[3] See, for example, 1938b; 1949d; 1950b; 1964; 1971a; 1973a; 1976i; 1981h.

[4] Vitalis perceptively comments, that 'Ellul sees a long way and knowing as an historian of institutions a multitude of different historical societies he is better able to grasp the specificity of our society and to understand its depths' (Vitalis 1994:163).

This research is located between the permanent in the course of all history and the provisional, strictly episodic, and momentary (*Sources*, 43).

This tri-partite structure found in Ellul's early writing recurs throughout Ellul's whole corpus where he often draws an analogy with the ocean and its waves, currents, and depths.[5] The first and superficial level (the waves) is that of constantly changing current events and personalities and is the great concern of the media and, increasingly, academic social scientists. The third level (the depths) is that of extreme abstraction and the domain of the philosopher. Ellul's historical and sociological studies are focussed on the intermediate level (the currents) and only at this level can the fundamental contradictory forces constitutive of history's dialectical process be found. It is also only at this level that truly revolutionary social, economic and political change can be effected. Indeed, as Ellul had written a year earlier (1946) in *Foi et Vie*, 'without an exact stock-taking (*une prise de conscience exacte*) of this kind, it is absolutely vain to try to act in the political and economic realm' (*Sources*, 20-1).

This level of analysis, which I shall call 'global sociology', is qualitatively different from social scientific studies. These focus on the first level of social events and adhere to certain agreed 'scientific' and statistical methods of which Ellul is highly critical (*Déviances*, 91-2). Although he grants that micro-sociological studies have their place, Ellul is concerned that their increasing dominance 'leaves fundamental and decisive phenomena unstudied only because they cannot be expressed in mathematics' (1976g, 14).[6] He emphatically rejects the idea that it is possible to use the results of such studies to produce a global model of society as a whole. This is impossible not only because a sociologist cannot discover all the necessary variables but also because of the more fundamental methodological problem that the two levels of study are incommensurable.

It is even inexact to say that a series of microsociological studies, however scientifically advanced, could ever result, through accumulation, in an understanding of global phenomena...*There is a sort of qualitative change that comes about that one can never take stock of.* (1976g, 14; italics added).[7]

---

[5] See *False*, 159ff; *Hope*, 279ff; *Bluff*, 14; 1988e. Discussion of this can be found in Punzo 1980; Fasching 1981:55-7; Gill 1984b:91; Wennemann 1991b:3-10.

[6] A similar critique of much sociological method is made earlier in 1961b.

[7] The importance of this in historical study of society is evident from Ellul's comments on Weber's global sociology of the 'spirit of capitalism' and the use of micro-sociological data in relation to this debate (1964,11-12).

Any attempt to formulate a global sociology has, therefore, to acknowledge from the outset that it is 'necessarily conceptual and hypothetical' but, Ellul is quick to add, 'this does not mean that it must be inexact' (1976g, 14).

Ellul nowhere explicitly elaborated the method he used to get behind the superficial level of events, discern the fundamental structures, and so construct a contemporary global sociology. Nevertheless, some of its key elements can be discerned from scattered comments in his writing and from the structure and content of his sociological corpus. There appears to be one fundamental principle (personal reflection upon lived reality) aided by two main tools of analysis (study of commonplaces and the sacred).

Drawing on his contrast between the second and third levels, Ellul insists that the concrete nature of structures makes his form of analysis fundamentally different from that of the philosopher. The important structures of our civilization, precisely because they are not abstract, impinge directly on the average person's daily life and so they can be discerned within everyday experience

> One must not imagine…that these structures are essentially abstract, that they are ideas or principles. On the contrary, actually a structure is necessarily very close to persons. It concerns them directly…We will as a matter of fact recognize a structure by a last characteristic, which is that it concerns the individual life of persons…What will allow us to recognize a structure, then, will not be its material importance, its influence on the economic or political order, but rather its repercussions on the concrete life of the average person. A structure will be what shapes average people, what has a decisive force in the organization of their life, in the order of their thoughts, in their behavior, in their habits…It is in pondering these average people, where they live and whatever might be their race, formed by a universal civilization, that we can distinguish the great forces which hold [in their grasp] this entire civilization (*Sources*, 44-5).

From *Presence* onwards, Ellul therefore emphasised the necessity of personal reflection upon the *reality* of our world in order to discern the objective reality of life lived by people in our society (*Presence*, chapter four). A global sociology cannot be achieved by abstract theorising or the quest for 'objectivity'. It requires serious reflection upon one's own lived experience and concrete engagement with that of others.

> This reality ought to be grasped first of all on the human level…We must no longer think of 'men' in the abstract, but of my neighbour Mario. It is in the concrete life of this man…that I see the real repercussions of the machine, of

the press, of political discourses and of the administration…The intellectual who wants to do his work properly must today go back to the starting-point: the man whom he knows, and first of all to himself…All other knowledge of the world, through statistics or news, is illusory…(*Presence*, 99-100).[8]

This emphasis on the subjective lived experience is a constant through to the end of Ellul's sociological studies (*Déviances*, 91-2). It has three important corollaries for any understanding of Ellul's analysis. Firstly, it explains Ellul's scepticism about all sociological 'experiments'.[9] He believes it is impossible to recreate an environment or phenomenon accurately and so, in order to understand something properly, 'all the sociologist can do is try to be there when the phenomenon occurs, experience it, analyse it, and afterward attempt to understand it' (1976g, 17). Secondly, it confirms the importance of Ellul's biography for understanding his sociological studies. Indeed, Ellul claimed that 'in my description of the contemporary scene, behind each bare statement lies an experience; and I could support each statement with concrete examples' (*Presence*, 114).[10] Thirdly, this emphasis highlights the fact that, despite their wider applications, Ellul's analyses are reflections rooted in the experience of a provincial Frenchman and must (especially in relation to politics, *Illusion*, xiii) be understood as referring primarily to his French context. That does not, of course, limit their value to France as Ellul was eager to point out (*Conversations*, 116).

Ellul's fundamental method is therefore an avowedly non-technical and subjective one of reflection upon one's own life (and that of one's neighbours) in order to gain a global perspective on society and discern what lies at its heart. It depends on the sociologist developing a sort of sixth sense that Ellul (citing as an example his sense from a day in Rome that fascism was about to revive in Italy) describes in the following terms:

In the social and political world (but also the human world in general) the intellectual must leave a large place for intuition (*flair*). From my own experience, this is not inbuilt and spontaneous but relies on being imbued

---

[8] Towards the end of his life Ellul again described this method, explaining 'I analyse my own feelings which I later transpose. I use myself as a model of the average man, usually I react like any man in the street. I'm rarely mistaken…I really do believe that I am like everybody else' (*Conversations*, 50)

[9] A good discussion of these is found in the appendix to *Propaganda*, especially pp260-77 discussing the difficulties of measuring its effectiveness, a problem still faced in such contemporary debates as the wider social impact of pornography or violence on television.

[10] Again this method is reaffirmed at the end of his life – 'I've always based my reflections on personal experiences' (*Conversations*, 40).

with earlier registered experiences (*L'Homme*, 114-5 cf. *Conversations*, 100).

This intuition is central but in Ellul's work it is guided and assisted by two more specific forms of analysis that together enable a deeper understanding of society. First, there is a critical analysis of *les lieux communs*. This key phrase usually appears in English as 'commonplaces' but its importance is sometimes lost through being rendered as 'clichés' or 'stereotypes'. This method of analysis came to prominence in 1966 with the publication of *Exégèse des nouveaux lieux communs* (ET *A Critique of the New Commonplaces*, 1968) but Ellul used it from his first studies. Both the term and method are found in his 1930s writing. There, in '*Directives pour un manifeste personnaliste*' (one of his earliest pieces of extant writing and studied in more detail below), Ellul's definition of society is described as the result of 'une exégèse des lieux communs' of our society (*Directives*, §12) and he refers to 'les lieux communs' which reveal the modern world (*Directives*, §40).[11] He explains his use of 'les lieux communs' in the following terms:

> That is to say, facts without importance and phrases which in themselves are innocent but which are the expression of ideological currents common to all in society, which the whole world admits and which therefore indicate a general state of mind (*Directives*, §12).

This definition can be amplified by guidance on how to discern commonplaces in his book published three decades later: when a formula is constantly repeated in a great diversity of writings or is an implicit presupposition accepted without proof as self-evident, then it is a commonplace (*Critique*, 26-7). Such commonplaces are embraced by, and reflect, the thinking and life of a whole society. A commonplace provides everyone with a touchstone, a fundamental presupposition expressing a society's values which can provide it with justifications that will make an action acceptable (*Critique*, 13ff). By means of a purposefully unpleasant analogy, Ellul explains the merit of studying the commonplaces of our own society by comparing them to a body's excrement: they reveal our society's

---

[11] Another 1930s personalist piece ('Le personnalisme, révolution immédiate) concludes with a short piece headed 'Exègese des lieux communs. IL NOUS FAUT UNE MYSTIQUE par Bernard Charbonneau'. Immediately after the war the phrase appears in a number of articles (1946g, 408; 1948a) and in Ellul's third lesson for the Professional Protestant Associations (APP) which is entitled 'Les Lieux Communs' and offers thoughts on thirteen commonplaces.

staple diet, its values, philosophies, and education, and the diseases within it which will bring about its demise (*Critique*, 9-13).

It is, however, important to realize that (as these descriptions and the book as a whole demonstrates) commonplaces by no means offer an accurate representation of the material reality of any society. Analysis of commonplaces thus has to be critical because what the commonplaces offer is primarily an opening into the standard perception of society and the unquestioned assumptions (both true and false) that the sociologist is likely to share, perhaps unwittingly. Indeed, Ellul's sociological law of suspicion that 'the development of an abundant discourse about something is proof that what is spoken about does not exist' (*Déviances*, 66) suggests that a 'mirror-reading' of commonplaces is often the most helpful guide to the construction of a realistic global sociology.[12]

The second form of analysis required for the construction of a global sociology is a study of the locus of the sacred in society.[13] From his early writing, Ellul insisted that in penetrating to the level of society's structures and fundamental givens one is entering the realm of the spiritual and diagnosing spiritual problems (Presence, 27f, 101ff).[14] The link with the sacred appears in various articles and in some books before becoming one of the central themes in his 1973 study *Les Nouveaux Possédés* (ET *The New Demons*, 1975), a work Fasching has described as 'the Rosetta Stone of Ellul's work'.[15] In this work Ellul totally rejects the commonplace that, in contrast to earlier societies, 'the modern world is secular, secularized, atheistic, laicized, desacralized, and demythologized' (*Demons*, 18).[16] He argues that instead of viewing ourselves as living in a secularised society which has come of age by eliminating the sacred and religious which dominated past eras (cf. *Critique*, 75-81) our society can be classed as post-Christendom and post-Christian but that this is not equivalent to it being secularised and desacralised (*Demons*, chapter two).

In demonstrating this, Ellul, in line with his normal method, does not first define the essence of religious phenomena. Instead, using what he calls a

---

[12] Although not prominent in translated works, this basic belief appears often in Ellul's sociological works e.g. *Révolution*, 271; *L'Homme*, 110.

[13] The role of the sacred in Ellul's sociological method is discussed by Zorn 1971:92ff; Temple 1976:79ff; Boli-Bennett 1980.

[14] Marva Dawn both in her thesis (Dawn 1992) and her translation of early articles (*Sources*, chapters 1-3) has confirmed the importance of this not just in later work (e.g. *TWTD*, 155-8; 1960k, 83-4) but from his early post-war writing (cf. also 1946g, 421; 1948f; 1948e).

[15] Fasching 1994a:14.

[16] A fuller critique of this secularisation view appears later in 1976e.

'nominalist' method of analysis, Ellul examines the different experiences of the sacred across time and place in order to discern common functions and forms.

> I would like to specify the method to be followed here. It is not possible to give a definition *a priori* of the sacred, of myth, o f religion. There are as many definitions as there are authors. For a work on myth which I was impelled to do a few years ago I had collected, between 1960 and 1966, fourteen mutually irreconcilable definitions…It is necessary to begin with a consideration of the indubitable phenomena of the sacred, indubitable because qualified as sacred by those who lived in that world; with the consideration of myths which are indubitable myths and of religions which are obviously religions (*Demons*, 46).

Using this method, he believes it is then possible to recognise the same phenomena within the contemporary world. Ellul examines in detail the sacred, myth, and religion. Although myths can be of value in a way similar to commonplaces, which are their most superficial form (*Demons*, 96), it is the sacred that is of particular interest for the attempt to construct a global sociology. We attribute sacred values to what threatens us and what protects us in our encounter with the world. This is done in order to create (in relation to our experiences of space, time and our social group) some form of order to guide us, give us meaning, and set boundaries to our action. To fulfil these functions, the sacred regularly assumes certain forms which then aid its identification in the modern world: it expresses dark and destructive powers; it combines absolute value, rites of commitment and personal embodiment; it is ambiguously organised around opposite poles which, although they are conflicting, are considered equally sacred (*Demons*, 50-7).[17] This 'characterology' of the functions and forms of the sacred then allows the identification of the sacred in contemporary society and thereby provides a means to get below the surface level of events and discover the deeper currents shaping the modern world.[18]

Combining his reflection upon lived experience and an analysis of commonplaces and the sacred Ellul produces his global sociology. This global perspective is of such importance because another central aspect within his sociological method is his belief that a specific social phenomenon can only be correctly understood when set within the context of the whole society in

---

[17] An earlier account of this discussion of the sacred is to be found in 1963b.

[18] The parallel between the sacred and the intermediate level of society is confirmed by Ellul's analysis of the modern sacred as revolving around Technique/sex and the state/revolution (*Demons*, 70-87).

which it appears.[19] This important feature of his work again stems from Ellul's work as an historian (*Institutions* I, 5-6).

> I felt that one could not study law in itself, and that one could not explain it without studying at the same time the economic context, the ideological context, the dominant values, and the political connections of the time (*Season*, 184).

The importance of this bigger picture for any social analysis is explained in the foreword to his untranslated second study of revolution.

> Revolutions are different in different societies, in terms of content, process, conditions, objectives and even the very concept of revolution. I would go so far as to say that a sociology of revolution is, strictly speaking, impossible unless one begins not by a typology but by analyzing the relationship between what one globally terms revolution and a given type of society...Revolution is specific to a certain type of society...(*Révolution*, 7-8).

The perception of the global social context of any phenomenon is therefore crucial but it will necessarily be both hypothetical and highly subjective. In addressing how to overcome these difficulties, Ellul dismisses the possibility of applying common 'scientific' criteria such as validation through experimentation or methodological rigour (1976g, 16-18). Instead he argues that there is only one reliable test for a global sociology: 'I maintain that the only 'proof' of scientific quality for a work in such areas is subsequent events' (*L'Homme*, 83)

Global sociological studies whose structure makes them untestable by this criterion (e.g., because they are highly abstract) therefore cannot be taken seriously as an account of social reality. Any realistic global sociology must contain either implicit or explicit predictions within it.[20] This is because a global sociology is really a snapshot within the larger context of historical development and the fact that society is a historically changing phenomenon composed of different and competing elements means that 'any sociological study must include a statement concerning the probable evolution of the phenomenon under consideration' (1976g, 20). The criterion of verifiability by subsequent events therefore ultimately enables a rigorous testing and development of all sociological analyses of our society. Although future events may falsify an originally accurate theory (*TS*, xxx) and Ellul indeed

---

[19] For Ellul's application of this method to revolutions see e.g. *Révolution*, 7-8.

[20] These conclusions are discussed in 1961b & 1979k.

writes in the hope that human action may change the natural development of society as he analyses it (*Changer*, 288), this criterion remains an important test. On the basis of it Ellul praises the work of Raymond Aron (1983l) and defends himself against the critique of André Dumas.

> Dumas seems to put in doubt my sociological observations. I am used to this…I simply wish to recall that the only possible test of a method's accuracy is agreement between its results and what the evolution of the social body progressively reveals. Now, anyone can go back over all that I have written since 1945 and they will see that everything (apart from two articles) has been confirmed…(1973d).

In the light of the earlier account of Ellul's conception of history and society it is clear that a decisive factor in the predictive value of any global analysis will be its choice of the key determining factors in society and its conception of their dialectical relationship with one another and other factors. Here, in addition to the methods discussed above, Ellul offers two questions which help in the selection of the most important element(s): 'Which factor accounts for the greatest possible number of data?' and 'What seems to orient the process of development or the decline of a group or society?' (cf. 1976g, 23).[21] It was his answer to these two questions and his wider Marx-inspired methodology which gave Ellul's own global sociology it specific form:

> I was actually a Marxist in 1933-34. And I asked myself then: If Marx were alive today, would he be so disposed to cite as the crucial social phenomenon of history the ownership of property ? What would he cite as crucial ? And I decided that it would be the phenomenon of technique.[22]

Ellul's Sociology: Modernity, Civilization and Technique

Ellul's analysis of Technique has been the area of his work most examined and criticised, especially in the extensive literature on philosophy and technology.[23] In addition to his classic text *La Technique* (*The Technological*

---

[21] See also *TWTD*, 164ff and the more focused discussion in 1967f & 1969c. Wennemann 1991b:63-85 discusses this approach.

[22] Quoted in Menninger 1974:209. *Season*, 175-6 relates his wartime planning of his writing project to a similar question.

[23] A brief note on terminology: I use 'Technique' (capitalised) for '*la technique*' in line with Ellul's own desired usage (1984a). The usual English term 'technology' is not used because for Ellul this term signifies discourse about the technical phenomenon rather than the phenomenon itself. The meaning of Technique in Ellul's work is discussed below.

Society), he produced two further books specifically relating to Technique and technology (*The Technological System* and *The Technological Bluff*) and numerous articles devoted to the subject. As the concern of this book is to provide an account of his thought as a whole and (in Part Two) his political writing in particular, comments on his analysis of Technique and detailed interaction with this important secondary literature is here kept to a bare minimum.[24] However, in order to make sense of his contemporary Christian ethic and understand his studies on law, politics and the state, Ellul's wider analysis of the modern world needs to be sketched. In particular the origins, structure and central features of his global sociology must be correctly perceived. What follows demonstrates that, in addition to his claim that Technique is the new determinant of modern society, Ellul's sociology is structured by another belief which has received much less attention: that Technique today is qualitatively different from earlier techniques and so the modern world constructed by it is fundamentally different from and indeed antipathetic to, traditional Western civilization. The opening part of this section sets Ellul's classic text in context by examining the generally ignored but vitally important years of Ellul's sociological analysis prior to writing *La Technique*, particularly highlighting his role in the 1930s personalist movement. It is followed by an account of the central argument of that book and the key subsequent developments in Ellul's perception of the novelty of Technique and its effect on the modern world.

Before La Technique

Long before 1947 when he began work on what became his most famous work, *La Technique ou l'enjeu du siècle*, Ellul, together with Bernard Charbonneau, was attempting to construct a global sociology. This, in the tradition of Marx, aimed to go beyond surface analysis and diagnose the roots of society's problems with the hope that, as a result, revolutionary change could be effected. The evolution of this analysis can be traced through his largely unpublished writings for the 1930s personalist groups and then his various newspaper and other articles prior to the completion of *La Technique*

---

[24] The major theses and books on Ellul and Technique are (chronologically), Mitcham 1969; Miller 1970; Mulkey 1973; Christians 1974; Menninger 1974; Ihara 1975; Temple 1976; Winner 1977; Wren 1977; Schuurman 1980:125-58; Lovekin 1991; Chastenet 1992:29-42 (summarised in Chastenet 1994e). In addition there are numerous articles on the subject. Several are dismissive but among the best are Mitcham & Mackey 1971; Cérézuelle 1979 & 1980; Mesthene 1984; Weyembergh 1989 and the many contributions to Chastenet 1994d.

in 1950.[25] There one finds the context and basic framework for Ellul's study of Technique and thus for the whole of the sociological strand of his writing, including his political analysis.

Ellul's earliest sociological analysis, which set the direction of his post-war thinking, is best outlined through an account of the central features of 'Directives pour un manifeste personnaliste'. This important document has only recently become more widely available with its publication by Patrick Chastenet.[26] Also known as 'Manifeste en 83 points' some uncertainty still remains as to its origins. In relation to authorship, although credited to both Ellul and Charbonneau and undoubtedly a jointly developed document, the manuscript Chastenet received from Ellul's son is entirely in Ellul's hand with only minor amendments from Charbonneau. Chastenet dates the document to 1935 although Ellul has himself, on different occasions, given at least four different dates.[27]

The first part of the manifesto and, in this context, the most important, is entitled 'Origin of our revolt' (*Origine de notre révolte*). It opens by giving an account of the birth of their consciousness of the need for revolution and their realization that the new world taking shape is characterized by anonymity and not properly understood or controlled by anyone.

> A world was organised without us. We entered it as it was beginning to lose its balance. It obeyed deep-seated laws we did not know, which were not those of earlier Societies. No one took the trouble to ferret them out, because this world was characterized by anonymity: no one was responsible, and no one attempted to control it. Each person simply kept to the post he was assigned in this world, which came into being by itself, through the interplay of these deep-seated laws (*Directives*, §1).[28]

In this new situation everybody is rendered impotent in the face of such powers as banks, the stock exchange, and production. As a result, the revolutionary struggle must take a new form. 'One cannot fight man to man as

---

[25] For background to the writing of *La Technique* see 1988b, 37-8. The importance of this period in Ellul's thought is now being made clear in the work of Patrick Chastenet. Loubet del Bayle 1994 presents a fascinating account of the analysis of technique and society in the wider personalist movement (especially Ordre Nouveau, for which see also Aron & Dandieu 1993) but refers to none of Ellul's own writing prior to *Technique*.

[26] The manifesto is to be found in Revue française d'histoire des idées politiques (1999), 9:1, pp159-77 and appears in the secondary bibliography as Charbonneau & Ellul 1999.

[27] The dates given have been 1934 (*Autopsy*, 292n), 1935 (*Conversations*, 18n53), 1936 (*Season*, 36) and winter 1937 (Roy 1992). For more details see part one of the bibliography of unpublished writings by Ellul.

[28] This translation is taken from Hanks 2001:4.

in previous societies, nor fight ideas with ideas' (§2). Ellul and Charbonneau proceed to offer their definition of this society as marked by two key characteristics which they name *fatalités* and *gigantisme*. As examples of the former they cite war, fascism and disequilibrium in production, while 'gigantism' is seen in the concentrations of production, the state, capital and population (§13-15).[29] These two elements engender and mutually reinforce one another due to human refusal to control them (§15,19,20). The kernel of the problem is then identified in the manifesto's seventeenth point:

> The means of realization of this concentration is *la technique*, not as an industrial procedure but as a general procedure (§17).

Here, in line with his later analysis, Ellul explicitly expands his understanding of Technique to include intellectual, economic, political and juridical technique as well as the machine. He then offers this assessment:

> *La Technique* dominates man and all man's reactions. Against it, politics is powerless... (§21).

There follows another characteristic Ellulian argument with 'proofs' that all three contemporary political and economic systems (capitalist, fascist and communist) are essentially the same (§22-26). The first part then draws some conclusions. What is being witnessed is the disappearance of the consciously acting human being as people become like machines, submitting themselves *en masse* to the orders of abstract powers. This is described as 'social sin (*le péché social*)', 'sin against the spirit (*le péché contre l'esprit*)' and the refusal to live (*le refus de vivre*)'. In language that explicitly reappears nearly fifty years later as central in Ellul's 1982 book *Changer* this is said to represent 'the fact that man is becoming totally proletarian' (§28-31). There is, therefore, a fundamental revolutionary necessity and 'the Revolution will not be made against people but against institutions' (§33).

The second part of the outline is entitled 'Direction pour la construction d'une société personnaliste'. It provides the outline of the personalist revolutionary programme, offering an account of the relation of a personalist society to the wider society, the character of its members, and the form of its various political, economic, and cultural institutions (§34-80). Of crucial importance here is the extent and categorisation of these proposals. Ellul

---

[29] Reflecting the general concern of the decade, which saw the majority of the French population for the first time becoming city dwellers (Berstein 1988:7ff), Ellul was already concerned with the problem of *la grande ville* as shown by his unpublished article 'La Formation des villes modernes' dated in the Wheaton Archive as 1935 (Cf. 1970e).

writes of the personalist revolution being 'a revolution of civilization...'
(§36), a description that is reiterated in the climax and concluding appeal of
the piece:

> All that we have said up until here shows that the problem of revolution is
> raised not only on the political or economic level but also on the level of
> civilization itself...(§81).

> Let those who believe they have a role to play in the Revolution that is
> coming (against a civilization which lives only by our death), prepare
> themselves...(§83).

The persistence of this analysis and the depth and range of the problem
Ellul perceived becomes clear in a piece written on the brink of the Second
World War. Although an ardent opponent of Nazism and those who
collaborated with it, he could also write boldly of the similarities between
France and Nazi Germany even asking if it was really possible to oppose
freedom in France to slavery in Germany and stating his belief that both
suffered forms of dictatorship due to *la technique*. He claimed that 'the
spiritual oppression is less overt' but 'almost equal in them both' (1939b,
178).[30]

This radical view is not challenged by the experience of the war and recurs
in one of his earliest post-war pieces (*'Victoire d'Hitler?'*) where Ellul
implicitly acknowledges the failure of his earlier attempts at revolution and
the resultant deterioration in the situation.

> Whoever says I exaggerate does not see the reality under the garlands and
> the chatter. When one simply compares the economic, political, social and
> administrative life of 1935 to that of 1945 one will see the gigantic step
> accomplished in ten years...Hitler's victory – not in its forms but in depth. It
> is not the same dictatorship, the same mysticism, the same totalitarianism,
> but it is a dictatorship, a mysticism, a totalitarianism, which we are laying
> the ground for with enthusiasm (1945e, 3).[31]

The numerous newspaper and journal articles which follow in the next five

---

[30] A strong objection to this was raised in response by Diétrich 1939. *Conversations*, 107ff
provides Ellul's reflections on this near the end of his life.
[31] This theme of the victory of Hitler and Nazism continues as a rhetorical ploy throughout
his books from *Presence*, 16 ('the triumph of the Nazi spirit that we see everywhere in the
world today') through to *Violence*, 29 ('Hitler won his war after all') and *Faith*, 215 ('The
democracies learned at Hitler's school').

years all reiterate this sense that Western society is taking the wrong course and elaborate the analysis found in his 1935 manifesto. Some of these are now available in Dawn's translation of key writings from this period (*Sources*, chapters one to three) but for a long time the most accessible and significant of Ellul's post-war pieces was his contribution to the 1948 WCC Amsterdam Conference (1948f). This, especially when read in the context of his occasional writings over the previous three years and his earlier personalist thinking, provides a powerful synthesis of the central elements of his thought at this time. Three features of Ellul's writing stand out as crucial for understanding *Technique* and all his later thought about contemporary society.

First, there is a sense that the world has undergone fundamental change. The belief that the situation is radically new and contemporary society qualitatively different from all preceding societies, is heightened and appears throughout this period. In 1946 he speaks of forces that 'give to our time its radically new character' (*Sources*, 20). A year later, Marx's valuable work is considered no longer valid because 'general conditions have changed as much in one century as [they had] in the three centuries that preceded Marx' (*Sources*, 39). In fact, 'people today no longer have anything in common with (*n'a plus aucun point commun avec*) people in the sixteenth century, for example, in their reality' (*Sources*, 70). The point is perhaps most explicit in the following extract from 1946.

> We are at an absolutely decisive point – such as there has never been before. And it is as a historian that I write that sentence...Our time is incommensurable with the rest of history...(*Sources*, 15).[32]

The problem, as in the personalist manifesto, is still seen in terms of human subjugation to impersonal forces and institutions with their own laws functioning independent of human beings. This is examined by Ellul in most detail in relation to the economy (1947b) but is applied more widely as shown by his WCC Amsterdam paper. This experience is now increasingly described not in terms of 'fatality' but of 'necessity' – 'man must subordinate himself to the necessity of things' (1948f, 56) – and is already being used in relation to propaganda (1947c, 1) and the state (1949e, 2).[33]

Most important, and the *second* key feature of works in this period, is that this situation is interpreted as nothing less than a crisis of civilization. In

---

[32] This theme of novelty was again prominent in the 1930s when Charbonneau wrote, 'There is between our civilization and the civilizations of the past a gulf such that ancient Egypt was closer to eighteenth century France than we are' (Charbonneau 1936:9).

[33] The fullest account at this stage is given in 1950i where comparison with *Directives*, §14 shows that the same phenomenon is being discussed.

December 1945 Ellul is clear of the challenge being faced – 'Our world is dying. Two solutions are possible: either the end of the world or a new civilization is going to be born' (1945c). A year later he writes of living through 'an end of civilization' (1946f) and again starkly sets before his readers the same choice.

> At stake is a problem of civilization that can be posed very simply thus: EITHER our civilization will continue on these same foundations, with its same dominant ideas, the same basic structures, and then humankind will die – spiritually and perhaps also materially. OR rather life will triumph within humankind, and then civilization with change its foundations and its structures. We are at an absolutely decisive point – such as there has never been before...(*Sources*, 15).

In 1947, doubtless reflecting on his own post-war political experience, Ellul writes of the dangers of political realism, warning that it 'leads to the annihilation (*un anéantissement*) of civilization and of humankind' (*Sources*, 67). It therefore comes as no surprise to read in his 1948 presentation in Amsterdam that

> We see European civilization breaking up into anarchy before our eyes...The traditional values of civilization are no longer moulding civilization today...Our task...is to discover values of civilization which – with the material elements of our world – will enable us to build up a civilization...It is possible that a new, authentic civilization may not materialize... (1948f, 51, 52).

This theme of a civilizational crisis also appears in Ellul's books dating from this time, most prominently in *Presence* whose original French sub-title was 'Problems of post-Christian civilization'. It regains prominence much later (as with the terminology of 'the proletariat') in his *Changer* which speaks of our crisis of civilization. Despite this, the theme has gone largely unnoticed in discussions of Ellul.[34]

Once again, there are important parallels here with the wider personalist movement of the 1930s.[35] Indeed, asked about the significance of such themes in this movement, Christian Roy, confirmed that,

---

[34] Ihara 1975 is a notable exception to this omission and Hanks 2000 now includes 'civilization' in her subject index listing over 50 books and articles, the majority prior to 1951 and many relating to the publication of *Changer* in 1982. Even Dawn's commentaries on the key articles in *Sources* fail to highlight the significance of this theme.

[35] Loubet del Bayle 1969:248-67, 1994 & 2001. The post-war writing of Bernanos also highlights this theme (Loubet del Bayle 1983; Chastenet 1992:76-7).

Yes, 'the crisis of civilization and the total novelty of the modern world' are not only regular themes in it, but its very premise, common to the whole generation of intellectuals christened *Les non-conformistes des années 30* by Jean-Louis Loubet del Bayle'.[36]

The elements of this civilizational crisis are examined by Ellul in a number of articles. As in the inter-war years, various phenomena are identified as the underlying material forces of this civilization in crisis: the state, the city, war, production, and the economy generally.[37] Our civilization as a whole is categorised as materialist, totalitarian, post-Christian, and global.[38] Within this rather extensive and diverse analysis, the *third* and most famous feature becomes prominent as *la technique* is already identified as the most important force and the root of the problem.

In 1946 Ellul speaks of being placed in a technical civilization (1946g, 411) and in analysing the economy he has already diagnosed a central problem.

It is becoming purely technical...that is to say that in it one is exclusively preoccupied with the absolutely best means of attaining a certain end...one doesn't seek the good, but the efficient (*l'efficace*)...(1946e, 25-6).

A year later a similar analysis is offered of politics in terms of political realism and the dominance of means.

Realism invites us to play a strange game. It sends us off in an infinite search for means...It persuades us that all means are good; it suffices to be the means to do something in order to be right and valid. One can no longer say that the end justifies the means, for within realism there is no longer any end; there is only the fact that the means succeed and that is all...What does that mean? Simply that the means are effective (*efficace*), have an effect, no matter what effect (*Sources*, 59).

By 1948, a whole chapter of *Presence* is devoted to this feature of the contemporary world but the Technique itself and its effects on society receive little detailed examination in the writings of the late 1940s. That task, essential for an accurate understanding of the novelty of the present situation and the challenge it presents to Western civilization, is undertaken in Ellul's

---

[36] Personal letter from Christian Roy to the author, 20th July 1995.

[37] The most accessible are *Sources*, 45 and 1948f, 53ff. but see also 1947b (the economy) 1949e & 1949c (the state) and 1950j (later part of *City*, being written at this time).

[38] 1946g; 1947b & f; 1948 e & f; *Presence*.

most famous book, written in the late 1940s in the forest of La Coubre while listening to the Brandenburg Concertos (*Conversations*, 87, 100). Originally entitled *La Société Technicienne* it was eventually published (after rejection by a number of publishers) in 1954 as *La Technique* (possibly an echo of Marx's *Le Capital* as it sought to do for the twentieth century what Ellul thought Marx had done so well for the nineteenth century).[39] It grew out of Ellul's life and thought in the inter-war and immediate post-war years and, as he acknowledged in the inscription of the copy he gave Bernard and Henriette Charbonneau, was as much their work as it was his own.[40] It had a clearly defined aim.

> I have attempted simply to present, by means of a comprehensive analysis, a concrete and fundamental interpretation (*prise de conscience*) of technique (*du phénomène technique dans son ensemble*). That is the sole object of this book (*TS*, xxxvi).

La Technique and Beyond

DEFINITION OF TECHNIQUE AND THESIS OF THE BOOK

Throughout his sociological studies, Ellul is reticent to offer a full definition of the various phenomena he analyses and this applies even to Technique. The 1954 French edition of *La Technique* nowhere offered a clear and full definition but for the U.S. edition in June 1963 Ellul added a 'Note to the Reader'. This offers what has become the accepted definition of Technique in his work:

> The term *technique*, as I use it, does not mean machines, technology, or this or that procedure for attaining an end. In our technological society, *technique* is the *totality of methods rationally arrived at and having absolute efficiency* (for a given stage of development) in *every* field of human activity (xxv, italics original).[41]

---

[39] The book's French subtitle (*l'enjeu de siècle*) refers to the stake which gamblers put down when making a bet. 'Le siècle' could refer either to the twentieth *century* or to the *age* in which Ellul lived. There may also be an echo of his favourite biblical text which shaped his writing of *Presence* around the same time – 'Do not be conformed to this present age' (Rom 12.1).

[40] Roy 1992:98

[41] Throughout this chapter, page references in parentheses refer to *TS*. Similar definitions of Technique are 'the coherent ensemble of absolutely efficient means for a given state of the economy and the social body' (1979g, 13) and 'the quest for and application of the most efficient means in every area' (1982c, 13). The fullest discussion is found in the first

In conformity with his general 'nominalist' sociological method discussed above in relation to the sacred, this definition was reached 'by examining each activity and observing the facts of what modern man calls technique in general, as well as by investigating the different areas in which specialists declare they have a technique' (xxv). Despite statements such as these and numerous treatments of Ellul's writing on the subject, there remains much debate about Ellul's understanding with one writer commenting that 'there are almost as many views of what Technique means as there are reviewers'.[42] In order therefore to clarify what Ellul does and does not mean by Technique in our society *five* significant elements of this definition should be noted.

Firstly, by speaking of the *totality* of methods, Ellul clarifies that Technique is qualitatively different from individual techniques taken independently. It is a universal, an overarching and complex entity embracing specific techniques and with certain defining characteristics which are discussed below. Ellul himself compares the relationship between 'Technique' and 'techniques' to that between 'dog' and 'boxer', 'spaniel' etc. (*TSys*, 23).

Secondly, as a universal, Technique embraces a number of different *methods*. This term is significant because, particularly in his earlier writing (most notably *Presence*, chapter three), Ellul often used *la méthode* and, more often, *le moyen* as shorthand when writing about Technique. 'Means' lies at the heart of Technique and therefore in beginning to formulate a definition in the original French edition of his book Ellul goes so far as to say 'technique (*la technique*) is nothing more than *means* and *the ensemble of means*' (19, italics in original ET).

Thirdly, the difficulty with translating *la technique* as 'technology' is made explicit in Ellul's insistence that the methods that Technique embraces are found in *every field* of human activity. He is adamant that we must understand the term *technique* in a broad sense.[43] Although the machine is 'the most obvious, massive, and impressive example of technique' (1), Technique must not be limited to machines. It now embraces all areas of life - psychology, art, sport, politics, law, economics, organisation etc.

Fourthly, Technique is not, however, simply the sum of all human means across these different activities. In a further important clarification, Ellul includes only those methods *rationally* arrived at. Human means can be based simply on tradition, instinct, and imitation of nature and Ellul classes these as

part of *TSys* (pp23-121) entitled 'What is technology (*la technique*)?'.
[42] Wren 1977:58-9.
[43] The breadth of Technique is emphasised from the start e.g. *Directives*, §17; *Presence*, 89ff.

part of the technical operation (*l'opération technique*) defined as 'every operation carried out in accordance with a certain method in order to attain a particular end' (19). A decisive change takes place in history when human beings become properly conscious of the techniques they use and apply reason to them. There then appears what Ellul calls the technical phenomenon (*le phénomène technique*). Humans now begin to explore alternative ways of accomplishing their desired end and to discriminate between the different means available. The result of this is a diminution in the role of the irrational and spontaneous in the means people use. One of Ellul's earliest statements of this pattern is found in his unpublished personalist writing on law from 1934/5.

As soon as any human phenomenon becomes conscious (i.e. we become aware of it), it enters into a network in which it loses its character of spontaneity. Once people have become aware of it, it becomes obvious and then understood. Once understood, it becomes reasoned. Once reasoned, it becomes willed. Once willed, it ceases to be real and becomes instead a process. Examples abound in confirmation of this thesis, such as regionalism (*Pour un Droit Vivant*, 1).

It is in this process that one finds the origins of modern Technique.[44]

The *fifth* and final defining characteristic of Technique is that the rational methods it encompasses are those that have *absolute efficiency*. '*Efficacité*'

---

[44] There is some confusion over the consistency of Ellul's terminology here. It is clear that he views the technical operation as a constant of human history but less clarity over the historical appearance of the technical phenomenon and whether this term is applicable only to the distinctive modern form of Technique. Mitcham & Mackey 1971:107 hold that Ellul does not view the presence of the technical phenomenon as distinctive of modern society and Temple 1976:117f agrees. Others, however, see the technical phenomenon as unique to modernity (Verene 1984:103; Wren 1977:64). The disagreement is clearest in the 1980 *Research in Philosophy and Technology* symposium on Ellul. Ellul's former pupil Cérézuelle writes that 'until the eighteenth century...humanity remained in the stage of "the technical operation". With the industrial revolution, the movement to "the technical phenomenon" began...' (Cérézuelle 1980:168). However, Temple, the author of one of the best theses on Ellul, writes, 'The technical phenomenon exists in any society and certainly is not distinctively modern' (Temple 1980:226). The problem, as so often, lies with Ellul himself who, on the one hand could write, 'Acknowledging that the technical phenomenon is a constant of human history, is there anything new about its present aspect?' (61) but then later stated, 'I am using "technological phenomenon" (*le phénomène technique*) in the sense that I gave it in *The Technological Society*, distinguishing it from technological operation (*l'opération technique*), which has always existed throughout history. The technological phenomenon has been specific to Western civilization since the eighteenth century' (*TSys*, 79).

and '*efficace*' frequently function for Ellul as the central defining characteristic of Technique and Clifford Christians comments that, 'The one feature that best characterises Ellul's <u>arche</u> is efficiency'.[45] It is when the application of reason to means leads on into the quest for the perfection of those means and the elimination of less effective means that Technique in its fullest sense appears. Uncharacteristically, Ellul turns to English to express this important point.

> C'est ce 'one best way' qui est à proprement parler le moyen technique...(*Technique*, 18 cf. *TS*,21).

Obviously what counts as this 'one best way' will vary in time and hence Ellul's definition includes the qualification 'for a given stage of development'. However, what always characterises the technical phenomenon is that 'in every field men seek to find the most efficient method (*la méthode absolument la plus efficace*)' (21).

In the light of this five-fold clarification of Ellul's subject matter, it is necessary to outline the purpose and claims of *La Technique*. Contrary to the impression given by Wilkinson in his Translator's Introduction and by certain subsequent writers, Ellul is not attempting to offer a *philosophy* of Technique in this work although an implicit philosophy can be derived from the work. Ellul explicitly states that 'we shall be looking at technique in its sociological aspect' (xxv).[46]

The book arises from the context outlined above: Ellul's long-standing perception of a *sociological* crisis of civilization and the need for fundamental revolution. In writing it, Ellul views himself like 'a physician or physicist who is describing a group situation in which he is himself involved. The physician in an epidemic, the physicist exposed to radioactivity' (xxvii). He aims to provide an account of the nature of modern Technique and the society it is in the course of creating. He hopes that he will thereby present the reader with a warning and a call to recognise the destination of the road on which she is travelling unless she changes course (xxvii-xxxiii).

The book's central and best-known argument is summed up in its opening sentence.

---

[45] Christians 1974:8. Latouche 1994:104 refers to 'obsession with efficiency (*l'efficience*), in opposition to the quest for effectiveness (*l'efficacité*) (efficiency versus effectiveness)' although Ellul's preferred terminology for what he critiques appears to be that of *le plus efficace* and *l'efficacité* rather than *l'efficience*.

[46] Lovekin ignores this statement in his attempt to justify treating Ellul as primarily a philosopher (Lovekin 1991:10). In fact, Ellul rarely refers to more philosophical approaches to technique although see 1984b and 1988b.

No social, human, or spiritual fact is so important as the fact of technique in the modern world (3).[47]

This argument is, however, combined with a second and equally important claim. This has gained much less prominence in studies of Ellul's work despite its great significance for Ellul's whole sociological corpus and its reiteration throughout the book.

The old characteristics of technique have indeed disappeared; but new ones have taken their place. Today's technical phenomenon, consequently, has almost nothing in common with the technical phenomenon of the past (78).[48]

The following section presents Ellul's historical perspective on the technical phenomenon and is followed by a summary of his characterology of modern Technique and his claim that it has altered the structure of our civilization. The full extent of this is shown in the next section which examines Ellul's understanding of Technique as man's new milieu. Finally, after noting that Ellul perceives a change in the nature of all social phenomena due to Technique, the significance of this analysis for the crisis of civilization discussed above is examined.

HISTORY OF THE TECHNICAL PHENOMENON

A central feature of all Ellul's historical and sociological studies is his insistence that phenomena be studied within their overall historical and social context. The reason for this is illustrated by means of a powerful analogy. Ellul explains that the explosion of a shell always has roughly the same internal, objective physical and chemical characteristics but its external results are radically different when the explosion occurs not in a desert but in the middle of a platoon of soldiers. A different relationship with the external world will similarly fundamentally alter the character and the effects of any social phenomenon (63-4). This method is particularly important for the technical phenomenon where there is a continuity of intrinsic characteristics but major changes become evident when one examines its situation in society.

The most dramatic historical change in the role of Technique is not

---

[47] Ellul's fullest defences of describing the modern world as 'technical' as against other characterisations are *TSys*, 1-20, 51-75; 1967f and 1969a.

[48] This theme can be seen throughout the opening chapters of the book (e.g. 14, 77-8, 125, 128) and in the introductory pieces (e.g. xxv, xxix, xxxiii). Among discussions that give this attention are Holloway 1970b; Mitcham and Mackey 1971; Comte 1973; Wilson 1975:482ff; Rumpf 1976; Cérézuelle 1979 & 1980.

discussed in *La Technique* but appears in a later article examining the relationship of Technique to nature. Ellul there explains that, in contrast to the present, nature originally dominated man. In that context 'the artificial (and technique) are the expression of human freedom and the road to this freedom' so that it is even possible to say that 'man becomes man...by making tools...man wins his freedom through artificial means, in the realm of the artificial' (1980q, 274). Ellul's criticism of many analyses of the modern technical phenomenon and his rebuttal of those who accuse him of being opposed to all technology and techniques lies in his belief that 'history has changed course' and an 'unbelievable reversal' has occurred in the role of Technique.

> They are missing (*and this is the meaning of what I have been trying to shed light on from the beginning*) the radical newness of our age - the fact that technique today has nothing at all in common with previous forms of technique (1980q, 275; italics added).

In *La Technique* this novelty of modern Technique is expounded by contrasting it with technique in civilization. On the basis of a short survey of the development of technique (23-60) Ellul argues that until the eighteenth century Technique in society was constantly limited in several ways. It was limited to certain spheres of life (e.g. magic and war) and did not affect the whole of society. Furthermore, the number of technical means was relatively small and no attempt was made to perfect them. Techniques were also geographically limited, and the development and improvement of techniques was slow and guided by a diversity of factors (64-77). This has all now totally changed as 'in our civilization technique is in no way limited' (78).

In earlier social contexts, humans were able to choose between a diversity of techniques and different societies and cultures developed and utilised a variety of techniques. Human beings here showed their dominance over Technique and it is this that is central to the difference between the past and the present.

> Evolution was not, then, a logic of discovery or an inevitable progression of techniques. It was an interaction of technical effectiveness and effective human decision (*une interaction de l'efficacité technique et de la décision efficace de l'homme*). Whenever either one of these elements disappeared, social and human stagnation necessarily followed (77; italics in original French)

In seeking to explain this overturning of the traditional relationship between Technique and society, Ellul highlights five factors in the eighteenth and nineteenth centuries (47-60), a period more fully analysed in the fourth and fifth volumes of *Institutions*.

First, the many preceding centuries of technical development were a necessary antecedent condition for the technical mutation of the last two centuries which can be seen as a development waiting to happen when other social conditions were ripe.

Second, the demographic changes of the period gave an impetus to technical expansion. The rise in population increased both the demand for technical growth (through increasing needs which only technical development could meet) and its potential supply (as technical research could be intensified because there were more potential technicians).

Third, the economic environment was supportive of rapid technical growth. It was both stable (so providing a constant on which technical research could focus) and also in flux (so able to adapt to technical development).

Fourth, the plasticity of the social environment produced a permissive mass society in which two central social limits on Technique were eliminated. Social taboos disappeared (whether those arising from Christianity or those such as the inviolability of social hierarchy) and natural social groups (e.g. families, guilds, religious orders) came under attack thereby removing the major brake upon technical development and creating the necessary mass society.[49]

Fifth, a clear technical intention appeared for the first time. Ellul defines this as 'a precise view of technical possibilities, the will to attain certain ends, application in all areas, and adherence of the whole of society to a conspicuous technical objective' (52) and it is clearly the condition for his narrower understanding of the technical phenomenon. He believes that the most important cause of this widespread movement to embrace Technique was the existence of special interest. Initially the state, and then the bourgeoisie, discovered how they could benefit from Technique. Its triumph was then assured when simultaneously Marx identified Technique as the means to the workers' victory and the masses began to gain benefits from new techniques. By the beginning of the twentieth century, 'a common will developed to exploit the possibilities of technique to the maximum, and groups of the most conflicting interests (state and individual, bourgeoisie and working class) united to hymn its praises' (55).[50]

Two features of this account particularly stand out. As would be expected from one inspired by Marx, it is materialist and sociological rather than

---

[49] Ellul's concern about mass society is most fully studied in Wren 1977 and clear in his statement, 'I have always been against the mass society' (*Conversations*, 83).

[50] Ellul's view of the relationship between Technique and the bourgeoisie, marked by the ideology of happiness and the quest to assimilate everything, is explored in *Métamorphose*.

philosophical and related to the history of ideas.[51] Little is said, for example, about the philosophical underpinnings of the creation of a mass society. Ellul simply refers to 'a systematic campaign waged against all natural groups, under the guise of a defense of the rights of the individual' (51) and in his fuller account in *Institutions* clearly sees material change as primary.

> The liberal ideology which dominates this period [1815-1914] is directly linked to economic growth...It is the conception best adapted to an era of rapid technical and economic progress (*Institutions*, 5:216).

Similarly, the appearance of a technical intention is subordinated to special interest and its intellectual roots in Hegel and Marx downplayed (52).

Ellul also minimises the influence of Christianity and the Reformation (32-8). This is in sharp contrast with other modernity critics who view Christianity generally as a major cause of technical progress in the West and the Reformation as of particular importance in the creation of the modern world.[52] It should, however, be noted that Ellul later modified this position. By the 1960s he was writing that 'technical activity was able to grow as it did from the eighteenth century because the Reformation had desacralised nature' (1964,13-14) and he acknowledged that 'it is Christian morality, in the form which it took from the sixteenth century on, which has been preparing the way for the development of technological morality' (*TWTD*, 185).[53]

Although these questions are highly significant,[54] differences in the historical analysis of the development of the modern world are not of primary importance here as the aim is simply to understand the basic structure of Ellul's argument and its wider impact on his sociological studies. The crucial fact for Ellul is that the eighteenth and nineteenth centuries raise a vital question:

> Why, after such slow progress for centuries, did such an eruption of

---

[51] *TS*, 46-7 offers Ellul's brief critique of those who focus on philosophical causes for the growth of Technique from the eighteenth century. This emphasis in Ellul is George Grant's major criticism of his work (in Schmidt 1978:146) and Grant blames it on the anti-philosophical character of Ellul's Reformed background. Other discussions of this omission in Ellul's account include Mitcham and Mackey 1971; Badertscher 1978; Temple 1980.

[52] See for example Grant 1969a:19ff & 1985:61; Arendt 1958:248-53; Voegelin 1952:133-61. George Grant confessed himself surprised that, despite his Calvinist background, Ellul offered such a penetrating critique of modernity (Schmidt 1978:146).

[53] See further 1958a; 1959a (now *Sources*, 137-61) & 1976e.

[54] Rapp 1994 critiques Ellul's limited account of modern Technique's origins and development.

technical progress take place in a century and a half ? (44).

Different explanatory causes may be offered and the various answers are able to shed new light on our current situation. However, Ellul is surely right that 'the ultimate reason escapes us' (44) and that it is the historical change any theory attempts to explain which is of greater significance. This monumental change prompts a yet more fundamental question in Ellul's work.

> Acknowledging that the technical phenomenon is a constant of human history, is there anything new about its present aspect? (61).

MODERN TECHNIQUE

Faced with the historical choice offered by the question of whether there is something new in modern Technique, Ellul emphatically rejects those who like Mumford answer in the negative: 'In the book *Technics and Civilization* …he says the relation between technique and society is the same nowadays as in traditional society. But I say that is not so' (1983i, 194). Instead, he insists that

> In opposition to this resolutely optimistic position, there is another which maintains that we are confronted with a genuinely new phenomenon. There is nothing in common (*il n'y a aucune commune mesure*) between the modern technical complex and the fragments of it which are laboriously sought out in the course of history to demonstrate that there has always been technique (62).

This opposing position is initially justified by an application of Engel's law that a certain level of quantitative change in a phenomenon can produce a qualitative change of nature. It is subsequently supported by a more detailed survey of the distinctive characteristics of modern Technique (77-147). Ellul simply notes with little comment the two most obvious and frequently recognised characteristics of modern Technique. Rationality (*la rationalité*), as noted above from his early personalist writing on law, is a process 'which tends to bring mechanics to bear on all that is spontaneous or irrational' (78-9). Artificiality refers to Technique's opposition to and destruction of nature and although this is a major concern in Ellul's work it is not his primary critique of the contemporary technical phenomenon.[55] These two features are, strictly speaking, characteristics internal to the technical phenomenon rather than features relating to Technique's external relationship with wider society

---

[55] *Contra* Mitcham 1969:60ff. 1980q is Ellul's fullest discussion of artificiality and the relationship between Technique and Nature.

in the modern world. Ellul's major concern is the analysis of this wider relationship and here he offers five more controversial characteristics of Technique in our society.[56] Ellul first argues that there is automatism of technical choice (*automatisme du choix technique*). This is because modern Technique imposes itself as absolute efficiency. As a result, the ability to choose between techniques which humans had in all earlier societies is eliminated (79-85).

Technique not only imposes itself on human beings, it also effectively engenders itself apart from humanity. It does this by a process of self-augmentation (*l'auto-accroissement*) whereby each new technical innovation in turn makes others possible and so extends Technique further (85-94).

As a universal category, Technique is also characterised by its monism (*unicité* or *insécabilité*). This is evident in the fact that the technical phenomenon forms a whole encompassing differing techniques. It invalidates any attempt to divide Technique into specific techniques that can be understood or addressed without reference to the whole. It also leads Ellul to reject the commonplace that humans are masters over neutral techniques and what matters is not Technique but how people use each technique (*Critique*, 226-35). Because Technique is also self-augmenting, a situation has now been produced where each new technical breakthrough engenders others and all the various technical innovations are embraced within the monistic system of Technique (94-116).

There is no also longer any limit to this phenomenon because Technique is now marked by technical universalism (*universalisme technique*) which takes two forms. Foreseeing what is now called globalisation, Ellul writes of a geographic universalism as no part of the globe is immune from Technique's development and growth. In addition, as every area of life and of human civilization is subordinated to Technique, there is also a qualitative universalism (116-33).

Finally, and at the centre of Technique's hegemony, there is its autonomy (*autonomie de la technique*). By this Ellul means that no other sphere (e.g. the economic, political, or moral) is now able to control Technique which is, in practice, even free from humanity itself (133-46).[57]

---

[56] Ellul offers a brief summary of these characteristics and his general thinking on Technique in 1962c, 35-6; 1979g, 13-6. Fuller discussions can be found in Miller 1970:167-81; Mitcham and Mackey 1971:108-10; Zorn 1971:14-37; Ihara 1975:210-226; Wren 1977:69-131; Benello 1981; Lovekin 1991:157-76; Chastenet 1992:33-5; Dujancourt 1994:29-33. Some authors refer to six characteristics, including the linking together of techniques (111ff), but this is not a distinct characteristic according to Ellul but the product of other characteristics (79).

[57] The rest of *La Technique* defends and illustrates this autonomy which has received much

These five characteristics are all examined further in Ellul's 1977 work, *Le Système Technicienne* (ET 1980 *The Technological System*).[58] This extends *La Technique* by showing how, instead of being simply a phenomenon shaping society, Technique itself has become a system with these characteristics within wider society.[59] Finally, in 1988, in *Le Bluff Technologique* (ET 1990 *The Technological Bluff*), Ellul turns his attention primarily to how we speak and think about Technique (i.e. technology, strictly speaking). Here he develops one further attribute of Technique – the characteristic of uncertainty (*l'incertitude*) - which he had briefly expounded in earlier articles but not in any published books.[60] This encompasses four features: the ambivalence of technical progress, the unpredictability of development, the double feedback which is constituted by the originating factors of technical progress, and the internal contradictions inherent in the system (*Bluff*, 33-121).

None of these subsequent developments contradict the original argument of *La Technique* or the central conclusion Ellul there drew from his 'characterology'.

The characteristics we have examined permit me to assert with confidence that there is no common denomination (*il n y'a aucune commune mesure*) between the technique of today and that of yesterday. Today we are dealing with an utterly different phenomenon. Those who claim to deduce from man's technical situation in past centuries his situation in this one show that they have grasped nothing of the technical phenomenon. These deductions prove that all their reasonings are without foundation and all their analogies are astigmatic (146).

It is these new characteristics, particularly Technique's universalism and

---

discussion in the literature beginning with Winner 1977 and later in Carpenter 1980; Weinstein 1981; Coninck 1994; Vitalis 1994.

[58] Although published in 1977, *TSys* appears to have been largely written several years earlier as implied by the dates (Avril 1968-Août 1977) at the end of the French edition (p360), the closeness of chapter three to 1967f, and Ellul's footnote comment at 1972g, 271 that it would be his next book. Some earlier characteristics appear under different names (autonomy, unity, universality, totalization, self-augmentation and automatism) and two new characteristics are added to describe the progress of the technical system ('causal progression and the absence of finality' and 'the problem of acceleration').

[59] Ellul's later account on this development is 1982b, 17ff. See further Cérézuelle 1980; Temple 1980; Weyembergh 1994a&b.

[60] The main earlier discussion of uncertainty (under the terminology of ambivalence) is 1965 whose importance is shown by its inclusion in the 1990 Economica edition of *Technique*.

autonomy, which provide the basis for Ellul's argument that Technique is not only *a* new and powerful determining social phenomenon but also *the central* determinant in our society. The central problem in our world is therefore that Technique, free from human control, is bringing to an end the crucial dialectical play of different forces found under the surface in all previous societies.[61]

The fundamental historical change that has occurred is that Technique no longer belongs to a civilization but encompasses the whole of our civilization. We now live in what Ellul calls technical civilization (*la civilisation technique*).

> *Technical civilization* means that our civilization is constructed *by* technique (makes a part of civilization only what belongs to technique), *for* technique (in that everything in this civilization must serve a technical end), and *is* exclusively technique (in that it excludes whatever is not technique or reduces it to technical form)...Herein lies the inversion we are witnessing. Without exception in the course of history, *technique belonged to a civilization* and was merely a single element among a host of nontechnical activities. Today *technique has taken over the whole of civilization*...(128).

The majority of *Technique* comprises a study of the society that Technique is in the process of creating, its economic life, its political life and the life of humans within it. Ellul's whole sociological corpus which follows this book is 'part of the detailed analysis of this technical society' (*Season*, 176). The absolute novelty of this technical society remains a central theme throughout these analyses. Its importance is highlighted by the fact Ellul often immediately draws this to the attention of his theological readers who may not know this central conclusion in his sociological work:

> The world in which we are living is very complex. It raises difficult questions, sets up barriers and lays numerous traps. Above all else, this world is terribly new (*False*, 2).

> What, in this connection, are the features of sin today, in the reality of the present time? What is the current form, the contemporary expression, of man's alienation from God? I believe that we have entered, in fact, upon a human condition which is new (*Prayer*, viii).

The nature, scope, and effect of this totally new social situation are the

---

[61] *Faith*, 192ff; *WIB*, 46, 184-7. For discussion of this theme in his work see Boli-Bennett 1980; Temple 1980:238ff & 1985:38-9; Clendenin 1987:45; Lovekin 1991.

subject of the following two sections.

TECHNIQUE AS MILIEU

The full extent of the historical and social transformation brought about by Technique only becomes explicit in Ellul's much later writing when he develops his idea of the formation of a technical environment or milieu (*le milieu technicien/technique*). The seeds of this concept are already present in *La Technique* (e.g. *TS*, 79) and throughout the following decades Ellul returned to this theme of the contrast between the natural milieu of humans and our new technical milieu (e.g. *TSys*, chapter two).[62] It is, however, not until 1979 that the idea is elaborated into a more comprehensive interpretation of humankind's historical development. This theory is subsequently fully expounded in his 1987 *Ce que je crois* (ET 1989 *What I Believe*).[63] There Ellul argues that humanity's milieu provides a starting point for an understanding of history as the human adventure. Three relationships define this milieu: it is that which provides us with what we need to live; that which also threatens and endangers us; and that which is immediate to us.

Ellul proceeds to claim that three crucial stages are distinguishable within human history on the basis of people's changing milieu. Originally, in the pre-historic period, our milieu was nature (*WIB*, 104-14). Then, around 3000BC, a gradual change occurred so that the milieu became society (*WIB*, 115-32). The distinctiveness of the modern world is therefore best summarised in the statement that 'in the last two centuries the social environment in turn is being replaced by a new one, the technological environment (*le milieu technicien*)' (*WIB*, 101).

The gulf separating our contemporary world from all that went before it is now made clear. The crisis of modernity is seen to be of much greater significance than that of any previous historical crisis. It is not a social, political or economic crisis but a crisis arising from a change of milieu. The nearest and only comparable event is one of which we know very little because humanity experienced it about five thousand years ago when we passed from the milieu of nature into the historical and social milieu.

> The crisis that we are approaching today is of yet another order. For it entails the transition, not from one form of society and power to another, but to a new environment. For approximately the last five thousand years we have lived in the environment...of society, in which politics plays the major role...But everything is now changing. The present crisis...has nothing in

---

[62] In addition to numerous articles (e.g. 1962c; 1963b; 1965a; 1967l; 1970e & k; 1972a) there is also the untranslated *Métamorphose*, 270-2 and *Révolution*, 347.

[63] For earlier developments see 1979a & c; *Perspectives*, 59ff.

common (*n'a rien de commun*) with previous historical crises...(*WIB*, 132).

This theme of the absolute novelty of our modern world and the crisis it is experiencing originated in Ellul's earliest work of the 1930s and was particularly prominent in the immediate post-war years. In his writings on our milieu in the 1980s Ellul powerfully summarises this belief and demonstrates that in his later writing the crisis has become even more significant. No longer is it a matter of Technique fundamentally altering its characteristics and becoming the new dominant factor within society. Society itself has now ceased to be our milieu. We have witnessed the arrival within human history of something never before experienced: a technical milieu.[64]

TECHNIQUE AND CIVILIZATION

One major consequence of this fundamental structural change in our very milieu is that our problems are different from those of the past. As a result, Ellul believes the past is of little value in any attempt to understand or overcome them.

> It is precisely one of my constant theses that our problems are not those of yesterday, from which it follows that yesterday's answers are of no help. I do also think that our problems are more difficult than those of the past, but above all that they are *of another order* (1966c, 94-5, italics in original French).

Not only Technique but all social phenomena that were features of historic Western civilization have therefore radically altered. Four of the most notable examples from Ellul's work can illustrate this universal and fundamental change that lies at the heart of his sociological studies.[65]

First, Ellul acknowledges that *propaganda* has always existed in some form within the Western world. However, in his untranslated history of the phenomenon, he insists that what we call 'propaganda' in the past is totally different from propaganda today because 'contemporary propaganda presents characteristics which are not able to be found in any of the political

---

[64] Ellul's response to this new situation is to follow the pattern established by humans when they overcame the natural milieu: artifice. He speaks of the Second Level of the artificial which is the ethical (1980q), elaborating the elements of this new universal ethic in 1980r.

[65] Many others subjects could be added to this list, e.g. morality (*TWTD*, 190ff), the ideology of happiness (*Métamorphose*, 76-7), information (1967c, 1969i & 1970r), language (1959c; *Humiliation*), the economy (1947b), social deviance & control (*Déviances*, 24, 50ff, 62).

phenomena of the past' (*Histoire*, 5). In his unpublished 1951/2 lecture course
he therefore opens with this warning

> We must immediately make the following remark: we must not 'compare'
> contemporary propaganda with that of the past or draw inferences for one
> from the other...Contemporary propaganda is radically different from that
> of the past...There is no common denominator (*il n'y a aucune commune
> mesure*) between propaganda enterprises in the past and the current
> system.[66]

His published and translated study of propaganda in the modern world also
constantly reiterates this, insisting that 'propaganda was not the same in the
past as it is today...its nature has changed' (*Propaganda*, 88).

A similar claim is found, *secondly*, in Ellul's untranslated study of *art* in
our society. There he writes that art today is 'radically different from all that
until now has been attempted in producing a work of art, from all that which
has been called "art"...The innovation lacks any commonality (*est sans
commune mesure*) with that which has gone before' (*L'Empire*, 22,23).

This view that there has been a change in the nature of phenomena so that
there is no common measure between our world and that of the past applies,
thirdly, to *images*.

> Images today are very different (*il n'existe aucune commune mesure*) from
> those in earlier societies...No comparison is possible between what people
> have traditionally known of images and what we are now exposed to
> (*Humiliation*, 112, 113).

Finally, as is shown in more detail in chapters six and seven below, Ellul
believes that all the elements of the modern *political world* (law, the state, and
politics) are fundamentally different from those of earlier centuries. So, in
another untranslated study, this time of revolution, he writes that 'the total
novelty of technical society renders the pathway of revolution totally new'
(*Révolution*, 377).

These drastic changes in our society are, however, not the result of the
revolution in civilization that Ellul sought from the 1930s onwards. His
diagnosis and appeals at that time were ignored and so the essential novelty of
modernity arises from the fact that the society Ellul then sought to challenge
has continued on the same foundations and with the same fundamental
structures. As Ellul lamented in 1980,

---

[66] *La Propagande* (1951/2), p2. See section three in the bibliography of unpublished
writings.

I am sick over the world I shall leave behind, sick at heart, physically and intellectually sick. I had been so hopeful when at the age of twenty I first committed myself to action, when we hoped to change the course of the world. In 1930 we could already see the oppression and disorder of that world taking shape. And we had the absurd hope of turning it away, however slightly, in a different direction, toward humanity and freedom, toward justice, toward a true democracy. I tried everything… (*Faith*, 211-2).

In the immediate post-war period, Ellul claimed that the consequences of failure would be deadly. He spoke of 'the end of the world' (1945c) and warned that 'humankind will die – spiritually and perhaps also materially' (*Sources*, 15). He predicted 'the annihilation of civilization and of humankind' (*Sources*, 67) and the creation of 'a society that will not be a civilization' (1948e, 3).

In the 1960s Ellul returns to this theme which was so prominent in his earlier work. He explains that, despite the fact that he himself writes of a technical civilization (*la civilisation technique/technicienne*), Technique and civilization are strictly speaking incompatible and we are therefore presently witnessing nothing less than the end of civilization.[67]

The origin of the problem lies in the fact that Technique, almost spontaneously, leads to a total questioning of traditional civilization (1970k). Everything is radically changed and we face a global transformation in which it is necessary to ask if a radically new, technical civilization can be born. To answer this question it is first essential to clarify what is meant by 'civilization'.

Ellul argues that those who speak of a technical civilization are often committing the basic error of equating society and civilization (1960k, 77). This is mistaken because most historic societies have not led to the creation of a civilization. Civilization is a complex and qualitative phenomenon that, given the right conditions, can be slowly created by humans within society. Influenced by Toynbee (cf. 1952a) and echoing some of the language used in his personalist manifesto, Ellul argues that every civilization is a sign of human greatness and the human vocation to surmount the obstacles facing us.

Every civilization was always the fruit of a victory over some fate (*une*

---

[67] See, for example, 1967d, 27. The fullest discussion is, of course, his later *Betrayal* where Ellul opens by explaining that 'our civilization is being challenged, rejected without due consideration' (*Betrayal*, vii). The original French refers to the classic personalist perspective of a crisis and uses one of Ellul's own key phrases, speaking of 'la crise que nous traversons…la mise en question de notre civilisation' (*Trahison*, 7).

fatalité), whether that be an economic or a geographic fate. Indeed often it is exactly in order to respond to some fate of this order…that, in the final analysis, humans have built a civilization (1960k, 83).

Ellul claims that civilizations are marked by a certain number of works and values and that, like the personalist revolution he sought, every civilization is both a collective and a personal, individualised phenomenon. The following dual definition is therefore offered:

> There is civilization in a society when that society is capable of integrating thoughts, activities, and institutions (its works) into a holistic synthesis which is submitted to certain values…There is civilization when society gives individuals the capacity to be themselves through the interplay of tensions between that society's diverse forces (1967d, 9 cf. 1960k, 73).

Ellul further claims that historically there have been certain necessary conditions for the creation of civilization. These relate to people's relationship with space (which must be rooted and local), to time (where an equilibrium between lived rhythm of life and that of the milieu is required) and to work (where a synthesis of work and values must occur) (1967d, 10-14). The first fundamental contradiction between Technique and civilization appears at this level. The changes brought by Technique have eradicated these necessary conditions and, once again, we find that 'we are in the presence of irreducibly new situations' (1967d, 13). As a result

> If there must be a technical civilization, this will be in the absence of all those things which have been considered indispensable factors in civilization…Nothing in either the thought or the behaviour patterns of the past is able to assist us. We must contemplate a human intervention that will be creative of a new way of being and a new type of civilization (1967d, 13-4).[68]

This contradiction between modern Technique and historic civilization goes deeper than the lack of necessary conditions. It is located in three decisive differences between Technique and civilization.

Firstly, technical society is a society focussed on quantitative improvement, on facts, and on objects. It is therefore in essence an anti-humanist society that cannot create a civilization because civilization focuses on the qualitative

---

[68] Cf. 1960k, 74-7 where Ellul concludes from the universality and autonomy of Technique that, 'it therefore seems to me impossible to say that one can hope to build a civilization on a technical foundation'.

advance of man.

Secondly, Technique is a means of power and the inverse relation between power and values renders it impossible for Technique to produce a civilization where works are subject to values. Instead of creating the social equilibrium and shared values of a civilization, the twentieth century world devoted itself to the exaltation of Technique as a means of power. In consequence, that century brought about an unprecedented level of suffering for humanity.

> As an historian I can say – and this is not to glorify the past – that never has humanity reached such heights of power or such universal depths of suffering and despair (*Faith*, 211).[69]

Finally, Technique is unable to make humans free but instead has become humanity's new destiny. It therefore cannot give rise to a civilization because the essence of civilization is the overcoming of fatality.[70]

In the light of this analysis, Ellul's conclusion about the relationship of Technique and civilization in our modern world is bleak but unavoidable.

> We can say that there is an infinitely small chance that a civilization will be born from Technique or even including Technique...We are headed towards a society which is organised, solid and satisfying from certain viewpoints but totally sterile in relation to civilization (1967d, 27 cf. *Hope*, 61).

Conclusion

It has been widely acknowledged that all Ellul's analyses of the modern world can only be properly understood by reference to his conception of Technique and its dominance. Much study has gone into his understanding of this phenomenon and its impact on our world but very little attention has been paid, to the context out of which Ellul developed this analysis and the larger canvas on which this central feature is set.

This chapter has offered a new interpretation of the heart of Ellul's sociological writings on modern society, proposing this as the context within which all these works must be set if readers are to understand both their coherence and their purpose. It has shown that, not least because Ellul is

---

[69] In *Si*, Ellul even goes so far as to write that the most radical condemnation of the modern world is that it has invented a suffering that Jesus did not know (*Si*, 66).

[70] 1960k, 81-3; 1962c, 40-2; 1967d, 15-27. A further contradiction is that a technical culture is impossible (*Bluff*, 132-48) but 'culture...is the central pivot of a civilization' (1960k, 81). Cf. Hottois 1994a.

primarily an historian, these studies are to be interpreted within a broader historical time-frame as an attempt at a global analysis of the fundamental underlying structures of our world which shape and direct the everyday lives of individuals and the flow of current events. By drawing on previously neglected and unpublished material it has been shown that, from the 1930s onwards (and in agreement with the wider French personalist movement) Ellul viewed the contemporary world as suffering from what, in his last sociological study (1992), he still called the crisis of civilization (*la crise de civilization*, *Déviances*, 142).

Ellul traced the origins of this civilizational crisis to the material changes in the eighteenth and nineteenth centuries that brought about a fundamental transformation in the relationship between Technique and society. Unchecked by humans, this led to the creation, through the twentieth century, of a totally new world lacking common measure with that of the past where humans have become progressively subject to the ever-intensifying power of Technique and the necessities it engenders.

From this perspective, the common subject matter of political debate, much sociological analysis, and the turbulence of events on the surface of history are radically relativised as they often simply mask the deeper unity of modernity. Even such apparently significant changes as the defeat of Hitler and Nazism and the process of decolonisation failed to alter this underlying uniformity and bring about the revolution necessary to redirect the world away from its denial of human persons and civilization. All social, political, and economic phenomena have been fundamentally transformed by the unprecedented crisis and effective destruction of historic Western civilization that the last century has witnessed as a result of Technique.

The aim of Ellul's sociological corpus is to explain, and make his readers aware of, this crisis so that they can question their world. Then, he hopes, they will seek a genuine revolution that will resist the development of this new world and lead to the creation of a new civilization.

In the immediate post-war years he believed that, as in the 1930s, the situation was still relatively fluid. A real choice could still be made.

At the present moment we are confronted by a choice: either a mass civilization, technological, 'conformist' – the 'Brave New World' of Huxley, hell organized upon earth for the bodily comfort of everybody – or a different civilization, which we cannot yet describe because we do not know what it will be; it still has to be created, consciously, by men. If we do not know what to choose, or, in other words, how to 'make a revolution', if we let ourselves drift along the stream of history, without knowing it, we shall have chosen the power of suicide, which is at the heart of the world (*Presence*, 31).

Even when the world chose decisively for technological, mass civilization and Ellul realised the ineffectiveness of politically organised revolutionary change, he nevertheless continued to criticise this path. He persisted in his long-standing desire for a personal and social revolution, organised from below, in order to create a new civilization. All his sociological writing is driven by that desire and a determination to share his critique and alternative vision with others.

My personal aim has been to help one generation of men and women to preserve their sense of criticism *vis-à-vis* technical civilization, but the step from that rearguard action to a fresh departure is a long one. New civilizations do not evolve overnight, nor are they the work of a small number of men. Ours too, if there is to be one, will be the result of a slow and laborious process, with many false starts and setbacks... (1972b, 102).

CHAPTER 4

Ellul's Dialectic of Sociology and Theology

The opening three chapters have provided a general introduction to Ellul's life and work and laid the foundation for the more detailed studies of violence, law, the state, and politics which follow in Part Two. The importance of Ellul's biography and the necessity of recognising the two different strands of his work is already evident and will become more so in the following chapters. In addition, it has been shown that both his theology and his sociology have a distinct, coherent, core structure. This brief concluding chapter to Part One addresses the vexed question of the relationship between the two strands of Ellul's corpus. In particular, it needs to be asked whether it can be legitimately argued that his sociology shapes and distorts his theology[1] or, as is more commonly alleged, his theology drives his sociological analyses so that they amount to 'the barely camouflaged judgment of a Huguenot prophet'.[2]

The difficulty in discerning the relationship between Ellul's theology and sociology arises from two features of his thought. On the one hand, Ellul's first and fundamental allegiance in life is to God in his self-revelation. As Chapter One demonstrated, when (in the 1930s) Ellul found his political and sociological judgments diverged from Mounier's this disagreement was connected to their theological disagreements. On the other hand, Ellul has also always insisted that he seeks to prevent his sociological analyses being dependent on his theology. He claims to purge these studies of any purely theological foundation that would make them unconvincing to a non-Christian. Thus, in one of his last major public speeches, responding to the November 1993 Symposium in his honour, Ellul again spoke of the two domains of his books and the distinction between them.

My work was located in two domains, which led to the two domains of my books, sociology and theology. What is their relation? First, a scrupulous

---

[1] The influence of his sociological studies on his theology and in particular the thought of Karl Marx is a common criticism of Ellul's work by conservative theologians e.g. Berthoud 1982; Bauman 1992a&b.

[2] Margolis 1984:146. A similar critique is in Merle 1965; Ihara 1975:41; Wilson 1975; Wren 1977:29. Chastenet 1992 and Temple's writings are more helpful and reject this view.

distinction: I have always tried to prevent 'my' theology from influencing my sociological research (Calvinism) and my comprehension of the world from distorting my reading of the Bible. These were two domains, two methods, two distinct interests. Only after the separation, one begins to perceive relationship (1994b).

That this distinction is successful is perhaps supported both by the vehement opposition to his sociology from many Reformed Christians and the constant similarity of his sociological conclusions to those of his non-Christian soul mate, Bernard Charbonneau.

The key to unravelling the difficulty many find in understanding how the two strands of Ellul's work fit with each other is to be found by examining two of the central themes highlighted in the previous two chapters: his theological account of the world which lacks communion with God and his sociological account of modernity. Ellul's sociological studies are clearly an examination of what theologically is the world of ruptured communion. They are, however, focussed on the intermediate level of a given society's determining structures and Ellul's central claim is that these structures make the modern world qualitatively different from earlier periods of the world's history.

Nobody seriously argues that Ellul's theology could lead him to the numerous (often positive) conclusions he draws about historical societies and their evolution throughout his *Institutions*. Similarly, nothing in his theology could lead him to the two conclusions central to his sociological works. Nothing theological leads him *either* to his conclusion of the novelty of modern society *or* to his choice of Technique as the determining factor of the modern world and his detailed analyses of Technique and its effect on other social phenomena. Both these conclusions are the fruit of 'natural' and not 'revealed' knowledge. As the previous chapter has demonstrated, they were first reached in the personalist movement of the 1930s. They derive from perceptive insight and painstaking historical and sociological analysis influenced by men such as Weber, Marx, Durkheim, and Charbonneau. They are the result of Ellul's *prise de conscience* of the world in which he lives and that capacity of recognising the reality of the world in which we live is not exclusively reserved to Christians.

> Recognizing my determinations is not conditioned by recognizing the liberty that is given me in Christ. It is not the natural result of this, even though only freedom in Christ enables me to have a full and decisive knowledge of alienation. It starts elsewhere and is possible for a non-Christian. When a Christian attempts it, this sets him among other men. He is like them in his alienation and in bearing the cost of the fight for liberation. Any man can

take this course... (*Freedom*, 231).

However, because the world analysed in Ellul's sociology is also the world his theology describes in terms of its rupture from God, this theological belief inevitably places certain limits on his sociological analysis. Ellul acknowledges this in discussion of the relationship between social reality and theology of law.

> A first theological given, well known and very necessary if we are to understand the world correctly is that the world is the product of the fall...social reality is included within that universe which wishes itself to be separated from God. It is always necessary to interpret it in relationship with that separation...and that allows a precise situating of the possibilities between definite positive and negative frontiers (1962b, 47).

The *task* of Ellul's sociological analysis can therefore also be expressed in the terminology of Christian theology as an examination of the contemporary forms of sin and of man's separation from God.

> What are the features of sin today, in the reality of the present time? What is the current form, the contemporary expression, of man's alienation from God? (*Prayer*, viii).

In addition, the independently reached *conclusions* of Ellul's sociological reflection can be given a theological interpretation within the structure set out in chapter two and four central theological judgments about modernity then follow.

Firstly, in terms of the elements of the fallen world, the dangerous novelty of the modern world can be expressed in the terms of human subjection to the powers and the correlative experiences of the sacralisation of human works and the worship of idols. Although not explicitly stated in exactly these terms, this is also the conclusion drawn from Marva Dawn's study of the powers as the connection between Ellul's sociology and theology.[3] This theological account of our current situation appears as early as *Presence*.

> Because our civilization is more than human, we must perceive that it is not made by 'flesh and blood' but by 'the principalities...and...powers...the world-rulers of this darkness', Eph 6.12 (*Presence*, 103).

The theme then recurs throughout Ellul's later writings which portray the

---

[3] Dawn 1992.

modern world as the creation of the powers Christ has defeated but which are now unleashed in the world.

> Christ has conquered the powers, thrones, and dominations, he has despoiled them, but without annihilating them. The city is one of these powers. It has been conquered. And we could ask ourselves if the enormous proliferation of the modern city is not the reaction, the savage response of its vanquished spirit still struggling and building a monstrosity because it has no future...(*City*, 132).[4]

The modern world is therefore nothing more than the extreme exaltation of man's will-to-power (*Freedom*, 217-9, 242-3).[5]

Secondly, the distinctive and threatening nature of modernity also leads Ellul to describe the world as increasingly dominated by the four characteristics that resulted from the rupture with God.

Not least because the powers lead the world to suicide, Ellul describes our world as one marked by and destined for *death*.[6] Furthermore, the totalitarian nature of the modern world represents the climax of man's attempt to construct his own uniform world without reference to God.

> Our societies, without exception, become all-engulfing, nothing can escape their control. We are confronting the increasingly familiar process of 'integration-exclusion'...(*Faith*, 193).[7]

This *integration* and *exclusion* is now so total that Ellul will even use this conclusion from his sociological studies to argue that, if there is to be change in the world, there must be a God who is truly transcendent and Wholly Other.

> Since totalitarian society turns everything to its own ends, the only possible challenge to it is the proclamation of a radical Wholly Other and the intervention of the Wholly Other through this proclamation (*Humiliation*, 110).[8]

---

[4] Similar themes appear in *City*, 166; *Prayer*, 140ff; *Hope*, 65ff; *Freedom*, 157-8; 1973l.

[5] *Métamorphose* (especially, pp.93-7) argues that the bourgeois quest for self-justification and happiness has made our world and this also relates to the powers' dominance.

[6] *Presence*, 22, 31; *Faith*, chapter eight; Part 2 of *Métamorphose* examines this ideology (*l'idéologie du Néant*) and earlier in the book Ellul writes of death's take-over (pp.192-202).

[7] This argument is central to *Métamorphose* (e.g. 109-64) & summarized in *Révolution*, 223.

[8] The major case for this is put in *Faith*, 189-97 and *WIB*, 180-7.

In agreement with Jean Brun, Ellul also argues that our world is a world characterised by *Eros* (1969j). In *Betrayal*, Ellul argues that historic Western civilization is so significant because ancient Greece and Rome displayed the power of Eros and it was into this culture that the revelation of Agape came in Jesus Christ thus producing the dialectic necessary for history. In our contemporary world, however, we are witnessing the end of history with the triumph of Eros in the West and its spread across the whole globe (*Betrayal*, 68ff). Part of this is due to the influence of Marx, Freud, and Nietzsche who represent the opposite of merciful Agape *(Hope*, 52). As a result, we live in a civilization that exalts power and tends to expel Agape and replace it by Eros (*False*, 69).[9]

The fourth characteristic of the fallen world is particularly prominent in our age. Despite Christ having brought freedom into history, our own world clearly reveals that history has not thereby become the triumphal march of freedom (*Politics*, 187). In fact, we see the increased power of *necessity* weighing down upon people in our society (*Métamorphose*, 277).

> I have...the sense that, over the last two centuries, we have been in the course of passing from a world of relative freedom to a world of necessity...The laws of gravity are always the same but if a feather falls from the top of a wall, a person can change its course by their breath; if it is a ball, by catching it; but if it is a 50kg rock it is better not to try and stop it. That is the current situation (1950i, 37-8)

Although in his sociological studies, Ellul presents our modern world as fundamentally different from previous societies in history, there exists a theological continuity between our situation today and that of the world throughout history. In the past, the present, and the future it is always the world of ruptured communion with God which sociology is studying. Now, however, we suffer from having given expression to the full effects of that break with God in a way which has never before been witnessed. One interesting sign of this perspective is found in places where Ellul reads Scripture's ancient witness as prophetic of distinctive features of the contemporary world. He finds this especially in relation to political propaganda in the example of Rabshakeh (*Politics*, 145) and the two beasts of Revelation (*Apocalypse*, 92). It is perhaps most obvious in relation to the city, the human work which symbolizes the world.

---

[9] Again *Métamorphose* regularly refers to this e.g. the bourgeois as a man of power who has bequeathed a world of power (49) and the development of power to a pure state (280-4).

The greatness of the scriptural doctrine of the city seems completely out of proportion with what the city really was in the tenth century BC...There is such profound understanding of urban reality that it appears to be taken from an observation of our modern cities...The Scriptures speak of the city in exactly those terms, whose complete reality we only know today. In that sense the biblical doctrine is truly prophetic (*City*, 41, 42).

Ellul is so critical of theologians who speak of modern man as 'man come of age' because for him modern man and the modern world are nothing more than the lived reality of the biblical revelation that humans have broken from God and are full of pride and power. (*Violence*, 40-3).

Thirdly, once it becomes clear that the modern world is to be understood as dominated by the powers and that it reveals the consequences of man's rupture of communion with God, Ellul offers one of his most controversial and most misunderstood theological conclusions.

Within Ellul's theology, the world is restrained from the full consequences of ruptured communion by the dialectic produced through the presence of God's Word in human history. As chapter two demonstrated, this Word counteracts the work of the powers and, seeking to re-establish communion, makes present in the world that life, otherness, agape love, and freedom which it lacks. Ellul's sociological analyses see any fundamental dialectical processes in the modern world being brought to an end. His theological reflection upon this state of affairs can only lead to one conclusion concerning our contemporary situation: the Word of God is no longer active in human history.

I had for a number of years intended to write a book on 'The Age of Abandonment'. It seemed to me that our society in its sociological evolution, as well as the individual in this society in his psychological outlook, were types of what the Bible says happens when God turns his back and is silent...My purely sociological and historical intellectual approach had led me into a blind alley. There was nothing to say to a person beyond a stoic exhortation to keep going in God's abandonment...(*Hope*, vi, viii).[10]

By reference to the death of Christ, Ellul expresses the same theme even more starkly, giving theological expression to both the essential continuity of the fallen world and the radical novelty of our age.

---

[10] The fullest discussion of Ellul's belief about the silence of God is Holland 1986 who strongly criticises his conclusion but fails to do justice to the logic of his position as described here.

There is no doubt that Jesus was crucified in about the seven hundred and seventieth year after the foundation of Rome; there is no doubt that the Lamb of God is being crucified each day, and will be until the end of the world. Yet it is as if now the crucifixion has at last become fully a historical reality. It is in our day that Jesus is, in the fullest and most radical sense, being rejected by everything – I mean literally everything – and in every area of man's endeavours: his thinking, his willing, his undertakings, his building of his world, his consumption etc. It is in our day that Jesus is being in the fullest and most radical sense, humiliated...It is in our day that Jesus is, in the fullest and most radical sense, being put to death...Now Jesus has truly been crucified, in the fullest sense that the word 'crucifixion' can have as the sign and symbol of scorn, derision, unimportance, failure, abandonment...The cross of Jesus, which was meant to be the sign of God's unconquerable love, has now become purely and simply the sign of his failure...God has fallen silent (*Betrayal*, 78, 79).

Fourthly, and finally, Ellul's theological reflection upon modernity leads him to the confession that Christians ultimately bear responsibility for our present plight (*Presence*, 17). They have been like Jonah, asleep in the boat, as he failed to heed God's call and 'the tragic thing...is that if conditions cease to be normal, it is not the fault of the sailors, the pagans; it is the fault of the Christian who has sailed with them...the storm is unleashed because of the unfaithfulness of the Church and Christians' (*Jonah*, 30).[11]

Christians are called to preserve the world by living out their communion with God and faithfully incarnating God's Word. By living the Word, Christians resist the world and so enable a true dialectic to exist within human history. In order to understand how the present world came to be, it is therefore necessary to see that there has been a subversion of the Christian message. This has resulted in Christians failing to fulfil their proper and unique calling, failing to make Christ and his victory over the powers present in the world. This is the underlying rationale of *Subversion* (cf. 1985b) where the primary question is not how the subversion of the gospel produced Christianity but rather how our terrible current situation in the modern world has arisen from the 'Christian society' of Christendom.

How has it come about that the development of Christianity (*la société chrétienne*) and the church has given birth to a society, a civilization, a culture that are completely opposite to what we read in the Bible ?

---

[11] The fullest discussion of the effect of Christian failure is Ellul's writing on negative responsibility (*Freedom*, 274-92), applied to the environmental crisis at 1974g, 154-5.

(*Subversion*, 3).

Ellul believes the Reformation rectified some of the errors of Catholic Christendom by again desacralising the world and firmly re-establishing the distinction between the church and the world. However, because it failed to produce an ethic which encouraged the incarnation of Christian faith, the Reformation ended up making the world's situation even worse (*Subversion*, chapter three) as 'the world, following its own law without any Christian presence, becomes worse than ever before' (*Money*, 28).[12]

Turning from Ellul's theological and sociological *diagnoses* of the modern world's problem to his proposed *solutions*, it becomes clear that in both strands of writing he is a dissenter and social critic who resists the world and has revolutionary aims. A distinction must, however, be drawn between the two strands.

On the one hand, Ellul offers a radical theological critique of the modern world as part of the historical world which has broken its communion with God and which therefore shares the characteristic features of the world of ruptured communion. This is complemented by the universal Christian calling to be a revolutionary presence living out God's word within the fallen world. The exact form of this theological critique and this call will vary from time to time and place to place. Its details will always therefore be significantly shaped by sociological reflection. Nevertheless, the structure of Ellul's theology and ethics means that in every period of history Christians should take a critical and resisting stance towards the world.

On the other hand, Ellul offers a sociological critique of the modern world and his revolutionary response to this situation. This is based on the belief that a fundamental transformation has destroyed the features and equilibrium of historic Western civilization. Ellul's revolutionary response is therefore specific to the present situation and is addressed to all people, whether they are Christians or not. It demands engagement in a personalist revolution that will work to restore the dignity of the human person and to challenge and transform the institutions and forces that currently destroy human beings.

In conclusion, a brief summary can now be offered of the nature of the dialectic between Ellul's theology and sociology. His theological dialectic of communion and rupture in the historic relationship between God and the world is derived from revelation. This dialectic is primary. Indeed, the lack of communion between God and the world can be seen as the foundation for Ellul's distinction between theology and sociology because God and his world are now ruptured from one another.

---

[12] On the Reformation's failure see *Sources*, 317-61; 1945d; 1976e; *TWTD*, 244.

Between my two series of books there was a caesura, what is more, an opposition, which gives expression to the dialectical confrontation of the Natural and the Revealed (1966c, 96-7).

Revelation can therefore be of assistance in the task of understanding our contemporary world because of what it reveals about humans and their world apart from God and because of the hope it gives to those who receive it. Ellul refers to this as a form of Christian realism about society and clearly believes Christians are better equipped, because of their faith in God's revelation, to understand the world (*Sources*, chapter seven and *Violence*, chapter three). He even suggests that 'no realism concerning the actual reality of the world is possible except from the standpoint of the promises of God' (*Prayer*, 136).[13]

Revelation cannot, however, provide either a sociological method or comprehension of any particular society's structures and evolution. Katharine Temple was therefore perfectly correct, in discussing Ellul's 'consistent distinction' to argue that

Ellul does not claim any special status, based on revelation or theological assumptions, for the content or methodology in his chosen discipline. In his own words, 'Revelation cannot be the first principle for anything'.[14]

In attempting to understand these limits it could be argued that Ellul's theology of the world of ruptured communion is similar to the third level within his trichotomous analysis of social reality, which he describes as the concern of philosophers and analogous to the depths of the ocean. The characterisation of the world sketched in chapter two therefore relates to the constant features of all societies and is not sufficient for understanding the determinative features of any particular society (the second level and focus of Ellul's sociological analysis).

Despite the primacy of revelation and the theological dialectic of rupture and communion in the relationship between God and the world, Ellul therefore must be exonerated from the charge of letting his theology determine the conclusions of his sociological analysis. He quite legitimately claims that his sociological studies of our contemporary world stand or fall on their own and are not simply the product of his theological presuppositions.

Quite honestly I believe that my theological convictions and stance in no way interfere with the way I study society. I do everything within my power

---

[13] On Christian realism about society see *Sources*, 94-109 and 1962b, 46-52.

[14] Temple 1985:41.

to keep the influence of my faith separate from both my sociological analysis and my work as a historian.... (*Conversations*, 113).

It would, however, misrepresent Ellul if it was only stated that his theology is the primary category and that it influences (albeit in a non-determinative manner) his sociology. His sociological conclusions themselves feed back into the other strand of his writings because these are written for Christians living in the world described by his sociology. Ellul's sociological works therefore help to provide concrete conclusions to his ethic for Christians. As chapter two has shown, his overall theology provides a theological account of the Christian life and a general pattern for the Christian living within the world of ruptured communion. Ellul is, however, insistent that any genuine ethic must always be related to the here and now. This was part of his rationale for emphasizing the study of social sciences in his reforms of theological training and was central to his criticism of Barth – 'I was not satisfied with his volumes of ethics and politics, which seemed to be based on an insufficient knowledge of the world and of politics' (1978d, 24). Ellul's general description of life in communion with God must therefore be placed alongside an analysis of the contemporary context in order to yield any specific ethical counsel for Christians.

It is now clear why Ellul faces critics in both disciplines and has been accused of corrupting his sociology with theology and *vice versa*. His account of modernity is mistakenly perceived by some as the inevitable pessimistic vision of the world given his theology of human sin. Others dismiss his revolutionary theology and ethics and his criticism of much traditional Christian social and political thought as a Christian façade for a basically Marxist world-view. Although there are grains of truth in these common perceptions, they are essentially caricatures of Ellul's thought which fail to do justice to the fundamental structure of his corpus. Ellul's work must be read and understood as a whole where each strand of writing has its own internal method and intellectual consistency but is in dialogue with the other strand, influencing, but never determining its conclusions.

On the macro-level of Ellul's global thought which has been examined thus far, the influence could be said to be primarily from his theology to his sociology: the modern world studied in his sociology is always part of the world of ruptured communion described in his theology. However, even here his theology does not, indeed cannot, explain the central themes and claims of his sociology any more than it could explain his social analyses of other periods of human history. In fact, his sociological conclusions owe more to the personalist movement than to any alleged Calvinistic pessimism about the world.

On the micro-level of Ellul's reflection on particular issues and social phenomena (to which we now turn in Part Two) the primary direction of influence could be said to be in the opposite direction: from his specific sociological analyses to his theology and ethics. Here Ellul seeks to reflect theologically upon the phenomena analysed in his sociology and to present more concrete conclusions as to the proper contemporary Christian ethical response. Once again, however, it will be clear that neither strand is simply reducible to the other. In each of the areas examined in the following chapters, his theology and his sociology will be seen (even amidst changes and developments) to have a certain internal consistency and integrity, to make sense within his own life story, and to cohere with the introduction to Ellul's thought that has been offered in Part One.

PART TWO

STUDIES IN ELLUL'S SOCIAL

AND POLITICAL THOUGHT

CHAPTER 5

Violence

This first case study in the micro-analyses of Ellul's thought offered in Part Two focuses on his study of violence, one of Ellul's best known and most criticized books. Close attention to Ellul's work in this area is demanded by four factors. Firstly, there are important questions concerning how his book on violence fits within his overall writing and the structure of his thought as outlined in Part One. Secondly, an understanding of his thinking in this field provides a helpful background for the next two chapters as they study law (with its use of sanctions) and the state and politics (where issues of coercion and force play a prominent part). Thirdly, faced with the analysis of the modern world which Ellul offers, and his call for a revolutionary response, many would naturally turn to political violence. It is, therefore, important to understand Ellul's analysis of the phenomenon of violence, especially in the modern world, and his assessment of how effective violence is in securing the forms of social and political change he wishes to see. Fourthly, the subject of Christian responses to violence has been a central one in the tradition of Christian political thought and remains a major area of debate in the contemporary church where Ellul's contribution should be heard.

Before turning to Ellul's sociological and theological reflections on the subject of violence the questions of the literary and intellectual integration of Ellul's work on violence with his wider writing and thinking must be briefly addressed. The literary difficulty is the easier of the two. Ellul's study of violence stands out in his corpus because, unlike most of his other published volumes, there are no obvious signs in earlier publications that violence is a central Ellulian concern. Furthermore, the book is not preceded by a number of articles developing its argument and it appears as a theological work lacking any obvious sociological counterpart. All this suggests that the study, first published in English in 1969 as *Violence: Reflections from a Christian Perspective* and then in French only in 1972 (entitled *Contre les violents*), is one of Ellul's *ad hoc* works and not part of his original plan of writing. Both the book's content and its much more apt French title support this thesis.

The book draws on Ellul's life-long reflection upon historical and contemporary political violence and revolution. This is also evident in *Autopsy* which also first appeared in 1969 (in French) with some material in common with *Violence*, and throughout his untranslated five volume *Institutions*.[1] It also, like all his work, is connected to his own personal first-hand experiences of violence of which the most prominent are the anti-fascist movement of the 1930s, the Resistance and the quest for vengeance after it, and his work with young delinquents and against state bureaucracy in the Aquitaine (see chapter one). Nevertheless, despite this background, it is undoubtedly one of his more contextual and polemical works, apparently provoked by Christians (perhaps particularly some linked to the World Council of Churches) who, though sharing Ellul's desire for revolutionary change, also justify the use of violence in defence of their political goals.

The intellectual, as opposed to literary, difficulties with the subject arise in the light of the introduction to Ellul's thought offered in chapters two and three. In relation to his sociology, it is initially unclear whether Ellul has any sociological reflection of violence or any account of the novelty of violence in modernity. In relation to his theology and ethics, his book seems to prove the validity of the simple framework of a dialectic between freedom and necessity that Clendenin has most extensively elaborated but which chapter two critiqued.[2] The difficulty is that when interpreted in this way Ellul's Christian writing on violence appears incoherent. The fact that the book is primarily a short, critical response to Christian advocates of revolutionary violence at least mitigates some of these problems but they need further examination.

This chapter therefore presents an account of Ellul's thinking on violence that draws not only on *Violence* but also on other books and articles in order to address these difficulties. The first section, on Ellul's sociological analysis, opens with a defence of reading Ellul's study of violence non-theologically and presents a summary of his methodology and 'laws of violence' as the heart of his sociological analysis. It is followed by an examination of Ellul's treatment of violence in the modern world. The second section then studies Ellul's theological reflections on violence. After an account of Ellul's critique of traditional Christian positions, it is argued that the interpretation of Ellul's theology provided in chapter two offers a better understanding of his thinking

---

[1] Ellul described himself as 'an historian who for a very long time has focussed on researching revolutionary and anti-establishment movements since antiquity' (1977h, 18).
[2] Clendenin 1987.

about Christian resistance to the world of violence than the limited freedom/necessity dialectic. On this basis, Ellul's own proposals about how the Christian can live in obedience to God's Word and resist a violent world are discussed.

Ellul's Sociological Reflections on Violence

An Ellulian Sociology of Violence ?

An initial reading of *Violence* could lead to the conclusion Ellul offers only a theological analysis of the phenomenon of human violence. The book is clearly one of his theological rather than sociological works and the fullest account of the phenomenon of violence in it draws on Scripture references and appears in a chapter entitled 'Christian realism in the face of violence'. However, that chapter's methodological principle is 'to get as clear and exact an understanding of the facts (*la réalité*) as possible' (81).[3] This form of realism is a demand for serious sociological enquiry and the book's analysis of violence is therefore fundamentally a sociological one. This is confirmed by Ellul's 1973 *Réforme* article that not only summarises some of the laws of violence found in his book but also restates his method more explicitly.

> Violence, being a sociological phenomenon, bears specific characteristics that it is possible to determine, analyse and prove (*cerner, analyser et démontrer*) on an historical and sociological level without appealing to morality (1973k).

As in his other sociological studies, Ellul adopts the twin principles of 'nominalism' and 'realism'. The nominalist method leads Ellul to accept as violence anything experienced and categorised as such. As a result, he unfortunately offers no clear definition of the phenomenon[4] and classes a great diversity of actions as forms of violence. This latter feature of his work is also due to his realism. Based on theological beliefs about the character of the world broken from God and a Marx-inspired belief in the ability of the powerful to use ideology to mask reality, this insists on going beyond mere appearance and common perceptions. It is, he argues, vital to uncover the full extent of violence. As his analysis (88-90) of the deep-rooted and long-

---

[3] All numbers in parenthesis in this chapter are page references to *Violence*.

[4] This is a common criticism (Gaffney 1975:187; Konyndyk 1981:256; Sturm 1984:581) and Ellul apparently later regretted the lack of definition in this work (Hanks, T. 1985:30).

standing violence present in American society demonstrates, 'the natural man fools himself about fact (*se cache la situation*), cannot bear to look at a situation as it is, invents stories to cover up reality' (84).

This determination to get below the surface shows that, as in relation to Technique/techniques and many other social phenomena, Ellul is not so much concerned with particular concrete instances of violence as with its more fundamental and universal characteristics. However, Ellul's study of violence differs from his other sociological analyses because, in the terms of his schema of analysis, violence is not on the intermediate level of societal structure (the currents) but rather on the third and deepest level of social structure (the depths). Violence is a form of human activity which constitutes a basic and constant social phenomenon 'inevitable in all societies' (93). His sociological account of violence therefore does not (unlike his analysis of Technique discussed in chapter three or his treatments of law, the state, and politics discussed later) take the form of a characterology of its distinctively modern form. Instead, Ellul offers (with little historical defence) five universal laws of violence (93-108). Taken together these constitute the backbone of his sociological account of violence.[5]

The *first* law of violence is *continuity* – 'Once you start using violence you cannot get away from it (*il arrive un moment où l'on ne peut plus s'en dégager*)' (94). This law is based on the fact that because violence gets results by simplifying complex situations there is no reason to cease violence once one has had recourse to it. It functions as a reminder that violence constantly reappears in new forms and, by highlighting the difficulty involved in securing even a de-escalation in violence (let alone an ending of violence) warns of the dangers inherent in initiating any form of violence, however laudable its goals.

The *second* law is *reciprocity* – 'Violence creates violence, begets and procreates violence' (95). This shows that every act of violence can explain and seek to justify itself as a response to an earlier act of violence. It therefore warns against a naïve view that violence can be used as a limited means to a desirable end without thereby provoking a cycle of reciprocal violence.

The *third* law of *identity* (or *sameness*) is central to Ellul's sociology of violence. This law acts as the essential foundation for the other four laws and much of his critique of traditional accounts of violence. Simply stated, it claims that 'every violence is identical with every other violence' (97). Although Ellul fails to distinguish them, there are in fact two distinct 'identities' within his account. There is the *phenomenological* identity uniting

---

[5] Some of the laws appear in passing in his other writing e.g. *Révolution*, 105-6,292-9. For discussions of the laws see Ray 1973:344-54; Ihara 1975:145-56; Burke 1980:156-63; Konyndyk 1981:257-8.

all types of violence (physical, economic, psychological, individual, national, international etc.[6]) and the *moral* identity which prevents any distinction between 'just' and 'unjust' violence or 'violence that liberates' and 'violence that enslaves' (108-15).

Ellul fails to explain the basis of these two forms of fundamental identity, uniting all forms of violence. This is unfortunate given that most people would wish to distinguish clearly between different levels and forms of violence rather than treating as identical the physical restraint of a dangerous criminal against his will and the dropping of nuclear weapons on civilian populations. However, certain statements, and the strong influence of personalism on his thought, suggest that Konyndyk was right in his claim that 'for Ellul violent behaviour is coercing someone in a way that violates his personhood'.[7] In other words, every act of violence is the same as all others in that all violence rejects a true I-Thou person-to-person relationship. This is because violence 'simplifies relations with the other completely by denying that the other exists' (94) and 'always breaks and corrupts the relation of men to each other' (113). This explains why psychological violence is therefore also violence for Ellul because 'the victim…is led to do what he did not want to do, so that his capacity for further personal development is destroyed' (97).[8]

The most important political implication of this law is that Ellul adamantly rejects the widely held distinction between 'violence' and the coercive actions of those with political authority that are usually re-classified as 'force'. This distinction sets the context for many ethical discussions as recognised by Jonathan Glover who, like Ellul, wishes to undermine it and opens his discussion on the ethics of war with the words, 'It is widely held that killing in war is quite different. It is not, and we need to think about the implications of this'.[9]

For Ellul, the state's coercion is the same as all other acts of coercion and must therefore also be referred to as 'violence'. This is particularly important in Ellul's work and the fullest defence of his position appeared prior to his

---

[6] Ellul mentions various forms of violence throughout the book e.g. pp 84ff, 97-8,112-5, 131ff.

[7] Konyndyk 1981:256.

[8] Mulkey 1973:69 unfortunately limits his explanation of Ellul's use of 'violence' to collective violence while Gaffney 1975:187 inexplicably defines violence in Ellul as 'an unjust use of force against the exercise of freedom' thus implying that Ellul distinguishes between just and unjust force.

[9] Glover 1977:251. Macfarlane 1974 attempts to overcome the standard statist bias in the use of terms but still uses 'force' and 'violence' to distinguish legitimate and illegitimate coercion.

study of violence in the second chapter of his 1965 sociological study of politics (*L'Illusion*, 69-82). Unfortunately, the 1967 English translation (*Illusion*, 68-82) undermines Ellul's argument here by constantly referring to 'force' whereas he clearly prefers 'la violence' and not 'la force' as demonstrated by the French title of the chapter's first section, 'Le monopole de la violence'.

Here it again appears that Ellul's beliefs may be traced back to his youth.

> The desire to disassociate force and violence reminds me of the finest idealist chatter of my law professors in 1930. It is, on the contrary, fundamental to remember that every social use of force, whatever the model of society (whether economic or something else), is necessarily an act of violence (1977h, 18n1).

The *fourth* law of violence asserts that *only violence results from violence* – 'Violence begets violence – nothing else...Violence can never realize a noble aim, can never create liberty or justice (100, 102). The heart of this law is found in one of Ellul's earliest articles on violence where, in relation to war in Algeria, he argues that war is abominable to a Christian, the rule of violence alone which can only engender violence (1957d). The law is, nevertheless, also one of the most confusing of Ellul's laws, not least because he earlier contradicted (or at least weakened) it when he recognised that although only reciprocity of violence is certain, there are other possible results of violence such as 'equal rights, legitimate defense, liberation' (96-7).

Placed in the wider context of his book and his own belief in the need for a revolution to change society, perhaps one of Ellul's aims in formulating this law in this way is to give some simple expression to his fundamental belief that although revolutionary changes are needed in society 'the use of violence, the means of violence will resolve none, absolutely none, of the problems posed (*Révolution*, 105). In fact, Ellul is quite clear about the effect of violence.

> My study of politics and sociology has convinced me that violence is an altogether superficial thing; that is, it can produce apparent, superficial changes, rough facsimiles of change. But it never affects the roots of injustice – social structures, the bases of an economic system, the foundations of a society. Violence is not the means appropriate for a revolution 'in depth'...The belief that violence can effect decisive change arises from a dangerous idealism that promotes violence and produces illusions of the worst kind (117-8).

The *fifth* and final law is that of *justification* – 'The man who uses violence always tries to justify both it and himself' (103).[10] This claim is probably among the least controversial although Ellul's further assertion that justification derives from the need to provide an ideological mask which hides the inextricable bond between violence and hatred is much more contentious. This law draws attention to the universal character of justifying the use of violence and implies that the diverse ethical quests for criteria to discriminate between acts of violence so as to justify some but not others are simply an inevitable corollary of the phenomenon of violence itself.

Overall, this bleak sociological analysis amounts to a determined undermining of the Western tradition's attempts (supported and arguably initiated by Christian beliefs) to limit violence by political and juridical means. Ellul's realism here is stark and shocking.

> According to me, once you have decided to go to war you have to go all out and use every means at your disposal. This is the case that applied in Algeria. Everyone was shouting their heads off against the torture that was going on. But the real problem was not the torture but the war itself. There is no morality in war. If you want to win you must pull out all the stops (*Conversations*, 39).[11]

The analysis is also a fundamental critique of all theoretical reflections on violence that are influenced by the basic principles underlying traditional Christian just war theory. Ellul is adamant that 'there has never been a just war…All wars are unjust' (*ibid*) and he sees the fundamental failure of such approaches based in the fact that they are

> based on the conviction that man can retain control of violence, that violence can be kept in the service of order and justice and even of peace, that violence is good or bad depending on the use or purpose it is put to (5-6).

In stark contrast to such analyses, Ellul offers a globalistic and quasi-deterministic account of violence as a seemingly autonomous force beyond human control. It is, therefore, unsurprising that, although never explored in detail, in his theological writing Ellul occasionally classes violence as one of the powers (e.g. *Money*, 79; *Prayer*, 174).

Ellul is insistent that everyone, especially Christians, must face the reality

---

[10] This self-justification, and the futility of violence in the quest for true revolutionary change, is discussed more fully in *Révolution*, 295-9.

[11] For Ellul's comments on Algeria at the time, including the use of torture, see 1957d & e; 1960b, c, f, g & h; *FLN*.

of violence in the world. Violence has its own momentum (First Law), engenders further violence (Second Law), and cannot be subordinated to any end (Fourth Law). Furthermore, and fundamental to the whole argument, all the distinctions constantly sought between acts of violence and all attempts to evaluate violence on account of its form or the end sought in its use, fail to acknowledge its fundamental identity (Third Law). Finally, the whole exercise of drawing moral distinctions between acts of violence (pursued by its practitioners, philosophers, moralists, sociologists, and theologians) is only a consequence of violence itself because all those who use violence always look to justify it and themselves (Fifth Law).

Violence and Modernity

In contrast with all the other social and political phenomena he examines, Ellul's emphasis in his sociology of violence lies not on its novelty in the modern world but on its continuity throughout history. In fact, in a foreword added to the French edition of his book, Ellul explicitly rejects the belief that there has been a quantitative or qualitative change in violence:

> We know well that history has always been the fruit of violence and there has always been a contradiction between a moral imperative and the reality of violence. We have changed nothing. Our time is not more violent than any other...Relationships of violence have been constant (*Violents*, 7).

However, although nothing appears anywhere in the English edition of *Violence*, Ellul does elsewhere focus on the distinctive features of violence in the contemporary world. These take two forms: the widespread consciousness of violence and its effects, and the changes (particularly in the violence of war) that have resulted from the wider civilizational crisis affecting the modern world discussed in chapter three.

KNOWLEDGE OF VIOLENCE AND VIOLENCE AS TECHNIQUE

The opening sentence of *Contre les violents* reads, 'Today is not the time of violence but of the awareness (*la conscience*) of violence' (*Violents*, 7). In the past, violence was always experienced directly as an animal instinct and could even be described as the human condition. This has now changed as people are aware of the use of violence which is presented as a global spectacle.

This new consciousness of violence then creates a general climate of fear because everyone is now much more aware of violence in society even if they do not experience it directly themselves. This knowledge and fear then in turn engenders more violence. One particular form of this phenomenon which Ellul often highlighted, especially after his work on the Peyrefitte Commission in the 1970s, was the desire of citizens to grant greater powers to the forces of law and order or to defend themselves against crime (*Faith*, chapter twenty).[12]

Furthermore, the recognition of the reality of the universality, identity, and reciprocity of violence which Ellul delineated in his laws has led to a belief that every act of violence can be justified because the perpetrator has himself suffered some prior act of violence. This brings with it the temptation to seek recourse to violence in response to violence which can then be developed into a whole strategy based on the conscious and controlled use of violence to achieve one's ends (*Violents*, 10). Whereas, in the past, political violence usually erupted as the expression of popular discontent and despair in the form of revolt, today it regularly forms part of a carefully constructed revolutionary programme or organised terrorist campaign. In short, our modern consciousness of violence has inevitably led to it becoming a highly developed political technique and part of the wider modern phenomenon of Technique.[13]

VIOLENCE IN THE MODERN TECHNICAL WORLD

Ellul also argues that, despite its own essential historical continuity, violence is affected by the new environment of modernity brought about by Technique, propaganda, administration, and the state. The rapid technical development of the last two centuries and the spread of new techniques to the general public has resulted in 'the democratisation of evil (*la démocratisation du mal*)', a phenomenon discussed by Ellul in relation to a variety of factors. His argument concerning violence is simple.

If violence increases in our countries, it is not that people are more violent (quite the contrary, I believe). It is because there are much easier and simpler means of practising violence. Even a very weak impulse toward violence is going to produce extremely violent effects... (1981i).

In addition to the accessibility of means of destructive, physical violence, Ellul and the Peyrefitte Commission highlighted the increasing forms of

---

[12] This emphasis also appears in a number of articles e.g. 1978c; 1980w; 1982k and is reported in Anonymous 1976.

[13] *Autopsy* (especially chapter one) and *Révolution* (especially pp292-9) are major discussions of this phenomenon while *Violence*, 27-43 examines modern arguments to defend revolutionary violence. Ellul credits Lenin with the development of violence as a political and revolutionary strategy (1946i; 1970g) although the assassination campaigns of nineteenth century anarchists are also cited. On modern terrorism see *Déviances*, 79-81; 1968g & 1983e.

hidden violence that progressively structure modern society.[14] It is a feature of our modern society that violence is often less blatant and physical because it has moved onto the spiritual level (*Hope*, 44), something Ellul views as the worst and distinctively modern form of terrorism (1968g).[15] Here Ellul has in mind such violence as that exerted by the growing machinery of modern state administration which he experienced in his own work with young delinquents and in defence of the Aquitaine region. This form of violence, which Ellul also sees at work in the police and the modern city, can lead even relatively pacific people to turn, in desperation and fear, to material acts of counter-violence (*Faith*, 231-3).[16]

> I have become more sensitive to social violence than to the individual violence of young people. The phenomenon of social violence – administrative violence, violence of the judicial system, and so on – has been for me the frightening discovery of something against which we are totally helpless (*Season*, 132-3).

In looking at violence in the modern world, Ellul particularly delineated some of the changes in the violence of war. An early and constant critic of the development of nuclear technology, Ellul's analysis is not, however, restricted to the simple observation that the creation of such weapons of mass destruction has qualitatively altered the destructive potential of war (1982n).[17] His discussion of modern warfare sets it within the societal changes wrought by Technique and propaganda.

While Ellul emphasises the permanence of war and its constant characteristics in history he insists that the *causes* and *scope* of modern war have changed. It is now total war driven by propaganda. In the past, war was caused by the immediate experiences of a community or was the play of princes involving primarily professional soldiers or mercenaries. Today, in the modern state (particularly in democracies), the people as a whole must be involved and war can therefore no longer depend on governmental decisions alone.

---

[14] See 1977f & 1978c.

[15] Ihara 1975:152 correctly comments that 'Violence in the modern age, while still present on the physical level, has been transferred to the spiritual realm...Spiritual violence is the way of life in the modern age...'.

[16] Further discussions of this form of violence appear in *Déviances*, 86, 129ff and 1980s.

[17] Ellul's views on nuclear weaponry are discussed in Johnson 1982. For a much more developed critique of the novelty of nuclear weapons and the whole modern philosophy of nuclear deterrence see O'Donovan 1989.

It is because the whole people has become political, because it incarnates liberty in its entirety, because the nation has the value of a democracy, that defense cannot be left to a few and all men must rally to protect democracy and freedom. Pseudo-liberty has engendered total war (*Freedom*, 286).

However, nations are so large that no natural, human reasons can unite a whole people and propel them to war.[18] As a result, war increasingly depends on propaganda providing myths and justifications that draw on natural instincts of violence and offer causes and objectives for war. Propaganda thereby unleashes the tendencies to violence and mobilises public opinion in support of any conflict. Already in *La Technique*, Ellul was describing how this phenomenon was at work in the United States to bring about their involvement in the Second World War (*TS*, 365f). He returned to the theme in both his study of propaganda and his later study of modern politics (*Propaganda*, 121-38; *Illusion*, 76-7) and in a short account of propaganda in the Algerian war (*FLN*). His argument is summed up in an important 1953 article on the subject.

In the current state of the world, if there were not propaganda there would be no cause of war; or to be more exact, all the present causes of conflict would disappear (1953h, 52-3).

This was, of course, written at the height of the Cold War and has in view such events as the Korean War and the Berlin blockade. Throughout this era, by applying his analysis, Ellul consistently criticized Western propaganda claims that the Soviet Union was intending to invade capitalist countries and engage them in military conflict. He thus later claimed that 'in the period when all the intellectuals were shivering and frightened, faced with the threatened war with the USSR...I was alone writing and proclaiming that there was no threat of direct war' (1973d).[19]

Finally, reflecting on the experience of the Second World War, Ellul drew attention to two new characteristics of modern war both of which have been confirmed by subsequent conflicts (1948d). The development of modern weapons technology renders war increasingly impersonal as the means of killing can now be as abstract as pressing a button with no enemy in sight. No human relation of sympathy is therefore possible between combatants and so

---

[18] On the link between the nation and war see 1960d, 207. Ellul always argued that only true federalism could reduce war e.g. 1948b (where he argues that world government, far from being the solution to world conflict would simply mean that what today we call war would be replaced by police operations which would be as dangerous) and 1982m.

[19] The proof of Ellul's position is found in 1951e; 1953e; 1955b & 1956a.

killing is not done with hate but with indifference as combatants do not even know if they have killed. It is, for example, difficult to imagine much modern warfare inspiring a poem such as Wilfred Owen's 'Strange Meeting'. While the increase in the number of non-combatant deaths in modern war is an evil, the impersonal massacre of an undifferentiated mass of 'enemies' is also a real atrocity.[20]

This dehumanisation of conflict relates to the second new characteristic deriving from the propaganda-based causes of war: a transformation in the notion of the enemy. In the past an enemy was someone who posed a real, live threat, somebody against whom one needed to defend oneself because they wished to do you harm. Now, propaganda and the weapons of war require that the enemy become, through belonging to a certain group, nothing less than the incarnation of Evil. Those who oppose the enemy thus view themselves as an incarnation of the Good.[21] Once again the possibility of any personal relation is eliminated and war becomes a new sacral duty.

> Justificatory propaganda (and all propaganda is this in some way) has this double link with war: on the one hand it makes war necessary in order to purge society of evil...on the other hand it charges war with a sacred content, making it inexpiable and totally inhuman...(1953h, 62).[22]

In conclusion, although Ellul primarily draws attention to sociological laws of violence applicable in all times and places, he also acknowledges that the pattern and character of contemporary violence has been affected by the civilizational crisis that has taken place. In the course of the twentieth century we have gained a new awareness of the reality of violence. This has, however, not led to a humanising control of violence but rather to the enhancement of its autonomy. As a result, violence is experienced on a higher, abstract, spiritual level and the unleashing of its full depersonalising power occurs in modern warfare so that 'a person no longer chooses their war, it is no longer

---

[20] The conflict in the Gulf (especially the infamous 'turkey run' on the Basra road in which thousands of retreating Iraqi conscripts were murdered) and the aerial bombardment of Kosovo and Afghanistan provide recent examples of this phenomenon.

[21] This self-understanding was quite explicit in the Kosovo conflict in the attitude of Tony Blair who, after the bombing had started and the expulsion of refugees began, declared that 'This is no longer just a military conflict. It is a battle between good and evil; between civilization and barbarity' (quoted in Rawnsley 2001: 263).

[22] In relation to World War Two and its aftermath Ellul discusses this hatred in 1945b and relates it also to the use of law at Nuremberg (1946a & 1947d) and in relation to the Oradour massacre (1949a & 1953d). He refers to his role at this time explicitly in 1978f, 110 and regularly speaks of all modern war as religious (*TWTD*, 158; *Hope*, 78; *Faith*, 24f).

his personal affair, it isn't even any longer a matter for his group, there is an enormous machinery which leads him into it...(1953h, 51).

Conclusion

It is clear that, despite first impressions, Ellul's thought does contain a significant amount of sociological reflection upon the phenomenon of violence. The heart of this is his five laws of violence. These are presented as universal laws, valid throughout history. Although Ellul discusses distinctive features of violence in the modern world, his treatment of these is neither as central nor as detailed as his analysis of the novelty of Technique discussed in chapter three and his writings on law, the state, politics, and other phenomena in modernity.

There are a number of reasons for this different emphasis in his writing on violence. Firstly, the structure and central concerns of Ellul's sociological thinking originated in the 1930s personalist movement. There, despite the breadth of their interests, neither Ellul nor Charbonneau appear to have focussed much attention on the question of violence, although they were clearly aware of the issue given their revolutionary aims and for a time accepted the necessity of violent action, although they never directly engaged in violence as a group (*Season*, 41-3). Even at this stage Ellul seems to have had little faith in the value of violence to effect real change, seeing its potential as primarily symbolic. So, explaining his thinking about the possibility of bombing the Bourse, he comments, 'it would not destroy capitalism but it would serve as a symbol and a warning' (*Anarchy*, 11). The failure of Ellul and Charbonneau to concentrate their thinking on the subject of violence at this stage is probably in part because they knew that, even if their personalist revolution could snatch the world from the embrace of modern Technique and reconstitute its political structures, no revolution could ever eliminate violence from society. Given that all Ellul's major sociological concerns develop and extend his thinking from the inter-war years and seek to make readers aware of their world so they can change its present structures, this omission of violence from the personalist agenda for change combined with the impossibility of any alternative to a world of violence, make it unsurprising that Ellul's attention to the subject of violence in his sociological works is limited.

Secondly, Ellul's sociology of violence is also limited because violence unlike most of his other concerns cannot be treated as a distinctive determinant of the modern world (i.e. Ellul's normal intermediate level of societal structure). Violence is a fundamental constant phenomenon of human relations throughout history, albeit one whose contemporary features are sometimes distinctive because of the wider civilizational crisis described in his other sociological studies.

Thirdly, the major reason for the distinctive features in Ellul's sociology of violence are, however, that his book on the subject is generated primarily by his ecclesial context rather than his own sociological project. This makes violence the one subject where theological concerns are clearly the context for the presentation of Ellul's sociological reflections. Furthermore, in contrast to his theological reflections on other subjects where Ellul's sociology significantly shapes an ethic for today, Ellul's theology provides unambiguous conclusions about all violence and so sociological analysis of the contemporary context is less important in giving concrete shape to his Christian ethic.

Ellul's Theological Reflections on Violence[23]

Christians and Violence: Ellul's Critical Account of Traditional Positions

Ellul's book on violence opens with a brief account and critique of three traditional Christian positions. The first and the third represent different political outlooks but both comprise Christian defenders of violence. They are strongly rejected by Ellul whose views are closest to the second Christian tradition he discusses, that of 'non-violence', although (as so often in his writing) Ellul is also critical of this group to which his own position is closest.

The first group, which Ellul classifies under the heading of 'compromise', embraces all Christians who affirm that violence can be legitimate when used by those with political authority (1-9). Since about the fourth century (Ellul places great emphasis on the Council of Arles in 314 as marking the major change in the church's position[24]), this has been the dominant theological account of violence in the Christian church. Its classical (but by no means sole) biblical source is the use of the sword granted to political authority in Romans 13 and one of its fullest and best know expressions is traditional just war theory.[25] Ellul sadly never engages with the detail of this tradition whose

[23] For other discussions see Philp 1960; Ray 1973:338-73; Ihara 1975:145-56; Burke 1980:152-75; Outka 1981; Konyndyk 1981.

[24] Fullest discussions of this change in the church's position are *Institutions* 2:506-7, 525-7 and *Anarchy*, 91-5.

[25] Key texts from the tradition addressing such issues are now collected in O'Donovan and O'Donovan 1999 and O'Donovan 1996 offers a contemporary appropriation of this tradition. In relation to modern just war theory see the classic writings of Paul Ramsey and

historical development he views as one of church compromise with the world, a compromise he later argued was extended by the influence during the Crusades of Islamic jihad thinking (*Subversion*, 100ff).

The third group Ellul identifies simply in terms of 'violence' (17-23). This includes all Christians who participate in (or justify) violence against unjust tyrannous political authorities and/or violence against the wealthy by the poor. It is the contemporary manifestation of this tendency that Ellul is primarily concerned to challenge in his book. This emphasis is in part because Ellul sees the growing influence of this group in the church in the 1960s through some liberation theologies and the World Council of Churches. Ellul also concentrates on it because of his own revolutionary sympathies and (as shown in his critique of Christian Marxists) his tendency to direct his strongest attacks against those with whom he has much in common. Central to his critique here is that this stance is to be understood as fundamentally politically rather than theologically motivated.

Both these views are doubly flawed from Ellul's perspective. Sociologically, he believes that they are unrealistic about the nature of violence. By seeking to distinguish between forms of violence and by justifying violence in the pursuit of what they each understand to be justice, they fail to acknowledge the laws of violence discussed above. Theologically, Ellul also believes them to be in error, not least in aiding humans in their rebellious quest for self-justification (140). Before seeking to understand his own distinctive theology and ethics of violence, however, Ellul's critical comments on the second group in his categorization – 'non-violence' (9-17) – need to be noted.

Ellul clearly has most affinity with the stance of non-violence that he argues is the oldest Christian tradition in relation to violence. For at least the first three centuries of its existence the church almost universally condemned violence and was broadly speaking pacifist in outlook, although debate continues concerning the exact details of the early Christian position.[26] Its origins, however, clearly lie in Jesus' own teaching and practice as is increasingly confirmed by recent historical Jesus studies.[27]

Ellul is fully aware of the diversity of formulations of non-violence.[28] In

---

also Johnson 1999.

[26] On this see Helgeland *et.al.* 1985 and Hornus 1980, to which Ellul often refers.

[27] Among New Testament scholars see Horsley 1987, Wright 1992 & 1996, Hays 1996 and Hays 1999 on Wright. Discussion of the use of Scripture in support of non-violence is found in Swartley 1983:96-149.

[28] John Howard Yoder, who along with Stanley Hauerwas (e.g. Hauerwas 1984) has proved the best exponent of Christian non-violence in recent years, sketched no less than twenty-nine varieties of religious pacifism (Yoder 1992).

order to distinguish his own position he raises (in his book and elsewhere) four concerns about certain expressions of this position. *First*, non-violence cannot be solely a political stance but must be founded on a personal repudiation of all forms of violence. In his later 1977 critique of a document from a non-violent political movement Ellul focuses on this. He argues, with echoes of his 1930s personalist agenda, that any political stance must be combined with a moral and spiritual transformation of the human person.

> Here is the centre of my disagreement. The authors of this project are very violent against the moral and religious aspects of non-violence. They wish to separate non-violence from this foundation in order to offer a political analysis and an effective, realistic political project and they view all other forms of argument as idealistic and false. Unfortunately, the authors themselves are idealist and falsely realistic as everything which they propose presupposes a change of everyone's personality, a moral and spiritual conversion...And, I am sorry to say, such a mutation of personality will not come from a political programme, nor from new institutions, nor from a movement, but precisely from an individual work (not an individualist one !) which is moral and spiritual. To tear up that root, which is a preliminary foundation, is to reduce all the rest to nothing. We need to recall that as soon as the Christian foundations, motivations, and speeches of Martin Luther King were disowned, the movement became violent...(1977h, 17).[29]

Second, non-violence is not an effective political tactic. In fact, 'there are practically no long-lasting non-violent movements in history!' (1977h, 18n1). Ellul argues that when one studies the cases which claim to show the success of non-violence it will be found that any success always comes from a certain weakness or uncertainty on the part of the adversary or from their respect for some moral and juridical principles. He is quite clear that, without this context, non-violence either fails or else explodes into violence.[30]

> Because of my spiritual convictions I am not only non-violent but I actually advocate meekness (*la non-puissance*). Non-violence is certainly not an effective method (*une technique efficace*). From a realistic point of view, force (*la puissance*) will always win. But for me, it is at this point that faith

---

[29] This is simply the application of his long-standing position on the inter-relationship between personal and social change and between means and end (sketched in *Presence,* 64ff). For a response see Muller 1977.

[30] Ellul relates this to Gandhi and other examples (*Violence,* 14-6) and made similar arguments on the occasion of the assassination of President Sadat (1981m). A recent attempt to argue for the effectiveness of non-violence in political struggles is Wink 1992, especially pp243-57.

comes into the equation. Jesus Christ, who acted without force (*qui a été révélé comme la non-puissance*), ended up as one of the prime movers in history. God is on the side of the meek (*non-puissants*) so they are the righteous but that does not mean that they succeed (*Conversations*, 28).

Third, non-violence must never become a form of justification. This refusal of justification is a central theme to which will we return and it is clear that for Ellul the refusal to justify one's actions must not only apply to those who have recourse to violence in the face of injustice and evil.

> In face of the tragic problem of violence, the first truth to be discerned is that, whatever side he takes, the Christian can never have an easy conscience and never feel that he is pursuing the way of truth (138).

Ronald Ray is, therefore, right when he says that faced with his own question about how one can say one loves the poor and exploited of South Africa when one refuses to do anything that involves violence (130) Ellul's response is to affirm that 'even the Christian position of non-violence involves guilt'.[31]

Fourth, Ellul believes that non-violence is not a truth that can be advocated in itself. Any Christian appeal for non-violence therefore cannot be made apart from Christ and his work.

> We cannot separate our objectives from the person of Jesus Christ. Peace and justice...have no importance or value in themselves. They are not objectives to be attained in isolation. They have no meaning except as Jesus is the prince of peace, the sun of righteousness...Any true proclamation of the gospel will entail work for peace, although pacifism both doctrinally and ethically makes no sense and is not intrinsically a serving of Jesus Christ (*Politics*, 138).

Ellul's Understanding of the World of Violence

In the light of Ellul's rejection of Christian defences of violence and his critiques of certain forms of non-violence, his own theology and ethics of violence must now be examined. One of the distinctive but rarely commented on features of his treatment is its relationship to the biblical witness. Ellul is usually eager to root his ethics in Scripture and, because he is convinced Scripture is dialectical, he usually finds contradictions within the Bible to be a means of gaining insight rather than an excuse for ignoring the biblical text.

---

[31] Ray 1973:196, n3.

Thus, in relation to money, he claims that 'we should not be disturbed that the Bible contains contradictory texts about wealth, for it contains opposing texts on almost every subject' (*Money*, 35). Similarly, in relation to death, he wrote an article on the Bible's contradictions on the subject (1981q). It is, therefore, surprising that he uses the lack of a united biblical witness on the subject of violence to reject emphatically the option of basing his theology and ethic of violence on biblical texts. He therefore begins his discussion of the Christian approach to violence with this stark disclaimer.

> If we want to find out what the Christian attitude toward violence should be, we cannot proceed by deducing the consequences of Christian principles or by enumerating biblical texts. The Bible does frequently condemn violence, but it defends violence just as frequently – even in the New Testament. So this is not a good method of seeking an answer to our question (81).[32]

Given his rejection of violence, Ellul is self-confessedly embarrassed by Scriptural texts advocating violence (*Anarchy*, 13) and insists that 'war is brought about by the will of man. It is not God who starts off wars' (*Conversations*, 104). However, in earlier discussions of passages such as the *Herem* (e.g. Deut 7) Ellul does not shy away from these but instead appeals to the transcendent freedom of God and offers them as among instances of the divine suspension of the ethical and so to be spoken of as 'good' because an expression of God's will (*TWTD*, 206-9; *Faith*, 150).[33]

Instead of any sustained engagement with the biblical text, Ellul's primary category for the theological analysis of violence is one of the four characteristics of the fallen world discussed in chapter two: the phenomenon of necessity (*la nécessité*).

Ellul argues that violence is universal and, citing Hobbes, claims this is because violence is man's natural state (87f).[34] This, however, cannot be used to pass moral judgment on violence as either legitimate or as evil. The laws of nature are also universal, natural, and of the order of necessity but nobody asks if gravity is good or evil (91). This is an argument Ellul frequently uses in his studies of violence.

---

[32] David Gill, who has produced the most detailed studies of Ellul and Scripture, unfortunately does not address this disclaimer in his study of the Word of God in Ellul's ethics (Gill 1984b).

[33] It is, presumably, this perspective that leads Ellul to the unelaborated qualification in his statement that 'apart from the inspiration of the Holy Spirit, the use of violence is always and a *priori* contrary to the will of God' (*Freedom*, 406).

[34] On Ellul's relationship to Hobbes see Stanley 1981.

To take another example of necessity: I inevitably obey the laws of Nature. If I trip up and fall I am simply obeying the necessity of the law of gravity: but that is not to say that it is good or just that I fall over...(1973k).

For Ellul, therefore, the proper judgment in relation to violence is that it is part of the order of necessity and as such escapes moral judgment. This initially shocking statement is fully in line with his theology and ethics as outlined in chapter two. It is simply the re-formulation, in terms of necessity and the natural, of his theology of the good as the will of God which cannot be determined in the world of ruptured communion apart from revelation which re-establishes communion with God.

Given this analysis of violence, Ellul's advocacy of radical Christian non-violence and resolute opposition to all justifications of violence appears to derive simply from his dialectic of freedom and necessity. Unsurprisingly this has been proposed by Konyndyk as the interpretive key for Ellul's understanding of violence. Konyndyk acknowledges Ellul offers other more traditional arguments for his position but sums up his central and original argument against violence in the following terms which he correctly states to be repeated in various forms throughout the opening section of chapter four of Ellul's book.

A. Violence is of the order of necessity.
B. The Christian's role is to shatter necessity and to reject all necessities (to reject anything of the order of necessity).
C. Therefore, the Christian must reject violence.[35]

Konyndyk's own careful critique of the syllogism and of its wider use by Ellul raises doubts as to whether this really does provide the best framework for understanding Ellul's thinking. Of particular importance here are the other examples of necessity and freedom mentioned in *Violence* and elsewhere in Ellul's work. Ellul writes that the order of necessity also embraces the human actions of ownership, work, and eating. Therefore, following the logic outlined above, he argues the Christian must combat and fight these necessities. The possible means are then shown us in God's dealings with Israel: eating ceases to be necessity by the act of fasting, work by keeping the Sabbath, and ownership by the establishment of the landless Levites (128).

Ellul appears unaware that all these examples undermine his argument for a total rejection of all violence by all Christians. In none of the cases cited does the act of freedom require a total, universal abstention by the whole people of God of that which is classed as of the order of necessity. It appears that, with

---

[35] Konyndyk 1981:259.

the sole exception of violence, some partial refusal for a period of time or by a group within God's people can act as a sufficient sign of freedom and the refusal of necessity.[36] With this strong counter-argument from within Ellul's own work, it must be concluded *either* that Ellul's absolute rejection of violence has little or no foundation within his theology as a whole *or* that Konyndyk's syllogism is an inadequate account of the theological basis of Ellul's critique.[37]

Chapter two has argued that Ellul's concept of necessity is simply one of four inter-related characteristics of the world that has ruptured its communion with God. Instead of approaches which reduce Ellul's thinking to the important necessity-freedom dialectic, its alternative proposal for the centre of Ellul's theology (the relationship between God and the world organised around communion and rupture) provides a much more solid theological foundation for Ellul's theology of violence.

The major flaw in Konyndyk's argument becomes clear once it is realised that not all elements of the order of the necessity are equivalent. This is because *all* elements of human life, although lived in freedom within creation's communion with God, are *now* lived as part of the order of necessity that arises from the rupture of that communion. There are, therefore, human activities (such as eating and working) which are *now* experienced as part of the order of necessity but which are not reducible to that order. Such activities are primarily expressions of human finitude which occur even in communion with God and so, although now part of the order of necessity, these are not solely marks of our ruptured communion with God. As Ellul wrote elsewhere,

> We do have to distinguish, of course, between the domain of man's finitude and that of his sin. Finitude means that man has a body, that he is limited by space, that he is conditioned by such functions as having to eat. That he is set in nature to work there is also part of his creatureliness. The point is, however, that the body becomes a passion and eating an all-consuming concern. The appetite for material things becomes insatiable. Man comes to be possessed by his body and what can satisfy it. Thus the simple mark of legitimate creaturely finitude becomes a slavery that results in separation from God. Similarly, work becomes a law, a constraint, a way of dominating

---

[36] This has, of course, been the Christian tradition's usual response to violence so, for example, paralleling the example of the Levites and property, clergy were not to bear arms.

[37] The dilemma may not be quite this sharp because Ellul has other theological arguments for total non-violence and he might also argue that the power of necessity is so strong with violence that, in contrast to these other examples, freedom can only be expressed by total refusal.

others, a mortal duty in virtue of its own domination, or the fabricator of idols and hence a delirious passion whereby what ought to be a joyous exercise is a bondage resulting from separation from God (*Freedom*, 48).

In some cases, therefore, the order of necessity is related to something which is a created experience of human finitude and which exists even in communion with God. In such situations it is reasonable to call for an expression of Christian freedom from the necessity experienced in the world of ruptured communion not by total abstention but by a limited non-participation such as fasting or the Sabbath. These acts of freedom acknowledge that freedom here is to be freedom from idolisation and control by the activity concerned.

In contrast to eating and working, however, violence is not an aspect of finitude which had a place in the good communion of creation but which now, in the world of the rupture, becomes necessity. Violence is wholly a consequence of the rupture in communion between human beings and God.

In the original created relationship of communion between God and the world, people were called to be the image of God's love and freedom in the world over which they were granted dominion. It must not be forgotten that the dominion in communion was one of love and not violence:

> It cannot be a rule (*une domination*) by violence, by constraint, by power, because God does not rule and does not direct the world by constraint, by violence and by power. God directs the world by love. And if humans are the image of God, their rule over the world can only be one imaging that of God, that is to say, rule by love (*Genèse*, 75-6).

The exact and specific form of human rule when in communion with God is the word - 'humanity must fulfil its royal function in the midst of the animals through the word, and not through the violence of implements' (*Humiliation*, 67). Violence therefore appears in our world only because the world of communion in creation was shattered by the Rupture. It is in the world of ruptured communion with its orders of necessity and nature that humans rule the world by power and violence and this is a reversal of their position and role when in communion with God. Ellul argues that this becomes clear by comparing the original divine mandate and the similar pronouncement to Noah after the Flood in Genesis 9.1,2. There is a complete rupture evident here as humans become the centre of fear and not love within the world (*Humiliation*, 68). Violence has therefore now become our natural condition whereas in communion within creation this was not so.

One result of this change is that we can no longer appeal for the universal fulfilment of humanity's original calling. That calling was a commission for the totally different world in communion with God. However, in Christ, God's Word has taken human flesh and entered the world of ruptured communion. Ellul argues that Christ reveals the reality of the world's violence now it has broken from God. He cites Jesus' words (e.g. 'All who take the sword will perish by the sword', Mt 26.52) to support his laws of violence (95, 99) and he refers to the cross as a revelation of the reality of human sin.[38] Christ also shows God's way of working in the world is one of non-violence and non-power.

Ellul's arguments for Christian non-violence are not as explicitly Christocentric as those found in writers such as Stanley Hauerwas. Nevertheless, by drawing attention to Jesus' consistent refusal of his disciples' desire to use violence (129-30) and stating that 'in his person [Jesus] manifested nonviolence and even nonresistance to evil' (9), Ellul demonstrates the significance of Christ in his ethic of non-violence.[39] Through union with Christ, Christians are restored to communion with God and so they can break with the ruptured world's way of life. As shown in chapter two, Christians are called to live out God's holy, loving, free, and non-violent presence and so resist the naturally violent world. It is therefore quite understandable that Ellul should write that 'The Christian *in imitation of Jesus Christ* must be non violent' (1980w, 2, italics added).

The account of Ellul's theology and ethics set out in chapter two therefore overcomes the apparent contradictions that appear to be present in Ellul's argument when (as in *Violence*) it is based only on the freedom-necessity dialectic. It now becomes clear that violence is primarily not a sign of necessity but of the world's ruptured communion because 'the order of necessity is the order of separation from God' (128). Ellul's rejection of violence rests upon the non-violent method of God's own free and loving rule made known in Christ. Humans were called to mediate this within the communion of creation but their rupture from God prevents them from doing so. Christ, however, obeyed this calling in the world and it is now also to be fulfilled by those who follow Christ and through relationship with Him re-enter communion with God and live His Word within the world they are called to resist.

This wider perspective on Ellul's understanding of violence in the world

---

[38] Although Ellul only ever refers to his work briefly, a dialogue between Ellul and the analysis of violence found in the work of his fellow French polymath René Girard (e.g. Girard 1978) would be illuminating and provide further support for Christian non-violence.

[39] Discussions of the temptation of power and violence are also found in the untranslated *Si*. For a discussion of Jesus and violence in Luke's gospel in relation to the parable of the pounds (Luke 19) see Goddard 1994b.

assists in clarifying some other important features in Ellul's account of Christian responses to violence. He offers what he calls a dualist ethic in which he offers contrasting assessments of the use of violence by Christians and violence in the world. He also seeks to offer a theological account of the irresolvable conflict of the Christian's position in the world which can become manifest in Christian recourse to violence.

Ellul's Non-Violent Ethic for Christians

On the basis that violence is natural for the world of ruptured communion but Christians are not to be of the world, Ellul proposes a dualist approach in his ethics of violence, contrasting this with the traditional Christian positions which are all, in his view, monist (23-6). In other words, there is an ethic for Christians alone as those in communion with God and a separate account of the use of violence by non-Christians whose communion with God remains broken (131).

The heart of Ellul's ethic for Christians is clear and unambiguous: the Christian's calling is totally incompatible with all forms of violence. Violence must therefore always be rejected with absolute intransigence whatever its source, even if this requires personal sacrifices and withdrawal from certain positions in the world. This theme runs throughout his writing, although he is wary of making it a cause of division within the church (*False*, 99). It shapes his understanding of prayer (*Prayer*, 173ff) and his form of anarchism (*Anarchy*, 13ff). Even more importantly, Christians must absolutely reject all justifications of violence, particularly those which purport to be Christian (139ff). Combining this emphasis with his wider theology and ethics, Ellul offers four concrete suggestions as to *how* the Christian can express this calling and live out the Word of God and resist a violent world.

Firstly, because she is to be present in the world even as she remains a distinctive witness to the Wholly Other God, the Christian must be willing to participate in movements using violence. This must, however, be a non-conformist participation. In addition to a personal refusal of violence, this could take such forms as always openly questioning the justifications of violence offered by one's allies within a group (and so undermining their recourse to violence), ensuring they do not believe a Christian presence is a sign of God's approval, and being willing to change sides and be present with the opposition in the conflict. By means such as these the Christian will relativise the cause that claims human devotion and appears to demand violence in its defence. She will therefore challenge the movement's idols.

The sole important task in the liberation of man is the relentless relativizing of all great causes, of all beliefs and ideologies...We have to be clear about it that the Transcendent, existing of itself, has its being without the need of any oppression, violence, or victory...Only the rigorous insistence on the Transcendent, maintained, believed, and obeyed, assures the relativizing of everything in the name of which man kills and oppresses other men. As long as one is dealing with facts, values, and theories known to be strictly relative, passing, uncertain, and inadequate it is much more difficult to kill and oppress others (*Hope*, 244, 245).

Secondly, in their participation in the world Christians must remember that worldly rule is characterised by violence but rule in communion with God (as evident in creation) is rule by the word. Ellul therefore argues that Christians should, in contrast to the world, rely on the power of the word. They should show support for the poor and oppressed not by participation in their violence but by a resolute representation of their cause before the powerful (150ff).

A *third* distinctive calling of the Christian is to be a watchman in the world. This requires him to discern nascent conflicts and attempt to draw attention to them so that some relatively just and consensual solution may be found before the full destructive power of violence is unleashed. Ellul, as noted in chapter one, sought to achieve this in relation to Algeria. This important task is based on the belief that, although it may be possible to weigh the respective claims of the parties and seek some agreement in the initial stages of a dispute, when war breaks out and violence escalates the means used invalidate any alleged just cause.[40]

Fourthly, Ellul speaks of an acceptable form of violence which is only open to Christians: the spiritual violence of love. This is

violence that makes us intransigent toward ourselves and insistent in our demand that the other live – I might say, "that the other live in a manner worthy of God's image" (166).

At the heart of this violence of love is prayer rooted in faith, an act totally incompatible with any form of physical or psychological violence (169f). In a line of argument that follows the pattern of reasoning later developed by Hauerwas in many of his writings, Ellul argues that it is experience of this Christian practice of prayer that eliminates the common argument that violence may sometimes justifiably be used as a line of last resort.

Violence, we are told, is legitimate when the situation is such that there is

---

[40] In addition to *Season*, 103-5 see also *FLN* and Marlin's introduction to that volume which explains the rationale of Ellul's critique of FLN propaganda once violence began.

absolutely no other way out of it. The Christian can never entertain this idea of 'last resort'. He understands that for the others it may be so, because they place all their hopes in this world, and the meaning of this world. But for the Christian, violence can be at most a second-last resort. Therefore it can never be justified in a Christian life, because it would be justified only by being really a last resort. The Christian knows only one last resort, and that is prayer, resort to God (170).

It is clear that for Ellul a Christian practice of non-violence does not mean withdrawal from the world. On the contrary, as the concluding sentences of his study make clear, it is non-violence that involves real Christian presence in the fallen world.

Will it be said then, that the Christians are absent from the world? Curious that 'presence in the world' should mean accepting the world's ways, means, objectives; should mean helping hate and evil to proliferate! Christians will be sufficiently and completely present in the world if they suffer with those who suffer, if they seek out with those sufferers the one way of salvation, if they bear witness before God and man to the consequences of injustice and the proclamation of love (174-5).

In such a response to violence in the world the Christian follows Christ in a pattern of life that is true combat with the spiritual powers. Ellul acknowledges that such rejection of violence often leads to apparent failure and even death (1981m) but he insists that the Christian's distinctive non-violent pattern of life also has great potential power as an alternative to the world's use of violence. It does not leave the world unaffected.

Choosing different means, seeking another kind of victory, renouncing the marks of victory – this is the only possible way of breaking the chain of violence, of rupturing the circle of fear and hate (173).

Christian Responses to the World's Violence

For Ellul, the Christian calling to choose for non-violence is a matter of living the Word of God. It therefore cannot be demanded from those not restored to communion with God in Christ. It is, then, important to consider what the Christian can and should say and do in relation to violence in the fallen world.

In relation to the world, Ellul sees the Christian's first task is to be realistic. This means admitting and accepting that non-Christians use violence. Indeed, Scripture teaches that 'what is normal now that man is separated from God is war and murder...' (*Politics*, 178).[41] None of these acts of violence are ever good, legitimate, or just. Nevertheless, within this universal negative judgment and despite his laws of violence, Ellul wishes to discriminate in some ways between different forms of worldly violence. Unfortunately, the nature, criteria, and implications of these distinctions within the world's violence are often left unclear and seemingly contradictory.

Ellul's judgment on the secular state's use of violence, especially its coercive force in relation to law and judgment (issues to which the following two chapters give more attention) certainly appears to develop in his writing. His generally negative judgment on state violence appears to be tempered when the use of violence is necessary for the state to fulfil certain functions. (*TWTD*, 105ff).

In Ellul's earliest work the necessary state functions were related to the act of judgment and Ellul here comes closest to anywhere in his work to a position of 'justifying violence' akin to the mainstream Christian tradition that he later labelled as 'compromise'. Discussing Mt 26.52 and Rev 13.10 and their relation to Rom 13.4 Ellul comments that

> The use of the sword in itself is not condemned...The use is subject to eventual condemnation...which will become a reality only if the sword...serves either the obstruction of justice or the spirit of power (*le moyen de l'esprit de puissance*). Within this eschatological perspective, man's judgment in the realm of law assumes its rightful value. His judgment is the reason why the use of the sword will not be condemned. Any use of it apart from man's judgment runs counter to God's will...It is law which, before God, permits the use of force (*Law*, 113).

Ellul fails, however, to develop this understanding of a form of non-condemned coercive force in his later work. There he not only insists that the language of violence is more appropriate than that of force but he increasingly places more emphasis on the necessity of the state to use violence to preserve itself and defend its own people rather than to pursue just judgment.

> To ask a government not to use the police when revolutionary trouble is afoot, or not to use the army when the international situation is dangerous, is to ask the state to commit hara-kiri. A state responsible for maintaining order and defending the nation cannot accede to such a request... (159).[42]

---

[41] See further *Reason*, 235ff on war in human history.

[42] 1960b claims that from the point of view of the state there are legitimate wars and he contrasts Belgian and French action in the Congo and Algeria with illegitimate US intervention in Formosa and the USSR in Hungary.

More widely, Ellul clearly believes some violence is understandable and speaks of violent actions that are not to be condemned. Thus he claims (133) that although as a Christian he 'cannot call violence good, legitimate, and just' there are specific conditions where he finds its use 'condonable (*compréhensible, acceptable, non condamnable*)'.[43] At times he appears to go even further in his sympathy for the world's violence.

I fully understand the insurrection of the oppressed who see no way out...the revolts of the slaves, the violent workers' strikes of the nineteenth century, the rebellion of the colonized peoples...I understand these explosions and, what is more, I approve of them (*je les approuve*). The oppressed have no other way of protesting their human right to live; and they think, too, that by rebelling they can change their situation for the better, if only to some small degree (68-9).[44]

Ellul's language here is clearly rhetorical and slippery. In places he is plainly contradictory as he later states that although (because of the fallenness of world) violence may be understandable (*compréhensible*), it is nevertheless always to be condemned - 'la violence est *toujours* condamnable' (*Ethique III*, 166; italics original).

Although the exact nature of Ellul's more nuanced judgment on certain forms of violence is unclear, the conditions which lead him to render more qualified judgments on some acts of violence are more carefully stated. Ellul is more understanding of violent acts that are acts of despair due to the lack of any perceived alternative or unmask a hypocritical situation claiming to be just and peaceful. In contrast, he emphatically states that making violence part of a strategy (as in terrorism) or hypocritically claiming it will produce order and solve people's problems is always and only to be condemned (133ff).[45]

Despite these rather blurred distinctions in his assessment of worldly violence, the heart of Ellul's stance is that the Christian must never offer a justification for the world's acts of violence (even when he understands them), nor must he think he can instruct the world with an ethic of violence such as traditional just war theory. On the contrary, when those claiming to be

---

[43] *Violents*, 170.

[44] It is important to note that Ellul immediately goes on to say that he cannot condone Christian association with such actions or, even worse, Christian affirmation that it can truly change things. This is because 'Christians do not have the reasons for believing this that the oppressed have' (69).

[45] In explaining these mitigating circumstances Ellul acknowledges his debt to Sorel, cf. *Révolution*, 295 on Sorel.

Christians are in positions of power and may be tempted to have recourse to violence, they should be called upon to fulfil their Christian calling in the world and reject violence and its justification. So, 'it ought to be possible to tell a President Johnson that his faith forbids any use of violence' (160). When, however, people do not profess to be followers of Christ, Christians should recognise that violence is the norm in the world of ruptured communion and that the world will remain the world broken from God until its final judgment and recreation in renewed communion with God. The Christian response of a personal rejection of violence is therefore combined with an acknowledgment that the world's violence can only be ended by re-establishing people in communion with God in Christ.

> At least [Rap] Brown and [Stokely] Carmichael are men who made a real choice, who did not even attempt a shabby reconciliation, and who saw clearly that violence is radically incompatible with faith in Jesus Christ. They chose violence; that was their privilege. All that a Christian could do would be truly to convert them to Jesus Christ (158-9).

The Christian's Necessary Sin ?

Faced with Ellul's challenge to reject violence the Christian should always be able to avoid *justifying* violence, whether his own or that of the world. Refraining from *using* violence is, however, a much more difficult task. Chapter two showed Ellul's emphasis that the Christian is the meeting point of the world which has ruptured its communion with God and the God who seeks communion with the world by his Word. As the person in whom the will of God and the will of the world meets, the believer is *simul peccator et justus*. Although not made explicit in his book on violence, a consequence of this perspective is that the total rejection of violence will in practice prove impossible for the Christian to achieve in the fallen world.[46]

In *Violence* Ellul acknowledges Christians have often used violence in the past and that they continue to do so today. He comments that our response to this shouldn't simply be to condemn them and say that such behaviour is impossible and unacceptable (137). Rather, in such circumstances the crucial factor is the Christian's attitude to their acts of violence. This must never be positive or even neutral in the face of their succumbing to violence.

The important thing is that, when he uses violence, the Christian knows very

---

[46] As is clear in the discussion that follows, there are parallels here with Lutheran ethicists (such as Helmut Thielicke and his borderline situations) who develop Luther's famous 'sin boldly' counsel to Melanchthon (see Higginson 1988, chapter seven).

well that he is doing wrong, is sinning against the God of Love, and is increasing the world's disorder (even if in appearance he is fighting against it)...The important thing is that here the Christian cannot have a good conscience...He is no longer a man conformed to God, no longer a witness to truth...He is once more travelling the rutted roads of this godless world...There can never be any satisfaction or acceptance of violence before God but only the humble recognition that one couldn't do otherwise...That is why the Christian, even when he permits himself to use violence in what he considers the best of causes, cannot either feel or say that he is justified; he can only confess that he is a sinner, submit to God's judgment, and hope for God's grace and forgiveness (137-8, modified).[47]

When Christians have recourse to violence there should be an acknowledgment of a bad conscience and a steadfast refusal of any form of self-justification. Yoder therefore rightly sums up Ellul's position as one where 'the Christian will have to use violence but will know that it is sinful'.[48]

This question of necessary sin in the Christian recourse to violence inevitably raises questions about Ellul's own life and use of violence. Unfortunately, some of the important published material on this has proved highly misleading. One of the fullest discussions by Ellul was a 1970 letter he wrote to *Christianity and Crisis*. Stephen Rose's review of Bethge's biography of Bonhoeffer had referred to Ellul's participation in the Resistance and commented,

Ellul's recent book, *Violence*, would seem to place an interdict on any and all attempts to justify violence as Christian...Has something happened between those war years and now to modify the grounds on which Christians can assent to violence?' (Rose 1970a, 154).

Ellul's reply opens by correcting Rose's misinterpretations of his work and restates the heart of his ethic as outlined in this chapter. There follows a clear statement of the inevitability of Christian involvement in injustice and Ellul then apparently sanctions Christian violence by stating 'we can join with them in violent actions'. This cannot, however, amount to moral legitimation because Ellul proceeds to describe such actions as 'blameworthy before

---

[47] The passage is here modified from the ET which loses the sense of the French (*Violents*, 174-5).

[48] Yoder 1992:177, n16. On this see *Ethique* III, 166 which explicitly states that, because we live in a sinful and fallen world, sometimes one must be associated with violence while knowing that what one is doing is evil.

God'.[49]

When Ellul turns to respond to the question of his own history of violence, his comments become practically impossible to understand.

> I have been asked if I have changed my opinion since the Resistance (1940-1944). I reply that I have participated in several revolutionary movements, in several wars and in the Resistance, but I have always maintained the same position. I could not help but think that these actions, which I thought necessary but not just, were consistent with what Jesus tells us about the relations among men and liable to bear witness to the love of God or the nearness of the Kingdom. In other words, these necessary actions are of the order of sin, and so I must repent and rely on the grace of God, even for that which I believe useful and indispensable on the political level (1970b).

His description of these actions as 'consistent with what Jesus tells us about the relations among men' may be explicable in descriptive rather than normative terms as elsewhere he argued that Jesus reveals the necessity of violence and the laws of violence in the world. However, the passage then includes an incoherent statement equating actions liable to bear witness to the love of God and the nearness of the Kingdom with actions that are of the order of sin. Even the most skilled interpreter of Ellul, schooled in the complexities of his dialectical manner of thinking, must here admit defeat and conclude that what Ellul said must have been lost in translation, perhaps simply by the removal of a negative. This is confirmed by Ronald Ray in his unpublished doctoral thesis where he writes

> In a letter to this writer dated September 14 1972, Ellul agreed that there had been a translation mistake in a letter from him published in Christianity and Crisis...As published, it appears that he believes that violent conduct can witness to the love of God and the nearness of the Kingdom. Quite to the contrary, he says that he believes that violent conduct, though sometimes humanly necessary, is an inappropriate means of witnessing to Christ. Of course, God in His sovereignty can accomplish His purposes even in and through the world's violence, and thus can use violence to effect His purpose of love. To Ellul this fact is not to be confused either with the notion that violence can conform to God's intentional will or with the idea that violence witnesses to God's love (Ray 1973: 367n).

---

[49] The original French probably read '*nous pouvons*' and could be seen as merely descriptive of what Christians are able to do in the world or permitting Christians to be part of groups who engage in violence. It may perhaps be permissive in the sense that Ellul means we 'can' because even such blameworthy acts are still within the forgiving love of God.

It would appear that when Ellul's letter concerning his involvement in the Resistance and other forms of violent political action refers to having maintained the same position this is better understood in terms of the sad inevitability of Christian participation in violence given above. This is supported by his 1957 comment that 'it is necessary to admit that the Resistance (1940-1944) was unjust, just as every other war...but I think that it was necessary' (1957d) and his explanation to Chastenet near the end of his life that, although he didn't have a theoretical position on the subject of non-violence at the time of the Resistance, 'I was perfectly well aware that if I got involved in the fighting I would be crossing over into the realm of necessity but if I had to I was quite prepared to give up my freedom' (*Conversations*, 77).

Ellul nowhere presents a sustained treatment of the complex theological and ethical issues raised by the existence of 'necessary sin'. This reticence may be because he fears that discussing the issue will encourage those who, adhering to the commonplace that 'you can't act without getting your hands dirty' (*Critique*, 38-48), then accept, tolerate, and justify compromise, excusing themselves beforehand. Instead, he says that the Christian must refuse defining an acceptable compromise and instead repent of any sinful action (*Presence*, 124ff). However, by drawing on the argument of chapter two and occasional comments in a number of articles it appears that, apart from the obvious and uncontroversial fact that Christians are imperfect and sometimes fail due to their sinful nature, Ellul presents two deeper reasons for the inevitability of the use of violence by Christians.

Firstly, there is the possibility of a true dilemma where the calling to reject violence conflicts with another Christian calling. Ellul recognizes, for example, that Christians sometimes have recourse to violence in order to defend others ('he can say that he is fighting *for* others', 137). He does not, however, explicitly state this in terms of a moral dilemma nor use it, as just war theorists, have done, to justify certain forms of violence [50]

Of more significance to his political thought is a 1960 article on war and desertion. Ellul there affirms that as a Christian it seems to him that participation in war is totally impossible but that he also holds that Christians must obey the authorities. He therefore accepts the existence of true and irresolvable ethical dilemmas where the Christian, by obeying one commandment, will have simultaneously to disobey another. He refuses to develop a casuistry that would enable one commandment to be given priority.

---

[50] The just war theory is best defended by relating it to the command to love our neighbour and viewing limited 'violence' as the form obedience to that command must take when one neighbour is unjust and oppressing another neighbour (e.g. Ramsey 1961).

The Christian may therefore choose to use violence because not to do so would be to disobey another of God's demands. Even in these situations, however, the disobedience must never be justified but simply confessed as sin.

> At the level of the individual it will be said to me 'and what about the obligation to obey the authorities?'. Indeed, we are here faced with one of these conflicts which are woven into the Christian life, one of these conflicts which seem unthinkable to good consciences which always wish to be just and pure...That contradiction is in every case there in order to teach us again that total obedience to the will of God is impossible for us by ourselves, obeying at one point implies that we are disobeying on another. That therefore shows that we are never able, whatever attitude we adopt, to have a good conscience, to be at ease (*tranquille*) before God. If we refuse to participate in war, we are disobeying those authorities which come from God – and we cannot take such disobedience lightly, still less claim that it is those authorities which are in error! If we obey the State, we are disobeying the loving will of God. That contradiction necessarily brings us back to grace alone: whichever attitude of obedience we adopt, our only recourse is the pardon that is in Jesus Christ by the grace of God alone (1960b).

The impossibility of total non-violence is, secondly, to be understood in terms of the nature of Christian existence in communion with God in the world of ruptured communion. Ellul examines this most fully in relation to the wider issue of the church and power. He radically rejects all Christian involvement with power but again must address the question of whether it is possible to avoid such involvement. He concludes that this is not possible:

> We are unable to get ourselves around this unjustifiable, always illegitimate, evil. The Church can therefore only in effect choose between this compromise and that compromise, destroy in herself the expression of the spirit of power (*l'esprit de puissance*), and repent constantly for being forced into compromise with all the powers (*tous les pouvoirs*), seeking constantly to detach herself, but knowing that *if she wishes to be present in the world, she cannot avoid being mixed up in structures of power* (*des structures de pouvoir*) (1972f, 19; italics added).

One standard response faced with this situation is to say that at night not all cats are grey and to develop a means of distinguishing between levels of compromise. Ellul, although willing to make difficult choices, absolutely rejects this approach.

As soon as one has chosen the best colour of cat, one is at ease (*tranquille*). One has done the best that one could...It is when she has made a *good* choice, and opted for the best, the most just, the truest of the forms of power (*des formes du pouvoir*) that the Church is most caught in a trap (1972f, 19).

Applying this analysis to violence it becomes evident that for Ellul the Christian must confess that the very fact of living in the world enmeshes him in relationships of violence and that he can never escape these. He cannot exonerate himself or seek to salve his conscience by justifying his position or comparing himself favourably to others. He must simply do all he can to resist violence. He must acknowledge he is truly *simul justus et peccator*. He must confess his sin rather than justify it. He must constantly seek God's forgiveness.

Conclusion

It is clear that although in his book Ellul's Christian reflections on violence are structured around the poles of freedom and necessity, his theological understanding of the phenomenon is better understood when set within the wider structure of his theology discussed in chapter two. When the world and God are in true communion, as in creation and in the new creation, there is no violence and humans rule the world in love and freedom by the word. Violence is a sign that communion with God has been ruptured but it is now a permanent, constituent element of the world broken from God. Violence is therefore woven into the fallen world's four central characteristic features. It is, as Ellul regularly emphasizes, part of the order of necessity. It is often provoked by fear of death. It represents one aspect of the will to power and human eros. It is always the denial of the other as other. As such Ellul is insistent that violence can never be legitimate, just, or good. It must, therefore, never be justified by Christians even if recourse to it is more understandable in some situations than in others.

In this world of violence, God continues to be present through his living creative Word. That Word became incarnate in Christ, revealing the full horror of human violence, and overcoming the world by a distinctive, non-violent life of freedom and love. The Christian disciple is now called to live out his communion with God in an agonistic life, torn between the will of God and the inescapable reality of living as a sinner in a world that remains broken from God. He must never attempt to formulate a compromise between God's Word and the way of the world. Nor should he ever justify the world's violence (as the church has often sought to do through theories of just war) by distinguishing legitimate coercion by political authority from illegitimate violence, or by supporting the violence of the oppressed. Instead, the Christian must seek faithfully to live out God's Wholly Other Word of love and freedom, resisting all the world's forms of violence, while constantly confessing his own incapacity to fulfil this calling and seeking the forgiving grace of God.

CHAPTER 6

Law

Even among those who know Ellul's work well, many are unaware that his primary academic expertise was in the area of law and very few know his writing in this field. Apart from his first published book, *Le fondement théologique du droit*, (1946, ET 1960 *The Theological Foundation of Law*) there is little sign in his many published volumes that law is a major interest and, in comparison with his discussion of most other areas, even that book has received limited attention in the secondary literature.[1] There is therefore no significant English language discussion of Ellul's writings on law and this chapter seeks to rectify this lacuna in Ellul studies by providing an account of Ellul's work in this area which integrates it with the account of his life and thought as a whole offered in Part One.[2]

In fact, Ellul wrote extensively on law, throughout his life. In addition to his early theology of law there is the untranslated five volume *Histoire des institutions* and over thirty journal articles discussing the sociology and theology of law. His thinking on law, most notably in his theology of law, is, however not as constant or fixed as much of his other work. As he confessed in his significant but unfortunately unelaborated April 1987 confession

> I'm astonished sometimes when I find things I've written twenty years ago, to say to myself, 'I still think like that'. But there's one point where I was constantly changing my interpretation: the law. I had four successive theories (1988a, 27).

---

[1] The four published theses on Ellul's work (Fasching 1981; Gill 1984b; Clendenin 1987; Lovekin 1991) contain no serious treatment of this part of his work. This omission has recently been partly rectified by an edition of both the Ellul Forum (July 1999, #23) and *Foi et Vie* (April 2000) devoted to issues of law and human rights in the light of Ellul's work. Discussions of Ellul's writing on law can be found in Aultman 1972; Holmes 1975 & 1981; Dengerink 1978:27-30; Lavroff 1983; Henry 1983:402-35. Among unpublished theses Zorn 1971:71-6,161-7; Ray 1973:143-54; Ihara 1975:163-80; Temple 1976:410-5 and Fasching 1978:179-85 treat aspects of Ellul's juridical thought. Important reviews of his book are Guisan 1947; Pascal 1948; Schrey 1952; Orsy 1961; Ehrhardt 1962.

[2] The only major studies of Ellul's legal thought are in German (Schüller 1963:160-256, a Roman Catholic perspective on *Law*) and French (Dujancourt 1989).

As in the previous chapter, we begin with Ellul's sociological (and in this case also historical) reflections on the phenomenon of human law. Faced with his account of a crisis of civilization due to Technique, one obvious response would be to turn to human law as a means of controlling and resolving at least some of the difficulties. Throughout the history of Western civilization, under the influence of both the Judaeo-Christian tradition and that of Roman law, a juridical response has regularly been sought to major social problems. To assess this response it is necessary to understand both what law is and how it works and how it has itself been affected by the wider crisis of civilization.

Turning to Ellul's theological reflections on law, he is well known as a long-standing critic of the Christian tradition of natural law and this proves to one of the (relatively few) constants in his writings on the theology of law. Confirming his reference to 'four successive theories', this chapter outlines four phases in Ellul's theology of law which, through their developments, highlight some of the central issues that Christian theology must address in any account it offers of the nature and task of human law.

Ellul's Sociological Reflections on Law

The most important factor shaping Ellul's non-theological juridical thought is the structure of his sociology outlined in chapter three. His thinking on law derives from his wider analysis of the modern world which, from the 1930s onwards, argued that the dominance and novelty of Technique was creating a wholly new situation that had to be challenged because it was destroying the human person and the central features of civilization.

Alongside this must also be placed the influence of Ellul's legal training and the wider jurisprudential debates of the period. During his studies, Bordeaux University's law faculty was still marked by the thought of its recently deceased *doyen* Léon Duguit (1859-1928).[3] Influenced by Durkheim, Duguit had developed the sociology of law and the school of sociological positivism whose theorists also include Ehrlich, Jèze and Ihering. This school rejected natural law theories but, rather than relating law to the state, emphasised law's relationship to the wider society within which it functioned.[4] It is within this broad school of thought that Ellul developed his own distinctive sociology of law.[5]

---

[3] On Duguit see Duguit 1921; Laski 1921; Markovitch 1933; Du Pasquier 1967:255-6.

[4] On this school see Ehrlich 1936; Brethe de la Gressaye & Laborde-Lacoste 1947; du Pasquier 1967; Paton 1972:19-36; Gurvitch 1973; Dias 1976:Chapter 19; Hunt 1978.

[5] Ellul's own lecture course at Bordeaux entitled *'Philosophie du Droit'* covered matters also discussed in his writing from 1960 onwards. In a personal letter of 3 March 1994 Ellul

In law, as in most areas of his thought, Ellul's sociology shows greater continuity over time than his theology. It is, nevertheless, helpful to distinguish two phases in his sociological reflections on law because a definite shift in focus and certain changes in content occur from 1960.

Ellul's First Phase: 1935-60

From his earliest writings Ellul emphasised the centrality of law within the modern crisis of civilization and the significance of law and legal institutions for the personalist revolution.[6] His first sociological reflections on law reveal his concern that law is becoming increasingly technical and detached from the spontaneous lived reality of human persons and society in which it has its foundation and where it originally developed and thrived. His aim is to give an account of this development and to seek its reversal by re-establishing the place of custom in law.[7]

Ellul argues that law, like religious, ethical, and other social rules, originally arises spontaneously from man's experience of living with others. This living law (*le droit vivant*) thus has its foundation in a social consensus about how to live together.[8]

> Law is born at the same time as human relationships. Law arises with contact between two people for it is made for people. It arises with spontaneity...In effect, it is the expression of a common but often tacit rule because it issues from a common juridical conscience...(*Droit Vivant*, 2).

Law is therefore always originally custom and is fully integrated into human social life from which it spontaneously arises and in tandem with

---

explained to me that 'this was more of a course on the sociology of law than strictly a philosophy course: I have never been a "philosopher" in the technical sense of that term!'.

[6] The majority of the unpublished '*Le Personnalisme, Révolution Immédiate*' deals with the legal institution and Ellul there claims to extend Hauriou's conception (on which see Brethe de la Gressaye & Laborde-Lacoste 1947:360-2; du Pasquier 1967:256-9). Institutions become an important element in Ellul's later theological writings and are discussed in that context below.

[7] The materials drawn on here for ideas prior to the publication of *Law* are (a) the unpublished early personalist article 'For a Living Law (*Pour un droit vivant*)' and (b) 'Law (*Droit*)' (1939a), a paper from the Fédé conference on a Christian university. This was recently republished in *Foi et Vie* (Ellul 2000) and this more easily available version will be cited throughout this chapter.

[8] The phrase 'living law' originates with Ehrlich 1936 (first published in 1912). Basing law on a collective consciousness derives from Duguit and the French sociological school of jurisprudence (Brethe de la Gressaye & Laborde-Lacoste 1947:17-21).

which it naturally develops. As societies grow in size and evolve, social life becomes more complex and differentiation occurs between different social relationships. A transformation inevitably takes place as law 'begins to become aware of itself (*commence à prendre conscience de lui-même*)' (*Droit Vivant*, 5). There then arises juridical technique (*la technique juridique*) involving the elaboration of the rule of law (*la règle de droit*) in jurisprudence and case law. This initiates a process in which a superstructure of law is created on its original foundation in society's common consensus.

Strictly speaking, Ellul claims that law cannot be said to exist until there is this self-conscious technical element differentiating it from other social phenomena. The dialectic between juridical technique and custom therefore becomes central to law's evolution.

> The evolution of law can be presented in terms of a tension between the depth (*le fond*), the popular conscience, and the form (*la forme*), juridical technique. At the beginning, conscience is everything…gradually technique (*la technique*) appears and this is the critical phase of law (2000, 13).

An equilibrium can be achieved between these two opposing elements (Ellul cites Roman law in the second century BC and thirteenth century canon law as examples of this equilibrium which he later calls the period of natural law). However, it is always precarious and constantly under threat from technique's ability to detach law from social reality and systematize it so that it regulates more and more of human life. If this is not checked, law eventually negates itself and becomes a source of conflict and injustice within society.

> A rupture of equilibrium is produced to the benefit of technique that renders law dead and powerless. Hence the adage is true *summum jus, summa injuria* (2000, 14).

Ellul appears to view this pattern of evolution as inevitable unless overcome by a major historical event disrupting law's normal development.

In his personalist writing, Ellul argues that contemporary French law bears all the marks of this corruption of law by technique and he sketches the features of an alternative *droit vivant*. This will necessarily be local law for a small community. It will be flexible (*souplesse*) and, rather than being abstract and thus experienced as a constraint, it will be 'internal and personal to everyone, a force shown sacred respect' (*Droit vivant*, 16). This characterisation leads Ellul to conclude that what is needed is a revival of custom.

The only form of law which perfectly fulfils these demands, is custom (*la coutume*)...Custom fulfils all the conditions of a living law and does so to the exclusion of a technical law...Customary law (*droit coutumier*) absolutely fulfils the characteristics required for law to live without overriding the facts or deforming human life (*Droit vivant*, 17, 26).

Among the advantages of *droit coutumier* is that in its application, which is where law's real value is found (*Droit Vivant*, 22), it is almost impossible for there to be injustice. This is because the judge will be applying custom and 'that custom is a popular law (*un droit populaire*) in which all the people will show an interest' (*Droit Vivant*, 23). Despite his fears about modern society, Ellul insists there is the possibility of re-creating such a living law for French society in the 1930s.

In *Le fondement théologique du droit* (1946) Ellul develops this account into a more detailed theory of the historical evolution of law through three stages (*Law*, 17-36).[9] He argues that, at its origin, law is always religious although there is no clear distinction between law and religion and religious precepts themselves take juridical form. This period gradually disappears as law becomes secular (*se laïcise*) and religion and magic become clearly distinct from moral and juridical rules. The classic example of this laïcisation is the *Lex Duodecim Tabularum* (*Institutions* 2, 284-92). This evolution is aided by the appearance of a power other than the religious power (*un pouvoir d'Etat*) and leads to the crucial period in law's evolution that Ellul calls the phase of natural law (*droit naturel*).

In the period of natural law, law arises as a spontaneous creation of society under the influence of economic, political, and moral factors. It is independent of the religious power but still not created by the state. Although the common will may not yet be consciously directed to the creation of a juridical phenomenon, there is a consciousness of law and adherence to it in a pattern of habit and obedience. At this time, the basic similarity of legal systems becomes even more marked and even when detailed technical rules differ they always refer to the same institutions and juridical realities such as marriage, property, and slavery. Ellul here cites the *Collatio legum Mosaïcarum et Romanarum* which in the second century compared the ancient Hebrew law with contemporary Roman law (29-30).[10]

This 'natural law' is a truly human work in which people spontaneously construct a system of law even though they lack explicit theoretical principles to guide them. The fact that this work has common features across different

---

[9] In this chapter page references in parenthesis in the text are to *Law* where no other book or article is cited.

[10] On this see also 2000, 6; 1974i, 207.

societies witnesses that these unconscious principles are common to all and that a common notion of justice is discernible in all primitive systems of law (35-6, 70-2). Once conscious of this 'natural law' man begins to develop *juridical* theories of natural law in order to account for it. Ellul here draws a sharp distinction between philosophical/theological theories and juridical theories of natural law (20-4). The former (e.g. those of the Stoics, Aquinas, later Thomists, and Calvin) he dismisses as lacking juridical importance. The development of *theories* of natural law is repeated in different times and places in response to the *experience* of natural law and Ellul focuses on the juridical natural law theories of ancient Rome and the Enlightenment (24-6). All such *juridical* natural law theories deal not with a moral ideal but a given legal reality and they do not claim to provide a criterion of justice but rather 'an aggregation of institutions and rules' (26).

This consciousness of the phenomenon of natural law is, however, the beginning of its destruction. Humans are no longer living spontaneously within the law but distinguishing law from lived reality, making it an object of speculation, and attempting to rationalise and organise it. The third stage of law's evolution has now been reached and 'law is about to become a creation of the state' (19). The creation of law (*droit*) is no longer a matter of custom and spontaneity but requires the definition of juridical principles and hierarchies, the co-ordination of different laws (*lois*), and the creation of a juridical technique (*une technique juridique*). Law thus ceases to be the concern of all society and becomes the speciality of jurists. In the immediate post-war period (when Ellul is writing) he sees Europe experiencing this transition which, as the negation of natural law, is marked by five characteristics (31-6).

First, law becomes detached from the norm of justice and reduced to technical rules applied in a logical manner to all areas of life. It is now a form of regulation and control (*réglementation*). By removing justice as the counterweight to juridical technique, the equilibrium of natural law is disrupted resulting in the negation of law (*summum jus, summa injuria*). *Second*, juridical technique, neutral in itself, serves the ends of those with power. *Third*, the state becomes the judge of law and is no longer judged by it. *Fourth*, because there ceases to be a common measure between law and people in society, law ceases to be observed and respected. As a result, it increasingly relies on sanction which is no longer the reaction of society against those who disturb it but the technical decision of the state experienced as an external constraint. There follows an increase in policing and penalties and the elaboration of another, popular law, distinct from that of the state. *Fifth*, there often arises an attempt to revive natural law artificially but this cannot be done as the relation between people and law has, in concrete social reality, been broken.[11]

Ellul believes this evolution is a feature of all developing societies. Furthermore, fitting with his wider analysis of the post-war situation discussed in chapter three, he argues that once the third stage is reached a fundamental personal, social, and civilizational change must occur for law to take a new form.

It is impossible to go backwards and to recapture a new spontaneity of law, as it were, 'behind' such juridical technique. A wilted flower cannot blossom again. But the rosebush on which it grew can bring forth a new flower. Likewise society when it is totally renewed and launches a new civilization, can produce a new body of law…What would be needed is a simultaneous transformation of the inner existence of man, conditioning his adherence to society, as well as of the outside, on the part of the state and of the law. But this would spell the end of a whole phase of civilization (19-20, 35).

Following an article characterising modern law as highly technical and arguing technique can only be effective when rooted in *un droit vivant* (1947a), Ellul's most famous work *La Technique* (1954) provides a more detailed study of law and technique by approaching the question from the perspective of the relationship between justice (*la justice*) and juridical technique (*la technique juridique*). Unfortunately the relevant section of the English translation (*TS*, 291-300 cf. *Technique*, 265-72) translates 'juridique' throughout as 'judicial' rather than 'juridical' and as a result becomes totally incomprehensible when Ellul distinguishes *l'élément judiciaire* from *l'élément juridique* (*TS*, 294 cf. *Technique* 267).[12]

Ellul argues that juridical technique is less certain than other human techniques because the quest for true justice has no fixed, pre-determined, and defined end. Justice therefore cannot be transformed into pure technique. Drawing on his 1939 argument and combining it with the terminology of *Law*, Ellul claims that 'a certain equilibrium is produced between the pursuit of justice and the juridical technique which flourishes in a period of natural law' (*TS*, 292). Juridical technique is, however, a matter of the *creation* and not

---

[11] This final feature is the fundamental juridical reason for Ellul's dismissal of the revival of natural law theory in the post war period (22). It is supplemented by three other features of modern law: the shift from private (*droit privé*) to public law (*droit public*), the fact that law increasingly appears as an historical phenomenon not an abstract norm, and the appearance of numerous new domains of law unknown to natural law theory (9-10).

[12] The translations that follow are therefore modified where necessary although reference is still given to the English translation.

just the *adaptation* of law.

> The great task of juridical technique then is to arrange the elements
> furnished it by the political function in order that the law not be merely a
> verbalism, a dead letter. And this takes a whole arsenal of proofs, civil and
> penal sanctions, guarantees, in short, the whole detailed mechanism created
> to secure the realization of the ends of the law (*TS*, 293).

This juridical technique is directed to the end of popular obedience and
shares with every other technique the central characteristic of an artificial
quest for efficiency. Ellul highlights the effects of this on law. The juridical
and judicial elements become separated. The judicial element becomes a
matter of organisation with the task of applying laws (*les lois*) rather than
seeking justice through the creation of law (*le droit*). This task can become
totally mechanical as it simply requires a good legal technician. The
importance of the juridical element then increases. It becomes more and more
technical and, divorced from concrete problems, it enters the hands of the
state. The norm of justice remains a difficulty for this technique but it ceases
to be a practical demand in the face of individual problems and instead
becomes an abstract idea. Eventually, law ceases to be based on justice but
rather sees its end and foundation in factors more readily reducible to
technique such as order or security.

All of this characterises modern law arising from the flourishing of
juridical technique and modernity's quest for efficiency. Law, once taken over
by the technical mentality, is then invaded by other techniques and comes to
be viewed as nothing more than technical norms, obedience to which is
secured by extra-juridical means. Laws then proliferate due to the merging of
juridical and political techniques and the technician's concern to foresee and
determine every aspect of life by eliminating the human element so vital to
law. Law can no longer be simply principles and general rules with which the
judge creates truly living law and the judge is instead bound by increasingly
complex regulations.

The equilibrium of natural law has now been destroyed and law becomes
simply an instrument of the state and so is really dissolved. This dissolution
leads to confusion between law and the process of administration because
everything the state does becomes a matter of law and the state, in turn, is
freed from control by law.

> The law at present is an affair of the state. The state, whenever it expresses
> itself, makes law. There are no longer any norms to regulate the activity of
> the state…The state is a law unto itself and recognizes no rules but its own
> will. When, in this way, technique breaks off the indispensable dialogue

between the law and the state, it makes the state a god in the most theologically accurate sense of the term: a power which obeys nothing but its own will and submits to no judgment from without (*TS*, 299).

Separated from justice and based on order, law loses its end and specific domain because order is the same as effectiveness (*l'efficacité*). The tragedy is that, in consenting to this, humans renounce one of their highest callings.

This is a much more detailed analysis of juridical technique than in Ellul's earlier work. The overall argument of *TS*, as shown in chapter three, also clearly implies that law's modern technicalisation is qualitatively different when compared with the change that has occurred from natural law to technical law in previous societies. It is, however, not until the 1960s that the unique features of modern law become a focus of study for Ellul. In the years prior to that, his *Institutions* was published and there his rather abstract sociology of law and theory of law's evolution take more concrete form in an historical study tracing the development of legal institutions from antiquity to the nineteenth century. Its breadth makes it, in line with his theory of law, more the history of society through its law than a history of law (*Season*, 185) and its detailed historical research provides the foundation for the second phase of Ellul's sociological reflections on law.

Ellul's Second Phase: 1961-94

The second phase of Ellul's juridical thought originates in his contribution to the 1961 theme edition of *Archives de Philosophie du Droit* on reforming the study of law (1961a). He there implicitly sets a double agenda which he follows over the next thirty years: on the one hand, the need for a properly elaborated theory of law and its function in society and, on the other, an account of the distinctive characteristics of modern law.

The article's stated aim is to discern the conception of law implicit in the teaching reforms. Ellul hopes this may result in an understanding of our society's common judgment regarding law. The fundamental problem is that the reforms amount to the effective dissolution of law. The two related presuppositions that have led to this are the dominance of the category of 'science' and the preoccupation with concrete facts. Law still exists today, but only as a fact and it is therefore no longer truly law.

> The assimilation of law to a pure social fact ruins its authority, its capacity to give form to a society, its continuity, the hold on the future, the legitimacy of contract. In other words we have definitively observed the removal (without any exception) of all the specific characteristics of law (1961a, 9)

The reforms fail to recognise that law is a normative discipline and this failure reflects the evolution of modern law. What is urgently needed, therefore, is a fuller understanding of the development and novelty of 'law' in the modern world *and* an account of the juridical phenomenon as normative that clarifies its specificity and provides a basis for an alternative way of teaching law.

In over a dozen articles between 1962 and his death in 1994 Ellul undertakes this dual task and, because it is more detailed and provides the context for his argument about the non-juridical character of modern law, his sociology of law will be examined first.

ELLUL'S SOCIOLOGY OF LAW[13]

In a number of articles Ellul offers an account of the structure and function of the juridical phenomenon as it appears in society throughout history. Within academic debate between schools of jurisprudence, he describes his work (in the opening sentence of his 1965 contribution to a Festschrift for the Dutch Reformed legal philosopher, Herman Dooyeweerd) as an attempt to overcome what he sees as the sterile opposition between idealist theorists and positivists (1965d, 249). He acknowledges that in this dispute both sides have significant strengths as well as weaknesses. The 'idealists' such as natural law theorists examine law's foundation and rightly insist that its authority and its meaning and significance (*signification*) rest on more than its mere promulgation. However, in seeking an absolute standard for law such thinkers tend to refer to some abstract law and lose sight of law as a sociological phenomenon. As a result, their philosophical reflection does not relate to law in reality and is of little juridical value. In contrast, the 'positivists' correctly assert that only positive law counts as law and that no system or law functioning as the law of a social body should be excluded from reflection upon law. Their problem is that they refuse to see any deeper truth to law or to consider its relation to normative values.[14]

Underlying both approaches Ellul sees two shared presuppositions that his alternative method rejects. There is an abstract vision of law as an isolated phenomenon and also a concept of humanity that denudes people of their

---

[13] Very little of this sociology of law appears in Ellul's books although passing comments reveal his conclusions (e.g. *Violence*, 85; *Hope*, 34-5; *Perspectives*, 51-2; *Conférence*, 58). The fullest discussion appears in his last and untranslated sociological study, *Déviances* (especially pp.159-70). Many of the themes discussed in detail in earlier articles appear there in summary form and Ellul stresses, as in the 1930s, the centrality of law in solving the modern world's problems. Dujancourt 1989:15-57 covers many themes discussed in this section.

[14] 1962b, 36-7; 1965d, 249.

complex reality in order to schematise them and relate them to law. Ellul insists on examining the complex phenomena of humans and law within their social reality, focussing on their inter-relationship.

It seems to me that the problem must be addressed on the level of the relationship between people and the law. But only on the condition that this is not an ideal, theoretical, general law but law such as we see it existing concretely in diverse societies and also on the condition that we do not take an abstract, generic humanity but the individual and social person in all his singularity and complexity…If I am examining a given historical system of law, and the individuals within that society, what is the relationship which exists between them? It seems to me that precisely in the phenomenon of the lived relationship between people and the law there may be a possible way of getting beyond the doctrinal conflict and developing an explanation of law's authority (1965d, 251).

In this context, a central question is the relationship between law and social reality. Law must be directly related to social reality but the nature of its relationship raises two fundamental questions, one of which is basically abandoned by each of the two dominant schools of thought Ellul is trying to transcend.

On the one hand, how can law spring from society, express it, give an account of it? On the other hand, how can it be in touch with social reality so as to structure and inform it? (1962b, 36).

Ellul's project can therefore be viewed as a quest to understand law's specific characteristics and function in society. He undertakes this by means of a study of the relationship between human beings and law in lived experience. By viewing people as both creators of law and subject to law this reveals how law both arises from social reality and, in turn, shapes it.

The final preliminary issue is Ellul's definition of law. Once again he applies methodological principles found in his other sociological studies: 'nominalism' and 'functionalism'. Ellul's nominalist method means accepting as a juridical phenomenon anything which any society designates in juridical terms.[15] He therefore refuses to offer any *a priori* definition in contrast to his earlier writing (2000, 9). He also rejects the categorisation of any functioning legal system as 'non-law' when its content fails to conform to our moral

---

[15] 1973i, 9-11 is the fullest discussion of this method and includes a reference to its application to law. It is first explicitly stated in 1959d, 35 and other explanations are found in *Autopsy*, ix-x; 1971b, 225; 1981e, 70-1.

standards.

This method is, of course, only applicable in societies where the juridical phenomenon is recognised and categorised in juridical terms. Ellul, however, refuses to restrict his study to such societies and therefore applies his functionalist method elsewhere. This means that any social phenomenon with the functions and characteristics found in relation to what is called law in other societies can itself be treated as a society's law even if it is not classed in juridical terms by that society.[16]

Not until 1981 does Ellul make explicit the characteristics and functions which amount to his definition of law:

> I enumerate seven points which appear to me to be constitutive of this phenomenon: (1) a framework (*ensemble*) of organised rules, (2) held to be necessary for the life of the group, (3) more or less internalised, (4) relative to an authority or power organised by these rules, (5) ruling certain areas (more or less extensive) of social relationships (family, exchange, property etc), (6) supplied with some level of sanctions, and (7) finally expressing values in which the group believes, to which it is attached, and in which it recognises itself. When these seven traits are combined, I declare that there is law (1981e, 70-1).

Ellul's sociology of law can now be examined in relation to law's *creation and evolution*, its *applicability*, and its *specificity*.

Law's Creation and Evolution

Ellul's study of the historical lived relationship between man-in-society and law led him to three fundamental conclusions. *First*, law is an *artificial human creation* and not something given to humans in nature (1963d and 1965e). It is therefore another human tool or technique (1973a, 78). *Second*, law is a *universal human phenomenon*, found in some form in every human group and society in history (1981e, 71). *Third*, law is always *normative* – 'every time that humans have created or discerned rules which have been called 'Law' it is a matter of a normative activity' (1963d, 21). These three observations lie at the heart of his theory of law's creation and evolution.

The universal existence of a human artefact such as law must be based on universal human experiences and Ellul claims that the only such experiences are those of time, space, and relationships. These are not stable phenomena bringing comfort to human beings but ones in which we meet incoherence, disorder, and threats. Law is therefore the human attempt to master and order

---

[16] 1973i, 11-13 is Ellul's fullest discussion of this method in relation to law. It is applied in relation to sacred, myth and religion at *Demons*, 46-7.

them and bring them under control.[17]

In their experience of *time*, people are faced with constant change, perpetually altering relationships, and an uncertain future. Law enables them to create stability through an artifice that makes time stand still and so grants a hold on the future. By defining and fixing certain situations law ensures that human life does not become pure process. Similarly, in relation to *space*, law enables people to demarcate an area of their hostile natural milieu within which they are relatively secure and in control rather than being subject to unknown forces. Finally, people's *relationships with each other* are inherently uncertain, frequently changing, and potentially dangerous. Law again acts as a means of protection, formalisation, and stabilisation as it organises human relations.

The juridical phenomenon is therefore humanity's attempt to bring order and stability into communal life. Its goal is the creation of a new environment in which human beings can live in relative social peace and stability. Thus Ellul writes that, 'it seems to me that in reality law is made in order to establish a *liveable* situation in the midst of conflict and disorder' (1965e, 205). Although law can be made to serve additional ends, the great variety of often mutually contradictory laws and legal systems share this common foundational and universal goal of maintaining human life in society. It can therefore be said that at the heart of the creation of law lies the attempt by humans to establish their own order in the world and thus to escape the alienation experienced within their natural and social milieu (1975a, 198-9).

Law's normativity is therefore partly explicable by the fact that from its origin law has been a *sine qua non* for human attempts to escape alienation and organise their own social world. This theoretical account of law's origins is, however, insufficient to ground law's normativity. Ellul's method also demands an account rooted in law's role throughout history.

Historically, law has a specific role because of three elements within the intention of those who create it: a distancing from reality which involves a refusal to accept it as it is, an attempt to manage and develop (*aménager*) the social milieu, and the proposal of a model for human relationships (1973a, 77-80). Underlying these three goals are a society's values. This decision to relate human law to human values rather than simply to justice is one of the major changes in this second phase of writing compared to his earlier work where although the theme of values appears it is not prominent.[18]

---

[17] 1971b, 225-8 summarising the argument of 1963d & 1965e which reappears in detail in 1981e, 72-9.

[18] Cf. Dujancourt 1989:40-2. The fullest discussions of values and law are 1961a, 16-8; 1965d, 253-5; 1965b; 1973i, 17ff; 1975a, 200ff. In earlier writing see 1947a, 488; 1947d, 109ff.

In addressing the question of values, Ellul distances himself from those who insist there must be some fixed, absolute value or values. He argues that such metaphysical concerns are irrelevant within a realist historical approach to law that concerns itself with what any particular human group values. Historical experience shows values are a human creation, variable across time and space and it is this artificial character that gives them their significance.

> They are values because created by man. If we take man seriously, if we consider him as a subject who expresses himself in history, then we have to take his works with a decisive seriousness and, above all, the whys of his works, that which expresses at the same time the model, not yet realized of what he wishes to be, and the imperative in relation to which he judges himself. That is what I term a value. It is this phenomenon of projection of his absolute model and of his self-critical capacity that seems to me justly the admirable element in values...(1965b, 56-7).[19]

Values therefore shape people's representation of what they as a person wish to be and what any society wishes to be. These values are projected into law when the creator of law accomplishes the three elements of his juridical intention outlined above and this projection is crucial for law's normativity. It is also inevitably risky because for the law to function properly its creator must express not his own values but those found within the social body as a whole and those values within the whole which the social body wishes to be given juridical form (1973i, 19). The values of any particular society are therefore an integral part of its juridical system and it is the variability of values and yet their essential normativity and universality as a phenomenon that explains why, despite being a human artifice, law is always normative.

> It is in the measure in which law is representation of value that it can play its normative role in the most profound sense (1965b, 64).

> Law is never normative in itself but exclusively through its reference to values accepted in the social group (1973i, 17).

In order to complete the account of law's creation and evolution, consideration must finally be given to society's history and the present reality of social relationships. Here law is created to act as a mediating structure.[20] Arising from a number of socio-cultural factors, law is not a simple reflection

---

[19] On values see also *TWTD*, chapter eight.

[20] On this feature see 1973i, 28ff which also characterises law's task vis-à-vis values as one of mediation between social reality and meta-social project.

of these factors but a synthesis of them and mediator between them. By incorporating diverse and conflicting factors within itself law offers a means of conciliation to prevent the social disintegration and *anomie* that occurs when different groups assert their independence. In addition to this generic mediation between the components of every social body, law must also recognise the specific tensions and contradictions which, in a particular society at a given time, threaten a community's social life. It must then perform a mediating function between these which allows a viable compromise to be reached.

Areas of conflict and contradiction within a social body inevitably change as society evolves and law must adapt to these changes. This raises the wider problem of law's evolution and its relationship to social change. Here the difficulty lies in the fact that part of law's rationale requires it to ignore change in order to provide a stable, ordered structure for people and a hold on the future. However, it cannot so detach itself from reality that it denies social change and refuses its own evolution. Were it to do this it would cease to be able to fulfil its functions as law (1971b). Law must, therefore, provide a means of coming to terms in a controlled manner with the inescapable reality of social evolution and yet it must do this without becoming subservient to that evolution and so ceasing to be normative. This balancing-act is achieved by means of legal procedure (*la procédure*) through which law includes within itself established juridical processes by which it can be altered.

Procedure is the most decisive part of law because it is the system by which one claims to know in advance how to make changes to the situations and structures in which law has formalized reality. When a legal system does not foresee the procedures of its own transformation then it brings about a debacle having struggled in order to remain the same despite the facts and this is a social disaster (1971b, 228).

Such procedural processes enable law to evolve in an orderly fashion in response to social change but they are not the only means by which juridical changes occur. This is clear from the difficulties faced by attempts to explain the history of law and legal institutions (1973a). In addition to logical evolution by procedural means there will also be changes in any legal system that are wrought by social crises through which it becomes clear that law has become too detached from changing social reality. These crises, usually focussed in an unexpected and disruptive *événement*, put existing law into question. They result in a radical revision, almost a re-creation, of the juridical institution in which law is re-founded in relation to present social reality.

The event (*l'événement*) is for me...the intervention of the unexpected, the wholly other (*tout autre*) – that which requires a departure from the normal foreseen evolution, which demands a change of a way of life, a social system, a scale of values. It can be an obstacle or challenge which leads to an awareness (*prise de conscience*) of something one did not previously know. The event is always more or less the appearance of an unforeseen mirror in which one discovers one's true face (1969d, 7n1).

In relation to law's creation and evolution, therefore, Ellul views law as an artificial human creation originating in an attempt to counter the uncertainty and alienation people experience vis-à-vis time, space, and relationships with others. Law is created in order to provide a mediating structure in society which enables people to live together and to give an expression to a society's values which imposes on it a certain orientation. Although law seeks to provide an element of constancy within ever-changing social reality, it must recognise the need for self-adaptation and so it establishes procedures by which it can be changed. Despite this, its very nature will lead it to become distant from social reality and, when this happens, a major social crisis can occur which revitalises the creative juridical function and produces a new system of law, better adapted to society.

Law's Applicability

Humans create law intending it to be normative but this is not sufficient to ensure that law modifies people and their social reality. If law is to *function* as normative then it must be applicable. It is only when people, as subject to law, accept and apply the created law that law can fulfil its purpose and be truly normative.

> Law is not just an abstract science or a theory that remains true even if not applied. Law has meaning only in application or at least in applicability. A law that is not applicable is not law (1973i, 18).

The central question is therefore why this human creation is accepted as normative and applied within a social body. Law's applicability clearly does not depend upon the law in itself as laws can be applied in one society and not others. Furthermore, what we consider an unjust law may well prove applicable while a just law remain inapplicable. This question of the applicability of law can therefore only be properly addressed within the wider framework of the global relation between people-in-society and that society's law.

In thinking about non-application of law, two forms of this phenomenon must be distinguished. Every society and juridical system must deal with individual acts of disobedience and a minority of 'outlaws' who consider themselves outside the legal system. Although it could be said that the law is not applied here, this non-application is in a limited and accidental sense and does not render the law as such inapplicable. This is qualitatively different from when society as a whole rejects a juridical system and the average person no longer recognises the law as authoritative. This latter sense of inapplicability is the significant one because the law is not primarily made for the criminal but to provide the order for society as a whole.

This distinction within non-application explains Ellul's refusal to give legal sanctions a central place in his account of law. Historical experience shows that laws with harsh sanctions can remain unapplied by society whereas those without sanction may be applied. Personal experience of obeying the law confirms this as most people do not normally obey the law simply because of its sanctions.

> We know that it is not because of the existence of a sanction that we most frequently obey a law, or more precisely, we know that we apply it without asking ourselves a question as to the sanction, in an entirely spontaneous way as if it was self-evidently right to do so. It is not the threat of punishment which makes us respect the law…'Normal' man lives by a kind of spontaneous adaptation to the legal system (1965b, 55).

In contrast to some of his earlier writing, Ellul now minimises the importance of sanctions.[21] Indeed, by 1979, in an important change of perspective, he not only rejects the traditional view that sanctions distinguish law from morality, but goes so far as to argue that sanctions are strictly outside law and the recourse to them represents law's failure and an act of violence by political power.[22]

Ellul argues that the acceptance of law and its applicability in society are only explicable by a theory of law-as-representation and an account of the relationship of this law-as-represented to society's values. The truth is that the ordinary citizen is largely ignorant of law's complex reality and what is important is that which the average person sees and understands of the law, the vision he has of it, 'the representation which he himself makes of this law' (1965d, 255). It is this popular representation that determines whether the law that man has created becomes living law (*droit vivant*), generally accepted and applicable to society as a whole.

I am not speaking here of the theoretical or doctrinal reactions that wider

---

[21] The change in Ellul's approach to sanctions can be seen by comparing 2000, 9 & 19 and *Law*, 27-8, 92, 125ff with 1961a, 7; 1962b, 57 and 1973i, 22.

[22] 1979b, 63-5 in opposition to *Law*, 125f. Dujancourt 1989:15-20 notes this change.

opinion can have, generally the result of propaganda, on this or that point of law…It is a much more global and deeper phenomenon of the vision that a people has of its law and which conditions its agreement or opposition…A matter of an adopting (*'reprise'*) of the law as its own. This is the fundamental question: can the people accomplish that adoption and consider the law as their own?…Much is said about 'living law'…What makes the law living is this act of adoption by the people (1965d, 255).

This acceptance of the law is so crucial in fulfilling law's purposes that Ellul (standing firmly in the tradition of Ehrlich, Duguit and the school of sociological positivism) argues that it is this law as subjectively represented by people-in-society and not the objective written law which should be considered the true law. This explains why, historically, reforms of the law to make it acceptable to society can fail because the popular vision of the law remains unchanged by objective reforms as seen, for example, in Louis XIV's reforms after 1775 (see *Institutions* 4, 250-62).

It is at the level of representations that the law can finally influence the course of society…I am not wanting to say that here there are two realities or two stages: the object which is the law and then a more or less inaccurate representation in the people's idea of the law. I want to say that *it is that representation which is the law*…It is the representation that people have of a juridical system that is the true law and it is at this level that we must situate ourselves in order to understand a juridical problem (1965d, 256, italics original).

Law's applicability depends, therefore, on the common representation of law. More specifically, it depends on the values perceived in this law-as-represented. Law is applicable in society when it is itself viewed as a value and this occurs when it is seen to have assumed, and so to represent, society's values (1973i, 18). Although law cannot itself realise the values it has assumed, it can offer society the possibility of achieving the realisation of its values by proposing these values as an objective. The individual then thinks, 'If I obey this legal rule which expresses a value which I recognise as mine, then I create a situation of justice or of order or of peace' (1965b, 64). If, in contrast, the citizen does not accept the values that the law-as-represented presents to him, he will cease to adhere to the law and if this attitude becomes widespread, the law will become increasingly inapplicable as we see today in relation to many young people (*Déviances*, 87-9).

The decisive factor in law's applicability is therefore people's representation of the law and its values. This representation is most influenced by personal contact with the law. The most important element in law is therefore juridical procedure in its widest sense, incorporating not only judicial procedures but also police, administrative, and legislative procedures (1965d, 257). Here people gain a perception of their society's law and decide if they wish to appropriate it and live it as their own. An experience of law as something abstract and specialist which excludes participation, or a perception that juridical procedures (either in their form or their results) fail to conform to the values expected, will result in a negative representation of the law and undermine its applicability.

In conclusion, Ellul argues that for law to be applicable and to direct society it is necessary that the society as a whole has a positive representation of its law. This will be gained primarily through the experience of juridical procedures and is focussed on law's values. It can lead citizens to appropriate the law as their own and to believe that through adherence to it their values will be realizable. When this process does not occur, law will become increasingly inapplicable and so will cease to fulfil its social function.

Law's Specificity and the Threat to Law: Centrality of Values & Procedure
These sociological reflections on law were, it must be recalled, initiated by Ellul's impression that law as a distinct, specific entity was dissolving in the contemporary Western world and it is now therefore necessary to show what Ellul believes to be unique about the juridical phenomenon.

As an artificial human creation law appears similar to other techniques (1973i, 8). It must, therefore, be differentiated from them if it is to retain its specific identity and vocation. Its distinctiveness lies in its constant claim to be normative and its acceptance as such by those in society. This has been shown to be based on its relation to a society's values which distinguishes law from organisation, administration and all other human techniques. It means that when law is reduced to being only juridical technique it ceases to be law.

Law, by the fact that it cannot be dissociated from the values in relation to which it is elaborated, distinguishes itself from all methods and techniques which have nothing to do with values. It seems to me to be essential to recall that, as a result of that unity of the juridical phenomenon, there is no dissociation in law between ends and means. Law is not a technical apparatus which allows the attainment of a certain number of ends which are external to it...Law is never only a juridical technique or rather it is when it is reduced to that it cease to be law (1973i, 21).

Ellul is aware that by speaking of law ceasing to be law and of modern law as 'non-law' he appears to be contradicting his 'nominalist' method, but he insists such a conclusion must be drawn and that it does not deny his basic methodology. It does not do so, he argues, because this conclusion is not his own individual judgment but that of the social body. This can be seen historically because whenever law is reduced to juridical technique it is no longer respected and lived as law (1973i, 21).

Law's specificity cannot, however, be reduced to its assumption of values or else it would be indistinguishable from morality. Its technical aspect must therefore also be included in its defining features:

> The law appears as a complex (*un ensemble*) of procedures destined to realize values. It is therefore characterized by the choice and elaboration of ways and means to bring values to a certain degree of effectiveness (*efficacité*). Law is effectively what establishes a simultaneous relationship between people's values and their conduct and creates the milieu in which these values can be realized. The law is like the bridge or the intermediary between the two (1973i, 22).

Law therefore goes further than morality or casuistry by laying down commonly accepted procedures to obtain the desired result and so 'it is procedure which seems to me to be the essential fact of law which defines the juridical nature of a situation' (1973i, 23-4). It is *la procédure* that enables law to be a means of mediation. It also guides and structures change by establishing agreed processes, protects individuals (for without procedures the recognition of a subjective right is meaningless), and co-ordinates diverse rights and juridical organs. The establishment of procedure is therefore what takes society beyond mere vengeance into the realm of law.[23]

> The specific role of law appears to me to be the imposition of delays, procedures and mediation. That the victim does not take revenge immediately, themselves, by pure violence, but after a certain delay, through somebody acting as intermediary (an arbiter, a third party, a tribunal etc.) and according to established forms is the very simple but crucial example from which one must assess the whole of the rest of the juridical world (1979b, 74).

Although this procedure is part of juridical technique it also cannot be pure technique because it must itself be measured by the values law assumes. When this ceases to be case (e.g. when the police are driven solely by the quest for effectiveness and efficiency), a negative representation of law is inevitably created and true law begins to dissolve.

Procedure, as the feature distinguishing law and the means by which law is

---

[23] In the immediate post-war period when Ellul critiqued the Nuremberg Trials (1947d, 104-5) he claimed that vengeance was the situation that is primary in all law.

put into play in society, is therefore the critical point of law. It follows that 'if procedure does not fulfil its role, all the law fails' (1973i, 25). Procedure may bring about law's failure in numerous ways and to avoid this it must walk a narrow tightrope. Law will fail if procedure, on the one hand, fails to provide juridical means for the realisation of some of society's central values or if, on the other hand, procedures seek to achieve too much by juridical means. Procedure may be so complex that the average person is incapable of gaining a positive representation of the law or it may produce decisions that are not consonant with society's values and so yield a negative representation. Finally, procedure may produce a law that adapts so readily to social reality that it ceases to be normative or, in contrast, it may result in a fixed law that ceases to evolve with society.[24]

In conclusion, Ellul is insistent that law is a unique phenomenon and that its specific features can be defined.

Law is specifically identified in relation to all other human enterprises by the fact that it assumes a certain number of the group's values, formalizes them (among other ways by means of norms) and supplies them with means which render them operational and effective in social control (1973i, 27-8).

Ellul is also aware that, because it seeks to integrate values and technique, law is an inherently precarious creation and that its distinctive characteristics are constantly threatened with the consequent danger that law will lose its specific identity, have its functions undermined, and witness its purposes fail. The other strand of Ellul's sociological writing on law in this period examines how such a dissolution of law has occurred in the modern world so dominated by Technique.

ELLUL'S ANALYSIS OF LAW IN THE MODERN WORLD

Ellul's early writing made clear that modern law had entered the period of technical law but his account of this remained largely theoretical and included little to suggest that the present was any different from law's technicalisation in earlier historical periods. Only from 1960 does Ellul draw on this earlier work, on his developing sociology of law, and on his reflection upon the contemporary French context, in order to present a more radical and concrete analysis of the transformation and dissolution of law in the modern world.[25]

---

[24] For discussion of these dangers see 1965b, 55; 1965d, 257-8; 1971b, 228; 1973i, 25-7.

[25] 1961a acknowledges his study arises out of the French experience but he justifies generalisation at 1963a, 3-5. The validity of Ellul's analysis for Britain in the early 1990s is vividly shown by the accounts in Booker 1994 and many of the issues were also central to the Scott Inquiry (Norton-Taylor 1995). Dujancourt's treatment of this central theme,

This analysis can be examined by a four-stage approach to the problem: an account of the *symptoms* and the *causes*, followed by a full *diagnosis* and the proposed *cures*.

Symptoms: The Characteristics of Modern Law

Ellul's fullest account of modern law appears in his January 1963 contribution to the 'Futuribles' series entitled 'Le Droit occidental en 1970 à partir de l'expérience française' ('Western law in 1970 from the viewpoint of the French experience'). This article and other discussion in his writings from 1961 onwards show four central, inter-related features dominating his perception of contemporary law.[26]

First, modern law is non-normative. It is rendered thus by two related characteristics of our world.[27] On the one hand, the exaltation of fact and science and the belief in historical progress (*Critique*, 28-37, 202-6) leads modern man to insist that the law must always be altered in the face of changing circumstances. This results in law ceasing to provide a norm by which people can shape their environment and assure themselves of a hold on the future. On the other hand, a desire for objectivity and a rejection of idealism has led to law detaching itself from society's values and it therefore no longer seeks to formulate a common objective for society to attain. However, as we have seen, law's relation to values is the factor that creates its normativity, specifically defines it, and renders it applicable. Law has therefore fundamentally changed and its application becomes increasingly dependent not on its relationship to a society's values but on sanctions applied by the state (1962b, 57).

Second, the state takes over law. This is what Ellul calls *l'étatisation du droit*. In the modern world there is increasingly no law apart from that created by a decision of the political power. This is evident in a variety of developments. Case law (even increasingly in England with its strong common law tradition) has less and less independent value. The judiciary are increasingly integrated into the functions of political power and the scope for a judge's personal evaluation is diminished by the production of detailed rules which can be applied automatically and are meant to eliminate any arbitrariness or subjectivity in passing judgment. In contrast to previous historical eras, custom is no longer a living and creative source of law within society and the private rules of associations, unions, and other social bodies are increasingly rendered valueless unless they are recognised by the public

---

which most closely relates Ellul's juridical thought to his wider sociology, is relatively brief (Dujancourt 1989:46-9).

[26] All that follows appears in 1963a so only further discussions in other articles are cited.
[27] 1961a, 5-10, 14-7.

powers and enter state law. This situation is now so well established that citizens find it hard to conceive any alternative to state-created law reliant on state sanction for its authority. (1962b, 57)

Due to this state takeover, the law ceases to be an effective means of controlling and limiting the state and protecting the citizen from state power.[28] The state can now alter the law in order to act as it wishes, even in some contexts establishing a special system of law (*droit d'exception*) granting it extra powers when it considers some crisis or state of emergency renders this necessary (1965e, 203-7). The law under state control and detached from wider society is also now forced to undergo constant change as political control of the state alters and a new set of politicians repeal the laws of the previous government and introduce their own politically motivated legislation. This denies law's permanence and renders it impossible for a positive representation of the law to be made by society as a whole (1965d, 259).

Third, there is an enormous proliferation of laws. This is due in part to the state's control of law but is also the result of a highly juridicised society which demands the legal establishment of all individual rights (*Métamorphose*, 77ff). In the contemporary world we see law being applied in increasing detail to more and more areas of life (1981p, 122-6).[29] This in turn results in the lack of any coherent set of principles underlying the law as a whole and the negation of traditional juridical principles such as the refusal of retrospective legislation (1947d).

The desire to ensure law's proper implementation across society also entails the production of a mass of legal texts that guide the application of more general laws. These, however, are often secret and may even undermine the intention of the primary legislation. The net effect of these developments is that the law becomes internally incoherent and incomprehensible to everyone except the legal expert and as a result the average citizen then absents himself from juridical life (perhaps turning to violence,[30] 1969d, 13-18) or else only uses the law for his own profit (1965d, 258-60).

Fourth, law can no longer follow its traditional paths of evolution as its internal mechanisms for change no longer function. This is because, detached from values and lacking normativity, the sole criterion by which law is judged is whether or not it is in sufficient conformity with social facts to be

---

[28] This analysis was confirmed by Ellul's subsequent personal experiences in relation to Aquitaine development (1981p, 135ff).

[29] Ellul notes that French health & safety laws cover 11,500 pages and university rules need 8,000 pages (1981f, 86). He contrasts this with the limited Roman law (1984c, 57-60).

[30] Ellul found recourse to violence happening in relation to Aquitaine development (1980s).

222 Living the Word, Resisting the World

applicable. As long as this is the case, the law will remain and as soon as it ceases to be the case, it will be replaced. There is, therefore, no longer any gradual adaptation of law or detachment of law from social change (1961a). The more radical path of change to the law provoked by social crisis also appears redundant. The state's dominance of law and legal institutions and the evacuation of values from the juridical realm now makes it impossible to initiate the constructive dialectic of institution and event (*l'institution* and *l'événement*) which is necessary for any genuine renewal of law (1969d).

In the light of these four characteristics of modern law Ellul draws two general conclusions that constitute a preliminary diagnosis. In the first place, law in the modern world is undergoing a major crisis. It is incoherent and powerless, bankrupt, devalued in the eyes of the general public, and no longer taken seriously.[31] Our present juridical system is 'paralysed, hardened, powerless and redundant' (1979b, 74). Indeed, the situation is now so serious that a second and even more radical conclusion must be drawn: what we still refer to as 'law' is really ceasing to be law as law has existed throughout western civilization.

> The law is in the process of becoming totally different (*tout autre chose*) to that which, in all Western society, has been called 'Law' since the Romans...(1963a, 11).[32]

Before examining how Ellul develops this conclusion, the three main causes that have produced these new characteristics and led to the transformation of law need to be delineated.

Causes: The Sources of Law's Transformation
Ellul's account of the origin of the juridical phenomenon described it is a means by which humans gain control and establish their own order in relation to time, space, and human relationships. Law can therefore be viewed as similar to other techniques. The present crisis is partly due to the fact that the ends that human beings originally sought to establish through law have now been more securely achieved by other techniques.

> The societies in which we are living have succeeded in taking possession of nature...Humans no longer need to delimit a space where their own order rules...Similarly in our society, the experience of time is no longer that of radical uncertainty...Here again, we see that law is no longer the privileged

---

[31] For these judgments on contemporary law see 1962b, 37; 1963a, 10-11; 1963d, 32.
[32] The novelty of this situation also noted in 1961a, 9; 1963d, 32; 1969d, 13,18-19; 1973i, 8.

means for laying hold of time but that this function is now replaced by organization. In fact, what humans attempted to accomplish in a partially illusory manner by means of the law, they now obtain effectively by diverse techniques (1965e, 200).

In this situation, people must realise that their changing milieu demands a transformation of law so that it still protects them against that which most threatens them. This is no longer nature but *la société technicienne*. Unless this problem is addressed, law is condemned to disappear (1965e, 200-3).

However, the distinctive characteristics of Technique in the modern world make any attempt to re-establish law even more difficult. Law was traditionally differentiated from other techniques by its reference to values but Technique has now become autonomous and itself the supreme value to modern man. Technique therefore steadily erodes traditional values rather than being controlled or limited by them (*TWTD*, chapter eleven). As a result, the modern world's evolution leads to the exaltation of law's technical element and its assimilation to that which now most threatens it and humanity.

This dominance of Technique is related to two other causes of the present juridical crisis: our modern conceptions of society and the state. As a result of technical developments, society has come to be viewed as a whole, all the diverse parts of which are rigorously inter-linked. The spontaneous solidarity of the social body through the actions of individuals and groups within it is therefore no longer acceptable because it cannot provide a coherent organisation of the whole. Traditional non-juridical means of social control are also declining in modern society (1963a, 21). However, some form of rationalised, systematised solidarity is deemed necessary because 'the activity of the social body must be all the more exact, precise and rigorous in response to the technical activities within society' (1963a, 13). The most obvious instrument to achieve this end is law.

The social body is not rational by itself but it is necessary to make it rational. It is not spontaneously organized in a coherent fashion and so it is necessary to impose that coherence on it...Law, in this perspective, becomes precisely the agent of that coherence, that rationalization, that rigour (1963a, 13-14).

This new conception of society leads, in turn, to a new vision of the state. Society now requires a single head which can express its rationality and direct the whole. The state is that head and it must therefore be given the task of law's elaboration in order to render society organised and coherent. A theoretical basis is given for this development in the belief that the state is based on the sovereignty of the people, thus establishing continuity between the social body and the state. The people, by granting their sovereignty to the state, effectively lose it. In relation to law, this means the cessation of the spontaneous popular creation of law (as in *droit coutumier*) because the state is now authorised to determine the law.

> The establishment of continuity between the State and the people leads to the negation of the people's power to question (*contester*) the law. Those authors who have constructed the theory *of law* in which law is nothing more and nothing other than the will of the State have correctly expressed (without generally acknowledging the fact) the counterpart of the theory of *the State* founded on popular sovereignty (1963a, 12).

Ellul acknowledges other causes of the changes in law but these three causes - the dominance and autonomy of Technique and changing conceptions of society and the State - are the most important. Their permanence is a sign that the crisis is not temporary but a fundamental and seemingly irreversible mutation in the juridical phenomenon.

Diagnosis: Modern Law as Administration and Regulation
Combining these analyses of symptoms and causes, Ellul's conclusion is that law in modern technical society has ceased to be law and become the means of state administration and regulation. This diagnosis runs as a constant refrain throughout his articles.

> The law becomes an instrument of social intervention and control, without reference to any value (1963a, 11).

> The radical crisis of law in our time is the transformation of law into an organizing power of regulation (1969d, 13).

> Modern law no longer plays its role: we have now arrived at something else, organization (1971b, 233).

> We are no longer faced in our modern societies with law but with pure regulation (which is something totally different) and a mechanism of linear organization (whereas all law is always dialectical)... (1981e, 79).

> There has been de-legalisation to the extent that what is produced are no longer laws but regulation. It is extraordinary when one compares the *code civil* with what we make now. There is nothing in common (*il n'y a aucune commune mesure*) (1984c, 61).

Modern law's objective is now to control technical actions with as much exactitude as possible and it therefore relates solely to facts and not to values. It takes the form of controls and regulations that seek to constrain human activity into the coherent, rational form necessary for the smooth functioning of technical society. When this combines with the will of the modern state to control everything and the fact that every technical activity (even the most private) now has a universal character, all action must be regulated and rules formulated in advance for all possible actions. This yields the proliferation of detailed laws devoid of legal principles whose goal is the *encadrement* of the masses. (1984c, 61). These laws are created by a bureaucratic state and the law itself takes on the character of bureaucracy and administration so the national plan and the administrative circular are the paradigm of modern law (1973i, 9).

Although rarely explicit, Ellul sees this transformation as central to the crisis of civilization the modern world is suffering and which he resisted from the 1930s. True law is a pre-requisite for civilization.[33] In contrast, organisation and regulation, which contain no reference to values and seek to control and bring uniformity to all areas of individual and social life, are absolutely destructive of civilization. Ellul himself therefore acknowledges the inescapable corollaries of his diagnosis.

> The juridical institution is a factor (and I think an indispensable element) in the creation of all civilization. Until we find proof to the contrary a civilization can only build itself up with and through a law (1969d, 19).

> This is for me the end of all that we have considered as civilization. I am not speaking only of Mediterranean civilization because you discover the same concepts among the Aztecs, the Incas, the Indo-Europeans, the Indians etc...(1981f, 96).

Cure ?: Actions Necessary for Law's Renewal

Modern law is in crisis and it can no longer evolve and renew itself in the manner in which law has historically undergone change. The juridical system has therefore reached an impasse (1969d, 19). In an attempt to unblock it, Ellul directs his challenge at the state's dominance over law and at the jurist's impotence.

The state's monopoly over law and law's resulting politicisation is a central cause of the crisis. This cannot be rectified by redistributing power within the present institutional structures. Instead, the whole ideology of the state's

---

[33] The link between law and civilization in Ellul's thought is clear from comparing the definitions of law at 1973i, 22 and of civilization at 1967d, 9.

subordination to law (*l'Etat de droit*) must be challenged and a new and radical separation of powers instituted (1981p, 135-7).

The formulation and application of law (the traditional tasks of the legislature and judiciary respectively) must now be totally separated from the political and administrative realm of the executive whose task should involve no juridical function (1965e, 202-3). The legislature, having been detached in this manner from the state power, must not then be re-integrated through the medium of political life.

> The creators of the law must be designated other than by partisan elections founded on political groupings. That is where the evil is to be found – the confusion between 'political parties – chamber representing these parties – production of law'. With this confusion we arrive at our current situation where it is finally the State and the political power which make the law for themselves. This will, evidently, be the law which they need and a law they will change to fit with their action. That is exactly the opposite of law (1981p, 137).

The judiciary (*la magistrature*) must also be constituted as a fully autonomous body outside of political or state control. This requires that there be no politician or government ministry at its head and no political interference in such matters as recruitment and promotion.

> The second condition…is the total independence of the judiciary and diverse types of jurisdiction…In other words, a true power which has its own head, is self-directed (*autocéphale, autogéré*) and financially independent, able to judge without interference, and capable of ruling against the administration and condemning it without any compromise (1981p, 137).

Ultimately, however, law's revitalisation depends on jurists recognising *their* function is to be the creators of law for society and not mere technicians who apply it.[34]

> The third condition…is that jurists rediscover the meaning and the value of their function. That is to say, they must cease to be pure technicians of law…in order to understand that they are the only creators of law. There is creation of law not when parliament votes for a piece of legislation or the Council of Ministers issue a decree but when each person performs a

---

[34] This is of course Ellul's experience during the Resistance, cited in chapter one and described at *Anarchy*, 18.

juridical act, when each jurist, notary, magistrate passes judgment and writes up a report: that practice of law is able to be effective and creative of the law's foundation. It was effectively such for centuries (*le droit coutumier*) and it simply needs a little courage to become such again (1981p, 137-8).

The jurist alone can fulfil this task because she stands at the crossroads between juridical technique and the citizen. It is the jurist who, through listening to the person in the street, can gain a sense of the common representation of the law, diagnose the problems, and apply her technical ability to reforming the system (1965d, 260-1). It is the jurist who, if properly trained in the philosophy of law, will be able (much better than any politician) to recognise society's values and give them the necessary juridical form (1961a, 16-7). It is the jurist who can adapt legal procedures to create a positive representation of the law so that the people feel involved in an accessible law that serves them (1965e, 202). Only by such means can the present crisis of law be overcome and law, once again, become a living law fulfilling its functions within society.

Conclusion

This section has examined Ellul's non-theological reflections on law in two phases although the differences between these relate more to their focus than to either their substantive content or method. The second period contains no explicit reference to the theory of law's evolution that was so central in his earlier writing but neither is that theory rejected. Indeed, it could be argued that Ellul's sociology of law examines the historical phenomenon of natural law while the study and critique of modern law evidently extends his earlier accounts of technical law.

The two significant changes in the later work relate to the accounts of law and technique and law's relation to justice. Ellul now classes law as, from its origin, equivalent to a technique and includes juridical technique in the form of procedure as a defining element of law. This contrasts with his earlier writing where technique's relation to law was seen in a more negative or ambivalent light. In addition, Ellul's initial writing consistently related law to justice whereas from the mid 1960s he views this connection as an historical accident and prefers to relate a society's law to its values more widely.

Despite these differences, essential continuity remains across the half-century of writing from the 1930s. As with his other sociological studies, Ellul attempts to understand the historical and contemporary reality of law in the light of history and what he perceives as a major crisis in Western civilization. On concluding that we now face a unique crisis in law, he presents a critique of its distinctive modern characteristics, and calls for its fundamental transformation. In particular, he consistently warns against law's technicalisation and subordination to the state and politics and, by developing the insights of the sociological positivists, he elaborates what could be described as a novel 'anarchistic' theory of law. This explains how law is properly the creation of society apart from the state and politics and it provides the basis for his revolutionary call for the contemporary re-creation of a living law (*un droit vivant*). Rooted in custom (*droit coutumier*), this living law will arise from the life of society as a whole, will effectively limit the state, and so allow law to fulfil its historic social functions once again.

Ellul's Theological Reflections on Law

Ellul's writing on the theology of law is marked by two constant emphases that arise from the basic structure of his theology. These are the intrinsic incommensurability of God's justice and human justice once communion with God is lost, and a legal positivism derived from his theological rejection of any higher structure of natural or divine law which could mediate (and thus enable some form of communion) between God and the world of human law. The attempt to construct a theology of law on this basis underlies Ellul's constantly changing interpretation.

By focussing on human law's theological foundation and on the juridical status of the Old Testament Law, four separate phases in Ellul's theological reflections can be distinguished. The first founds human law in conscience and the Torah interpreted as a system of law. The second presents a Christological foundation of law and refuses to accept that the Old Testament Law is juridical. In the third period, a number of articles apparently accept law's Christological foundation but introduce new emphases in the account of human law and once again view the Jewish Law as a legal system. This forms the transition to the final phase where Ellul refuses any theological foundation of human law and reverts to a non-juridical reading of Torah. An examination of the central features of these phases is the concern of the following four sections and a conclusion then notes the significant continuities and discontinuities and proposes reasons for Ellul's changing position.[35]

---

[35] Although this account of Ellul's theology of law is based on the same extensive primary materials as Dujancourt's treatment in Part Two of his thesis (Dujancourt 1989:58-94), it refuses to present a synthesis focussed on his book on the subject. Instead it takes seriously the major changes in Ellul's thought (1988a, 27). Dujancourt acknowledges but downplays the significance of some of these changes (e.g. pp.70, 75n95) while he does not even note other major changes (most surprisingly, the fact that Ellul explicitly changes his view on whether or not law has a Christological foundation between 1939 and *Law*).

Ellul's First Phase (1939)

Ellul's first published article on law, simply entitled 'Droit' appeared in 1939 and was republished in 2000 in *Foi et Vie*, the journal in which it first appeared. He opens by insisting that law must be distinguished from the state because law's sphere is justice not authority (3) but he refuses to found human law in *divine* justice because God's justice is incommensurable with human justice and law (4).[36] He also rejects any natural law theory, on the rather strange basis that all natural law theory negates Christian eschatology by claiming that law has a positive role in bringing about the kingdom of God on earth (18-19). These two themes recur throughout all Ellul's later writings but his 1939 article represents a distinct phase because he resolutely opposes any Christological foundation of law.

> Is the law included within the redemption by Christ? Has it a foundation in the Gospel? Is it part of the domain of justification?...Without question, the law does not receive its foundation from Christology, but from the Law. The effect of justification by Christ can only be the abolition of law...(19).

Human law's primary theological foundation is clearly understood to be the Old Testament Law (*la Loi*) and this 'is no longer a question of justice but strictly speaking of law...the organization of human justice' (5). The Torah's content and structure are essentially the same as those of contemporaneous juridical systems and it is therefore not the expression of divine justice and not to be taken as a perfect model. It must, nevertheless, be given a special status because 'it is ordained by God' (6).

Ellul distinguishes the Decalogue from other legislation, arguing that it provides the foundation for all Hebrew law and that the other laws, which explain it, are complementary to this fundamental law. It is the universally and eternally valid law as confirmed by the fact other societies' first legal expressions are the same as those commandments prescribing human relations. In contrast, the other Israelite laws are contingent and more human.

This divine origin of Israel's law is then conjoined with its similarity to neighbouring juridical systems in order to draw Ellul's most important conclusion: 'just as the Hebrew law (*droit*) was spoken by God, so also, given the similarities that we have been able to show, all law (*tout droit*) comes from God' (7).

It follows from this that what Paul says about the Torah can be applied to all human law. Four conclusions may then be drawn about law's purpose and

---

[36] Throughout this section, page numbers in parenthesis refer to the 2000 reprint of the article.

limits within human society (14-15). *First*, law is always given by God because of our sin and is totally the consequence of sin. *Second*, its end is to restrain and limit sin and not to deny it. *Third*, law is given to secure the minimum justice necessary to preserve life in society by preventing sin's full effects. *Fourth*, law is not redemptive because it can fight only sin's repercussions and means. As a result, all human law is only a sign of God's patience, lacking any eschatological significance. It will pass away with the coming of the Kingdom of God: 'One does not conceive of law in the heavenly Jerusalem...Here, I indeed speak of an abolition...'(19).

Ellul correlates his sociological and theological analyses by arguing that the link Romans 2.14 establishes between Torah and conscience reveals that the earthly foundation of human law is conscience.

> Law is recognized as a product of conscience. Here one sees that the jurists are not mistaken in their analysis and practically all they have said can be taken on board by a Christian except they lack the final foundation. For that conscience which is invoked...what is it if not the law written on the heart by God which, says Paul, allows 'Gentiles who do not have the law, to do *naturally*, that which the law requires' (Rom 2.14)? So then, just as we have seen the Hebraic law, founded on the Decalogue, expressly spoken by God, so now we see law in general founded on that conscience left by God to humans despite sin. That conscience, which is not recognized by non-Christians as given by God, is found almost identically among all peoples (15).[37]

A further connection is then made when Ellul counters the view that positive human law as it exists is directly inspired by God. This he claims ignores the distinction between law's divine foundation in custom/conscience and its human technical expression, and fails to recognise that law is also tainted by sin. Relating these two failures and appealing to Jesus' condemnation of those who added to the Law of Moses, Ellul makes one of his harshest theological critiques of technique, effectively equating it with human sin.

> For the Christian, human intervention in law brings sin into it...Humans, in seeking to express the law in a technical fashion, to reduce conscience to the juridical, thereby introduce sin (17).

This theology of law is complemented with an account of the Christian's

---

[37] Ellul's assertion that jurists view law as the product of collective social conscience reveals how wedded he is at this time to the sociological school of jurisprudence.

relationship to human law. This is significant because, although less prominent in his subsequent book, central elements reappear in his later writing. The essence of his view is that, 'there is literally an antinomy between the idea of the Church and the idea of law' (16, n3). This antinomy is made clear in numerous ways in Scripture. It is, he argues, evident in the explicit injunctions of the New Testament against Christian recourse to law. It is rooted in the opposition of justice and love stated in Christ's new commandment that requires the Christian to found her relationships with others not on justice but on love (15-16). It is also important to realize that 'if Paul can say that we have been freed from the law (*la loi*), how much more are we able to say that in relation to law (*le droit*)' (15).

Finally, three practical conclusions are drawn by Ellul from this account (18-20). *First*, it is wrong to formulate a 'Christian' law whether from some supposed natural law or biblical law. *Second*, the Christian is to obey human law but with indifference as she has the right of refusal. This detachment is to be shown by never seeking recourse to law or demanding respect for one's own interests and by ensuring that relations between believers are not ruled by law. The only reasons for obedience are the recognition of law's importance for the world that remains under sin and the avoidance of scandal to those who are not Christians. *Third*, knowing the divine origin and purpose of law, its true foundation, and the problems which arise when it seeks to go beyond its limited designated role, the Christian's unique responsibility involves maintaining and perfecting law as part of the God-given order of the world's preservation and challenging law when it goes beyond its ordained limits, expresses an existing state of disorder (*le désordre établi*), or claims for itself a redemptive function.

Ellul's Second Phase (1946)

In 1946, in his first published book, *Le fondement théologique du droit* Ellul offers his most comprehensive theology of law much of which will shape his developing thought over the next quarter-century. His study arose out of concern about the modern technicalisation of law and the recent experience of Nazi law and the Nuremberg Trials which led many to seek a revival of natural law theory to counter the problems of legal positivism. From a Barthian perspective, Ellul seeks to counter this by offering an alternative theology of law. Unfortunately, the book's structure makes it difficult to understand and English readers face added difficulties created by the translation (ET 1960 *The Theological Foundation of Law*). There is the acknowledged policy of translating '*justice divin*' as 'righteousness' and '*justice humain*' as 'justice' which can lose the element of similarity and difference found in the original French. There is also the more serious problem of nearly always translating '*droit*' as 'law' whereas the term, in fact, embraces both '*droit objectif*' (law) and '*droit subjectif*' (right) and Ellul's '*droit divin*' is better understood as 'divine right' rather than divine law. In order to avoid confusion, '*droit*' will be used below rather than attempting to choose between English translations.

Ellul admits that natural law theory is central to the Christian tradition's reflection on law but he still rejects it and even claims that it is not at any point a Christian doctrine. Ellul's theological objections to natural law theories derive from his wider theology (outlined in chapter two above) and can be summarised under five headings.[38]

1. They stem from a desire to discover a meeting place between Christians and non-Christians and this denies the separation created by revelation and grace (10-11).
2. They exclude the true, living God from consideration and reduce him to a distant original creator (11).
3. They present a picture of man that fails to acknowledge the radical effect of the Fall (60-2, 89f).
4. They postulate the existence of some eternal, universally valid 'justice' and so deny revelation's witness concerning divine justice (62-5).
5. They misconceive *la loi de Dieu* (65-7).[39]

Of more significance is the fact that Ellul also repudiates his own earlier argument that human law can be founded on the Old Testament Law. He argues that a radical opposition is created between Gospel and *Loi* if the Old Testament reveals the true law to us. He explicitly rejects the argument he had earlier advanced that agreement could be found between the Law and conscience (66). He seeks to avoid this opposition of the Old Testament Law to the gospel by de-juridicising the Torah in contrast to his earlier writing.

---

[38] Here, as throughout this section, all numbers in parenthesis are page reference to *Law*.

[39] Ellul summarises the opposition between his concept of *droit divin* and *droit naturel* in twelve statements (68-70) and in later writings adds further objections. Four in particular are raised at 1959d, 32-4: (1) No biblical text refers to natural law and Scripture's teaching opposes it; (2) There is no reference to Jesus Christ; (3) Natural law undermines the doctrine of justification; (4) Natural law theories transform the living event of revelation into principles for the elaboration of a philosophical system. These relate more to natural law in the moral than the juridical sphere as is evident from the fact that the pages from this article reappear almost exactly at *Vouloir*, 45-7 (*TWTD*, 51-3) with '*droit naturel*' interestingly replaced throughout by '*morale naturelle*'. For discussion of Ellul and natural law see Schüller 1963; Dengerink 1976; Holmes 1981.

Admittedly these God-given statutes (*cette loi*) can teach us something about law (*droit*) and social problems. But in themselves, they (*la Loi*) are neither law (*un droit*), nor a principle of law (*droit*), nor the content of law (*droit*). They do not constitute a juridical system, but are part of revelation…(66)

The Law, as revelation and not *droit*, cannot be separated from the Gospel as a different domain of God's action. It cannot be envisaged in itself apart from *all* of God's just action and it has meaning only as a preaching of Jesus Christ. The Old Testament Law can therefore only have value for juridical problems within a 'theocentric' approach that yields a wider account of *le droit divin*.

To speak of *droit divin* raises the problem that, as Ellul confesses in the first chapter's opening sentence, 'Our contemporary understanding of law (*Droit*) is foreign to the Bible' (37). In a vitally important statement, Ellul then states that, biblically, *droit* is the expression of justice. The first task for a Christian theology of law is therefore to understand justice.

Ellul claims the two Hebrew roots for justice have different meanings. On the one hand there is *Shpht*. This connotes judging and guiding (*juger, conduire*) and its various derivatives such as law (*droit*), statute (*loi*), and customs and manners (*coutume*). *Shpht* is 'justice in its human, external, social aspect' (38). On the other hand there is *Tsdq* which implies righteousness (*justification*) and its derivatives appear to go in opposing directions – justice, equity, truth versus grace, innocence and justification. This is 'justice in its divine aspect, that is the righteousness of God (*justice de Dieu*) which finds its supreme expression in mercy' (38). Divine justice is not something abstract, static, or definable but a specific decision of God in which he passes concrete judgment on a particular situation. In so doing, he expresses his will to re-establish what has been destroyed.

The most important acts of judgment which are revelatory of God's justice are those taking the human juridical form of a covenant (*alliance*) that combines judgment and grace. On the one hand, there is a covenant only due to the free grace of the God who is love and chooses to enter into relationship with man. On the other hand, the covenant is initially a divine condemnation to death for humans broken from God (what was described as God's 'No' in chapter two) and only after this does divine justice show itself as *for* humans (the divine 'Yes') by re-establishing them as God's free covenant partner and maintaining their life (50-4). In juridical terms, Ellul classes God's covenant as a form of *un contrat d'adhésion*, a contract requiring adherence. This implies an imbalance between the contracting partners but does not make human beings simply objects. Humans are called upon to accept the conditions necessary for life which God lays down but God also grants them rights and makes them legal subjects (*sujets de droit*).

With this framework in place, Ellul's theological conception of *droit* as an expression of justice must now be examined. Because *droit* is conformed to the *divine* justice described above there can be no question of an objective right/law (*un droit objectif*).

> This understanding of justice radically destroys the idea of objective law (*droit objectif*) and of eternal justice (*justice éternelle*)...Law (*Le Droit*) comes into being only by the judgments of God and these judgments are pronounced according to the rights of man (*droits de l'homme*)... (49).

A concrete account of *droit divin* is therefore only possible on the basis that God's justice is revealed in his covenant, a covenant where God lays down conditions for the continuation of human beings in their status as his covenant partner. These conditions are what give substance to *droit* in Ellul's definition of it as the expression of divine justice:

> The conditions laid down by God are the result of his judgment and the expression of his righteousness (*sa justice*). As such, they correspond exactly to the idea of law (*droit*) as developed earlier. This law (*droit*) is the prerequisite for maintaining the situation that God has re-established in his covenant (55).

God's covenantal judgments therefore 'establish a law (*un droit*), his law (*son droit*) over against man' (55) and *le droit divin* comprises the covenantal conditions of life laid down by God.

The centrepiece of Ellul's theology of law within this covenantal theology is now (in contrast to his earlier writing) Jesus Christ. God's judgments in Scripture show that his justice has the following characteristics (39-41).

> Divine justice demands that all faults be punished *and* it is bound up with mercy and forgiveness.
> Divine justice renders all human justice unjust *and* it accepts human justice.
> Divine justice is most fully expressed in the final judgment *and* it is God's rule over nations today.

These essentially contradictory characteristics are incapable of human synthesis. God, however, gives the synthesis in Jesus Christ and any theology of justice not founded on Jesus Christ must therefore be rejected.

> All the characteristics of God's righteousness (*la justice de Dieu*) are united

and embodied (*réalisés*) in the life, the death and the resurrection of Jesus Christ…What is important at this point, in the discussion of the problem of justice, including legal justice (*même juridique*), is the absolute centrality of the person of Jesus Christ (42, 44).

All God's covenants are founded on Christ because only in him do we see the full force of God's judgment of death upon humanity, his full and perfect re-establishing of human beings, and his founding of human rights. The difficulty is that this Christocentric account of *droit divin* apparently annuls and denies all human *droit* and *justice*:

> Before God's righteousness (*la justice de Dieu*) all human justice (*justice de l'homme*) is unjust. All that is not his righteousness (*sa justice*) is injustice (40).

> There is no secular law (*droit profane*). Anything man builds up under the name of law (*droit*), is precisely non-law (*Non-Droit*)...(49)

In response to this apparent dead-end in his attempt to develop a theological foundation of human law, Ellul establishes four inter-connected links which he argues found *droit humain* on *droit divin*.

First, human justice and divine justice can be distinguished but not separated. This is because *shpht* and *tsdq* are used interchangeably in the Old Testament and, throughout Scripture, divine justice renders all human justice unjust *and* accepts human justice. To reject human justice as unjust is therefore to oppose God's will (39-41).

Second, by his self-revelation in covenant, God makes the human person into a subject in the realm of *droit*. He establishes a meeting place between the justice of God and human beings. The very fact that God's covenant is in the form of human legal conventions demonstrates that he appropriates human law to make his will known to us and this has important implications for all human law.

> The very fact that God chooses this form in order to express himself informs the whole juridical system…The juridical system is saturated with meaning by the very fact of its being chosen…Law (*Le droit*) can no longer be interpreted independently of this divine choice…(50).

Third, because God's justice and covenant are founded on Jesus Christ, the foundation of human justice in *droit divin* is firmly established in Christ who is both God and man, the person in whom divine and human justice meet (43-5). Ellul therefore rebuts the accusation that his understanding negates the law of the earthly city (*le droit de la cité terrestre*). Fitting with his wider theology he rejects such a claim with the assertion that, 'to say this is to deny the Incarnation' (49). It is his incarnational theology of Christ's assumption of sinful humanity and all human works that also leads Ellul to give law the role within human justification he earlier rejected.[40]

Fourth, Ellul provides an eschatological link by arguing that God finally judges us according to our own form of human justice. Furthermore, and again in contrast to his earlier article, he draws law within the ambit of his doctrine of the eschatological recapitulation of human history and works. In fact, he even claims that law's value rests ultimately not in its relation with the covenant but because God will ultimately authenticate it and end the distinction between *tsdq* and *shpht* (94-9).

In summary, the relationship between divine and human justice is central to Ellul's argument because of the priority he gives to justice within *droit divin* and his belief that *droit humain* is in turn based on human justice. Despite their incommensurability, God's justice gives a foundation to human justice. This finds expression in the concrete judgment of God's covenants, is fulfilled and secured in the person of Jesus Christ (who is himself divine justice), and will be fully revealed in the eschatological recapitulation.

The relationship between *droit divin* and *droits humains* established, Ellul then asserts that 'according to the scriptures, three elements are present in law (*droit*). They are institutions, human rights (*les droits de l'homme*) and justice' (76). Although never explicit, Ellul appears to view these as elements of *droit humain* and also part of *droit divin*. Although the section is entitled elements of human law (*droit humain*), the definition of each element conforms to the earlier conception of *droit divin* as the conditions for life laid down by God. Furthermore, the statement quoted above speaks simply of '*le droit*' and Ellul proceeds to write of these three elements as 'also found in human law (*le droit des hommes*)' (76) while, in his conclusion, he refers to institutions and rights as the content of *droit divin* (139). Ellul acknowledges that other elements are also found within human law but claims that revelation shows these three to be the necessary constitutive elements of *droit humain*. Each must therefore be examined in turn.

Institutions (76-9, 107-9). An institution is defined as 'a body (*un ensemble organique*) of juridical rules oriented toward a common goal, constituting an enduring entity which is independent of man's will, and imposing itself on man in certain circumstances' (76). Ellul cites as examples such institutions as marriage, the state and property, noting that these may take a number of juridical forms and that their historical origins and apparent permanence and

---

[40] *Law*, 58 citing Barth's *Rechtfertigung und Recht* (*Justification and Justice*) known in English as 'Church and State' (Barth 1960:101-48).

universality are shrouded in mystery.

Ellul claims that the Bible reveals some institutions were created by God. As a fundamental reality of God's creation, they are completely independent of human will, and (as Colossians 1.16 reveals) have a fully Christo-centric character. They constitute part of the divine order to which human law must give form although their fragmentary character leaves humans with a certain freedom in this juridical task. Here Ellul distinguishes the form and reality of institutions arguing that there is a Christocentric reality under the forms revealed in Scripture and that human *droit* must observe that reality.

These institutions are then related to Ellul's wider theology and his belief (at this time) in a divine order of preservation that exists despite the rupture of creation's communion with God. They are a permanent feature of the world, and the necessary conditions for the maintenance of human life even though their concrete form will vary. Although Ellul's account is sketchy here, he clearly wishes to chart a *via media* between a theology which calls for the instantiation of a fixed divinely ordained order and one where human law simply adapts to the ever changing social environment, effectively creating its own order. He proposes that, in giving form to institutions, human law must acknowledge and take account of two factors: that the institutions are permanent creations of God (which renders certain forms inadequate) *and* that law has to function in an evolving political, social, and economic context.

Human rights (79-84). In his covenant, and supremely in his new covenant in Jesus Christ, God grants rights to people. It is on the basis of these rights that God himself judges human beings and their non-violation is a condition for the maintenance of human life. Contrary to modern conceptions, rights are not given to man as an abstract individual but to humans-in-society. They are not 'natural' rights but covenantal in origin, given so that people can take the place God has ordained for them in society. Indeed, Ellul claims that both Scripture and historical experience demonstrate that a conception of inherent individual rights removes any distinction between violence and justice and leads to the founding of rights on force. This opposes the whole teaching of Scripture where 'it is the weak who receives his rights from God (*un droit de Dieu*), which he may claim before God and before men' (84).

A fixed list of rights cannot be given because they are essentially contingent and vary with humanity's historical situation. They can, however, be determined on the basis that they are granted so that people can respond to God's word and enter into covenant with him. Furthermore, everyone can recognise their own rights out of an instinct of self-preservation and so, despite a demonic element in any claim to a right and the danger it will lead to the belief that humans possess these rights in themselves, such claims (particularly when made by the poor and the weak) must be taken seriously by

Christians seeking to discern the human rights given by God.
Justice (85-93). Ellul acknowledges it seems humanly impossible to agree a definition of 'justice' and, citing Pascal and Augustine, claims this scepticism as a traditional Christian position. He is also adamant that humans cannot know *God's* justice except as a gift, glimpsed in God's own judgments by means of divinely granted wisdom. Those who refer to Rom 2.14 to correlate human and divine justice are countered by claiming that this verse simply states that a pagan can, in ignorance, perform an action that is just because it conforms to the will of God. Ellul then argues that people are called by God to act and their action *may* prove to be just. Applied to law, this means that people do not know what justice is but simply that they must act and judge.

In all their juridical activity, people are therefore ignorant of divine justice (*tsdq*) and their human justice (the *shpht* which we have seen God respects, accepts, and provides with a foundation and meaning) is 'purely pragmatic justice, worked out by man for convenience's sake…a certain adjustment to convenient and pragmatic criteria, chosen by man for organizing the environment in which he lives' (91, 93). It would, however, be wrong to see this as totally relativistic because this human justice must produce a law that successfully maintains human life and so shows itself to be part of God's justice (91).

Following the pattern of *droit divin*, and its sequence of judgment-justice-*droit* (50), human justice is expressed by an act of judgment and gives rise to *droit*. This is because whenever humans are living in relationship with each other they find it necessary to pass judgment concerning institutions and human rights. Such judgment can take many forms (custom, judicial decisions) but any judgment is only true when it is relative to God's order and elaborates *droit*. Reflecting the great emphasis on the act of judgment by jurists that we saw in his sociology of law, Ellul argues that it is in this context of having to pass judgment and not as a definition of some absolute justice that principles such as commutative and distributive justice and the common good have their place. This is because such concepts 'are but instruments to be used in a concrete situation in order to pronounce a judgment. Such a judgment contributes to the elaboration of a body of law (*droit*)' (112, n9).

The value of this human *droit* is based on its situation between God's covenant and his final judgment. Although not all human *droit* will be accepted by God (for it too must pass through God's judgment), all human *droit* is given its value and its end by the fact that it has a certain end and purpose (*finalité*). This embraces both law's content (101-14, *l'expression du droit*) and its meaning or significance (114-21, *la signification du droit*).

In relation to its *content*, law is based on human rights (*droit subjectif* and *les droits de l'homme*) and hence on God's covenant. It must therefore grant people the rights they need to be able to hear and respond to the Word of God's covenant. Any law that renders the preaching of the covenant vain or places people in a situation where life is impossible for them therefore denies itself. In addition, because God's conservation of the world is with a view to his judgment expressed in his Word, law must also conserve the world for divine judgment and thus Ellul can express a double end for law – it is 'commissioned to express the covenant on earth, and to organize the world with a view to its preservation until the last judgement' (104).

This implies law must view itself as relative and subject to judgment. Ellul further claims that law must not have moral or religious content because it is an element of social organisation and not internal or spiritual direction. It is therefore to be secular (*laïque*) and the society it organises should be an open one. When human law serves this end and is created by man's judgment in response to the divine order of institutions and human rights, it becomes a means by which sinful human beings participate in God's work of conserving the fallen world.

The other strand of law's purpose is its *meaning*. In passing judgment, humans are faced with the question of justice and their own responsibility before God. This arises because in judgment a person puts into play a power from God's domain (justice), takes a role which is God's (judge), and performs an act which belongs to God (judgment). Human law can therefore be said to signify God's presence and to act as a prophecy of his justice but this, in turn, means that it cannot be separated from mercy.

As in 1939, this theology of law lacks any significant reference to political authority and the state. The reason for this is that law is now directly related to the justice of God and receives its authority directly from him. The state is clearly to be subordinate to law and not its creator. The state is created to serve law and would not exist without it. Ellul grants the state three functions in relation to law in his book (124-7). *First*, it can express or formulate law (although this is not biblically required). *Second*, it must sanction law (i.e. make it efficacious by force). *Third*, it must be law's guardian (which requires the state to obey the law and ensure it retains its true character and fulfils its proper role). Law cannot, however, be made effective by the state's power. Its effectiveness depends not on coercion or state power but on its relation to *droit divin*.

> Because human law (*le droit humain*) depends entirely on divine law (*droit divin*) and literally does not exist part from the God's righteousness (*la justice de Dieu*), it can be effective (*efficace*) only when the normal relationship between divine law (*ce droit divin*) and human law (*ce droit humain*) is maintained and when the conception of human law (*droit humain*) allows for this relationship. This means that an unjust law (*un droit*

injuste) before God is a law without authority (*un droit sans autorité*). A law indifferent to human rights (*un droit qui néglige les droits de l'homme*) will be a useless law (*un droit inutilisable*). A law disregarding institutions (*un droit qui néglige les institutions créées*) will be an incoherent law (129).

As Ellul admits in his conclusion, the book says very little about the concrete relationship between Christians and human law although a number of relevant points are made. Because God will judge human law and discriminate within it but has also given all human law validity in assuming it, Christians are to have a double and paradoxical attitude towards human law. On the one hand there is acceptance of the totality of law as it exists *and* on the other hand there is non-acceptance and condemnation of the whole law (98-101). In taking this attitude, one of the church's tasks is to recognise valid claims made by people to their rights and to seek their establishment in law. This is because the divinely granted subjective right (*droit subjectif*) is law's constitutive element and the church is guilty of betraying people when it leaves them alone to claim and recognise their own rights which renders the law subject to incoherence and revolution (134ff). A further task Ellul now gives to the church (in marked contrast to his earlier antinomy between the church and law) is claiming its own right which is that of proclaiming the word of the gospel in all its fullness (131-2).[41]

The church must also examine and critique the existing law on the basis of what it knows to be law's theological foundation and purpose. This will involve affirming the law's concrete limits, judging and seeking to reform the juridical system, and, when necessary, opposing that system's present form. Finally, the church must teach Christians about law's foundation and end in order to form a true juridical conscience in them (136-7).

If the church properly fulfils this role and addresses the issue of law in the light of God's revelation then the law cannot fall under state control.

> Law (*Le droit*) becomes really independent from both state and Church and finally independent from man himself. It ceases to be the direct or indirect outcome of some human activity and becomes the autonomous power (*ce pouvoir autonome*) intended by God (138).

In such a situation the equilibrium of natural law can be maintained and that is vital because it is this natural law that acts as a witness to law's

---

[41] Here, as throughout this book, Barth's influence on Ellul's changing position is evident - 'all that can be said from the standpoint of divine justification on the question (and the questions) of human law is summed up in this one statement: the Church must have freedom to proclaim divine justification' (Barth 1960: 147).

foundation in *droit divin.*

Natural law appears as a period of juridical equilibrium, It raises the problem of law, inasmuch as it is inexplicable and contains an element of mystery, and also inasmuch as it is an effective law (*un droit efficace*) which manages to maintain an organic order in society. For us it is the human proof of a certain relationship between the righteousness of God (*cette justice de Dieu*), the divine law (*ce droit divin*), and the laws governing human societies (*le droit des sociétés humaines*) (73).

Ellul's Third Phase (1947-67)

Over the next twenty years, in six articles on the theology of law, Ellul regularly repeats the main conclusions of his earlier book and refers to it for fuller treatment of issues.[42] There are, however, three significant new emphases that foreshadow the radical change in the fourth phase of his thinking.

Firstly, Ellul consistently gives much greater prominence to his belief that law is a human work and part of the fallen world. In line with the wider theology sketched in chapter two the phenomenon of law must therefore be set within the wider relationship of God and the world.

Law is part of the whole that the Bible calls the world. To determine the Christian attitude in regard to law we must define the relations between the Church and the world (1959e, 134).

When discussing Barthian approaches to law he spells out the implications of this perspective in language that is more reminiscent of his 1939 article than his later book.

The whole of law (*L'ensemble du droit*) is part of that which Jesus Christ calls the World...Law is a necessary condition of human existence and as a result it belongs to the world of the fall. This law...has its origin in a situation of sin and cannot overcome the power of evil (1960a, 33,34).

This emphasis leads to the reassertion of a strong opposition between

---

[42] For example, 1947a on method, institutions, and rights; 1959d on natural law and law's proper relation with God's work in Christ (32-3), '*la justice de Dieu*' (36), the secular nature of law (37), and law's attachment to both justification and eschatological recapitulation (38); 1960a, 32-5 on method and conclusions; 1961c, 40-2 on law's meaning in Christ and law's relation to God's justice; 1962b, 54 on the existence of '*un droit de Dieu*'.

human law and the gospel which derives from the more fundamental opposition between God and the world of ruptured communion: 'the Gospel, because it is God's word and does not belong to the world, is opposed to *all* law (*tout le droit*) whether in our eyes it is good or bad law' (1960a, 33).

Secondly, and following from this, Ellul is much more explicit in contrasting law with love, grace, and freedom. He argues that law cannot be based on love because 'its statutory and imperative nature is contradictory to the freedom and spontaneity of God's love' (1959d, 36).[43] The proper relationship between grace and law is one of tension (1960a, 34).

Thirdly, rather than offering an elaborate theological account of human law in relation to *droit divin* (which it was implied in his book's conclusion was the next task to be undertaken) Ellul focuses more on the reality of the legal world. This now leads to an insistence on the need to be concerned with law itself and not supposedly Christian doctrines about law. It also entails acceptance of the law as it really exists, with an explicit refusal of any approach that rejects a system of law because its laws are 'non-Christian' (1959d, 34-5).

Those authors who are committed to strictly biblical thought refuse all possibility of a Christian philosophy of law…The Church has had very varied positions depending on time and place…The Christian can adopt diverse theories of the law (*la loi*)…He can be positivist, realist, historicist, or committed to natural law, but he can never say that that theory is the eternal expression of Christianity for the law (*droit*), can never attach an eternal value to any of these theories (1960a, 32-4).

In addition to these three developments, this phase's major contribution is Ellul's elaboration of a juridical ethic addressing more practical questions of the Christian's concrete relationship to human law. Its main principles are those of his Christian ethic generally which were sketched in chapter two. The Christian's unique responsibility involves the quest to find a living expression of his faith in relation to law which requires a proper sociological and theological understanding of law and an active engagement with law as presently constituted. From the late 1950s, Ellul regularly characterises the Christian's stance as one in which, as with the world generally, he is in tension with law and acts as a critical conscience, making demands of it, and engaging it in dialogue.[44] Within these general principles, there are two

---

[43] Ellul argues that the project undertaken by some Christians to relate law to love fails to acknowledge law's diversity and focuses on such realms as family and criminal law while ignoring others such as administrative law and contract law (1960a, 30-1).

[44] Examples at 1947a, 485-8,493; 1959d, 40-3; 1960a, 32,34-5; 1961c, 48-9; 1962b.

distinct emphases in Ellul's writing during this period: a concern to show how his theology of the elements of law can be applied and a desire to revitalise law by countering its modern technicalisation. This latter emphasis is best illustrated by reference to the opening and penultimate articles of this phase.

In 1947, when he was working on *La Technique*, Ellul's primary concern is Technique's destructive effect on contemporary law. He argues that the primary task of the Christian jurist is the rediscovery of the proper role and meaning of *la technique juridique* and thus the revitalisation of human factors in the law. This demands a true independence on the part of the judiciary and a re-creation of a juridical climate among citizens so that law is formed not apart from them but in their life and action. Jurists must therefore tackle the obstacles preventing popular participation so that the law is once again reasonable, living, and understandable to the average person in the street. They must undertake such tasks as the simplification of juridical forms and vocabulary and renounce their own monopoly through acknowledging that law is built using materials provided by the people. This work of overcoming the present divorce between the people and the law is, Ellul claims, one that only *Christian* jurists can accomplish (1947a, 490-3).[45]

Fifteen years later, Ellul examines in some detail the contradictory relationship between law and social reality and claims that the Christian's task is to make this relationship a positive and dialectical one. To accomplish this requires, as a *sine qua non*, that technique be restrained along the lines sketched above for 'it is only starting from law restored in its full grandeur (participating in the redemptive work of the Lord) and all its meaning and significance...that one can think about an effective relation' (1962b, 45).

In sketching how the Christian can do this, Ellul examines the relation between theology and social reality. He argues that biblical theology enables the Christian to understand the world as the product of the fall, to recognise that Christ allows us to see social reality as it is, to have faith in Christ in order to desacralise the real, and to bear reality without illusions and self-justifications. (1962b, 46-52) He then applies these conclusions to law arguing that Christianity should primarily enable the jurist to see clearly the world in which law must be applied.

> In the domain of law this leads us to consider that Christianity has a different function from that which it is generally given. Christianity must above all give the jurist a complete clarity concerning the world in which law must get organized, in which the values with which law must be composed are to be expressed and to become normative (1962b, 51-2).

---

[45] This emphasis on giving technique a proper, limited place in a profession is a major theme of A.P.P. which Ellul and Bosc were leading at this time.

On this basis the Christian can assist the double relation in which law arises out of reality and yet also structures it. On the one hand, by discerning social currents, individual needs, and legitimate claims, she can serve the elaboration of law. On the other hand, she can be of value in law's applicability to society. This should be her primary concern because the real problem of justice is the rule's application and not its formulation. Such an approach contrasts with much Christian juridical ethics that focuses on some definition of justice to which Christians should ensure that laws have to conform. Ellul explains his focus on people in their concrete situations and the application of law in these situations with three theological reasons. First there is a Christological motivation because it was the highest form of law - Roman law - that, *in its application*, led to the death of Jesus. Second, a soteriological parallel is drawn with the claim that just as faith is recognised and measured by works and not by some abstract criterion, so the rule of law is to be measured by its concrete consequences and application by police, courts, and administration. Third, such a priority conforms to the theological conception of divine justice elaborated in his book where justice is defined by God's concrete acts of judgment (1962b, 57-8).

In her concern with law's engagement with social reality the Christian has a triple role which takes shape as much from the conjoining of Ellul's sociological analysis and theory of law with his general theology and ethics as from his specifically theological writing on law.

Firstly, she must accept that law is inserted into the present social reality and not into some healthy social body already in equilibrium and order. Indeed, 'if the social body was good there would be no need of law, it is in the evil reality that it must act' (1962b, 59). The law must be related to reality and not so divorced from it that it relies on state sanctions for its applicability. Success here leads to law being experienced as a service rendered to all and will largely resolve the problem of law's applicability in society (1962b, 60).

Secondly, because law's applicability is threatened by the divergence of interests within society, the church's wider mission of reconciliation also aids the application of law by mediating between opposing parties.

Thirdly, because in eschatological perspective law is engaged in a process of successive tensions, Christians must oppose attempts to make law a means of producing unanimity and removing diversity.

> The church and Christians have to refuse every temptation to authoritarian uniformity. Law will apply itself much better when society is genuinely pluralist. Federalism leads to reduction in the sharpness of administrative and juridical conflicts because its respects the tensions (1962b, 61).

The earlier work on theology of law becomes much more prominent in the other major development of this phase, Ellul's application of his understanding of human rights and created institutions as the elements of *droit divin* which form a divine order.

The treatment of human rights is limited. Ellul states that Christians should understand, through biblical and sociological study, what rights God has conferred on people and should find the current form of these rights The Christian jurist is then to interpret and express those contemporary claims which are valid before God (1947a). In particular, love of neighbour and the calling to be on the side of the 'have nots' demand that the Christian jurist must publicly express the needs and claims of those who cannot be heard in society (1959d, 43). This is essential because there can be no true *droit* without proper recognition of subjective rights but Ellul believes that a false conception of rights means that nobody but the Christian can truly discern subjective rights.

In contrast with this limited development of human rights, Ellul offers two extensive accounts of the Christian's relation to institutions.

In 1959, at a conference on Christian revelation and the philosophy of law, he presented his fullest account of institutions which was published two years later (1961c). This addresses the question of whether it is possible to go beyond his general theological foundation of law and find Scripture of assistance in relation to specific institutions and laws within a system of law. Marking a shift from his book, Ellul answers by re-asserting his earlier conclusion concerning the Old Testament Law.

There is a law (*une loi*) in ancient Israel, a whole juridical system of institutions, and all that is contained in the Old Testament, in the revealed books (1961c, 42).[46]

Then, after dismissing those who attempt to differentiate juridical from moral and ceremonial laws, he rejects three other common approaches (1961c, 42-6). *Firstly*, Israel's institutions cannot be taken as models for both historical and theological reasons. Historically, they depend on (and are marked by) Israel's historical and sociological milieu. Theologically, as Israel uniquely is both a nation and a church (*un peuple-église*), her institutions are of no juridical value in themselves because they are the condition for the people of God to be able to fulfil their vocation. *Secondly*, it is also wrong to draw juridical content from revelation by analogy because historical experience shows all sorts of conclusions can be 'justified' by such methods

---

[46] This juridical reading contrasts with *Law*, 66 and is closer to his 1939 article (2000, 5ff).

and Ellul is here critical not only of medieval attempts to justify monarchy but also Barth's attempt to justify democratic government and open diplomacy.[47] *Thirdly*, the temptation to derive Christian principles or juridical norms from the Old Testament must also be resisted as this both distorts the personal, existential nature of revelation and forgets that law has to be acceptable to all within society and not just believers.

Ellul's disagreement with much traditional Christian juridical ethics is then neatly summed up.

> The Christian, it seems to me, is not in any way to state a content to positive law (*droit positif*), nor to insist on this or that juridical *form* which is to be given to an institution. I think that this must be a collective work, the work of all in the nation (1961c, 46).

In this juridical task a whole society formulates the best possible law which expresses, in a given context and state of civilization, what it considers to be most just. Ellul claims that Christians can accept great variety in the form of juridical institutions that may arise from this process because, 'I do not believe that the particular form of institutions, their procedure and their structure are to be the concern of our work as Christians' (1961c, 47). The Christian's concern should instead be at the level of the *functions* of institutions. The Old Testament proves of great value here because it reveals that institutions such as the nation, the state, family and property all have a function beyond the obvious and logical function which jurists recognise. It is this that Christians are to focus their attention upon and Ellul illustrates this in relation to property. He recognises the *form* of property will vary considerably but claims that

> We have therefore not to judge this or that form to be willed by God, but to decide for ourselves, given the present circumstances, what form of property appears best adapted to the function which it is assigned by God (1961c, 48).

A particular relationship is therefore established between the general elaboration of law within society and the demand of Christians who must constantly ask whether an institution is effectively fulfilling its biblical function. This is one aspect of the fundamental relationship of tension and dialectical movement that must exist between the legislator and Christians. This movement must be constant because institutions always change and there needs to be a progressive elaboration of law through the critical and

---

[47] Barth 1960:149-89.

dialectical relationship which Christians establish with society as it creates law.

The other account of institutions appears in 1962 where Ellul re-affirms that, 'The Old Testament furnishes us with a juridical system and a collection of institutions' (1962b, 53). He also argues that the Old Testament Law shows a clear juridical relationship with the laws of neighbouring countries and thus is not some abstract will of God but set in a certain social and historical context. However, a detailed study of the Old Testament shows that a new factor introduces ambiguity and distortion into Israel's institutions.

> I am certain that in all these areas one will arrive at the same result, namely the confirmation of the following double observation. Israel's law is a perfectly realist law which is adapted to a given historical, economic and sociological milieu (and as a result comparable to the law of peoples in the same sociological milieu!). It is an applied and applicable law, able to give form to social reality...The other observation is that this law at the level of its meanings, its human consequences and its purpose is not the same as that of these other peoples...There is always a different perspective on the same institution when it is found among other ancient peoples and when it is found in Israel (1962b, 54-5).

This difference in perspective is due to a particular conception of human beings and, although it may appear only a minor detail, the whole juridical system is thereby transformed because God has adopted common institutions to use them for his end. Comparative studies of ancient near eastern legal systems are therefore of value because of the difference they reveal in Jewish institutions. This difference is 'a sign of the intervention of God, of the summons that God has made of that juridical form, of the use by God of a human creation, and ultimately, it is a sign of the purpose (*la finalité*) which God attributes to law' (1962b, 55). Thus, while the legislative and juridical parts of the Old Testament have no intrinsic institutional value, they do provide the only example of what law *becomes* when God uses it, something most fully developed in Ellul's study of kingship in Israel (1967e). These examples can then provide a practical guide for Christians in their dialectical and critical relationship with institutions within contemporary law. Through a comparative study of the differences between Jewish institutions and those of other ancient societies Christians can gain insight as to how to incarnate Christian demands in a given historical situation. To do this they must 'understand the meaning, the value, the destination of these differences and in what way they are significant'. Once this has been done

> it is necessary, starting with existing institutions in our society,...to transfer

these differences in a way which gives to these institutions the same purpose and movement. This is really much more important than any struggle to adopt a particular law which one considers to be 'Christian' in terms of its content. And it is in this sense that Old Testament legislation can be taken as an example (1962b, 55-6).

Ellul's Fourth Phase (1971-94)

In articles addressing the theology of law after 1970 it becomes clear that another significant change of perspective has occurred in Ellul's thinking. He now places the opposition between God and human law at the centre of his theology of law. Law is now viewed as the means by which humans establish their own order over time, space, and human relations and this project is viewed as in continuity with the elaboration of religion which normalises and structures humanity's relations with the gods and the divine realm in a similar way (1971b, 225-31). The whole juridical enterprise thus stands in total contrast with God's self-revelation which (as Ellul most fully argues in *Faith*) opposes all religion.

> With Christianity, humans find themselves in contact with the God on whom one cannot place a mask because he himself has decided to incarnate himself and one cannot reduce Jesus Christ to a juridical *persona*. Here one finds oneself in a covenant that is no longer established in the norms and framework of law for it is this God who has taken the initiative and who has revealed himself in his incognito. He remains the one who does not enter into the juridical stabilizations, who establishes the relativity of all such enterprises and who invites humans to renounce such securities (1971b, 231).

Biblical passages such as God's preference of Jacob over Esau, his declaration that he gave unjust laws to his people (Ezekiel 20.25-6), and the parables of Jesus (especially the prodigal son in Luke 15.11-32 and the workers of the eleventh hour in Matthew 20.1-16), are cited to show that in a biblical theology of law, although *droit* isn't condemned it is excluded from grace (1981p, 118). *Droit* and grace are represented as two opposed orders that never coincide and so a theology of grace can never have any legitimation of the juridical. Indeed, 'every idea of *droit juridique* is the opposite of Grace' (*L'Autorité*, 20).

This opposition cannot be limited to human relationships with God. It also applies to relations between people. Jesus says that in their relations with others his disciples are to reproduce the gracious relationship that God establishes with them. In his own trial, he demonstrates this opposition by refusing to respond to juridical accusations and thus demonstrating that he is outside the juridical world (1981p, 121).

By so strongly opposing God and the juridical world, Ellul is forced to give a detailed account of the Old Testament Law and Scripture's apparent juridical terminology. In his most detailed study of Torah, Ellul insists its quasi-juridical elements cannot be separated from the whole which is not itself a matter of *droit* but rather of instruction and revelation. Echoing his claims in *Law* he writes,

> Torah is not a juridical document and the sections that concern juridical questions are not primarily assigned this character. Von Rad showed that Torah is not primarily Law (*Loi*) but Instruction and it is under this aspect that it is necessary to consider it - not as a juridical law (*loi*) but as the teaching of the Wise…The Torah is not a law (*une loi*) in the modern sense, it is not law (*droit*), it is not a juridical system. It is God's Word, never juridical, even if it relates to questions that we judge as juridical (1974i, 201).

Drawing on Barth, he argues that the biblical commandment is 'always here and now, ad hominem, establishing a personal relationship between the speaker and the hearer' (1974i, 201). Commandment in Scripture must therefore be distinguished from both *droit* and *loi* which both refer to an objective, non-personal system. The Torah's content stands in marked contrast to all juridical categories for it is not something objective but rather 'the specification of Israel in relation to other peoples and the establishment of a unique relationship with God' (1974i, 202).[48]

Ellul proceeds to further de-juridicise the biblical terminology of justice and covenant, explicitly classing these features of his work as developments from his book (1974i, 204n1). Drawing again on Von Rad he now claims *tsdq* is not a matter of justice as conformity to juridical decision but rather 'carries more the aspect of goodness (*bonté*) than of juridical justice' (1974i, 203). The other Hebrew root (*shpht*) contains the idea of 'lead' and again must have all juridical value removed from it. He thus concludes that it is an abuse of words to give these two terms a juridical connotation. Turning to the language of covenant which was so central in his book, Ellul confesses that on first sight it is a contract and even admits that 'one has often wished on that basis to found human law (*le droit humain*) on covenant, to give a divine meaning

---

[48] In his unpublished 1975 paper on authority Ellul repeats much of this analysis and when asked if his opposition of God and law applies also to the Torah he replies 'Indeed ! It concerns the Law (*Loi*) of Moses to the extent that one understands it as Law (*Droit*) but it was not Law (*Droit*)' (20).

to law (*un sens divin au droit*)' (1974i, 203). Now, however, he emphasises that the covenant is an act of God's free grace and love and therefore does not give birth to a juridical situation. Although some of Ellul's negative conclusions about 'droit' find parallels in his earlier book, their context is now much more thoroughly anti-juridical and hence destructive of the earlier framework.

> In reality, in the act of covenant God reveals himself and gives life. He re-establishes humans in their true condition as creatures in relationship with God. And if God establishes *un droit* it is *his droit*. But this is not a juridical system and nor is it able to be detached from God in order to furnish us with the natural bases of a juridical system. The *droit de Dieu* is useless (*inutilisable*) for the elaboration of *un droit humain*. Strictly speaking, in the Bible, there is nowhere *un droit*. One does not meet there the notion of *Droit*...speaking of *droit objectif*. There is not any juridical, legal, sanctioned etc system... (1974i, 204).

In none of these articles does Ellul refer to a theology of institutions and in relation to subjective human rights his position is now ambiguous. He initially maintains that there are *droits de l'homme* granted to humans in the covenant. (1974i, 205) but ultimately he concludes that the radical and irreducible contradiction between grace and *droit* means that, 'biblically there is never any question of having rights (*d'avoir des droits*)...Neither rights before God...nor rights in relation to other people' (1981p, 116).[49]

Even when he permits a theological basis for human rights, only negative implications are drawn concerning human law.

> This conception (of a person's *droit*) is radically destructive of the idea of *droit objectif*, of *loi sacrée*, of *droit divin*, of *justice éternelle*. That which is *droit* is that which God expresses in his judgment. All that people are therefore able to claim to construct under the name of *droit* is something else, and, by the measure of God's judgment, it is a *non-droit* (1974i, 205).

This conclusion is found, almost word-for-word, in his book (*Law*, 49) but there it was immediately counterbalanced by a detailed account of how God nevertheless accepts and gives foundation and orientation to human law, as shown by the juridical form of his actions. Ellul can no longer argue this given his de-juridicising of the language of Scripture. He therefore now offsets his

---

[49] Ellul does, however, speak of the recognition of a person's *droit* by their superior so the emphasis here may be on 'having rights' and a less lucid statement of his earlier position that rights are not inherent in the individual.

negative assessment in a quite different manner. Von Rad is again utilised in order to argue that many of Scripture's apparently juridical precepts are purely pragmatic in origin and describe the world and society as it is without any sacralising aura. The shift this represents in Ellul's outlook is made clear in citations from Von Rad and his commentary upon them.

> 'The social order is considered as established' as it is, it is *obvious* – but '*it is not theologically founded*'. It is not a social organization that is willed by God, neither this nor that type of government. It is not a case of demonstrating the theological basis of the Institution. The Institution must, on the contrary, be taken for what it is, which is useful and pragmatic (1974i, 205).

Ellul appeals to Von Rad's study of the wisdom literature which shows that in Israelite thought there are two types of rules: those of the experimental natural order and those from God. These two orders are neither confused nor opposed but instead there is a dialectic between them in which human responsibility and creativity is at work. Israel is therefore unique among ancient societies because she does not follow either of the two normal paths in relation to law: she is neither theonomous with a sacralised law nor is she totally secularised through a juridical operation that cantonises the sacred into the divine.[50] Israel's God is truly and wholly God and so his revelation enables the world to be desacralised by other than human juridical means.

> If *la loi* has the specific character of Torah, it is precisely…because the God of Israel is fully and totally God. It is because of holiness. But this is not a sacred…It is the presence of this God who desacralises the institutions and reduces *le droit* to its (irreplaceable, eminently useful !) value as something relative and pragmatic (1974i, 206).

This new understanding of the biblical material requires Ellul to explain the dominance of juridical categories in the history of Christian thought and the constant desire to provide some theological foundation for law. He argues that the impregnation of Western thought by Roman law, aided and abetted by an intellectual dislike of contradictions and dualities and the insecurity produced by an anti-juridical revelation, produced a situation where the juridical order

---

[50] Ellul's study of the role of the juridical phenomenon within sacral societies led him to argue for a contradiction between the sacred and the juridical operation ending in *la loi*. He believed, however, that the Old Testament Law shows ancient Israel was unique because desacralisation occurs in her through non-juridical means (1974i, 195-201).

was forced to enter a theological framework.[51]

This assimilation of the juridical and theological began by viewing Torah as a law similar to Roman law and reading Scripture through a juridical framework. Its climax was the argument that 'if Jesus submitted himself to the Roman magistrate, to the juridical forms of a trial, that gives an exemplary value to *droit*' (1974i, 208). Ellul adds that this was an argument made by Barth in 1935 without acknowledging that it was one that he himself used in his book (*Law*, 58) citing Barth as his source! All this assisted the bridge-building exercise between law and revelation but it was the notion of justice that provided the key to their integration.

Justice as a value is neither necessarily juridical nor necessarily found in law.[52] However, by focussing on justice, Christian theologians could connect the great human works of Greek philosophy and Roman law with Scripture. The result was two-fold: the fixing of the correlation between law and justice which dominates Western thought and a theological legitimation of law which failed to see that the 'juridical' aspect of the Old Testament is really a wholesale challenge to the juridical mindset.

> In effect, the formulation of *une loi* spoken by God is the very opposite of *une loi juridique* because the essential is the 'spoken by God'...The intervention of this living God destroys the security of the juridical (1974i, 11).

This whole process of juridicisation is an element of the disastrous path that Ellul later called the subversion of Christianity.[53] Its consequences included the encouragement of the view that our relationship with God conforms to a juridical model and the belief that ethical difficulties are to be seen in juridical rather than spiritual terms. In addition, important biblical texts came to be misinterpreted due to the dominance of a juridical mindset and the church viewed its juridical and institutional forms not as a painful necessity of the fallen world, but as the highest expression of ecclesial reality.

The culmination of this subversion was the elaboration of *un droit divin*. This is, of course, the terminology Ellul himself used in his book and he here adds an important note

> The *droit divin* of which I am speaking here corresponds to the normal idea and not that which I tried to analyse under this term in *Le Fondement*

---

[51] 1971b, 231-5; 1974i, 206-18.

[52] 1971b, 223-5; 1974i, 208-10.

[53] Law is a sub-theme in the later book where Islam is also blamed for Christianity's juridicisation (*Subversion*, 21ff, 69-70, 88ff, 95-99, 115-7, 130-2).

théologique du Droit. But I must acknowledge that that expression caused confusion and I was seriously at fault to designate the Proclamation of Justice and the covenant by that formulation (1974i, 215-6).

The institution of a divine law (in the usual sense of that term) represents for Ellul a fundamental denial of central theological truths. It amounts to the institutionalisation of our relationship of communion with God, the removal of divine freedom, and the translation of what is of the order of grace and love into the juridical terms of power and obligation.

The creation of *droit divin* from the givens of revelation is therefore not an innocent process. It involves the totality of the interpretation of revelation by the simple fact that it makes it enter into juridical categories with which it is rigorously incompatible. This is precisely because Holy Scripture shows us the extent to which relationship with God is strictly gracious and as a result situated outside of all *droit* and beyond all juridical form or expression (1974i, 217).

This critique may not initially appear to undermine Ellul's earlier work as he always opposed traditional conceptions of *droit divin* and *droit naturel.* However, Ellul's attack is now on *all* attempts to give human law a theological foundation. Despite its long Christian heritage and its debt to such great thinkers as Augustine, this is a pattern of thought Ellul now fundamentally rejects as the following passage from his unpublished paper on authority clearly explains.

What was terrible is that they justified and legitimated a practice of the world. The point of departure, the origin of this theory of natural law (*Droit naturel*), one can say is found in St Augustine...Augustine found himself faced with Roman Law (which was, in his eyes, the greatest creation of the human spirit) and of Greek philosophy and he said, 'how can one fail to admit that this admirable construction of human intelligence has a foundation in God?' From that position was drawn a whole network of ideas which led to the idea of natural law, law which was founded in God. I think that, on this point, Saint Augustine was profoundly mistaken in that he attempted conciliation and synthesis between human creations (admirable and positive creations) and Revelation. Our Christian life has always to remain in some way in counterpoint (not negative and contradictory condemnation) and in some sense opposite to that which exists in the world. We have not, and this is our permanent temptation, to add a small spiritual cap to that which exists. That is always the risk...But understand that from the moment where you engage in this system of justification, you commit yourself to justify everything (*L'Autorité*, 21).

This refusal to provide any form of theological justification now goes so far as to include rejection of even a Christological foundation.

> *Le droit* constituted in society must be purely human...and we must not be tempted to provide it with an assured theological content, nor to justify theologically this or that juridical form. We must leave this *droit* its own function and its own peculiar nature...It is no longer founded on an eternal word! (1974i, 217).

A methodological shift has therefore occurred in Ellul's approach so that he re-centres his thinking on the principle that the Christian is to live in tension with the world (1981p, 116). This leads him to reject or significantly revise central elements in his earlier theology of law. He is now rather dismissive of his earlier view that law's end is to be a means by which God conserves the world until judgment. His study of law leads him to reject this view as divorced from reality.

> I know well the immediate traditional response: *le droit* is one of God's means...for the conservation of the world until judgment. Within the body of classical theology that may perhaps appear satisfactory and indeed it is not false but it does seem to me to be very elementary and rather suspect. By such an interpretation we are in the presence of the assimilatory tendency of theology...Concerning *le droit* one is obliged to take it as something other than it really is and obliged to assign it a task which it does not fulfil, to reclothe it in a garment which is not its own (1971b, 235).

Ellul still holds that law has an eschatological orientation but this (as noted in chapter two above) applies to all human works. It is now understood not in objective juridical terms but rather in the more subjective terms of law as experienced by human beings and law as the embodiment of human hopes.

> *Le droit* is assumed by God not as a work in itself but as something which attests to that which humans finally had the intention of doing, as a bearer of human hope and the human project, and at the same time as a witness of failure and disillusion...That which humans intended to do through *le droit*...will finally be fully realized, given by grace, in a new relationship with time and space (1971b, 238).

Finally, the full implications of removing law's Christological foundation become clear in the explicit reduction of law to the realm of necessity and the category of the useful and Ellul's confession that he is in fact not far from viewing law as demonic.

> I will not go quite as far as to say...that *le Droit* is of the essence of the demonic, but I am not very far off and in one sense there is reason for such a view. *Le droit* is, in every case, of the order of necessity...It is indeed necessary to organize oneself and to have juridical rules...It is extremely useful, but it is purely and simply in the domain of the useful. The authority that establishes itself juridically and expresses itself juridically simply marks that which is of this world...But the authority that makes droit shows by this very fact that it is of this world and belongs to the form of the world which is passing away. And at this very moment there arises always the demonic temptation of replacing the relationship of love and grace by a juridical relationship. In other words, *le droit* becomes demonic when it claims to occupy the whole place and unfortunately *le droit* always finally claims to occupy the whole place (*L'Autorité*, 20).

Now that law is viewed as only a useful work of the fallen world without theological foundation, Ellul's account of the Christian's relationship to law must also be revised. The Christian's task is restricted to examining the present reality of law and acting as a check, resisting its 'demonic' tendencies. This is primarily achieved through a life bearing witness to the opposition between God and law. Ellul illustrates this in his 1981 study which shows signs that, despite his new method, there nevertheless remains a desire to offer some theological foundation for his understanding of law's proper role. In a manner similar to his 1939 article, Ellul argues that the Christian is outside the law and should not make a complaint to the police or pursue a debt. She is 'without rights' and must work to place all human relationships outside the juridical (1981p, 120). This is a distinctive action benefiting society as a whole because the universal demand for rights and the juridicising of all relations has disastrous consequences for a community: it arouses suspicion of all non-juridical relations and gratuitous actions, fosters a denial of personal obligations and responsibilities unless one is faced with someone who can claim them as their right, and encourages the regulation of all human life (1981p, 123-6).

When Ellul turns to the Christian's positive relation to law, certain inconsistencies arise in his argument. He makes claims about law's proper social functions based on conclusions from his sociology of law. Thus law is not necessarily related to justice, its task is to set a framework within which people can live together, to consecrate relative values which the group considers useful, and, by providing accepted procedures, to act as a mediator in times of crisis (1981p, 128-32). All this is stated without reference to any theological or biblical foundation. Ellul also continues to insist there can be no theologically based relation between *droit* and justice, that Torah is not strictly speaking law, and that Christians cannot invest human law with a divine inspiration. Nevertheless, he incorporates a theological appeal within his juridical ethic by claiming that in Scripture a person's right is always founded on its recognition in the particular on the part of a 'superior'. He also notes that, although non-juridical, the Torah's function in Israel parallels that of law in society as it marks out the area within which there is life.

There is, then, a certain confusion here over whether the form of law Christians are to seek has any theological foundation or solely a sociological one. This becomes most evident in the passage concluding the discussion of law's functions and introducing Ellul's concrete proposals for Christian action in relation to law. There Ellul claims that his conclusions necessarily arise from the nature of a properly functioning *droit* but also slips in otherwise unsubstantiated appeals to the Christian gospel.

> *Le droit* allows the avoidance of the crisis of rupture...But this obviously leads to a fundamental attitude demanded by the very existence of *droit*: the recognition of the *droit* of the adversary. In other words, if the Gospel forbids us from claiming our *droit*, it leads us into a double recognition of *droit*: *le droit (objectif), as possible reducer of crisis* and *le droit of my adversary that I have to acknowledge and consider.* Now this put us up against the wall (like the Gospel!) for at this moment *le droit* has the major function of protecting the weak against the strong (and of course the Old Testament gives us numerous examples!)...*Le droit* is exactly from an evangelical viewpoint that which must compensate for a weakness (1981p, 132, italics original).

Finally, although the theoretical basis of the Christian's calling is now unclear, its content is not. The Christian is to demand the social body recognises the right of the weak. When the existing law supports the strongest in society, the Christian is to oppose it and seek to restore law to its proper place in order that it may regain its social legitimacy (1981p, 133). This makes it essential for the Christian to be active in the present juridical context. The technicalisation of law has led to it ceasing to be truly law and the state's dominance requires action to defend the right of the individual against political power and administration. This campaign is, however, not limited to Christians because its foundation is not primarily theological and others can recognise the contemporary failings of law. It is, however, a calling Ellul believes only Christians can truly accomplish because they alone will be motivated to act without an interest in demanding or assuring their own *droit* (1981p, 136-9). His fear is that the church's politicisation has led it instead to seek *political* means to defend the poor rather than recognising that, in relation to the weak and powerless, the gospel demands that the church engage in a *juridical* struggle.

Conclusion

In contrast to Ellul's sociological reflections on law, his theology of law is marked by a number of significant changes. By focussing on law's theological foundation and the status of the Old Testament Law, four phases can be distinguished in Ellul's work which may represent the 'four successive theories' to which Ellul referred in relation to his writing on law.

Before highlighting the significant developments and suggesting reasons for the changes in Ellul's theology of law, two important elements of continuity need to be recalled. Deriving from his overall theological framework where the world has broken from God and the rupture is overcome only in Christ, Ellul always seeks to construct a theology of law which recognises the essential incommensurability of divine justice and human justice and he rejects any higher structure of law such as natural law which may mediate between God and human law.

In his 1939 article Ellul attempts to develop his theology of law by placing law's theological foundation in a juridical Torah and in human conscience. This produces a denial of any Christological foundation for law, a rejection of any eschatological significance for law, and an antinomy between human law and the Christian church.

Ellul's major study of law (1946) explicitly repudiates this approach. He no longer believes there is any *droit objectif* in Scripture and, by re-focussing his theology of law on an account of *droit divin*, he argues the gulf between human and divine justice is overcome by God's action, supremely his incarnation in Christ where he assumes human justice and law.

Three major reasons can be suggested for this shift. *First*, his earlier more negative view of the Christian's relation to the Old Testament Law is now replaced by a desire to avoid any fundamental opposition between Law and Gospel (perhaps the influence of his year studying Calvin and his discovery of Barth in contrast to his earlier affiliation with the Lutheran Kierkegaard). *Second*, although his earlier article rejected natural law theory, he now recognises that his interpretation of Rom 2.14, his basing law on conscience, and his argument that the Decalogue is universally valid, make his position tend towards something very similar to natural law. *Third*, instead of rejecting any relationship between human law and the work of Christ and viewing human law as part of the present evil age from which we are redeemed, Barth's influence leads Ellul to place Christ and his redemptive work at the centre of his theology of law.

The two decades following *Law* mark the next and third phase in his thinking. Here Ellul apparently still accepts the Christological foundation of law but his stress on law as part of the fallen world and his insistence that the Old Testament Law is a juridical system mark a break with his argument in that book. Ellul's major contribution here lies in the two detailed discussions of institutions. Neither of these, however, repeats his earlier claim that institutions are created entities constituting a divine order of preservation which human law must respect. Instead, the first piece distinguishes form and function within institutions (perhaps a re-formulation and elaboration of *Law*'s form and reality distinction). It claims Scripture reveals a divinely ordained function for each institution although Ellul gives no hint as to the institutions' ontology. An even clearer break with the original account is found in the second discussion which speaks of institutions as human creations God uses, arguing the Old Testament reveals how God's action modifies these institutions within Israel.

These developments are part of Ellul's broader theological rejection of an elaborate order of preservation for the fallen world discussed in chapter two. There may also be two more specifically juridical reasons for his shift in this period. The writing during these years follows Ellul's detailed historical analysis of legal institutions and his awareness of their diversity and relativity may have contributed to his re-thinking on this subject. Towards the end of his life he commented,

> Of course all human beings keep their specificity before God but I do not believe that there is a natural law governing human nature...What leads me to challenge this idea of human nature is the prodigious diversity of customs and institutions. If there was really only one sort of human nature then all these customs and institutions should be the same. As it turns out one finds institutions that are entirely specific to one given social entity compared to others (*Conversations*, 111).

In addition, despite his protestations in *Law*, Ellul's original theology of created institutions to which law must give historical form is clearly similar to certain theories of natural law. Ellul himself had initially acknowledged this in one of his first discussions of institutions, an unpublished paper from the 1930s personalist movement.

> The institution is a factor of constant progression in society (in parenthesis, this is indeed a sort of natural law (*une sorte de droit naturel*) which one gets back to here, but not natural law as it was understood in the 18th

century, a natural law which will be the expression of the human person)...[54]

As with the transition from the first to the second phase, this change may therefore be partly the purging of any traces of natural law from Ellul's theology.

In the fourth and final phase Ellul reverts to a non-juridical interpretation of the Law. He then extends this principle even further to remove all juridical connotations from Scripture and to reject the formulation of any theological foundation for law. Instead, he centres his theology of law on the fundamental incompatibility between God and juridical phenomena in the world.

This new position arises from a number of factors. Ellul's historical studies of law and his sociology of law led him to conclude that law is not necessarily based on justice and that it is essentially anti-historical. Furthermore, he now views law as a human artifice that originates in an approach to the world that also produces religion and is incompatible with God's transcendence, freedom, love, and grace. As a result, Ellul sees a much starker contrast between God and the whole human juridical world.

In addition, Ellul is now fundamentally opposed to all attempts to provide a theological foundation for law. Among the theological reasons for this is his belief that the introduction of law and juridical categories into the church's life and thought undermined revelation. The fundamental transformation of law in the modern world away from the pattern he described as natural law into a totally technicalised law (which is truly non-law) may also provide a sociological reason for rejecting any theology which could be seen as justifying contemporary law.

Finally, immediately prior to this period Ellul became a universalist and, though never explicit, the changing view on the nature of God's judgment that this represents and his new emphasis on the triumph of God's grace and love may have contributed to his sharper dichotomy between the form of God's action and that of the human juridical world.

All these changes in his theology of law clearly had an impact on Ellul's juridical ethic. Once again, however, the changes should be set within the continuity of Ellul's wider account of the Christian's role in society. As sketched in chapter two, the Christian is someone who is 'in but not of the world' and so the Christian's relationship to law is always one of dialectical tension. In the first and last of the four phases identified here, Ellul places greatest emphasis on the Christian's personal detachment from the juridical world but throughout his writing he emphasises the Christian's function as a

---

[54] '*Le Personnalisme, Révolution Immédiate*', p.8. Hauriou (who developed the legal theory of institutions Ellul alludes to here) was a Catholic advocate of natural law.

critical conscience within society.

The most significant changes in his juridical ethic relate primarily to the basis for the Christian critique of law. In the first three phases Ellul clearly believes revelation provides some insight into the proper function of human law, institutions, and human rights, although the theological foundation and scope of this insight changes in each phase. Throughout these writings, therefore, Christians are called to apply this insight in their stance towards law. In the final phase, however, the basis for the Christian's critique derives not from a theology of law as such but rather from a combination of Ellul's sociology of law and his wider revelation-based Christian ethic of living the Word and resisting the world.

Despite these changes, two constants in Ellul's ethic must be noted as they represent, on the one hand, a critique of much traditional Christian thinking and, on the other, an important and original contribution to the church's calling in relation to law. *First*, even when he has a theological foundation for law, Ellul consistently opposes any attempt by Christians to establish a 'Christian' law and argues that law must be secular (*laïque*), created by and acceptable to the whole of society and not imposed in any sense by the church. *Secondly*, in line with his sociological analysis, Ellul always calls on Christians to oppose law's modern technicalisation and its subordination to the state and to revitalize the role of legal practitioners in the creation and evolution of a living law.

In conclusion, the most distinctive feature revealed by this chronological account of Ellul's developing theology of law is one we shall find mirrored in chapter seven in the examination of developments in his theology of the state. This is his increasing unwillingness to provide any theological foundation for law or to view law as a divinely ordained phenomenon for the world's good. Instead, in the course of his writing, law becomes merely a human creation which can be positive or negative (even demonic) but which can be changed by the distinctive work of God in tension with the world through his faithful people who live his Word.

CHAPTER 7

State and Politics

This final case study in Ellul's political thought builds on the studies of violence and law to examine his sociological and theological reflection on the state and politics and his advocacy of a form of anarchism. In order to do this it is first necessary to clarify Ellul's use of terms and his distinction between state and politics.

Ellul attacks those who, by abusing the fact that 'politics' can be used in a variety of ways, reach invalid conclusions which extend the scope and the importance of political life (*False*, 158f). He also criticises Christians, including Barth, who think a theology of the state is equivalent to a Christian political ethic.[1] For Ellul, the state and politics can both be subsumed under the broader category of power (*la puissance*) but they must also be distinguished. Although strictly speaking the state (*l'état*) is only one particular form of his wider concern, namely the directing power within society (*le pouvoir/le pouvoir politique*), Ellul generally uses these terms interchangeably. Following this pattern, 'state' and 'political power' are (unless clearly distinguished) treated as equivalent in this chapter. The political realm (*le politique*) is the general sphere of public interests administered and represented by the state. Politics (*la politique*) is then defined in a number of ways not all strictly interchangeable. In the broadest sense, 'politics' refers to any action relative to the political domain including leadership of political groupings or influence upon such leadership.[2] More narrowly, politics and engagement in political activity (*faire de la politique*) is restricted to the pursuit and maintenance of political power:

> *La politique* is neither the search for the common good nor participation in the polis. It is not an idea of justice etc. It is solely a matter of power (*de puissance et de pouvoir*). We must accept the conception of *la politique* given by most political scientists: '*La politique* is the ensemble of means employed in order to gain power (*conquérir le pouvoir*), and once one has

---

[1] *Politics*, 14; *Ethique* III, 100-2 (cf. *Freedom*, 369f).

[2] On definitions see opening note in *Illusion*, 3 and the citation of definitions at *Ibid.*,15, n6.

gained it, to keep it'. *La politique* is nothing other than that…(*Ethique* III, 101).[3]

This distinction between the state as an institution, and politics as the aspects of human life within its sphere and the forms of public action aiming directly to influence or control it, shapes both sections of this chapter. In the study of Ellul's sociological reflections, attention is first focussed on the novelty and growth of the modern state and then on Ellul's account of politics in the contemporary world. The section concludes by offering a brief history of his anarchist beliefs and outlining some of his concrete proposals for political action and for challenging the state. The second section opens by tracing Ellul's shifting theological perspective on the state and his proposals for the Christian's attitude to the state. The question of the Christian's proper role in politics is then analysed before, finally, the relationship between anarchy and Christianity in his thought is clarified in the light of his wider sociological and theological reflections.

Ellul's Sociological Reflections on State and Politics[4]

The Modern State

In order to understand Ellul's conception of the modern state it is necessary to set it within his wider interpretation of the historical development of political power in Western society. His untranslated *Institutions* helpfully presents a detailed account of the diverse historical forms of political power and their development. Further insight can also be gained by reference to Charbonneau's work *L'Etat* which was written in the late 1940s and reflects their common analysis stemming again from the 1930s personalist movement.[5]

---

[3] Given the discussion of chapter three, this makes *la politique* a form of Technique. For similar accounts see *Faith*, chapter twenty-one; *Anarchy*, 62; 1978f. Seurin 1994a presents an important critique of Ellul's political writing based on this definition being too reductionist.

[4] In addition to the detailed study of Chastenet 1992 (summarised in Chastenet 1994e) there are a number of articles examining Ellul's political thought (Holloway 1970b; Nisbet 1970; Temple 1980; Stanley 1981; Sullivan & Di Maio 1982; Weyembergh 1989; Seurin 1994) and a number of unpublished theses (Zorn 1971:37-70; Mulkey 1973; Menninger 1974; Ihara 1975; Wren 1977). Important reviews of his main sociological study in this area (*Illusion*) include Merle 1965; Michel 1965; Thorson 1968.

[5] Asked towards the end of his life if Charbonneau's book influenced him Ellul replied, 'Not at all because it brought me nothing new. We had worked on it together…We had

In his five volume study of institutions in Western history, Ellul sees the state as a distinct form of political power which historically originated when Rome's political institutions had to be transformed from those designed for a city to those able to direct and administer a vast geographical area of diverse peoples.[6] This was one of Rome's major bequests to the Western world.

> Rome created a certain number of institutions and juridical forms that have marked the West in a decisive fashion...It seems that the original creation of Rome which has influenced the entire West is the concept of the State (*Institutions* 3, 18).

Ellul reads the history of Western institutions from the crises of the fourteenth and fifteenth centuries as one of the state's steady rise in the midst of other constitutional and social revolutions.[7] Thus, of the French Revolution he writes,

> In reality, only one element will remain – the State. This, as a centralizing political power, hasn't ceased to grow since the fourteenth century. The revolutionary crisis did not alter this tendency. On the contrary, with the change of constitutional structure, new progress occurred in the institution of state control. The Revolution appears as the crisis in the course of which the political power succeeded in gaining a hold on the whole Nation. This power becomes more rational, more centralizing, more organising, more unifying than before, but the course of its evolution is not changed in any way (*Institutions* 4, 310-1).

In the course of the nineteenth century, the state took the form of the liberal state (*L'Etat libéral*) which Ellul's first widely circulated article argued was the precursor of fascism (1937).[8] Although Ellul's account of the history of Western political institutions is important, it is even more important that he

---

such a communion of thought that I could have said everything he said on the State and he everything I had to say on technology' (*Conversations*, 88). Ellul dedicated his main sociological study of state and politics (*Illusion*) to Charbonneau.

[6] *Institutions* 2, 367ff, summarised at *Institutions* 3, 19-21. *Apocalypse*, 193f is a summary of this view in English. For Charbonneau's discussion of Rome see Charbonneau 1987:21-8.

[7] These crises of the fourteenth and fifteenth centuries were themselves largely due to 'the rapid growth of state institutions and the destruction or subordination of autonomous institutions' (*Institutions* 3, 297).

[8] *Institutions* 5, 297-376 discusses *L'Etat libéral* and the closeness of Ellul's thought to Charbonneau's is here evident in the fact that the final chapter of *Institutions* has the same title as one of the sections of *L'Etat* (Charbonneau 1987:83ff).

finds little or no present value in analyses of historical forms of the state because of the total novelty of the modern state and the problems it raises.

There is no longer any question of a state in the classic sense. To think otherwise is a laughable error on the part of the majority of those who talk about the state, be they philosophers, theologians, publicists, politicians, or professors of constitutional law. They are speaking of the state in terms and forms appropriate to the state of the nineteenth century, or to that of Napoleon. The situation today is radically different (*TS*, 279).[9]

This section therefore focuses on Ellul's study of the modern state. He confesses this is rooted in the distinctive French political experience but he claims its general features are applicable to all modern technicised societies where the state has become, together with Technique, the determining factor.[10]

Following his general sociological method, Ellul goes beyond the usual forms of analysis of political institutions undertaken by social scientists. To maintain a focus on such traditional concerns as comparative constitutions and the varied forms, functions, and inter-relationships of the legislature, executive and judiciary is to lose sight of the deeper uniform reality of the modern state and its distinctive new features. Thus Ellul claims that in reality the American state in the 1960s had more in common with its contemporary Soviet counterpart than with the American state at the beginning of this century.[11] The modern form of the state is so different from that of previous eras that past political philosophy and many of the current political concerns deriving from it (e.g. the balance of power between the executive and the legislature) are passé.

This metamorphosis in the state's nature, power, and role derives from the changes in the relationship between society and Technique discussed in chapter three. The state always had recourse to various techniques but these were traditionally limited in scope and rarely fully utilised or perfected. This began to change with the rapid technical development of the late eighteenth and nineteenth centuries. The highly public nature of many of the new discoveries (e.g. transport, communication, and mass production), the large costs involved in their development and application, and their economic and

---

[9] Cf. *False*, 155; *Illusion*, 9ff., 136-8.

[10] *Illusion*, xiii-xxi. For an accessible account of the French state and political system and its distinctive features and dangers see Siedentop 2001. Interestingly Siedentop's earlier work was on De Tocqueville who highly influenced Ellul and Charbonneau (*Conversations*, 88).

[11] *Illusion*, 10; *TS*, 267-80.

social impact all required the state to take an active interest in the new technical phenomenon (*TS*, 229-47). Herein lies the key to the radical novelty of the modern world:

> From the political, social, and human points of view, this conjunction of state and technique is by far the most important phenomenon of history. It is astonishing to note that no one, to the best of my knowledge, has emphasized this fact. It is likewise astonishing that we still apply ourselves to the study of political theories or parties which no longer possess anything but episodic importance, yet we bypass the technical fact which explains the totality of modern political events, and which indicates the general line our society has taken…(*TS*, 233).

In the face of the widespread and fundamental societal changes being wrought by Technique, the state set itself up as the overseer of the whole of the nation's life and extended into areas which had previously been left to private individuals or other collectivities. However, despite its attempts to control Technique, the state soon found this impossible as Technique proved to have its own laws of growth and development. The state was thus forced to transform and perfect its own traditional techniques so they were as extensive and efficient as possible. It then adopted a wide range of new techniques (such as insurance, planning, and industrial techniques) which were originally devised and made effective by private initiative and had not traditionally been used by the state (*TS*, 247-55). The result of Technique's penetration of the state is that the state itself is transformed and 'the state as a whole becomes an enormous technical organism' (*TS*, 252).

The state can therefore no longer be viewed as the centralised decision-making organ within society that it was in the past. It has now become, on account of the multiple tasks expected of it and the complexity of modern technical society, a complex machinery of departments each of which is itself an enormous administrative organism of innumerable sub-departments and offices. The size and diversity of a single department let alone that of the full state machine makes knowledge of the working whole a practical impossibility and any claim to control the bureaucratic system an illusion.[12] Political scientists are aware of this reality but prefer to perpetuate the myth that control of the state is nevertheless achievable because administrative personnel are subject to their political heads who are, in turn, accountable to Parliament and the electorate. Ellul believes this is one of the major modern political illusions it is necessary to dispel (*Illusion*, chapter four). The idea of

---

[12] In relation to the United Kingdom today see Dynes 1995 for the complex structure of the modern state, since made more complex by constitutional changes.

political control is ridiculous because of the reality of the state bureaucracy and the position and task of politicians within it.

Modern bureaucracy is not the pragmatic, more personal, form of organisation and administration found in the past. It is a global system which can be shown to obey its own internal laws of functioning and development. Building on Weber's analysis, Ellul argues that any political chief is impotent within his department because of these laws of which he highlights three.[13] *First*, the law of continuity and stability means the administrative system remains fundamentally the same throughout political changes. *Second*, specialisation and rationalisation are signs that the state is controlled by Technique and 'bureaucracy...obeys the sole rule of efficiency (*l'efficacité*)' (*Illusion*, 146). Modern state bureaucracy cannot therefore concern itself with individuals, values, or ideology. *Third*, the whole process of decision-making is shrouded in anonymity and secrecy. Nobody can be held truly responsible because all ultimate decisions are independent of any one person, the result of a large number of separate agents' decisions and the application of numerous general rules of procedure. The personal and political elements of the bureaucratic state cannot be ignored but they must be seen as secondary and set within this rigidity and autonomy of the system.[14]

Political control of this system is further made impossible by the fact that politicians will inevitably be actively involved in only an infinitesimal number of decisions made by their department. Those matters they do personally approve will be able to receive little or no concentrated thought on their part (*Season*, 53f speaks of this in relation to Ellul's own political responsibilities). Even where politicians appear to have significant input and control, they will find themselves as amateurs facing complex problems and will rely almost totally on the advice of technical experts (*TS*, 255-67).

Not only does a small fraction of state activity depend on politicians but only a small fraction of time can be devoted to such matters. Their leading concern is maintaining and improving their own personal political standing. The modern political reality is that government ministers must primarily be skilled in propaganda techniques and the political techniques of building their own personal support within the party and the country. Taken together, all these factors mean that, 'the politician carries no weight with regard to the bureaucracy' (*Illusion*, 152).

Ellul grants that the extent to which this account is true, the exact forms

---

[13] In addition to references to Weber in *Illusion*, see 1966c, 97 and Ellul's review of Jacoby's *Bureaucratisation of the World* where he writes that one cannot chose a better master than Weber on this subject (1975d, 550).

[14] In relation to recent British politics see, for example, Norton-Taylor 1995 on the Scott Inquiry into arms sales.

state bureaucratic systems take, and the degree to which this transformation is obvious, will vary. Nevertheless, he holds that these general characteristics of the modern state are universal and that the direction of the state's evolution is set to confirm and strengthen rather than to challenge these patterns. Earlier forms of the state may appear to persist but they are vestigial. The underlying reality is the appearance of this new phenomenon of the technological state (*l'état technologique*) where the nature of the state is the omnipotence of the bureaucracy and administration (*Illusion*, 153-62; *TS*, 267-80).

In addition to these transformations in the internal nature of the state, the modern technical environment has also produced a qualitative change in the state's role and power within society. Originally forced, by the spread of techniques and their impact upon the social body, to extend its interests into more and more areas of national life, the technical mindset then took hold of the state. A totally new relationship was thus established between the state and the political society of which it was a part:

> The nation becomes the object of the technical state in that it furnishes all the different kinds of material substratum: men, money, economy, and so on. The state becomes a machine designed to exploit the means of the nation. The relation between state and nation is henceforth completely different from what it had been before (*TS*, 265).

On spreading its reach into more and more areas of life, the state did not restrict itself to controlling and limiting the effects of Technique. It found that Technique enabled the removal of the practical brake that had hitherto limited the state. Actions that in the past the state may have wished to pursue but was unable to perform (because it lacked the necessary means) suddenly became possible and thus, by the law of modern Technique, were realised.

Out of its relationship with Technique, the state therefore experienced exponential growth in a variety of forms

> The essential element that must be taken into consideration if we want to understand the total phenomenon of politization is a fact that is, if not the cause, at least the moving force of this phenomenon. The fact is the growth of the state itself. Governmental action is applied to a constantly growing number of realms. The means through which the state can act are constantly growing. Its personnel and its functions are constantly growing. It responsibilities are growing (*Illusion*, 9).

The state thus became not only *l'état technologique* but also *l'état totalitaire*, the totalitarian state totally absorbing and controlling all of life. Although the ugly face of this new phenomenon appeared in the regimes of

Hitler and Stalin, Ellul is adamant that liberal and democratic states are in principle no different. The varied scruples that currently restrain the full realisation of the totalitarian state in democracies will ultimately yield to technical necessity. In the meantime, the more brutal and inhuman characteristics of those infamous regimes are absent while the more subtle and dangerous reality of state totalitarianism progresses (*TS*, 284-91).

Despite the significance and impact of these changes on wider society, Ellul admits they have aroused little public opposition and no serious attempt has ever been made to control, limit, or abolish the modern technological-totalitarian state. Several factors explain this apparent indifference. The changes have taken place incrementally throughout the course of this century, spurred on by the two world wars but otherwise with no obvious sudden or unwarranted qualitative transformations. As a result, the formation of this new form of state apparatus was neither immediately obvious nor easily conveyed to the general public by the means of mass communication. It therefore attracted little attention. In addition, it is much easier and more comforting to continue utilising familiar categories of political analysis that retain a semblance of truth and enable questions of political power to be viewed in terms of established constitutional frameworks and procedures.

This refusal to face reality is further understandable because the increase in the state's power and bureaucratisation are simply part of the much wider civilizational crisis provoked by Technique. To address the specific problem of the modern state would therefore necessitate undertaking a fundamental re-assessment of the whole evolution of modern society. The failure to acknowledge this is one of the reasons why every 'revolution' of the past two hundred years has failed to restructure the state or reduce its power and has instead furthered its development.[15]

However, the primary reason the modern state has gone unchallenged is that it promises order and comfort and has become a new locus of the sacred in our society (*Demons*, 80-7). Although the modern state is now the cause of our alienation, any radically different alternative to our present political structures appears impossible to us.

> We cannot conceive of society except as directed by a central omnipresent and omnipotent state. What used to be a utopian view of society, with the state playing the role of the brain, not only has been ideologically accepted in the present time but also has been profoundly integrated into the depths of our consciousness. To act in a contrary fashion would place us in radical disagreement with the entire trend of our society…We can no longer even

---

[15] This is explored in *Autopsy* (especially 147-72) and *Révolution* with Ellul's attempt to overcome this difficulty most fully developed in *Changer*.

conceive of a society in which the political function…would be limited by external means (*un obstacle externe*)… (*Illusion*, 12).

The state has taken the place of God for modern man. It is the state that is held responsible for all that occurs and to which people now look for security, protection, and the solution of all their problems. The state in turn thrives upon this religious devotion, encourages it, and demands its citizens' full compliance with all its decisions.[16]

In conclusion, from his earliest analyses, Ellul has viewed the modern state as (together with Technique) one of the causes of the destruction of our historic civilization and one of the new structuring determinants of the modern world. Like Technique, it has spread from the West, where it first took its new form, across the whole globe. Uncontrollable, bureaucratic, totalitarian, and destructive of the human person, we must first become aware of the state's real nature and then vigorously challenge it if genuine revolutionary change is ever to occur in our society.

Modern Politics

Alongside the state's growth and transformation has appeared the phenomenon of politicisation whereby all problems are viewed as entering the political domain. This is largely due to the rise of the modern state and the consequent changes in our conception of the relationship between society and politics. If the state becomes totalitarian and society is viewed as dependent upon it for its direction (and even for its vitality) then, inevitably, all that happens in society is to be considered political. The political world has also taken on new significance because it is no longer the concern of a small elite. Due to such factors as population growth, mass communication, and the belief in popular sovereignty, politics has become a realm which private individuals cannot avoid and in which practically everyone views their own participation as both a duty and a right (*Illusion*, 11ff).

This expansion of politics is compounded by a totally new evaluation of politics. Active political participation is now viewed as necessary for human dignity and politics is assigned ultimate and religious value, the correlate of the state becoming sacred. As a result, traditional values become politicised and political beliefs (like religion in the past) arouse passions and a commitment to sacrifice which simultaneously defines other individuals as either friend or foe.[17] Across political divisions there is a basic consensus: political action will, somehow or other, solve any problem we face (*Illusion*,

---

[16] *Illusion*, 78ff, 187ff. Cf. 1961d.

[17] *Faith*, chapter twenty one; *Demons*, chapter six.

chapter six).

Ellul's account highlights *three* distinctive new elements in modern politics: its autonomy, its submission to either necessity or the ephemeral, and its illusory discourse.

First, despite the constant desire to subject the political world to the demands of morality, values, and faith, Technique's predominance in the modern world has led to the fulfilment of Machiavelli's political vision of a political realm which is autonomous, free from such controls, and guided only by the criterion of efficiency and effectiveness (*l'efficacité*).[18] Ellul insists he is not here proposing that politics is always autonomous and incapable of being moulded by other values than that of efficiency or that it *should* be autonomous. He claims to do no more than observe present reality: modern politics is saturated with talk of values and principles but this amounts to no more than an ideological cover and justification for a political world devoid of them.[19]

The principal sociological reasons for the development of this autonomy have already been discussed: the state's increased power and domination by autonomous Technique, its increasing control of law, its use of violence, and the general politicisation of life which leaves a constantly diminishing sphere of the non-political to act as a control on politics (*Illusion*, 68-82). Underlying these specific contemporary causes for politics' autonomy there is also the fundamental contradiction between power and values. Ellul believes it impossible to increase power in order to realise values and insists there exists an inverse relation between the two (1980d). The modern world's massive increase in its means of power has therefore diminished the ability of values to limit power. In addition, liberal democracies are generally marked by a lack of commonly held social values that can be imposed on political power. Democracy therefore tends to assist the autonomy of politics. Democratic theory refuses to acknowledge this is the reality of modern political life but such wishful thinking is dangerous as precisely that refusal was one reason for the democracies' failure to take Hitler and Stalin seriously when their political programmes violated generally accepted moral norms (*Illusion*, 86ff).

In theory it is possible for politics to be non-autonomous, subject to law and values. It is, however, an illusion to believe that such a situation is the norm. In fact, any past experience of this was 'an infinitely fragile thing, a rather astonishing human achievement, and one that had to be maintained by will-power, sacrifice, and constant renewal' (*Illusion*, 88-9). The

---

[18] *Illusion*, 68-71. In his earlier articles Ellul referred to this aspect in terms of political realism (*Sources*, chapter three). He claims Lenin most fully understood and utilised this new reality.

[19] *Illusion*, 5-7, 90-1 (the original gives examples from French politics, *L'Illusion*, 89-91).

contemporary political world is far from this reality and to return to it would require a reversal of all the trends of the last century.

> For the autonomy of political affairs to come to an end, it would be necessary that they be subordinated to common values; that the party machines and the state themselves have no autonomy – that is that they are not technicised; that acts and decisions inspired by moral reasons be clearly recognizable as such in the eyes of all. But the people's education has been proceeding in exactly the opposite direction...(*Illusion*, 93 modified).

The irony of modern politics is that, as more and more of life was drawn into its ambit and people increasingly placed their faith and hope in it as the solution to their problems, it became less and less capable of fulfilling its traditional role and effecting the changes necessary in society.[20]

Second, Ellul argues that two fundamental characteristics of traditional politics are lacking today: an effective choice between a number of genuinely possible alternative solutions and a mastery of time that ensures a certain longevity to the action (*Illusion*, 25-9).[21] These are no longer present due to the nature of modern technical civilization and politics is therefore reduced to the necessary and the ephemeral (*Illusion*, chapter one).

Necessary decisions are those that are simply the product of modern society's determining forces. They are made without any genuine alternatives being considered. Many factors can render major political decisions necessary, but the primary underlying cause is again the dominance of the technical quest for efficiency and an unquestioned acceptance of such general ends as technical development, economic growth, and increased standards of living.

Ephemeral decisions are those which are provoked by (and seek to influence) current events (*l'actualité*) but which leave no lasting mark on society. They usually focus on false issues raised by the media and involve little serious or sustained analysis of the problems they claim to solve.

These two features of modern political life combine in various ways. A decision may be both necessary and ephemeral but usually it will be the necessary decisions, primarily those necessitated by Technique, which last

---

[20] It may now be argued that such recent features in Western political life as increasing public disenchantment with mainstream politics and political apathy, evident in such factors as low voter turnout or voting for fringe parties, are a sign that the public have – over thirty years later - recognized the accuracy of Ellul's claims here.

[21] Politics is therefore like true law and so Ellul speaks of '*une prise juridico-politique sur l'avenir*' (*L'Illusion*, 34) although the ET fails to show this - 'real political positions with regard to the future' (*Illusion*, 28).

(even if originally controversial[22]) while those which appear to display an element of freedom by politicians will be proven ephemeral by subsequent events. As recounted in the opening chapter, Ellul had great hopes towards the end of the Second World War that politics could involve decisions which were acts of genuine freedom not dictated by necessity and which would secure lasting and fundamental change. His own political experience dispelled that illusion and he remained convinced that modern politics is incapable of initiating and accomplishing the fundamental revolution necessary in the modern world.

Third, this inability of politics to be a means of effecting permanent changes other than those necessitated by the structure and evolution of modern technical society is in large part due to the creation of a totally new political environment which amounts to an imaginary world detached from lived reality.

Prior to last century, two basic kinds of fact could be distinguished. There were local facts of immediate and usually personal interest and political facts of which the general population were largely ignorant and which had little direct impact on their lives. Today, a totally new category of fact dominates. This is something that is translated into words and images and then given a global character through transmission by mass communication. It then gains a colour it lacks for those who experienced it directly. Public opinion is created around such facts, some of which will become specifically political facts.[23]

For a fact to become political *either* the government or some powerful group in society must consider it such *or* public opinion must grant it a political status. For the latter to occur a fact must either challenge an established stereotype or else become part of propaganda. Simple information about events is never sufficient to create public opinion let alone lead public opinion to treat the event as of political significance.[24]

This change has fundamentally altered the nature of politics because political action is now restricted to being a function of political facts as known and perceived by public opinion. Even were those with political responsibility somehow able to discern modern society's real problems, they could no longer act on the basis of that reality. They must constantly conform their actions to the illusory world of public opinion and seek to mould that world by their own propaganda (*Illusion*, 112-24). Those encouraging mass

---

[22] Ellul cites the French Pierrelatte atomic energy installation (1962a) and the British Welfare State.

[23] *Illusion*, 96-112 discusses this phenomenon, explored further in *Propaganda* and numerous articles (e.g. 1957b; 1967c; 1969i).

[24] Ellul compares the killings of the Rosenbergs and Goettling (*Illusion*, 103-4) which he discussed at the time in relation to this problem (1953b & c).

involvement in politics fail to recognise that the participation they propose amounts to entering this fictional politicised world centred on the modern state, driven by global political facts, propaganda, and public opinion, and dominated by political parties which are only vehicles for careerist politicians seeking to seize political power (*Illusion*, chapter five).[25]

Taken together these three characteristics explain why Ellul views the political world as having undergone a transmutation due to the wider civilizational crisis of the last century. The frontpiece quotation of *Illusion* from Saint-Just sums up the heart of his analysis: 'The people will fancy an appearance of freedom; illusion will be their native land'.

According to Ellul, politics today lays claim to all and promises all. In truth, it is an autonomous world of lies and illusion which divides people and, rather than meeting their real needs, creates a false universe in which they can live unaware of the root causes of their problems. In this description of the nature of modern politics Ellul sees the signs of a deeper and more menacing reality. Politics today is not the means of redeeming the modern world that it pretends to be. Nor is it even any longer a normal human activity. Politics today has become nothing less than 'the realm of the demonic'.[26]

Anarchy as Ellul's Response to the Modern State and Modern Politics

Ellul's fears about the nature of the modern state and his anarchist beliefs can be traced back as far as the 1930s (*Anarchy*, 1ff). In 1979 he explained that a position favourable to anarchism and opposed to the state was taken by him, de Rougemont, Charbonneau and a small number of others, some forty years earlier (1979d). He later recalled that even in 1930-33 they sensed the dangers despite the apparent harmlessness of the French state

Looking back at the French state between 1930 and 1933, it seemed civil and well-intentioned. Nevertheless we sensed all the underlying dangers. A certain number of us experienced a feeling of dread at the increased power of the State... (*Conversations*, 23).

---

[25] Here in the 1960s we see Ellul discerning what has become the art of the spin-doctor now so prominent in political life (see Goddard 2000a for contemporary discussion of Ellul's work on the media). For recent studies of how this world functions see Bruce 1992, Rees 1992 and Jones 2000 & 2001. The rise of the career politician in Britain is well documented in Riddell 1993 and the phenomenon has recently become even more prominent.

[26] See 1978f and *Faith*, chapter twenty-one. The theme is discussed by Seurin who offers a critique of this designation.

About the time Ellul read Marx's *Capital* he also read and was impressed by Proudhon and continued to read writers such as Bakunin and Kropotkin through the late 1930s (*Conversations*, 87).[27] Although violently hostile to the capitalist system, he claims that even at that time it was primarily the state that he opposed and viewed through the same eyes as Nietzsche – 'the coldest of all cold monsters'.[28] Charbonneau shared these beliefs and the wider French personalist movement of the 1930s also nurtured them. *Ordre Nouveau* was strongly anti-statist and presented a radically federalist programme while the impact of Proudhon and other anarchist thinkers is also clear from Mounier's 1937 work, *Anarchie et personnalisme*.[29] This early anarchism was further strengthened by Ellul's personal contacts with anarchists during the Spanish Civil War.

Following the failure of his hopes that Resistance could lead into Revolution, Ellul's frustration with the political establishment appears in 1947 in his first published advocacy of anarchy, albeit an 'anarchy' quite different from that he would later espouse. *'Propositions Louches'* (Dubious Proposals), in the 28th June edition of *Réforme*, attacks the total failure of post-war French politicians and government. Ellul then writes, 'I maintain that *today and for a certain time in France*, anarchy is the only possible solution'.[30] This 'anarchy' is an attack upon politicians and would involve the removal of such political organs as the Council of Ministers, National Assemblies, and political parties. Intriguingly, in contrast to his later work, Ellul assures readers that the administrative machinery will remain and continue to run the country smoothly.

Four years later, Ellul's *Réforme* piece provocatively entitled *'Eloge du désordre'* (In Praise of Disorder), is more in line with his later position. There, although not explicitly referring to anarchy, he mounts a sustained attack on the dominance of organisation and the state in the modern world (1951b). That same year, Ellul's short review of Alain Sergent's *Les Anarchistes* reveals his interest and knowledge of this area of political thought (1951a).

---

[27] Although strongly influenced by Proudhon, Ellul again warns that his work can only be an inspiration today due to the absolute novelty of the modern world (*Révolution*, 256, n3). For a brief introduction to Proudhon see Marshall 1993:234-62.

[28] This phrase is used in other personalist writings of the 1930s (Aron & Dandieu 1993:52). It originally appears in Nietzsche's *Thus Spake Zarathustra* (quoted in Marshall 1993:160-1).

[29] Mounier 1966:88-191. These links between personalism and anarchism are discussed in Loubet Del Bayle 1969. Further on them see Aron & Dandieu 1993, especially the new Preface to this work (Tenzer 1993) and the 'Introduction'.

[30] 1947e, 1 (italics original). Note also the passing comment in the same year that 'there are many others apart from the Church who have spoken of this freedom and affirmed it and I think for example of the anarchists and the great anarchist experience...' (1947b, 52).

A number of passing remarks in *La Technique* reveal more about Ellul's anarchist leanings and begin to give an insight into what he means by the term. In a surprising designation, his historical account of the height of Christendom reads,

> The society which developed from the tenth to the fourteenth century was vital, coherent, and unanimous; but it was characterized by a total absence of the technical will. It was 'a-capitalistic' as well as 'a-technical'. *From the point of view of organization, it was an anarchy in the etymological sense of the word* with its law principally based on custom i.e. rigorously non-technical. It had no social or political organization based on reasoned, elaborated rules... (*TS*, 34).[31]

In addition to favourably contrasting anarchist thinkers to Marx (*TS*, 222), Ellul also drops a hint as to one of his reasons for opposing modern Technique when he remarks,

> It is contrary to the nature of technique to be compatible with anarchy in any sense of the word. When milieu and action become technical, order and organization are imposed. The state itself, projected into the technical movement, becomes its agent (*TS*, 198).

The most important clue to the nature of this anarchism is Ellul's description of what it would be for the workers to actively participate in the economy. This he describes as 'a non-capitalist liberalism, that is to say, anarchy' (*TS*, 210). Here, and in his praise for the early anarcho-syndicalists ('As far as I'm concerned I've always stayed faithful to anarcho-syndicalism as it was in the early days of the movement', *Conversations*, 120),[32] it is clear that Ellul's anarchism is not of a right-wing, free-market form.[33] To view those opposed to the state as automatically on the right is falsely to assume that all socialism entails a strong, centralised state and to forget that a critique of the state may be only part of a much wider, radical critique of modern society. Ellul always insisted he was on the left of the political spectrum and he places his anarchism firmly within the socialist tradition stressing, 'I regard

---

[31] I have added italics and modified ET slightly in light of *Technique*, 31. This interpretation is repeated in Ellul's history of institutions where he writes of medieval society as anarchic (*Institutions* 3, 131 and 4, 6).

[32] See also *Anarchy*, 21; *Métamorphose*, 128; 1950e, 5; 1977h, 18; *Institutions* 5, 349-51.

[33] For discussion of the various forms of anarchism (including their positions on the traditional left-right spectrum) see Marshall 1993 and, on a popular level, Rooum 1992. The practical outworkings are described in Ward 1988. On Ellul's position see Weyembergh 1989.

anarchism as the fullest and most serious form of socialism' (*Anarchy*, 3).[34]

Having sketched the historical development of Ellul's anarchism, highlighted the traces of it in his early writing, and noted its socialist stance, more details can now be given of his form of anarchy. It is important this is seen as a response to his understanding of the modern state and modern politics for, in his own words, 'I felt that the anarchists' response was right, not for all time but in the actual context of modern society' (*Conversations*, 87).

Although Ellul suggested possible reforms within the present political system, he believed a truly revolutionary and not a reformist approach was required.[35] The first step in this process is opposition to, and disengagement from, the present political system: 'the political game can produce no important changes in our society and we must radically refuse to take part in it' (*Anarchy*, 14). Ellul consistently opposed voting in elections, often writing newspaper articles during election campaigns to persuade readers that none of the established parties were seriously addressing the fundamental problems of modern society, that there was no great difference between the left and the right, and that the proper response was not passive abstention but an active expression of one's rejection of false democracy by spoiling the ballot paper.[36] Similarly, despite his longstanding activism in the environmental movement, he was hostile to the Greens because he believed one should not form and fight as a political party within the present system.

Ellul argues that it is necessary to reject the modern state and administration, advocating a wide-ranging policy of conscientious objection as the firstfruits of anarchy. This will include rejection of military service but it will be a much more extensive challenge to state demands and regulations including opposition to taxes, obligatory vaccination, and the established education systems (*Anarchy*, 15ff). Such actions need to be focussed and

---

[34] The most concrete account of Ellul's anarchistic socialism is the untranslated *Changer*, especially chapter six. For further discussion of this issue, including Ellul's belief that it was Lenin's victory which led to Marx's form of socialism becoming dominant, see 1959f; 1983a, f & j; 1983i, 195-7 & 1984c, 63.

[35] Possible reforms of the present system include holding officials and politicians publicly accountable for specific administrative decisions and punishing by fines and removal from office those responsible for waste and gross misjudgement (1979h; 1980g; 1982f).

[36] 1967j; 1973g; 1981a. See responses of Dumas 1967; Ferchaud 1981. Despite his claims 'I've never voted in my life…I've never participated in elections' (*Conversations*, 82) as chapter one showed, Ellul was in fact more active in the immediate post-war period. Although this stance is one many Christians find hard to accept, O'Donovan notes that 'the Gospel may raise serious difficulties for an order that conceives itself as democratic…Jacques Ellul waged periodic campaigns against voting: they deserve at least a respectful mention in the annals of Christian political witness' (O'Donovan 1996:225).

determined but his own experiences in defence of the Aquitaine demonstrate they are possible and that, even when unsuccessful, they at least reveal the harsh reality of the modern state.

A policy solely of withdrawal and refusal is, however, of little value and may result in the irresponsible flight into a purportedly 'apolitical' private life. A positive alternative therefore needs to be developed to both the state and modern politicisation. A programme of depoliticisation must involve a relativisation, demythisation and desacralisation of politics. This entails the development of new perspectives on the problems at the heart of modernity so they are not perceived and tackled as primarily political questions with political answers. It also requires a reformation of individuals so they can effect a personal *prise de conscience* and, from that, develop *une mise en question* of contemporary society and politics (*Illusion*, 199-206). As the opening chapter demonstrated, this was the primary purpose of all Ellul's sociological writings.

To challenge the modern state it is primarily necessary to resist its totalitarianism. It is this that leads the state to remove the power of all that seeks to be truly independent of it and to secure society's adaptation into the uniform, efficient whole which is sought and necessitated by Technique and state administration. This resistance requires the re-creation of those tensions and dialectic within the social body which are necessary conditions for its living diversity and development (*Illusion*, 206-23).

In the past, the state faced a number of intermediary and non-governmental associations, whether autonomous provinces, trade unions, the church, or universities. These have now ceased to be creators of social tension and it is useless reviving institutions that served this purpose in the past but now conform to the requirements of the modern state and Technique. New bodies therefore need to be created at the base of modern society that can fulfil this essential function.

This means that we must try to create positions in which we reject and struggle with the state, not in order to modify some element of the regime or force it to make some decision, but, much more fundamentally, in order to permit the emergence of social, political, intellectual, or artistic bodies, associations, interest groups, or economic or Christian groups totally independent of the state, yet capable of opposing it, able to reject its pressures as well as its controls, and even its gifts. These organizations must be completely independent, not only materially but also intellectually and morally...What is needed is groups capable of extreme diversification of the entire society's fundamental tendencies, capable of escaping our unitary structure and of presenting themselves not as negations of the state – which would be absurd – but as something else, not under the state's tutelage but equally important, as solid and valuable as the state. They must, that is, be poles of tension confronting the state, forcing the latter to 'think again' and limit itself to considering real political problems without being in a position of omnipotence (*Illusion*, 222-3).

The formation of such groups and participation in political activity outside the established state and party procedures lies at the heart of Ellul's conception of anarchy. As the opening biography demonstrated, it was a feature of his own life from the personalist groups of the 1930s, through his activities during the Resistance to, in the post-war period, his camps with students, the early work with young delinquents, his attempts to reform the university system, the formation of base groups to defend the Aquitaine from state-sponsored 'development', and the reform of the French Reformed Church.

Ellul is reticent about elaborating a detailed account of an alternative political system except to stress he does not share anarchism's traditional belief that a society can arise without organisation or political power. What is needed instead is the reinvention of all our current political institutions (*Anarchy*, 19ff). He prefers to focus on the anarchy described above as the form of political action necessary today and then to await the developments which will arise when the social dialectic is reinvigorated by this challenge to the state from outside mainstream political life. There are, however, signs as to the form of political life and institutions Ellul ultimately seeks - 'a truly democratic federalism'.

Ellul again traces his federalist beliefs to 1930, long before what currently and erroneously passes as federalism became fashionable: 'I have always been a federalist' (*Conversations*, 108).[37] For Ellul, true federalism is a reaction against the modern nation state and depends on its destruction in order to create small communities and regions the size of Luxembourg or a Swiss canton. These will then develop a minimalist and relatively powerless federal structure to enable peaceful co-existence, co-operation, and co-ordination

---

[37] 1949c, 1 traces Ellul's federalist beliefs to the 1930s, a claim supported by *Directives* §52-8,76b. On personalism & federalism see Kinsky 1979. In Ellul's view, contemporary federalism is really only a deconcentration of state power within the established statist system. Herron 1987 argues that among early European federalists there were, in addition to those in the Anglo-American tradition of 'international' federalism, advocates of an 'integral' federalism. Herron's abstract describes this as a view that 'rejected the fundamental assumptions of modern political philosophy, was based on the French traditions and theories of anarchism, personalism and royalism, and had the goal of creating a new type of political order for Europe built around 'functional' economic, social and political institutions'.

between the new political units.[38]

Within such locally based political structures, true democracy could be established based on the genuine freedom and participation of the individual person within his or her community (*Illusion*, chapter eight). Such democracy is incompatible with modern techniques of organisation and propaganda. Having progressed from nineteenth century 'political' or 'legal' democracy of constitutions and political institutions, through Marx's critique of this to the quest for 'social' and 'economic' democracy, Ellul argues it is now necessary to go further to 'human democracy' (*la démocratie humaine*). In our present society this is not a natural process. It supposes a radical questioning of all we accept and bless as progress. Not only must society therefore change but a radical conversion of each and every citizen also needs to occur if there is to be any hope of this democratic federalism:

What is needed is a conversion of the citizen, not to a certain political ideology, but at the much deeper level of his conception of life itself, his presuppositions, his myths. If this conversion fails to take place, all the constitutional devices, all studies on economic democracy, all reassuring sociological inquiries on man and society are vain efforts at justification (*Illusion*, 234).

Were such a revolutionary change of heart to occur there could then be formed the reasonable, respectful, questioning human person, conscious of her true situation and able to engage in genuine dialogue with others, who is indispensable for true democracy (*Illusion*, 234-40). The destruction by the power of Technique and the state of the possibility of forming such persons is what Ellul protested against and sought to halt throughout his life and his anarchist views must never be abstracted from this wider radical vision and pattern of resistance to the contemporary world.

I dream of a balanced society in which any ideologically motivated group would, by virtue of its numbers of followers, be able to stand up to and correct the state power. It is certainly not through the political system that we are going to be able to change the orientation taken by our industry or reduce the hold that technology has on our society. Politics can solve none of our fundamental problems. If we really want to come to grips with these problems we will have to make a complete change in our life style. We'll have to give up all the things that make our lives easier, and let's not fool ourselves we will have to go back to frugal ways (*Conversations*, 120-1).

---

[38] 1948b; 1949c; 1978b; 1979f; 1982g, i & m; Courtin 1949.

Ellul's Theological Reflections on State and Politics[39]

The Christian and the State

Ellul's theological reflection on the state (like his theology of law) developed significantly in the course of his writing. Unfortunately, the relative paucity of his theological work on the state makes it impossible to repeat the systematic periodisation and account offered in relation to law. Nevertheless, there is a clear development in his thinking towards a more negative account of the state which begins in the early 1960s and shifts further in the 1980s.

Ellul's earliest work contains his most positive theology of the state. In his 1939 article on law he even comments that the state may possibly have a place in the new creation (2000, 19). In *Law*, although his theological discussions of the state are largely limited to emphasising its subordination to law, he clearly believes the state, although it cannot be Christian, is a gift of God who grants it authority and the use of the sword. Although he speaks of the possibility of the state becoming unjust and of it as 'the sign (and not only the sign) of spiritual authorities' (*Law*, 123) these are not explicitly related to each other at this stage.[40]

In numerous articles throughout the late 1940s and early 1950s Ellul's regular comments and his use of *le magistrat* reveal he works with a Reformed theology of the state drawing on Calvin and Barth.[41] He believes the state is part of the fallen world in rebellion against God and can actively participate in that rebellion under the influence of the powers. However, he sees it primarily as part of the divine order of preservation for this world (discussed in chapter two) and within this order it has a specific and positive God-given task. Christians are therefore to encourage the state to act within this order and to challenge the state when, as is increasingly the case in the modern world, it follows the rebel powers and ceases to respect its divinely ordained function. The Christian's own submission to the state depends,

---

[39] See also Ray 1973:250-319; Fasching 1978:445ff; Van Hook 1981; Gill 1984b:126-55; Seurin 1994a&b.

[40] The main references to the state in this book are *Law*, 10-11, 113-4, 122-31. Although not explicit, Ellul could be read as implying that the state is a created institution (77). His position on the state's violence is more ambiguous than in his later work but he never explicitly says the state's action is just. The ET, 'it has received the sword, and we know how the use of this weapon is justified' (*Law*, 125) suggests too positive an account because the French (*Fondement*, 97) refers to self-justification which Ellul always views negatively.

[41] 1967i, 130-48 offers Ellul's later account of Calvin and Barth on the state. For an earlier account see 1959b.

however, not on this order of preservation but on Christ's lordship over the state.

Almost all this early writing is untranslated but Ellul's contribution to the 1948 Amsterdam conference of the WCC sums up his view in this immediate post-war period.

> We do not deny the value of the state. The state is willed by God, and has its own part to play in God's plan of salvation. Without it, an ordered life in society is impossible. But the state may fall prey to demons, if the power that it represents refuses to recognise the supremacy of God...(1948f, 53).

Clearly here the usual position is that the state is to be understood as part of the ordering of divine providence although it is recognized that it may deviate from this. The language used for this is 'falling prey to demons' which is related to the power the state represents. It is this theme of the powers (also discussed briefly in chapter two) which becomes central to Ellul's radical rethinking of the traditional position and his changing viewpoint.

As shown in chapter two, Ellul sees in biblical references to the powers a witness to the presence in various sociological phenomena of something more than a human, material institution. This 'something more' is also evident from the impossibility of providing a purely human and rational explanation of the state and other phenomena. His unpublished 1975 talk on authority demonstrates this line of his argument.

> I would say that the *exousia* seems to me to be the hidden background of human action and organization which invests an institution with an effectiveness (*l'efficacité*) and a dimension that it lacks in itself. We will never be able to explain authority sociologically, psychologically or logically. I think of the famous proof of the sixteenth century theologian, Suarez, on the subject of the state: if a man kills another man, he is a criminal; if two men kill a man, they are criminals, etc...but if the authorized power (*le pouvoir*) condemns a man, the State is not criminal. Something – some mutation – has taken place. But from where does the political power hold this right of life and death? From where does it draw its power (*pouvoir*) to command? And why do you obey it?...If all citizens decide to disobey the police, the State can do nothing. If we obey, it is because there is something more...The Bible tells us that this irreducible core is precisely a spiritual *exousia* which cannot be grasped or represented but which the Bible warns us is there...The Bible warns us that the *exousiai* are there and that each time that we are in the presence of a question of authority, the sociological, psychological and other dimensions are always subsumed by something more...(*L'Autorité*, 7).

Ellul's 1954 study of money is the first published book to present these powers in a strongly negative context and here Ellul begins to take a much more ambiguous view of the state. He can talk of the rule of David and Solomon as a sign and prophecy of God's kingdom (*Money*, 41), but he now also sees governments and kings as only the appearance and form of another power similar to that of Money/Mammon - *la puissance politique* (*Money*, 76-7). This is illustrated by a comparison between money and the state.

> In the material reality of the fallen world, however, where men and women are fallen, sinful and in revolt, money is effectively a rebel power of seduction and death belonging to Satan. The same apparent contradiction operates in the realm of the state: on the one hand, 'there is no authority except from God' (Rom 13.1); on the other, the state is the beast which ascends from the bottomless pit (Rev 17.8) (*Money*, 99).[42]

Ellul begins more detailed theological discussion of the state in 1963, with the publication of *Fausse*. The important changes and developments in his thought must be carefully delineated. Under the influence of Barth and Cullmann, Ellul has moved further from the traditional Calvinist view and says little on the state as a divinely ordained means of the world's conservation.[43] His emphasis is instead on the state's dual relation to God's work in Christ and to the rebellious powers. It is essential to recognise that henceforward Ellul is precise in his use of *le pouvoir* and *la puissance* although this is unfortunately lost in most English translations. *Le pouvoir* refers to particular, human institutional structures with some form of ordered power within society, most often *le pouvoir politique*. *La puissance* refers to power as a coercive force and is used for the means an earthly *pouvoir* may utilise. However, *la puissance* often refers to the spiritual power Ellul views as existing in and beyond *le pouvoir* and which was studied in chapter two as part of the principalities and powers.[44]

Ellul's thinking is now structured around the double biblical witness to the state evident in Romans 13 and Revelation 13 and his changing position becomes clearer by examining first the more positive and then the more negative aspects of this dual perspective.[45]

---

[42] This stress on the state's relationship with the rebellious powers also appears in Ellul's study of the city written about this time (*City*, 44, 50, 69, 85-7, 164).

[43] See Barth 1960, Cullmann 1963 and Ellul's own account of their work in 1967i.

[44] See for example *L'Apocalypse*, 252-3 where ET p235 translates '*la puissance*' as 'power' and '*le pouvoir*' as 'dominion'; *Feu*, 21; 1972f; Dawn 1992:335ff.

[45] Ihara 1975:174-80 fails to discuss this development, focussing solely on the more

In relation to the state as willed by God, Ellul initially (*False*, 101) still refers to it as part of the economy of the world's conservation but immediately adds that its significance must also be seen in the economy of salvation. Until the 1980s, even when emphasising the negative account of the state, he always speaks of *le pouvoir politique* as given by God.[46] However, he says little by way of explaining how it is given and increasingly rejects making this a legitimating theological foundation for the established state.[47]

In relation to the negative strand – the state and the powers - Ellul initially only deals briefly with the powers. In 1963 he presented for the first time his argument that, in the temptations, Christ accepts that Satan controls *les puissances politiques* (*False*, 16-7).[48] He also claimed that although the powers would finally be destroyed and have already been defeated by Christ they can revolt against him. Ellul's fullest discussion of these powers and their relation to the state is in *Apocalypse*. There he argues that the first beast in Revelation 13 cannot be interpreted as simply Roman imperial power (*le pouvoir impérial romain*) but must be universalised.

> If the first beast is actually incarnate in the Roman state, its symbolism is not exhausted in this simplistic allegory...I will not hesitate to say that the first [beast] designates authority (*la puissance*), political power (*le pouvoir politique*) in the global, universal sense...It is not Rome; it is what Rome has expressed in its political expansion, in its organization, what Rome has carried to a summit practically never surpassed. This is Political Power (*le Pouvoir Politique*) in its abstraction (an operation that Rome had been the first to effect), the absolute power (*la puissance absolue*) of the political...(*Apocalypse*, 92, 93).[49]

This *puissance politique* is the constant which leads the state always to

---

positive account of the state in *Law*.

[46] Among many examples see *Politics*, 83-4; *Apocalypse*, 149; *Violence*, 1-2; *Freedom*, 386; *Marx*, 170 (=1974a, 169); 1967i, 154; 1972f, 15.

[47] At *False*, 114 the gift of political power appears to be understood as historically specific and a gift of God's providence whereas Ellul's response to Cox suggests it could simply refer to God's general creation gift of various powers and abilities (*des pouvoirs*) to humans (*Feu*, 21).

[48] A similar statement appears at *False*, 111 but it is important to see that the ET here is highly misleading as it always speaks of 'the political power' whereas Ellul switches from *le pouvoir politique* to *des puissances politiques* in this reference to Satanic control and continues to use *puissance* in the discussion of Paul and Revelation (*Fausse*, 99-100).

[49] The translation of this passage demonstrates the problems in using English translations here as in translating *L'Apocalypse*, 92-3 the key terms *puissance* and *pouvoir* are both translated at different points as 'authority' and as 'power' (ET pp92-3).

demand devotion and worship and which re-asserts itself as each historical form of *le pouvoir politique* is destroyed and a new form instituted.

Ellul is now clear that this power cannot only be seen as the cause of the occasional perversion of the divinely ordained institution. This *puissance* inhabits all forms of *pouvoir politique*.[50] However, in Christ, God defeated this *puissance* and so, in contrast to Barth and his own first writing, Ellul now rejects the possibility of any form of *pouvoir* in the New Jerusalem.

> In that New Jerusalem it is often commented that there is no longer any Temple nor any King. However, Barth insists that only the Church disappears and that a political power (*un pouvoir politique*) still exists. But which?…Democracy is frankly an error because the word implies 'kratos': a power (*une puissance*) and a domination. No, the heavenly Jerusalem is not a democracy for the simple reason that there is no longer any form of power (*pouvoir*) nor any form of government! (*Feu*, 277-8).[51]

Christ's victory does not take effect automatically in history where Ellul believes that 'every manifestation of power (*puissance*) is an expression of the might (*la force*) of Satan…' (*Freedom*, 55).[52]

In the light of Ellul's interpretation of both the positive and negative strands of the biblical witness, further developments in Ellul's theology of the state can be mapped out by examining how he seeks to correlate these two conflicting emphases. He becomes increasingly critical of the traditional Christian understanding that emphasises the positive aspect and treats negative passages as referring to occasional historical perversions of the norm.[53] In his book on violence (1969), he insists that both accounts are equally true.

> The biblical perspective sees the state as ordained by God, in harmony with the divine order, and at the same time as the Beast of the Abyss, the Great Babylon; [at the same time] as wielder of the sword to chastise the wicked and protect the good, but also as the source of persecution and injustice. Instead of maintaining the balance (*la confrontation*) of both these truths,

---

[50] *Apocalypse*, 93ff, 192f.

[51] This is interestingly a later addition to the French version which is omitted from *City*, 195. See also *Apocalypse*, 200-1, 227-8 and the important note which not only critiques Barth but insists that only in the new creation is political power abolished and so 'no anarchist society is realizable or possible upon earth' (279, n18).

[52] The French adds in parenthesis a reference to Romans 13 - 'despite the "All authority comes from God"' (*Ethique* I, 64).

[53] Barth follows this perspective in writing, 'The State of Revelation 13 is, as H. Schlier rightly maintains, "the borderline of the possible State"' (Barth 1960:118, n23).

these theologians chose rather to validate the political power (*le pouvoir politique*) a priori on a global scale (*Violence*, 2).

Later he acknowledges the Christian authenticity of the traditional doctrine but argues that in reality *le pouvoir politique* is now a concrete enslavement of human beings (*Ethique* III, 199-200). He therefore explicitly repudiates the traditional view and instead highlights the state's attachment to the rebellious powers:

> We have to accept the fact...that no matter what the original intention of God may have been, all institutions have become forces (*puissances*) of alienation and enslavement...(*Freedom*, 452).

Although Ellul still desires to hold both strands together in tension, he has here clearly shifted the balance towards the negative account. In *Subversion* (1984) it becomes clear this can no longer be interpreted as a purely contextual shift in emphasis due to the distinctive characteristics of the modern state. A full-scale reversal of the traditional prioritisation of the positive over the negative aspects of the state has now occurred in Ellul's thought.

This change is implicit in Ellul's re-interpretation of two texts that were important in earlier accounts.

Firstly, he now interprets Jesus' remark to Pilate in John 19.11 as a reference to Satan's control of *le pouvoir*. The verse was initially cited to show that even Pilate was in some sense given his power from God (*False*, 113; *Freedom*, 283-4). That interpretation is explicitly reversed in *Subversion* where Ellul writes:

> Strangely, this text has been read as a validation of Pilate's power by Jesus, as though 'from above' were a reference to God. This inference is strange when one puts the saying in the context of the dealings of Jesus with Pilate...I believe that...the 'from above' does not denote either God or the emperor but the *exousia* of political power, which is a rebel *exousia*, an angel in revolt against God...(*Subversion*, 115).[54]

Here Ellul has taken a text he originally read in a more positive light and transferred it to the more negative strand of biblical witness that relates the state to the rebellious powers.

Secondly, in an important but easily missed change of terms, he reads the temptation account as demonstrating Satan's control not only of the spiritual

---

[54] The same interpretation is offered at *Anarchy*, 68-9.

powers (*les puissances*) but of *le pouvoir politique*.[55]

The theological issues raised by these exegetical changes are addressed when Ellul states that it is both true and false that state authority (*l'autorité de l'Etat*) rests on God's will.

> The idea that the social hierarchy, or the law, or the authority of the state or of owners rests on the will of God is thus at one and the same time both true and false. It is false inasmuch as all these things indubitably express the active, present power (*puissance*) of the prince of this world. It is true inasmuch as they are also means to limit the ultimate consequences of evil...I reject (*je retournerai*) the common theory that they are creations that conform to God's will (the state, law) but have been deflected from their true and valid purpose by the wicked action of Satan. No expression of power (*puissance*) or dominion (*domination*) either is or can be willed by the God of Jesus Christ...The spirit of power...is the spirit of the prince of this world. Every expression of power (*tout ce qui exprime...une puissance*) *on earth and in the course of human history* belongs to his domain...These products of the spirit of power can be deflected from what the prince of this world expects of them and can be used for other ends. The state can become a servant and law an instrument of justice when they are permeated by grace and evangelical truth. But this is the exception...a sign (and perhaps no more) that God has not given us up to the prince of this world (*Subversion*, 179-80).

Despite this negative account of the normal functioning of the state, there is clearly hope that some sort of transformation can take place. To understand Ellul's increasing stress on the state's domination by the powers and how that domination can be resisted, it is necessary to examine his account of political authority in relation to Christ and political power's theological foundation.

In *False*, where there was a more balanced position between the two strands of biblical witness, Ellul argued that political authority as willed by God is personal:

> The biblical teaching definitely indicates two things: that the political authority (*le phénomène de l'autorité politique*) has been willed by God as part of the plan of salvation, but that, at the institutional level, this applies to persons only (the ruler (*le magistrat*), the king)...(*False*, 110).

This New Testament emphasis cannot be attributed to the political context

---

[55] This shift in terms is clear by comparing the discussion of this passage in *Ethique* I, 63-6 with the later discussions at Subversion, 135 [ET, p.114]; *Anarchie*, 66-7 [ET, pp.57-8]; *Si*, 75-9.

of the first century because the Romans had elaborated an abstract doctrine of the state.[56] It must therefore be taken seriously along with its implication for the modern world that we cannot simply apply biblical texts referring to kings and magistrates to our modern state. Although never explicit, it appears Ellul at this point believed that the authoritative form of *le pouvoir politique* is purely personal and that when it becomes more abstract and permanent the rebellious powers are increasingly taking over the institution so that it depends on *la puissance* rather than *l'autorité* which comes from God.

The character of this personal authority is to be understood in the light of Christ's lordship and his possession of all authority (*Apocalypse*, 244-7). Reflecting the agape/eros dichotomy discussed in chapter two, Christ's lordship takes the form of service and stands in total contrast to political power in the world.

> Our reference is to the lordship of him who is the servant...His lordship is not the control (*la direction*) established by a king. Once again, there is opposition between that lordship and states, the world, political power (*le pouvoir politique*) exercised by humans. This is the lordship of Love. As a result, it does not use any constraint, is able to exert itself only in the reciprocity of love and so never takes the form of authoritarian control (*une direction autoritaire*)...(*Ethique* I, 95 cf. *Freedom*, 83).

As a result of God's self-revelation in Christ we have to reconfigure our whole understanding of power and authority for, as Ellul succinctly sums it up – 'In the Bible authority is always the authority of service' (*Freedom*, 55).

The fullest exposition of this appears in Ellul's three unpublished 1975 conference papers entitled *L'Autorité*. After discussing sociological perspectives on power and authority and his conception of the powers in Scripture, Ellul addresses Scripture's teaching on political authority. He argues two attitudes are called for from Christians: obedience and challenge. The call to obey political authority is, he says, total and not restricted to political authority judged to be good. This strand has dominated the Christian tradition. However, alongside this is a current of challenge, refusal and condemnation. Even a passage such as Romans 13 takes this form in its context because it reduces political authority to being God's servant.[57]

---

[56] 1967i, 156-60; *Institutions* 2, 367-441.

[57] Ellul unfortunately nowhere provides a comprehensive exegesis of Romans 13.1-7 and, given the changes in his overall position sketched in this chapter, his detailed interpretation of this passage probably changed. Its apparently wholly positive account of political power must, he insists, be set within both the wider context of Scripture's common critique of power and Romans as a whole where it is not an alien body in Paul's exhortation but part

Applying his earlier claim that Scripture personalises political authority, Ellul argues that texts calling for obedience relate to a personal authority while those calling for challenge relate to a general and abstract authority such as that of the state. This latter, although it can be used by God for his service, lacks legitimate authority.

Turning to authority's structure, Ellul claims that Christ's ministry and death provoked a reversal of the hierarchical, pyramidical structure of worldly authority because this structure of authority condemned Christ. Authority can therefore no longer be founded from above. It can only be founded from below as an authority which, like Christ's own, derives from the choice of non-power and the authority of the word.

> A theology of the Cross is consequently radically opposed to all political theology of the State. It is anti-establishment (*contestataire*) before all authority which declares itself superior. The Cross destroys all that authority wants to be in terms of domination, power (*puissance*) etc...(*L'Autorité*, 14).

Ellul turns to the practical implications of this in his third presentation where he insists that authority must be based on interpersonal relations. This means, for example, that all authority in itself and all institutionalisation of authority must be contested by Christians in order to establish a personal relationship with those in authority. Christians with some form of worldly authority must therefore constantly question it in the light of Christ because before God there is no hierarchical authority. True authority can only serve. By rejecting all constraint, *puissance*, and domination, true authority relies on the willing obedience of the other who recognises the authority that serves and so gives it the possibility of exercising itself. This is the fundamental reversal in Christ which means authority now truly comes from below.

---

of Paul's teaching on non-conformity to the world (Romans 12.1) and Christian love, particularly love for enemies (Romans 12.14-21). It is, therefore, primarily an attempt by Paul to temper Christians' natural hostility to those in political power who appear as their enemies. It is also an implicit critique of the established political power which is due only taxes and tribute (not fear and honour) and which performs a function of vengeance forbidden Christians and only necessary because of human failure to love one another. Although the text appears to grant a high status to the political power its aim is not to provide it with a theological foundation and, in fact, as Nero's recent claims on taking power illustrate, it acts as a major assault on the self-perception of the Roman ruler who is simply God's servant (like Satan in Job). See *L'Autorité*, 11-12; *Anarchy*, 77-90; 1967i, 166-7; 1972f, 15; 1990a. For recent discussions of this passage see e.g. Dunn 1986 & 1988; Wright, N.T. 1990 and Pilgrim 1999. For a novel reading of Rom 13 that relates it to synagogue rather than secular rulers and engages with Ellul see Nanos 1996.

This form of authority cannot be transformed into a political system for the fallen world which refuses to recognise Christ but it does provide the basis for Ellul's own theological reflections on the state's authority and foundation and his account of the role of the church as it lives God's word and resists the world of power.

First, Christians must not seek to justify and offer a theological foundation for the authority of established political power.

> Our constant temptation, which we must reject, is to add a spiritual gloss onto what exists. This is always the risk. State power (*le pouvoir de l'Etat*) exists – how can we explain this theologically and doctrinally ? The power (*le pouvoir*) of the head of the family exists (or rather, it no longer exists, it did exist), how are we able to justify that ?…You see, from the moment one enters into the system of justification, you start justifying everything…(*L'Autorité*, 21).[58]

Even in his earlier, more positive writing, Ellul rejected any religious or divine foundation for political power. He argued that Christ desacralised *le pouvoir* as seen in his comment to Pilate which shows 'Pilate is accorded no power (*pouvoir*) in himself' and reveals that 'for Jesus power (*le pouvoir*) is nothing in itself' (*Freedom*, 283). By affirming God's transcendence, Jesus breaks the usual integration of the religious and political and, despite appearances, his reference to *le pouvoir* as given from God does not re-establish it on a divine foundation.

> The fact that all power comes from God does not mean that the powers have a religious character or that power has a divine character or basis. Quite the contrary! The powers are not God nor is God in the powers. The fact that power 'comes from above' implies distance and difference. This means that power as such is secular and in ever sense human, relative, and secondary. What we have here, then, is the opposite of the other saying of Jesus: 'My kingdom is not of this world'…Kings and magistrates are not God. They are not divine. They are not even representatives of God. They are God's servants, but only as all men are called upon to be (*Freedom*, 284).[59]

The Christian must not, therefore, provide the political power with any foundation. If there is a foundation for political power it can only be that of the obedience of Christians (*Freedom*, 284f, 455-6).

Secondly, Christ's lordship means true authority is Christ's authority of

---

[58] Cf. *Freedom*, 391f; *Subversion*, 113f.

[59] Throughout this passage the French speaks of *pouvoir(s)* and not *puissance(s)*.

service, the word, and non-power. This authority is ultimately founded only on the willing obedience of the inferior. When, therefore, the political power seeks to secure authority and establish itself by using means of power it becomes detached from the source of authority and instead becomes enslaved to the Beast and *les puissances* (*Freedom*, 56f).

Thirdly, in the light of these theological reflections, the Christian's relationship to political power reflects the double character of the institution. Ellul regularly reminds Christians they are commanded to obey, honour, and pray for those holding political power.[60] These are absolute commands and depend not on some theological foundation for the state's political authority but on being commands of Christ.[61] Alongside this obedience, Ellul places great stress on the regularly ignored strand in Scripture which is critical and indifferent to political power. From his brief discussion in *False* through to the detailed account of *Anarchy*, Ellul regularly draws attention to the dubious origins of kingship in Israel, the Chronicler's evaluation of Israel's kings, the critique of power in the Psalms and Ecclesiastes, Jesus' attitude to political rulers, and the message of the Apocalypse.[62]

These two seemingly contradictory positions of obedience and criticism must, Ellul insists, go together in a genuine Christian stance to political power.

> As Christians we are called… 'to have as those not having, to possess as not possessing'…to live under authority as not having authority beyond us…It is truly in reality this permanent play of obedience-challenge (*contestation*) and we must not separate the one from the other: I can challenge only if I am obeying and I am only a Christian and obeying if – by my very obedience – I challenge (*L'Autorité*, 14-15).

Fourthly, at the heart of Ellul's understanding is his belief that the Christian is to be other than the state. He emphasises that although Scripture nowhere forbids the Christian to participate actively in *le pouvoir politique* neither does

---

[60] There are numerous examples of this e.g. *False*, 110, 180f; *TWTD*, 106ff; *Prayer*, 165ff; *Ethique* III, 101ff; 1967i, 155. There is no explicit statement of the requirement to obey in either *Subversion* or *Anarchy*. This may suggest the changes noted above led him to change this ethical stance but he recognises at least a limited obligation of Christians to rulers and acknowledges and does not repudiate biblical injunctions to obey (*Anarchy*, 59-61, 78).

[61] The command to obey authorities may, at certain points, contradict other commands of Christ and this places Christians in a true dilemma for which Ellul refuses to provide any casuistic guidance as was noted in chapter five in relation to violence and war.

[62] For discussion of these passages see, *False*, 109ff; *Politics*, 17ff; *Subversion*, 113-21; *Anarchy*, chapter two; *Si*, 75-9; 1970l; 1974a, 164ff.

it encourage this. Biblical examples of men such as Daniel and Joseph reveal 'the awkward compromises' (*False*, 113) which arise when Christians enter into what Ellul sees as the most dangerous and satanic domain.[63] Ellul himself concluded that

> I believe it is much easier to be a Christian acting in the political world without exercising power *(sans exercer le pouvoir)*…But to be both a person who exercises power *(un homme qui exerce le pouvoir)* and at the same time to be a Christian, that does not seem possible to me (1983m).

In fact, the Christian has a distinct and unique role vis-à-vis the state and this is defined by Ellul's wider theology and theological ethic. The political power stands as part of the world broken from God. The church is therefore to be in tension with it and act as the bearer and incarnate presence of God's Word (*False*, 178ff). The state's power is most effectively limited not by an internal separation of powers nor by the church's participation in the state or collaboration with it. State power is limited by the church establishing a relationship of dialogue where it represents something wholly other than worldly power and uses the means of love, namely the word.[64]

The church alone can limit the state in this way because she represents the Wholly Other. Other bodies are either part of the quest for worldly power or cannot seriously enter dialogue because they refuse to accept the necessity of the state. Ellul claims this dialogue can only properly be undertaken with the persons who have authority and not with the abstract entity of the state. It must be open and above board but it must not seek to attract publicity or arouse political agitation for then it becomes part of the political fray.[65]

In dialogue with the state the Christian must be rooted in God's Word but she is not to instruct the political power how to govern. This is because the state is to be secular and the church has no special technical expertise (*False*, 183ff). Instead, the Christian's function is prophetically to discern the signs of the times, warn of the consequences of political power's action or inaction, and oppose and resist all the political power's attempts to overstep its limits and sacralise itself.[66] The Christian should also insist that the political power takes its own words seriously (and so draw out the implications of, for example, the claims to be democratic or to seek justice and peace), demand the state truly conform its actions to such statements, and highlight the

---

[63] Cf. 1967i, 166.
[64] On this theme see *Ethique* III, chapter four (the earlier version in ET is *Freedom*, 385-98); 1967i, 174ff; 1983m.
[65] *False*, 192-5; 1967i, 158-9. A concrete example of this dialogue is discussed in 1976c.
[66] *False*, 202-8; 1967i, 176-9.

hypocrisy when there is divergence between deeds and words.[67]

The political power's response to such engagement in dialogue will vary considerably but it is only by means of this dialogue that the church is faithful to its calling within the world and acts in a manner which is ultimately beneficial for the world by providing a concrete limit to the political power. As an example of this in recent times Ellul cites the role of the Catholic Church and Lech Walesa in communist Poland.[68] If, as has been the historical pattern, the church rejects this calling and instead establishes itself as a worldly *pouvoir* with institutional connections to the political power then, although it may secure certain small-scale improvements in the social, economic and political realm, it will fail to act as the counter-weight necessary to limit the state and the growth of power.[69]

In the light of Ellul's view of the proper Christian stance towards the state, set in the context of his wider ethics outlined in chapter two, provides the framework for a brief examination of four characteristics he ascribes to political power when it is transformed and reflects Christ's lordship over the powers.

First, political power should be *laïque*/secular (1967i, 169-74). This is one of the most long-standing of Ellul's beliefs.[70] It refers to the non-religious or non-confessional nature of the state in two senses. In contrast to many Christians (and the various models of Christendom) Ellul argues there must be no institutionalised links between the state and any Christian church. This, however, is now a much less serious threat than the modern state's pretensions to be worthy of the religious devotion and worship of its people and to be able to solve all society's problems. The spiritual powers constantly seek adoration, total service, and a response of faith, hope, and love from man. Christians are to challenge every political power showing such tendencies.

Because it is to be secular, the state cannot give any special status to the church but neither can it interfere within the church, outlaw it, or claim to be able to judge upon matters of truth. Its task is to enable all opinions to be expressed and all quests for truth to have a place within society. This cannot be limited to granting freedom of conscience and speech but must apply also to belief's practical consequences. The full extent of the implications of this

---

[67] *False*, 198-202; *Ethique* III, 127-8; 1967i, 179-80.

[68] *Faith*, 135-6; *Ethique* III, 129; 1982h. Another modern example could be Archbishop Romero.

[69] This argument is already present in *False* and central to *Subversion*, especially chapter six.

[70] He claims to have been one of the first to stress this aspect (*Freedom*, 375n11) and 1949e is an early published article devoted to the subject.

are illustrated by Ellul's 1954 articles on the state and truth, the second of which strongly condemns the state for prosecuting parents whose religious beliefs prevented them seeking medical assistance for their sick child who subsequently died.[71]

Second, political power must be limited. In addition to the limits of its secular character, it must be a minimalist state that does not seek to extend its powers. The innate hubristic tendency of all power to self-augmentation and towards the destruction of that which is different from it lies at the heart of the biblical condemnation of power and always needs to be resisted and held in check.[72]

Third, the political power has a specific and limited task. Ellul says relatively little about the functions and powers which should be recognised as valid, perhaps because he does not believe these to be permanent and universal and sees little value in such an approach given the contemporary context. He defines the state's task in general terms as, 'to make a certain order rule which renders human life possible' and acknowledges that this specifically relates to the task of judgment for which the state has use of the sword (1967i, 164ff). However, he does not limit the state to this. He also recognises an organisational and co-ordinating function of the state within society.

> It will be a good administrator of things and of people, a good technician of 'infrastructures'. It must know well the complex patrimony which it administers – goods, services, interests which need to be brought together, equilibria which need to be established...(1967i, 173).[73]

This moves him closer to the Thomist rather than Augustinian tradition within Christian political thought and, in tension with his general emphasis, significantly increases the potential for state involvement in social life.[74]

Fourth, Ellul seeks to personalise political power because true authority can be recognised and exercised only by persons and a personal form of power avoids the dangers inherent in the permanent, abstract structure of the state.

In conclusion, although he never explicitly acknowledged this, Ellul's theology of the state clearly develops in a consistent direction, becoming

---

[71] 1954a. See his later comments on this in *Conversations*, 124-5.

[72] 1967i, 163-5, 174.

[73] *False*, 203; *Freedom*, 385; *Faith*, 49.

[74] Although Ellul defended the rights of the *écoles privées*, his own children attended state schools and he even encouraged the Reformed church to cease involvement in education and to leave this to the state (1983b).

increasingly hostile to political power. Until the early 1950s he appears, despite his antipathy to the modern state, to acknowledge a theological foundation for political power as a divinely ordained means for the fallen world's preservation, while recognising that it may at times be perverted and fall prey to rebellious powers. From at least his 1954 study of money these powers steadily dominate Ellul's thought and the references to a divine order begin to diminish. At first, the state is at the same time both willed by God and the expression of the powers. Then, although it is still in some sense from God, it is (at least in its modern form) dominated by the rebel powers and can claim no theological foundation or legitimate authority. Finally, the traditional position Ellul originally held is turned on its head and political power has its source in the rebellious powers although it may at times escape their grasp and express God's redemptive work in Christ.

Ellul offers no explanation for this final and most fundamental change in his position but a number of factors can be noted. It must, firstly, be recognised that the books in which this new stance is advocated are *Subversion* (1984) and *Anarchie* (1988) where Ellul presses a radical argument which could be significantly undermined if he elaborated any counter-balancing positive account of the state. The omission of such an account could, therefore, be partly explicable on rhetorical grounds. Similarly, Ellul's long-standing belief that the modern state is an incarnation of the powers may have forced him to conclude there was no longer any contemporary relevance in distinguishing *puissance* from *pouvoir* and speaking of *le pouvoir politique* as in some sense given by God.

Although explanations for the shift in Ellul's position that are based on the purpose of his writing and his convictions about the current sociological context are plausible, the more likely cause for this last development in Ellul's theology of the state is a theological one. It is suggested by the description of his final account as one that no longer accepts a fundamental distinction between *pouvoir* (in some sense from God) and *puissance*. As discussed in chapter two, Ellul's view of the being of the powers is ambiguous: at times he sees them having some form of existence apart from human beings while at others he denies this and sees them existing only by human determination as expressions of fallen humanity's *esprit de puissance*. This latter position dominates from the 1980s.[75] When it is combined with his earlier emphasis that *le pouvoir politique* is essentially a human phenomenon (*Freedom*, 284), the result is that '*les puissances*' no longer refers to something independent of humans and '*le pouvoir politique*' and '*la puissance politique*' thus become inextricably intertwined and effectively interchangeable terms. In other words,

---

[75] The fullest account is the untranslated *Si*, 16ff but see also *Subversion*, chapter nine.

Ellul's changing theology of the powers is, after he abandons his early belief in a divine order of preservation encompassing the state, probably a significant factor in the changes in his theology of the state.

The Christian and Politics

Ellul insists that Christian dialogue with the state, obedience to it, and prayer for it, are not strictly political activity. *Faire la politique* is a phrase to be restricted to the activity of pursuing and holding onto political power. Ellul hereby draws a distinction between a theology of the state and a political ethic for Christians and also distinguishes political involvement from the much wider category of social action with which it is often uncritically merged. If these distinctions are clear and accepted, it can be shown that Scripture has relatively little interest in Christian participation in politics.

Ellul believes there is a problem in Christian appeals to Scripture that focus too much on Israel's politics because Israel uniquely is both Church and State (*False*, 113). However, his critique of political power in Israel and his study of 2 Kings (where the politics of God is shown to be distinct from and often opposed to the politics of man) show that he views the Old Testament witness as radically relativising political action. In addition, the involvement of Israelites in the politics of the nations is rare and (Ellul believed) always leads to compromises.

Turning to the New Testament, Ellul condemns the loose terminology prevalent among Christians and exemplified by the title of Yoder's book, *The Politics of Jesus*. He insists that 'the texts of the New Testament show that neither Jesus nor later his disciples ever engaged in or showed any interest in politics' (*Freedom*, 371). This cannot be dismissed by postulating a political context so different from our own that it prevented popular involvement in active political life. As under any regime, there was the possibility of revolutionary political activity to overthrow the established power and there can be no doubt that Jesus could have joined or started such a movement given the prevalence of political dissent in first century Palestine.[76] Instead, Jesus refused to be Israel's political liberator and cleverly avoided being drawn into supporting any particular party on matters of political controversy. Drawing on his own expertise, Ellul also insists that there was an active political life within the Empire of the first century.[77] The epistles' omission of any injunctions relating to Christian conduct in politics is therefore of significance and confirms 'there is a great indifference with regard to politics,

---

[76] For recent discussion of these movements see Wright 1992:148-214.

[77] *False*, 115-7; *Freedom*, 372. Detailed support is offered in *Institutions* 2, 452-70.

and there is no encouragement to take part in them' (*False*, 116).

This biblical study leads Ellul to draw two important conclusions. *First*, there is no specifically Christian or biblical political doctrine, theory, or practice (1980t, 35). *Second*, politics is not a particularly favoured area for living out the Christian faith, quite the opposite (*Freedom*, 369n1).

The concrete problems raised when Christians get involved in politics are evident from the church's history. Such engagement has, in Ellul's eyes, proved to be perhaps the church's greatest temptation and, when yielded to, it has assisted the subversion of Christianity. The crucial event in the history of Christian political activity is Constantine's 'conversion' in the context of a wider attempt to convert those with political power and encourage them to carry out their political functions as Christians.[78] From this moment the church was inevitably involved in political life:

> No matter how independent the Church might wish to remain, she finds herself, from that moment on, inevitably tied to the decision of the power (*pouvoir*), since the latter (sometimes quite honestly) is seeking to put into effect a Christian truth. Under these conditions, how can the Church deny to the power her advice and support? (*False*, 119).[79]

This participation in power soon led to the institutionalisation of relations between the political power and the church and the development of a casuistic ethic to assist Christians involved in politics. It then became clear that, as long as the state or its personnel in any sense confessed itself Christian, the church had to take one of three political positions which Ellul attributes (*False*, 119-20) to three different key thinkers: to seek to guide the state (Augustinian political theory), to collaborate with it for the spread of Christianity (Charlemagne), or to subject itself to it (Marsilius).

Although Ellul shows great admiration for the tradition of Christian political thought throughout the period of Christendom, he judges it a failure.[80] It not only shows the impossibility of a Christian state in any sense but, more radically, demonstrates that 'the Church can make no valid judgment in politics' (*False*, 120-1). It demonstrates that involvement in politics leads to a betrayal of the gospel as the church is drawn into becoming one of the powers of the world rather than the incarnation of non-power. This

---

[78] The historical details are covered by Ellul in *Institutions* 2, 537-40.

[79] Ellul offers a similar account in his fullest discussion of Christendom in *Demons*, 15ff.

[80] *Freedom*, 289f discusses the tradition of Christian thought and claims that the thinkers of the eleventh to fourteenth centuries studied with great care all the issues which agitate the church today. On this great tradition in relation to political authority see now O'Donovan and O'Donovan 1999.

lesson can be drawn not only from the historic Christendom experience but also from studying the involvements of French Protestantism in politics and the wider experiences of, for example, the church under communism and the various forms of liberation and revolutionary theology.[81]

To use this biblical and historical evidence to draw the conclusion that Christians are therefore obliged to withdraw from all political life is, however, also fundamentally mistaken according to Ellul. It is, in any case, dubious whether this is possible, particularly in the modern highly politicised world. Certainly Ellul believes the church and the Christian will be inextricably involved in power relations of some form and therefore all the dangers and compromises entailed by political activity will have to be faced even were one to eschew politics (1972f, 18-9). Furthermore, such an attitude denies basic Christian truths, as the following classic piece of Ellulian dialectic and purple prose vividly demonstrates.

> When all is said and done, it seems as though politics (*le politique*) is the Church's worst problem. It is her constant temptation, the occasion of her greatest disasters, the trap continually set for her by the Prince of this world...*Yet we must continually remind ourselves that the opposite attitude has not more truth on its side.* The review of successive historical betrayals by the Church through political involvement (*engagements politiques*) does not signify that the Church ought to be spiritual, that the faith is a matter of the personal and the inward, that revelation is purely abstract, and that the contest for truth has no political implications and that the love imperative has no social significance. All that spirituality is just as false, treasonous and hypocritical as the taking of political sides condemned above. It is a negation of the incarnation, a forgetting of the lordship of Jesus Christ. It is to scorn one's neighbour...It implies that we acquiesce in giving a free hand to the Prince of this world. It is the rejection of everything Jesus tells us about the Kingdom of Heaven. It is the *other trap* which Satan lays in the path of the Church (*False*, 126).

The Christian is therefore placed in a difficult position. She must recognise the dangers involved in all political action but, nevertheless, seek a way of being engaged with the world of politics which is consonant with her calling to live out God's Word faithfully in the world. Contrary to the claims of many Christian political activists today, there is only one valid Christian motive for such political participation and that is to bear witness to Jesus Christ. This must shape the form of all Christian political activity. It may be that an

---

[81] *False*, 121ff. 1972e offers a commentary on the situation in France in the early 1970s and *Marx* offers Ellul's critique of some left-wing Christian political theology.

individual believer will conclude that fulfilling this demand in political life is impossible and so withdraw from at least certain forms of active politics. That, however, must be a matter of personal judgment and cannot be a general rule for all Christians (*Season*, 65). For politically active Christians, Ellul provides a framework for addressing the basic questions of Christian involvement in politics and offers guidelines as to the appropriate character of the Christian presence.[82]

Ellul's most important claim is that Christians must not seek to form a Christian political organisation. They should be involved across the political spectrum while never seeking to justify their chosen political affiliation on theological grounds.[83] Ellul insists there can be no Christian political stance because the available choices are between parties and organisations of the world that has broken its communion with God, and Scripture gives no clear teaching on this matter. So, despite his own political conclusions, Ellul can claim, 'I have found no Christian reasons, based on revelation, why I should be more right than left, or *vice versa*' (*Freedom*, 376). In addition, historical and sociological analysis reveals a great diversity of 'Christian' stances and internal inconsistency in the arguments offered in their defence. It also demonstrates that theological justifications for political choices are simply a cover for decisions made on separate, non-theological grounds. Once all this is recognised it can be acknowledged that in discussing Christian faith and politics 'it is a case of passing from an ethic of choosing between objects offered us by the world to an ethic of movement in relation to the powers (*pouvoirs*) of the world' (1972f, 19). Within this framework, an account can be offered of how, even in politics, it may be possible to live God's Word in a manner that resists the world. This, following the account of chapter two, involves being a distinctive and holy presence, overcoming necessity by freedom, and displaying agape love in the political world of eros and power.[84] Four features of this genuine Christian presence in politics recur throughout Ellul's writing.

Particularly in the modern world which places its faith in politics, the Christian must *first* heed the biblical critique of power and its pretensions and ruthlessly relativise the political realm and the stakes involved in political argument. This will mean refusing to move political debate from the simple

---

[82] For what follows see *False*, chapters five to seven; *Freedom*, 375-81 (*Ethique* III, 108-14); 1980t.

[83] The quest for theological justification of one's political stance has been regularly seen in recent British politics e.g. Gummer et.al. 1987; Alison & Edwards 1990; Bryant 1993 and, most famously, Margaret Thatcher's Church of Scotland speech which is printed and then mocked in Raban 1989.

[84] *Freedom*, 369 gives the triad of love, freedom, and holiness in relation to politics.

dispute over pragmatic questions of administration and management into the sphere of ideology and spiritual values where it can become an 'all or nothing' struggle with opponents. It will also entail (in the face of the extravagant claims frequently made by political activists) a frank acknowledgment of the very limited nature of the changes achievable by political activity.[85]

By relativising politics in this way, Christians will, *second*, humanise politics. This humanisation of political life is another unique task given to Christians who are to be agents of reconciliation, showing respect for political opponents. One form this will take is the witness of the fellowship among Christians of opposing political viewpoints. Instead of the modern scandal where Christians bring their political disputes into the life of the church and seek to condemn and even excommunicate their Christian political opponents, Christians should take their unity in Christ into the political world so that however great their political disagreements 'they are closer to their brothers in Christ in the opposing party than they are to non-Christians who share the same political view' (*Freedom*, 380). In addition, a Christian must seek reconciliation between non-believers in politics by challenging every action that fails to respect political opponents and by actively seeking to understand their views and explain them within his own party. This will build lines of communication and mutual understanding across political divides.

Third, within her own chosen political affiliation, the Christian is to be a permanent critical conscience, particularly scrutinising the *means* used in political action. She must be sufficiently disengaged from the movements in which she is involved so she can critically reflect on their decisions and actions. She can then perceive when the means being used are incompatible *either* with her own Christian faith (which would carry implications for her own continued involvement) *or* with the movement's stated aims (leading to public confrontation and protest). This is where the Christian will discover to what extent she is able to be active in her chosen form of political life and yet remain a faithful witness to Christ - 'it is in practice that the Christian will see if one can or cannot cooperate with this party !' (1980t, 39).

Fourth, in line with his own programme of sociological analysis, Ellul argues that Christians are not to focus on the usual issues of political concern and the surface phenomena of current affairs. Nor are they to repeat the everyday commonplaces of political discourse and the slogans of political combat. Instead, they are to focus on the deeper, long-term phenomena that are often a matter of consensus across the political spectrum and rarely questioned by anyone engaged in political activity. Christians should

---

[85] This appears in Ellul's early work at *Presence*, 81-9. Cf. *Freedom*, 381-5 on relativisation.

investigate such key determinants as economic growth, Technique, work, and the nation-state both theologically and sociologically. They can then be agents of true revolutionary change at this fundamental level of social, political, and economic structures.

Each of these four features will make the Christian's political presence in the world an alien and resisting one, especially in the modern highly politicised world. If the Christian lives the Word of God in this way she will inevitably arouse suspicion and hostility, whatever political movement she chooses, and she will likely find herself marginalized or excluded. These characteristics are, however, essential for a healthy and constructive political realm and Ellul believes that (although they frequently fail) Christians alone are able to realise them.

Anarchy and Christianity[86]

It is true of any book by Ellul that it can only be properly understood in the light of his other writings. This is supremely the case with *Anarchie et christianisme* (1988), the fullest single account within his corpus of his own Christian political thought.[87] In large part because it was commissioned by the Federation of French Anarchists and originally published by the small Lyon-based anarchist group *Atelier de Création Libertaire* (ACL) for a predominantly non-Christian, anarchist and libertarian readership, this short book is liable seriously to mislead innocent readers.[88] Vernard Eller in personal correspondence wrote to me in late 1993.

> Ellul would have been writing me not too long after he had a finished copy of my Christian Anarchy book – which would make it 1987 or 1988. He came on decidedly more upbeat than usual. His first sentence was something on the order of 'Whoever would have believed this one?'. It seems the Federation of French Anarchists had approached Ellul about doing a book for them. It would have to be short (which seemed to amuse Ellul) because

---

[86] For earlier discussions of Ellul's anarchism see Anonymous 1972; Eller 1973; Gill 1976a; Holland 1986:162-4,194-202; Hanks 1992. Ellul's position is often misunderstood e.g. Ray 1973:288 denies Ellul is an anarchist, Ihara 1975:293,316 sees his anarchism as driven by his theology and leading to quietism; Bauman 1992a sees it as pure Marxism with a veneer of Christian theology.

[87] For reviews see Temple 1989b; Clark 1993.

[88] In a personal letter from ACL in September 1993 they explained they are a small militant group who published mainly anarchist works but had links with others such as ecologists. Their readership is overwhelmingly libertarian or anarchist but they knew Ellul had written something on this subject and decided to publish it. For more information on group see their web site – www.atelierdecreationlibertaire.com.

120 pages was as much as they could afford. The book was to be *Anarchy and Christianity* – yet here is the consideration I think is all important for readers of the English edition to be aware of: it was written for an audience of anarchists in educating them about Christianity. It is not as with the other of Ellul's books – written particularly for a Christian audience. This should be kept in mind when reading the book...[89]

If Ellul's Christian political thought is to be properly understood this book must, therefore, be placed in the context of Ellul's wider sociological and theological analyses discussed above and his earlier writings on anarchy and Christianity.[90]

It is first necessary to clarify exactly what Ellul is and is not claiming when he writes of the relationship between Christianity and anarchy. *First* and foremost Ellul is not proposing anarchy as the true Christian political position. Although he himself has concluded that a certain form of anarchy is the political stance closest to biblical thought,[91] he believes no political creed or movement can claim to be Christian and is highly critical of those who seek to show a necessary correlation between Christianity and, for example, socialism or communism.[92] He explicitly denies this is his aim in relation to Christianity and anarchism. His much more modest goal is clearly stated at the start of his book. It amounts to questioning the longstanding misconceptions that have led both anarchists and Christians to believe anarchy and Christian faith are mutually exclusive. Rather than telling Christians they must become anarchists (which would fundamentally undermine his belief in Christian freedom), Ellul simply hopes to overcome the historic prejudice of Christians and show that, if Christians are to be politically active, they must not rule out anarchism in advance as a possible option.

Second, Ellul does not believe anarchy is, at all times and in all places, the best political option. His position here is quite clear.

I'm not against politics in general. I am only saying that today politics is developing in a certain direction. At another time, in other circumstances, I might say something completely different (1974d, 214).

As with any part of Ellul's ethics, his writing on anarchy has to be set

---

[89] Personal letter from Vernard Eller, Christmas 1993. See also Eller 1989b.

[90] The main earlier works on Christianity and anarchy are 1974a (reprinted, with very minor changes, in *Marx*, chapter seven) and *Ethique* III, 131-3 (earlier ET, *Freedom*, 395-8).

[91] Claims of this form are scatted through his book, *Anarchy*, 3, 4, 45-6, 103-5.

[92] The best instances of this are the pieces collected in *Marx*. See also 1981b & r.

within the context of his analysis of the contemporary world. So, in *Freedom,* he writes

> What I have to say is that for most men *today* the involvement which is most useful, and which best expresses Christian freedom, is involvement in anarchy…What reasons drive me to this view? I certainly do not say that it seems to me to be a direct expression of Christian freedom. What leads me in this direction is the constitution and development of the modern state…I am not trying to lay down what should be an intrinsic or permanent Christian attitude…Every modern state is totalitarian…That is why I maintain that no state *in the modern world* (*actuellement*) is legitimate. No *present-day* authority can claim to be instituted by God, for all authority is set in the framework of a totalitarian state. *This is why I decide for anarchy* (*Freedom*, 395, 396, italics added).

This stance was also clear in his book on Jesus and Marx first published in France in 1979. There, in one of very few amendments to the original 1974 article, Ellul clarifies that it is 'within the context of modern society and our concrete historical situation' (*Marx*, 177) that anarchism is the way to proceed. When André Dumas' review of the book failed to notice this, Ellul clarified his position most explicitly in a short article in *Réforme* where he states

> I wish to rectify two errors of fact concerning my taking a position favourable to anarchism and against the State. One consists in believing that I am making this a permanent and theoretical Christian attitude when I wrote exactly the opposite…Dumas has made the error of translating into a metaphysical option that which is an ad hoc positioning (1979d).

Similarly, although parts of his book on anarchy and Christianity may appear to undermine this position, even there Ellul stresses it is his perception of the current political and social environment that leads him to advocate anarchy (*Anarchy*, 21-3).

Third, Ellul is frank and open about his disagreements with much traditional anarchist thinking. Most obvious is his personal faith in Jesus Christ that was so inimical to Debord's Situationists that Ellul was prevented from joining their group when he wished to do so. This basic division has other more concrete consequences. In contrast to many anarchists, Ellul is emphatically opposed to all forms of violent protest. Much more fundamentally, he consistently rejects the anarchist claim that it is possible to establish an anarchist society without rule or hierarchy (*Anarchy*, 11-23).[93] For Ellul, anarchy can only be a means, given the present context of the modern state and administrative and bureaucratic systems, of opening up the possibility of an alternative socio-political system. Thus he writes, 'I have no faith in a pure anarchist society, but I do believe in the possibility of creating a new social model' (*Anarchy*, 21).[94]

Having clarified exactly *what* Ellul says about the relationship of anarchy and Christianity and removed some common misconceptions about his stance, it is necessary briefly to show *why* he reached these conclusions. In terms of his own biography, Ellul's opposition to the modern state and support for a form of anarchy originated in the 1930s with his sociological reflections on the modern world, his reading of Proudhon, and his personal contacts with anarchists. It is, however, wholly consistent with the general structure of his theology, his specific theological reflections on the state and politics, and his sociological analysis of the modern political world, that he should see anarchism as an acceptable political stance and encourage Christians today to support forms of anarchy.

In relation to the state, it has been shown that although Ellul's theology becomes increasingly critical of political power, he always highlighted the strong biblical current of suspicion and critique of all human power. He consistently stressed the church's calling is to be separate from the political power, seeking to engage it in dialogue, and challenging it when it becomes an agent of the rebellious powers. Within this framework, the obligation to respect and obey persons in authority clearly prevents certain forms of anarchy. Nevertheless, when the state appears more and more like the Beast of Revelation 13 there must be confrontation and firm opposition by the Christian church. In addition, the theological principle of the existence of the church as a body within society which is distinct from the state, questions it, and limits its power, provides a base for a wider and more radical contesting of established political power when this is necessary. This explains why in *Freedom* it is in discussing the modern form of the Christian's dialogue with the sovereign that Ellul introduces his support for anarchy.

In relation to Christian involvement in politics, by emphasising the strong anti-power and anti-political stance of Scripture, its lack of positive encouragement that Christians seek to gain any political power, and its failure to rule any concrete political position either obligatory or impossible, Ellul demonstrates that there cannot be an absolute proscription of all forms of anarchy. More positively, anarchism's essential refusal of political power and

---

[93] This account of the form of anarchy Ellul advocates is now available on the web at www.flag.blackened.net.

[94] On possible anarchist models see Ward 1988.

Ellul's own form of anarchy - eschewing the modern political process and the modern state's excessive power in favour of creating small groups on the fringes of society which seek to address its real problems - explain why Ellul can recommend anarchy as 'the only "anti-political political position" in harmony with Christian thought' (*Marx*, 157).

CONCLUSION

CHAPTER 8

A 20th Century Prophet for the 21st Century ?

As the Christian church in the West enters the twenty-first century, few would dispute that the challenges she faces are great. Her strength, numerically, socially and politically is in decline, some even claim terminal decline, although she often lives in denial of this fact. The heady days of Christendom are a dim and distant past and will not and should not be recovered. In society at large, despite a growing recognition of the barrenness of materialism and an ever-expanding market offering a diverse range of alternative forms of 'spirituality', the institutional church, particularly in its historic and traditional manifestations, seems increasingly irrelevant to most people. The church, in turn, seems to struggle to understand the sexual, technological and communications revolutions of recent decades which shape most peoples' lives and she often appears to have lost sight of her calling to be the bearer of God's Word in and for his world.

In such a situation the church needs to hear a prophetic voice which is able to discern the signs of the times and to show her, through both encouragement and rebuke, how to be a faithful witness to her Lord. Jacques Ellul was, during his life, often described as a prophet by those who read his work or knew his life, although it was not a designation he welcomed or encouraged. The portrait of Ellul offered here has shown why some used that categorisation. He was a revolutionary dissenter who, from the 1930s onwards, was inspired by his personalist convictions and faith in Jesus Christ to study Scripture and to analyse the modern world in order to hear and obey God's word. He wrote to encourage others to resist what he saw as the catastrophic path taken by twentieth-century man and to incarnate the word of God in the contemporary world.

In the light of Part One's account of the structure of his theology and his sociology and the relationship between them and Part Two's examination of the details and development of his thought in areas of social and political thought, a brief assessment can now be offered of Ellul's value for the church's life and thought. The first section examines Ellul's contribution to social and political thought and shows his sociological analysis is still of value in secular social analysis and can still help the church understand the world she is called to resist. The second section turns to Ellul's contribution to Christian theology and ethics to illustrate that his work still addresses the church as she seeks to hear and obey God's Word.

Resisting the World: Ellul's Contribution to Social and Political Thought

One of Ellul's central criticisms of the contemporary church was that it failed to understand the world it found itself in during the last half of the twentieth century. It was therefore unable to resist the world in faithful witness to God's Word. Ellul's own reading of the cultural situation establishes him as a radical critic of modernity whose work is a major contribution to the church and to the wider task of critical social analysis. His insights here are not uninfluenced by his theology but they cannot be dismissed as simply derived from prior theological presuppositions. In order to recognise the distinctive contribution and ongoing significance of the sociological strand of his work it is helpful to distinguish four aspects: its context, form, focus, and goal.

First, in terms of its *context*, Ellul's analysis and criticisms stand out as they are not those of a philosopher or of a Christian mourning the loss of Christendom. They are the work of an academic historian of legal and political institutions with a speciality in Roman law. From this location his perspective on the development of the modern world is quite different from that of most other modernity critics, whether secular or Christian.

Of even more significance, his writing in this sphere has been seen to originate in the context of the French personalist movement of the 1930s. This movement (in the words of the sub-title of Loubet del Bayle's major study) sought the renewal of French political thought. It did so through an emphasis on the novelty of the twentieth-century world and the crisis of civilization that this produced. Initially, it produced much original thought and influenced many thinkers but it failed to establish itself as an ongoing, recognised, and distinctive school of political and social criticism and has now largely been forgotten. Ellul's sociological works (along with the even more neglected studies of Bernard Charbonneau) represent the perpetuation, elaboration and adaptation of this set of ideas. Their revolutionary programme sought, at a critical time in twentieth-century history, to formulate an alternative to communism, fascism, and liberal democratic capitalism, but it then largely vanished from both the intellectual and political scene. As Economica recognised when it began republishing their writing in its *Classiques des Sciences Sociales* series in the late 1980s, Ellul and Charbonneau together present an extensive and innovative analysis of the malaise of our contemporary world that deserves much greater scholarly attention in the social science community.

Although it would be melodramatic and premature to compare the closing years of last century and the opening decade of this century with the turbulence and crises of Europe in the 1930s, there are interesting parallels between our contemporary situation and that in which Ellul's analysis was born. Having witnessed the collapse of communism, Europe is once again seeing the resurgence of extreme right-wing politics and widespread popular discontent with traditional political solutions and procedures. Both at home and abroad, the phenomenon of 'globalisation', the attempt of liberal capitalism to secure hegemony despite its obvious failings, and the recognition of the reality of an environmental crisis have all led to growing resistance and the creation of numerous 'fringe' movements protesting against the direction set by the major world powers. In such a situation, the origins of Ellul's work almost seventy years ago renders it not irrelevant and anachronistic but potentially of even greater value for those seeking to comprehend our complex world and to develop genuine new alternatives to mainstream political, social and economic programmes.

Second, the *form* of Ellul's analysis also marks him out as significant because, unlike many critics of modernity, he does not concern himself with tracing an intellectual history of ideas but rather attempts to offer what has been called a 'global sociology'. Although inspired by Marx's project for last century, he cannot be classed (and then summarily dismissed) as simply another Marxist social critic. Instead he offers a radical analysis and critique which acknowledges that Marx's analysis (despite its accuracy for the nineteenth and early twentieth century) is no longer applicable because of the novelty of the modern world.[1] Although Ellul values Marx's method he is highly critical of some of Marx's presuppositions and many of his conclusions and presents his own extensive alternative account of the determining phenomena and characteristic features of the contemporary world. Here he draws on and develops in an original manner the insights of earlier libertarian socialist and anarchist thinkers as much as the work of Marx and offers a perceptive analysis of our legal and political world which could revitalise radical political thought after the apparent demise of traditional socialism.

Third, the *focus* of this alternative account is, of course, Technique and although the credit for this insight is due at least as much to Charbonneau, Ellul's greatest contribution is certainly to be found in making this the focus

---

[1] In the untranslated *Métamorphose*, Ellul writes, 'Marx's explanation is not sufficient today…we are in the presence of a new relationship between man and the world, even a new relationship between men which lacks any continuity (*sans commune mesure*) with that of the past' (*Métamorphose*, 292, n2).

of his understanding of the contemporary world. If for no other reason, his work is worthy of attention because by the mid-1930s, as a law student still in his early twenties, Ellul had already concluded that Technique was the central determinant of our modern world and begun to warn of some of the likely consequences of this. At the start of the twenty-first century, many of the ethical issues with which we must wrestle can only be understood and responded to from within a recognition of our world's wider commitment to efficiency and technological development. This insight therefore classes Ellul as one of the most original and discerning (perhaps even prophetic) social critics of the twentieth century.[2]

The first fruit of this perceptiveness was Ellul's 1954 study *La Technique*, of which George Grant, another great critic of modernity and technology wrote, 'in that work, the structure of modern society is made plain as in nothing else I have read'.[3] The book's calibre is proved by the fact that, nearly fifty years after its completion, it remains an indispensable work for anyone wishing to understand our technological civilization. Furthermore, as shown here in relation to the state and politics and the much neglected area of law, Ellul's account of Technique and its effects provided him with a key which opened up the door to shed light on a whole range of other elements of our social and political world. Faced as we are today with such diverse challenges as legal regulation in more and more spheres of life, bureaucratisation in education, developments in assisted reproduction and genetic engineering, and the power of the mass media and political spin-doctors, Ellul enables us to get below the specific, surface issue and see the bigger picture.

Fourth, it has been shown that Ellul's social criticism was never solely academic. Its *goal* was always to ignite a desire to oppose the developments of the modern world and to work for revolutionary change. Here again Ellul's vision and work is distinctive because, while insisting on the need for a radical restructuring of contemporary society from its foundations, he rejected the possibility of accomplishing this by normal political means. Taking control of power systems (whether by violence or through established procedures) in order to change them from within through re-directing them to different ends was, in part because of his own post-war experience, rejected as a strategy. Although he sketched a vision of an alternative society (personalist, anarcho-socialist, libertarian, democratic, and federalist) this was also not his primary goal. His revolutionary programme focussed on making individuals aware of the character and structure of the modern world and their alienation within it and organising small groups, starting from a local community base,

---

[2] For an account of other respects in which Ellul's work foreshadows that of such other great names as Roland Barthes and Jean Baudrillard see Chastenet 1994a.
[3] Grant 1966:ix.

to resist the direction society as a whole was taking. These concentrated their external challenge on particular aspects of the established social system while internally they recognised the need for personal as well as social transformation if a genuine revolution was to succeed. In a context where new forms of political campaigning are developing (e.g. anti-capitalist, anti-GM crops) and new forms of church (e.g. cell church) are being sought outside established institutional structures, Ellul again remains a fruitful dialogue partner for both contemporary church and society.

Many criticisms can - and have - been levelled at Ellul's sociological work. Its weaknesses, especially within the norms of the academic community are evident: its polemical style; its eschewal of precise definitions; its indiscriminate, sweeping, impressionistic statements and lack of careful, detailed analysis; its global vision and apparent dismissal of any change as insignificant; its bleak prognosis and lack of positive solutions. Nevertheless, in terms of their context, form, focus, and goal, Ellul sociological studies remain a significant contribution to the task of contemporary social and political thought and a guide for both the church and the academy as they seek to understand the world. Perhaps the best evidence of his importance and the highest recommendation that can made is not only that his thought is highly original but that his analysis has, on the whole, passed his own rigorous test for any such work: most of what he said, even as long ago as the 1950s and 1930s, has been proved right rather than wrong by subsequent events and remains of relevance at the start of the new millennium.

Living the Word: Ellul's Contribution to Christian Theology and Ethics

In assessing the continued significance of the other strand of Ellul's writing - his theology and ethics, and particularly his Christian reflections on society and politics - two levels of contribution can be distinguished: the substantive content of his work and his overall method and approach.

The Content of Ellul's Work

Despite his lack of formal academic qualifications in the field, Ellul was not only widely read in theology, but developed his own distinctive theology and ethic. Combining a strong doctrine of the Fall with an emphasis on Christians as those who are restored to communion with God, his theology did not result in an ethic of denial and withdrawal from the world. Instead, Ellul developed a theological ethic of a revolutionary Christian presence and style of life within the fallen world because his emphases on sin and holiness were counterbalanced by the centrality of the Incarnation, the call to hear and obey God's Word, and God's eschatological recapitulation of human history.[4] This theological ethic did not lead to a sense of Christian superiority for Ellul believed that the Christian always remain a sinner and it is the church's failure to fulfil her unique calling and make the Word of God present in the world which makes her peculiarly responsible for the world's troubles, not least in their contemporary form. Turning to those troubles, Ellul's theological and ethical reflections on specific issues can both help to shape Christian social and political witness in our post-Christendom world and to serve the task of Christian political thought.

Ellul's work on violence is perhaps the least original area of his Christian political thought. He stands broadly within the well-established tradition of non-violence best represented by the Anabaptists and recently revived in the works of John Howard Yoder and Stanley Hauerwas. Nevertheless, he expresses this in an original and provocative manner due to the structure of his theology. Many of his particular concerns bring to the fore themes which can get lost in Christian debate over questions of war, violence, and pacifism: that violence be understood in the broadest sense and that, similarly, true peace must be both a personal and a social quality; a theological critique of the just war theory for its provision of justifications for fallen man; a recognition of the impossibility of wholly fulfilling the Christian's calling to reject all violence; a refusal to expect an acceptance of non-violence on the part of the world. These features, however, also demonstrate the major weakness of his approach and open him to the criticism that his ways of approaching the question of violence cannot assist in concrete moral decision making as they 'leave the deliberative question in paradox and so seem to have more rhetorical than conceptual persuasiveness'.[5]

In contrast to the stability of Ellul's perspective on violence, his theology of law was constantly changing. There is a theologically principled opposition to any attempt to ignore the qualitative difference between human and divine justice or to overcome it by privileging the category of 'law' and establishing a hierarchy of laws in which divine law or natural law guides human law. Instead, his writing presents a number of alternative approaches to the question and this regularly changing position demonstrates the difficulties that arise for his theology of human law as a result of his wider theological framework and emphatic rejection of the dominant Christian tradition.

Despite this problem, two aspects of Ellul's juridical ethic redress an

---

[4] Fasching explores this aspect in Ellul's work as combining Niebuhr's 'Christ in paradox with culture' and 'Christ against culture' models to produce 'Christ transforming culture' (Fasching 1990 & 1992:154ff).

[5] O'Donovan 1993:655-6.

imbalance in much Christian reflection on law and offer new ways the church can engage today with legal questions in wider society. Firstly, in contrast to many Christians, Ellul does not concern himself primarily with the questions of the authority, validity, and desirability of certain specific pieces of secular legislation. Instead, he encourages Christians to understand and to judge the legal system as a functioning whole and to focus on the individual's personal relationship to that whole and particularly the task of Christian jurists within it. Once correlated with his disturbingly accurate predictions of the regulatory and bureaucratic direction of the legal system, this sets a distinctive agenda for the church, not least in relation to the development of European Law.[6] Secondly, particularly in its first and last phases, Ellul's work re-emphasises the strong biblical and early church tradition of Christians placing themselves on the margins of (or even outside) the juridical world by refusing recourse to law and basing their own attitude to secular law not on some general obligation to obey human laws but instead on obedience to Christ as Lord.

It is perhaps Ellul's writing on the state and politics which is most interesting and significant for the church in the contemporary world. Although others have critiqued the dominance of a particular interpretation of Romans 13 in the Christian tradition's reflection on the state, Ellul's writing also highlights the strong current throughout Scripture that is critical of all human power. Then, by drawing on the work of Barth and Cullmann, his theology of the powers and the authority of Christ provides this with a theological underpinning. Despite his constant (and seemingly never fully resolved) struggle to find the proper relationship between this critical strand and the more positive biblical teachings on political authority, Ellul, once again, provides an important counterbalance to the mainstream within Christian political thought. When this is joined with his emphasis on the destructive novelty of the modern state he presents a strong case for a much more critical and resisting Christian stance towards the state and the possibility of some Christians finding certain forms of 'anarchism' acceptable.

Finally, in politics (as in law) Ellul moves the focus away from debates about specific political stances which still dominates much Christian political discussion. He instead presents a picture of the pattern of Christian witness in relation to political life as a whole while warning the church against uncritically accepting the modern world's politicisation of the whole of life and ignoring the extent to which all politics in the world is based on violence and the quest for power. By his radical relativisation of political questions and careful delimiting of the political realm, he emphasises the importance of the

---

[6] For a discussion of the European Union which is influenced by Ellul's political writings and touches on legal issues (pp18-9) see my Grove booklet on the subject (Goddard 1998).

non-political without thereby suggesting that political and social questions fall outside the witness of the Church.

Taken together, Ellul's work in these areas offer a provocative challenge to the church's traditional patterns of thinking and witness. Rather than seeking to maintain the vestiges of Christendom he calls the church in this new century to recognise its minority position and to embrace afresh its prophetic calling: to be other than the world, resisting the world while speaking God's prophetic word to it and living that Word out within it by a distinctive way of life.

The Method of Ellul's Work

In addition to the concrete proposals discussed above, Ellul's general method is also of help in the task of Christian social and political witness and the church's calling in the world. He offers answers to five central questions, three relating to the role of God's self-revelation through his Word, one to the historic Christian tradition, and one to the agenda we face today.

First, does Christian revelation help us understand our social and political world ? Ellul's answer to this question has already been discussed in some detail in chapter four's study of the relationship between Ellul's theological and sociological works. From a panoramic perspective, Ellul believes God's Word reveals our social and political worlds as part of that world which has broken its communion with God. They are therefore marked, to varying degrees, by certain features and characteristics (chapter two). In addition, revelation shows that human attempts to explain the world will often hide its harsh reality with myths and ideologies while it enables Christians to be realistic in their analysis by giving a hope not dependent on this world but on God and his Word of promise.[7] Ellul does not, however, believe that revelation helps explain how particular human societies are structured or even how we are to study them. Nor can revelation enable us to trace the historical development of phenomena or discern the determining structures of our contemporary social and political world.

These conclusions have two important consequences: Christians must not claim any special privileged position for their analysis of contemporary society and their accounts of particular social and political phenomena can and should be presented on non-theological grounds and in non-theological terms. As a result, there must be constant but critical engagement with secular

---

[7] In his sociological work Ellul discusses false consciousness and explains it in language reflecting his theology – 'since the world's fracture *(la rupture du monde)* through the exploitation of man by man, there is no longer any just praxis and so we live under the reign of false consciousness' *(Métamorphose*, 291-2, n2).

social science because the work of Christians attempting to understand our social and political world is a fruit of reasoned reflection on experience and not divine revelation.

Second, does Christian revelation instruct Christians how to live in our social and political world ? It is clear that Ellul's proposals for Christian living in relation to elements of the social and political world derive from his wider Christian ethic which (as chapter two showed) is based on his overall theology. Here we find the heart of the division in Ellul's corpus: although we *cannot* appeal to revelation for comprehension of the structure of our social and political world, we *must* appeal to revelation for comprehension of our calling as Christians within that world. Revelation will not provide a Christian politics or a Christian legal system but it will show the unique and distinctive pattern of life expected of those restored to communion with God in Christ.

In order to make this calling concrete, however, Christians must become aware of the actual structure of the world in which they live. Ellul's social and political ethic for Christians is therefore the product of both his general theology and ethics and his sociological studies of the modern world. This is of great importance in seeking to understand his work and develop it further for the future. It means that those who disagree with Ellul's concrete proposals for Christian witness will nearly always find their differences can be traced back into the basic structure and central emphases of his wider theology (chapter two) and/or his sociology (chapter three).

This insight can be applied more widely as the church seeks to discern the nature of its witness in the world as it suggests disputes over the Christian response to society's problems are best analysed and assessed by getting below the surface issues to identify the deeper, more fundamental areas of agreement and divergence in theological perspective and/or sociological analysis. The enterprise of Christian political and social thought and debates about the Church's witness in the contemporary world would therefore be greatly enhanced were those involved to take greater care to present the ethical, theological, and sociological presuppositions which underpin their analyses and their concrete recommendations.

Third, does Christian revelation help Christians tell the world what it should do ? This, as noted in chapters two, six and seven, is a most important areas where Ellul's thought underwent change with major implications. He always insisted on the distinctiveness and uniqueness of the Christian's calling and he consistently repudiated any attempt by Christians to structure wider society in order to conform it to their own calling as Christians. His stance was clear: the church is to be the church and the world is to be the world.

However, in his early work Ellul regularly refers to a divine order for the preservation of the world. Although few details of this are given and it is clear that humans are granted significant freedom to determine its detailed forms, this order is clearly quite elaborate. Furthermore, this order can be known (at least in part) without reference to revelation even if revelation helps the Christian understand it and his relationship to it. Within this phase of his thinking, Ellul therefore believes Christians can and should call on the world to form its structures in a manner consonant with the divine order of preservation.

A much weaker form of this view may still undergird some of Ellul's writing on the specific question of legal institutions in the 1960s but it generally fades from his work in the early 1950s. From that time forward, Ellul's focus shifts and it is a shift he believed much of the Christian church has still to make but must make. His aim becomes primarily one of enabling the Christian to be faithful to his own unique calling in the world and, through this faithfulness, thereby preserve the world from the full effects of the rupture of its communion with God. Instead of a Christendom model with the church instructing the world about its proper ordering from revelation, Ellul presents a dual Christian function vis-à-vis the world: the critique of the world and its self-justifications on the world's own grounds (e.g. its claims that war will solve problems, that its legal system produces justice, that its political system is truly democratic) and the prophetic warning to the world (partly on the basis of revelation) of the consequences of its chosen actions, particularly when it falls prey to the powers and sacralises elements of the world which should be secular.

This question of the grounds and content of any Christian proposals for wider society is highly significant in our liberal, pluralist society. The church in the West is now living after Christendom and (as the French subtitle of his seminal 1948 study *Présence* already acknowledged) in a post-Christian society. The Christian church is simply one voice among many in the market place of ideas and programmes. Apart from his earlier dalliance with a complex order of preservation, Ellul rejects any appeal to some universal and revealed divine order. He thus repudiates the idea that the church must constantly condemn the world for failing to conform to the revealed will of God and, as his thought develops, he increasingly expunges from it any idea that the church should provide solutions or justifications for the world and its problems on the basis of revelation.

Instead of a direct application of revelation to the world, Ellul's project envisions Christian revelation affecting the social and political world radically but indirectly. It does so by a combination of four factors that set a challenging agenda for the church today. First, Christians are to offer a distinctive and faithful witness to Jesus Christ in all walks of life. Second, they are to fulfil their role as a critical conscience within society which reminds society of its own proclaimed values and its failure to live according to them. Third, they are to exercise a prophetic ministry that draws the world's attention to the problems that need to be addressed and the dangers that lie ahead on its chosen path. Fourth, Christians are to call individuals within the world of ruptured communion to break with it and enter again into communion with God in Christ and embrace the Christian life that flows from such conversion.[8]

Fourth, can the Christian tradition of social and political thought help contemporary Christian social and political thought and witness ? The previous questions have all focussed on Christian revelation because the claim to be trustees of special revelation is the primary distinctive feature of the Christian church and because Ellul places greatest emphasis on revelation in his theology. There is, however, also the question of the value of the history of Christian reflection on society and politics. Here Ellul is peculiar. Despite being an historian and referring to traditional Christian thought (both positively and negatively), he neither makes much use of it nor pays much attention to its potential contribution to the contemporary task. Three reasons can be given for this omission of dialogue with the Christian tradition which, if accepted, cast doubt on the value of viewing the tradition as a significant resource for contemporary Christian social and political thought and witness.

Firstly, theologically, Ellul evidently admires the scope and thoroughness of past Christian thinkers but he also believes that their understanding of the relationship between Church and society was seriously in error. As a result, their work offers little of positive value for today. Secondly, their thought reflects their participation in historic Christendom which for Ellul not only casts doubt on its conformity to revelation but also renders it of little value for our society where the relationship between the church and wider civil society is quite different. Thirdly, Ellul views our modern world as radically discontinuous with historic Western civilization. The absolute novelty of the modern world therefore also undermines appeal to traditional Christian social and political thought in debates about contemporary Christian witness.

Fifth, what should be the focus of contemporary Christian political and social thought and witness ? Ellul calls on Christians to reject not only the answers but also the questions which are raised by the world in standard debates on specific issues. They should, instead, develop new agendas and new responses that will mark out Christian reflection from that of the world. Rather than responding to issues thrown up by current affairs, political debate,

---

[8] For a recent discussion (influenced by Ellul) of how this might shape evangelism and mission see Tomlin 2002.

and general academic discussion, Ellul argues that the church's special responsibility is to address the deeper structural problems in society. It must, in other words, tackle the areas where most people share in an uncritical consensus and take matters for granted.[9]

Ellul's claim for the absolute novelty of modernity and his interpretation of our present social situation as a crisis of civilization may be considered too extreme by some. Nevertheless, his work challenges Christians to consider seriously the possibility that the problems which so often concern them and the rest of society - issues such as crime, social dislocation, unemployment, globalisation, international inequality and poverty, divorce, abortion, the environment, reform of the welfare state etc. - are mere epiphenomena to which solutions will not be found by political means or specific social reforms. What is required is a deeper understanding and a more fundamental critique leading to a reversal of the overall direction and fundamental structure of our modern technical civilization.

Living the Word, Resisting the World: Jacques Ellul's Life and Thought

In conclusion, Jacques Ellul's work represents an extensive and complex contribution to both contemporary social science and to the task of Christian social and political thought and witness. Although parts of it are now gaining the attention they merit in the church and the wider academic community, Ellul himself warned of the dangers in highly selective appropriations of his work:

> It is perfectly legitimate, for a particular end or a limited study, to take this book or that book from among my books…but obviously one misses out then on a level of appreciation… (*L'Homme*, 29).

The breadth and length of Ellul's writing, not to mention its style or the limited availability of much of it, could give the impression Ellul never seriously expected anyone to treat his work as a whole. He was, however, insistent that 'I have certainly conceived my books as *un ensemble*' (*L'Homme*, 26), that each book was merely a chapter in the one book which was his oeuvre and, ultimately, that it was his whole life which was his true oeuvre and in the light of which his writings must be interpreted.

Readers of Ellul, especially those discovering him for the first time, constantly face the challenge of seeing both the wood and the trees. This study

---

[9] Examples of this were cited above in relation to each of the studies in Part Two.

has combined a global account of his life and thought with more specific and detailed studies of particular areas of his thinking in order to clarify that extra dimension which is present when his work is interpreted within the context of his own life and read comprehensively as Ellul intended. Amidst all the complexity, controversy, changes, and at times apparent chaos of his thought it has uncovered a basic coherence within the entire, unique project and the two strands of theology and sociology which comprise it. Above all, it has discovered in the remarkable and powerful witness of Jacques Ellul's words and personal life-work someone whose life and thought presents the contemporary church with a truly prophetic challenge: to live the Word and resist the world.

ABBREVIATIONS

All references to Ellul books in the text refer to the volumes by means of a single italicized word from the title or an acronym of the title. The works are listed here along with their reference in the following bibliography of Ellul's published books where full publication details can be found.

ENGLISH TRANSLATIONS

Anarchy	1991	Anarchy and Christianity
Apocalypse	1977	Apocalypse
Autopsy	1971a	Autopsy of Revolution
Betrayal	1978	Betrayal of the West
Bluff	1990b	The Technological Bluff
City	1970a	The Meaning of the City
Conversations	1998	Jacques Ellul on Religion, Technology and Politics
Critique	1968	A Critique of the New Commonplaces
Demons	1975	The New Demons
Faith	1983	Living Faith
False	1972a	False Presence of the Kingdom
FLN	1982a	FLN Propaganda in France During the Algerian War
Freedom	1976	The Ethics of Freedom
Hope	1973	Hope in Time of Abandonment
Humiliation	1985	The Humiliation of the Word
Illusion	1967	The Political Illusion
Jonah	1971b	The Judgment of Jonah
Law	1960	The Theological Foundation of Law
Marx	1988	Jesus and Marx
Money	1984	Money and Power
Perspectives	1981	Perspectives on our Age
Politics	1972b	The Politics of God and the Politics of Man
Prayer	1970b	Prayer and the Modern Man
Presence	1951	Presence of the Kingdom
Propaganda	1965	Propaganda: The Formation of Men's Attitudes
Reason	1990a	Reason for Being: A Meditation on Ecclesiastes
Season	1982b	In Season, Out of Season
Sources	1997	Sources and Trajectories
Subversion	1986	The Subversion of Christianity
TS	1964	The Technological Society
TSys	1980	The Technological System
TWTD	1969a	To Will and To Do
Violence	1969b	Violence: Reflections from a Christian Perspective
WIB	1989	What I Believe

FRENCH

Anarchie	1988a	Anarchie et christianisme
Autopsie	1969	Autopsie de la révolution
Bluff	1988b	Le bluff technologique

Changer	1982	Changer de révolution
Classes	1998	Les classes sociales
Conférence	1985	Conférence sur l'Apocalypse de Jean
Crois	1987a	Ce que je crois
Déviances	1992a	Déviances et déviants
Dieu	1991a	Ce Dieu injuste…?
Directives		Directives pour un manifeste personnaliste
Entretiens	1994	Entretiens avec Jacques Ellul
Ethique I	1973a	Ethique de la liberté Tome I
Ethique II	1974	Ethique de la liberté Tome II
Ethique III	1984b	Les combats de la liberté
Exégèse	1966a	Exégèse des nouveaux lieux communs
Fausse	1963	Fausse présence au monde moderne
Feu	1975b	Sans feu ni lieu
Foi	1980a	La foi au prix du doute
Fondement	1946	Le fondement théologique du droit
Genèse	1987b	La Genèse aujourd'hui
Histoire	1967a	Histoire de la propagande
Institutions	1950s	Histoire des institutions (5 vols)
Israël	1986	Un chrétien pour Israël
Jeunesse	1971a	La jeunesse délinquante
Jonas	1952	Le livre de Jonas
L'Apocalypse	1975a	L'Apocalypse: Architecture en mouvement
L'Argent	1954b	L'Homme et l'argent
L'Empire	1980b	L'Empire du non-sens
L'Espérance	1972c	L'Espérance oubliée
L'Homme	1992b	L'Homme à lui-même
L'Idéologie	1979	L'Idéologie marxiste chrétienne
L'Illusion	1965	L'Illusion politique
Métamorphose	1967b	Métamorphose du bourgeois
Oratorio	1997	Oratorio: Les quatres cavaliers de l'Apocalypse
Parole	1981a	La parole humiliée
Politique	1966b	Politque de Dieu, politiques de l'homme
Possédés	1973b	Les nouveaux possédés
Présence	1948	Présence au monde moderne
Prière	1971b	L'Impossible prière
Propagandes	1962	Propagandes
Raison	1987b	La raison d'être
Révolution	1972b	De la revolution aux revoltes
Si	1991b	Si tu es le fils de Dieu
Silences	1995	Silences
Subversion	1984a	La subversion du christianisme
Système	1977	Le système technicien
Technique	1954a	La technique ou l'enjeu de siècle
Temps	1981b	A temps et à contretemps
Trahison	1975c	Trahison de l'Occident
Violents	1972a	Contre les violents
Vouloir	1964	Le vouloir et le faire

Bibliography

This bibliography falls into five main sections:
- French Published Books – These are arranged chronologically under first year of publication. After publication a cross-reference is given to the relevant English translation where it exists. Details of reissues are also provided.
- English Translations – These are also arranged chronologically by year of first appearance in English and again a cross-reference is provided to the original French. US and UK details are noted as are significant reissues.
- Articles by Jacques Ellul – These are limited to articles referenced in the thesis and are arranged chronologically with relevant English translations noted where important. For a full bibliography here see Hanks 2001.
- Unpublished Writings by Jacques Ellul – see explanatory note in this section.
- Secondary Materials – works cited in the book and used in research.

French Published Books

1946 *Le fondement théologique du droit*. Neuchâtel: Delachaux & Niestlé, Cahiers Théologiques de l'Actualité Protestante <nos. 15/16>. 109 pages. **[ET: 1960]**

1948 *Présence au monde moderne: Problèmes de la civilisation post-chrétienne*. Geneva: Roulet. 202 pages. **[ET : 1951]**
1988 edition : *Présence au monde moderne*. Lausanne: Presses Bibliques Universitaires, Éditions Ouverture. 136 pages.

1952 *Le livre de Jonas*. Paris: Cahiers Bibliques de Foi et Vie. 104 pages. Also published as *Foi et Vie* Vol 50 No 2 (March-April 1952), pp81-184. **[ET: 1971b]**

1954a *La technique ou l'enjeu du siècle*. Paris: Armand Colin. 401 pages. **[ET : 1964]**
1990 edition : *La technique ou l'enjeu du siècle*. Paris: Economica, Classiques des Science Sociales. 423 pages. Claims to be based on 1960 manuscript and adds 1965 article as appendix (pp393-409).

1954b *L'homme et l'argent (nova et vetera)*. Neuchâtel: Delachaux & Niestlé. 220 pages. **[ET : 1984]**
1979 edition : *L'homme et l'argent*. Lausanne: Presses Bibliques

Universitaires. 229 pages. Adds a new 'Postface' (pp219-229).

1950s   *Histoire des institutions 1-2: L'Antiquité.* Paris: Presses Universitaires de France. 629 pages. **[No ET]**[1]

1950s   *Histoire des institutions 3: Le Moyen Age.* Paris: Presses Universitaires de France. 396 pages. **[No ET]**

1950s   *Histoire des institutions 4: XVIe-XVIIe siècle.* Paris: Presses Universitaires de France. 320 pages. **[No ET]**

1950s   *Histoire des institutions 5: le XIXe siècle.* Paris: Presses Universitaires de France. 381 pages. **[No ET]**

1962   *Propagandes.* Paris: A. Colin. 333 pages. **[ET : 1965]**
1990 edition : *Propagandes.* Paris: Economica, Classiques des Science Sociales. 361 pages. Adds two articles from 1970s as appendices (pp333-354).

1963   *Fausse présence au monde moderne.* Paris: Les Bergers et les Mages. 189 pages. **[ET : 1972a]**

1964   *Le vouloir et le faire: Recherches éthiques pour les chrétiens: Introduction (première partie).* Geneva: Labor et Fides, Nouvelle Série Theologique <no 18>. 218 pages. **[ET : 1969a]**

1965   *L'illusion politique: Essai.* Paris: Robert Laffont. 265 pages. **[ET : 1967]***1977 edition* : *L'illusion politique.* Paris: Librairie Générale Francaise. 383 pages. This omits original 'Annexe' on the democratisation of the economic plan and adds a September 1977 'Postface' (pp355-383).

1966a   *Exégèse des nouveaux lieux communs.* Paris: Calmann-Lévy, Coll. Liberté de l'esprit. 298 pages. **[ET : 1968]**
1994 edition : *Exégèse des nouveaux lieux communs.* Paris: La Table Ronde, Coll. La petite vermillon <no. 38>. 302 pages.

1966b   *Politique de Dieu, politiques de l'homme.* Paris: Éditions Universitaires, Coll. Nouvelle alliance. 240 pages. **[ET : 1972b]**

1967a   *Histoire de la propagande.* Paris: Presses Universitaires de France, Que

---

[1] For fullest details of the history of varied editions of these regularly republished five volumes see Hanks 2000: 23-26.

Sais-Je ? <no 1271>. 127 pages. 2nd edition in 1976. **[No ET]**

1967b   *Métamorphose du bourgeois*. Paris: Calmann-Lévy. 303 pages. **[No ET]**
1998 edition : *Métamorphose du bourgeois*. Paris: La Table Ronde, Coll.
La petite vermillon <no. 97>. 354 pages.

1969   *Autopsie de la révolution*. Paris: Calmann-Lévy. 354 pages. **[ET :
1971a]**

1971a   *Jeunesse délinquante: Une expérience en province*. Paris: Mercure de
France, Coll. 'En direct'. 307 pages. Co-authored with Yves Charrier.
[No ET]
1985 edition : *Jeunesse délinquante: Des blousons noirs aux hippies*.
Nantes: Editions de l'AREFPPI. 218 pages.

1971b   *L'impossible prière*. Paris: Le Centurion. 186 pages. **[ET : 1970b]**

1972a   *Contre les violents*. Paris: Le Centurion. 222 pages. **[ET : 1969b]**

1972b   *De la révolution aux révoltes*. Paris: Calmann-Lévy, Coll. Liberté de
l'Esprit. 382 pages. **[No ET]**

1972c   *L'espérance oubliée*. Paris: Gallimard. 286 pages. **[ET : 1973]**

1973a   *Éthique de la liberte Tome I*. Geneva: Labor et Fides, Nouvelle Série
Théologiques <no. 27>. 330 pages. **[ET : 1976]**

1973b   *Les nouveaux possédés*. Paris: Arthème Fayard. 286 pages. **[ET : 1975]**

1974   *Éthique de la liberte Tome II*. Geneva: Labor et Fides, Nouvelle Séries
Théologique <no. 30>. 209 pages. **[No ET]**

1975a   *L'Apocalypse: Architecture en mouvement*. Paris: Desclée, Coll.
L'Athéisme Interrogé. 274 pages. **[ET : 1977]**

1975b   *Sans feu ni lieu: Signification biblique de la Grande Ville*. Paris:
Gallimard. 304pp pages. Compared to earlier ET this has a longer
Preface ('Avertissement', pp9-17) and also adds a summary bibliographic
note (p18), notes on Comblin's book (pp19) and a note on Harvey Cox's
critique of the US edition (pp20-21). A Scripture index (pp299-302) is
also provided. **[ET: 1970a]**

1975c   *Trahison de l'Occident*. Paris: Calmann-Lévy. 224 pages. **[ET : 1978]**

1977   *Le système technicien*. Paris: Calmann-Lévy. 363 pages. **[ET : 1980]**

1979   *L'idéologie marxiste chrétienne: que fait-on de l'évangile ?* Paris: Le Centurion. 229 pages. **[ET : 1988]**

1980a *La foi au prix du doute: 'Encore quarante jours...'* Paris: Hachette, Coll. 'Littérature'. 330 pages. **[ET : 1983]**

1980b *L'empire du non-sens: L'art et la société technicienne*. Paris: Presses Universitaires de France, Coll. 'La politique éclatée'. 286 pages. **[No ET]**

1981a *La Parole humiliée*. Paris: Seuil. 304 pages. **[ET : 1985]**

1981b *A temps et à contretemps: Entretiens avec Madeleine Garrigou-Lagrange*. Paris: Le Centurion. 210 pages. **[ET : 1982b]**

1982   *Changer de révolution: L'inéluctable prolétariat*. Paris: Seuil, Coll. Empreintes. 291 pages. **[No ET]**

1984a *La subversion du christianisme*. Paris: Le Seuil, Coll. Empreintes. 252 pages. 2nd edn in 1994. **[ET: 1986]**
         2001 edition : La subversion du christianisme. Paris: La Table Ronde, Coll. La petite vermillon. 324 pages.

1984b *Les combats de la liberté*. Geneva & Paris: Labor et Fides & Le Centurion. 338 pages. Originally written in 1966 and revised in 1972, 1974 and 1980-82. **[ET : 1976]**

1985   *Conférence sur l'Apocalypse de Jean (suivi du texte de l'Apocalypse)*. Nantes: Editions de l'AREFPPI. 173 pages. **[No ET]**

1986   *Un chrétien pour Israël*. Monaco: Éditions du Rocher. 241 pages. **[No ET]**

1987a *Ce que je crois*. Paris: Grasset and Fasquelle. 290 pages. **[ET : 1989]**

1987b *La Genèse aujourd'hui*. Editions de l'AREFPPI. 221 pages. With François Tosquelles. **[No ET]**

1987c *La raison d'être: Méditation sur l'Ecclésiaste*. Paris: Seuil, Coll. Empreintes. 315 pages. **[ET : 1990a]**

1988a *Anarchie et christianisme.* Lyon: Atelier de Création Libertaire. 123 pages. **[ET : 1991]**
1998 edition : Anarchie et christianisme. Paris: La Table Ronde, Coll. La petite vermillon <no. 96>. 163 pages.

1988b *Le bluff technologique.* Paris: Hachette, Coll. 'La force des idées'. 489 pages. **[ET : 1990b]**

1991a *Ce Dieu injuste...? : Théologie chrétienne pour le peuple d'Israël.* Paris: Arléa. 203 pages. 2nd end in 1999. **[No ET]**

1991b *Si tu es le Fils de Dieu: Souffrances et tentations de Jésus.* Paris: Centurion. 110 pages. **[No ET]**

1991c *Subjectivité.* Bordeaux: Bibliothèque de Bordeaux. 5 pages. **[No ET]**

1992a *Déviances et déviants dans notre société intolérante.* Toulouse: Editions Erès, Coll. 'Trajets'. 173 pages. **[No ET]**

1992b *L'homme à lui-même: Correspondance.* Paris: Editions du Félin, Coll. 'Vifs'. 187 pages. With Didier Nordon. **[No ET]**

1994 *Entretiens avec Jacques Ellul.* Paris: La Table Ronde. 209 pages. Interviews by Patrick Chastenet. **[ET: 1998]**

1995 *Silences: Poèmes.* Bordeaux: Éditions Opales. 92 pages. **[No ET]**

1997 *Oratorio: Les quatre cavaliers de l'Apocalypse.* Bordeaux: Éditions Opales. 96 pages. **[No ET]**

1998 *Les classes sociales: Cours de Jacques Ellul à l'Institut d'Études Politiques de Bordeaux, 1966/67.* Talence: Institut d'Études Politiques. pages. **[No ET]**

English Translations

1951 *The Presence of the Kingdom*. Translated by Olive Wyon, London: SCM Press. 145 pages. US edition - Philadelphia: Westminster (1951). **[Fr: 1948]**
1967 edition : *The Presence of the Kingdom*. New York: Seabury. Includes 'Introduction' by William Stringfellow (pp1-6).
1989 edition : *The Presence of the Kingdom*. Colorado Springs: Helmers and Howard. Includes a new Preface (vii-xiv) and a January 1989 'Afterword: Notes on the Current Situation' (pp129-132) by Ellul. Reprints the 1967 Stringfellow Introduction as 'Foreword to the 1967 edition' (xv-xix). Daniel Clendenin adds a new introduction (xxi-xlii, see Clendenin 1989) and index (pp137-45) supplied.

1960 *The Theological Foundation of Law*. Translated by Marguerite Wieser, New York: Doubleday. 140 pages. UK edition from London: SCM Press (1961) and later US reprint from New York: Seabury (1969). **[Fr: 1946]**

1964 *The Technological Society*. Translated by John Wilkinson, New York: Knopf. 449 pages. Adds 'Statement from Publisher' (iii-iv), Foreword by Robert K. Merton (v-vii) and Translator's Introduction (ix-xxvi). Ellul himself gives a June 1963 'Note to the Reader' (xxv-xxvi) and provides a January 1964 'Foreword to the Revised American Edition' (xxvii-xxxiii) to supplement his original 1954 Preface (xxxv-xxxvi). The original Postface is extended with a section 'A Look At the Year 2000' which is lacking from all French editions of the book and an index is also provided. UK version from London: Jonathan Cape (1965) and a US reprint from New York: Knopf, Vintage Books (1967). **[Fr: 1954a]**

1965 *Propaganda: The Formation of Men's Attitudes*. Translated by Konrad Kellen and Jean Lerner, New York: Knopf. 320 pages. Adds an index to French edition and Introduction by Konrad Kellen (v-viii). Later US reprint from New York: Random House, Vintage Books (1973). **[Fr: 1962]**

1967 *The Political Illusion*. Translated by Konrad Kellen, New York: Knopf. 258 pages. Ellul adds a January 1966 'Preface to the English Translation' (xiii-xi) and Kellen writes a 'Translator's Introduction' (vii-xi). **[Fr: 1965]**

1968 *A Critique of the New Comonplaces*. Translated by Helen Weaver, New York: Knopf. 303 pages. **[Fr: 1966a]**

1969a *To Will and To Do: An Ethical Research for Christians.* Translated by C. Edward Hopkin, Philadelphia: Pilgrim Press. 310 pages. Foreword by Waldo Beach (vi-viii). **[Fr: 1964]**

1969b *Violence: Reflections from a Christian Perspective.* Translated by Cecilia Gaul Kings, New York: Seabury Press. 179 pages. UK edition from London: SCM Press (1970) and London: Mowbrays (1978). Includes index which did not appear in French edition. **[Fr: 1972a]**

1970a *The Meaning of the City.* Translated by Dennis Pardee, Grand Rapids: Eerdmans. 209 pages. Introduction by John Wilkinson (vii-xvi) and Preface by Ellul (xvii-xviii). Reprint from Bellingham WA: Regent College (1993) and UK edition from Carlisle: Paternoster Press (1997). **[Fr: 1975b]**

1970b *Prayer and Modern Man.* Translated by C. Edward Hopkin, New York: Seabury Press. 178 pages. Paperback edition appeared in 1973. **[Fr: 1971b]**

1971a *Autopsy of Revolution.* Translated by Patricia Wolf, New York: Knopf. 300 pages. **[Fr: 1969]**

1971b *The Judgment of Jonah.* Translated by Geoffrey W. Bromiley, Grand Rapids: Eerdmans. 103 pages. **[Fr: 1952]**

1972a *False Presence of the Kingdom.* Translated by C. Edward Hopkin, New York: Seabury Press. 211 pages. The original Preface appears in a slightly edited form and with a new paragraph addressed 'To The American Reader (v-vi). **[Fr: 1963]**

1972b *The Politics of God and the Politics of Man.* Translated by Geoffrey W. Bromiley, Grand Rapids: Eerdmans. 199 pages. **[Fr: 1966b]**

1973 *Hope in Time of Abandonment.* Translated by C. Edward Hopkin, New York: Seabury Press. 306 pages. **[Fr: 1972a]**

1975 *New Demons.* Translated by C. Edward Hopkin, London: Mowbrays. 228 pages. US edition from New York: Seabury (1973). **[Fr: 1973b]**

1976 *The Ethics of Freedom.* Translated by Geoffrey W. Bromiley, London: Mowbrays. 517 pages. Includes Editor's Preface (p5) and Author's Preface (pp7-8). US edition from Grand Rapids: Eerdmans (1976).

[Fr: 1973a & 1984b]

1977   *Apocalypse: The Book of Revelation.* Translated by George W. Schreiner, New York: Seabury. 283 pages. **[Fr: 1975a]**

1978   *The Betrayal of the West.* Translated by Matthew J. O'Connor, New York: Seabury. 207 pages. **[Fr: 1975a]**

1980   *The Technological System.* Translated by Joachim Neugroschel, New York: Continuum. 362 pages. **[Fr: 1977]**

1981   *Perspectives on Our Age: Jacques Ellul Speaks on His Life and Work.* Translated by Joachim Neugroschel, Toronto: Canadian Broadcasting Corporation. 111 pages. Edited by William H. Vanderburg who adds preface in Canadian edition (vii-xi). US edition from New York: Seabury (1981) and reprint from Concord, Ontario: House of Anansi (1997). **[No French edition]**

1982a   *FLN Propaganda in France During the Algerian War.* Translated by Randal Marlin, Ottawa: By Books. 30 pages. Randal Marlin provides 'Translator's Introduction' (pp1-12). **[No French edition]**

1982b   *In Season, Out of Season: An Introduction to the Thought of Jacques Ellul: Based on Interviews by Madeleine Garrigou-Lagrange.* Translated by Lani K. Niles, San Francisco: Harper & Row. 242 pages. Adds 'Introduction' to the American Edition' by David W. Gill (v-xiii) and Index (pp237-42). **[Fr: 1981b]**

1983   *Living Faith: Belief and Doubt in a Perilous World.* Translated by Peter Heinegg, San Francisco: Harper & Row. 287 pages. Adds 'Introduction' by David W. Gill (xi-xvi) and Index (pp279-87). **[Fr: 1980a]**

1984   *Money and Power.* Translated by LaVonne Neff, Downers Grove, IL: Inter-Varsity Press. 173 pages. Foreword by David Gill (pp5-8). UK edition from Basingstoke: Marshall Pickering (1986). **[Fr: 1954b (ET of 1979 reprint)]**

1985   *The Humiliation of the Word.* Translated by Joyce Main Hanks, Grand Rapids: Eerdmans. 285 pages. Adds 'Preface' by Joyce Main Hanks (vii-xiii) and indexes (pp274-285). **[Fr: 1981a]**

1986   *The Subversion of Christianity.* Translated by Geoffrey W. Bromiley,

Grand Rapids: Eerdmans. 212 pages. **[Fr: 1984a]**

1988 *Jesus and Marx: From Gospel to Ideology.* Translated by Joyce Main Hanks, Grand Rapids: Eerdmans. 187 pages. Adds 'Preface' by Joyce Hanks (vii-xvi) and indexes (pp181-7). **[Fr: 1979]**

1989 *What I Believe.* Translated by Geoffrey W. Bromiley, London: Marshall Morgan and Scott. 223 pages. Includes 'Translator's Preface' (vii-viii). US edition from Grand Rapids: Eerdmans (1987). **[Fr: 1987a]**

1990a *Reason for Being: A Meditation on Ecclesiastes.* Translated by Joyce Main Hanks, Grand Rapids: Eerdmans. 306 pages. **[Fr: 1987c]**

1990b *The Technological Bluff.* Translated by Geoffrey W. Bromiley, Grand Rapids: Eerdmans. 418 pages. Adds 'Translator's Preface' (ix-x). **[Fr: 1988b]**

1991 *Anarchy and Christianity.* Translated by Geoffrey W. Bromiley, Grand Rapids: Eerdmans. 109 pages. Adds indexes (pp106-9). **[Fr : 1988a]**

1997 *Sources and Trajectories: Eight Early Articles by Jacques Ellul that Set the Stage.* Translated by Marva J. Dawn, Grand Rapids: Eerdmans. 208 pages. Dawn translates eight articles only previously available in French (1946b, 1947g&h, 1954d, 1951c, 1959a, 1960l and 1968c) and provides for each comments on their background ('Sources') and later development ('Trajectories'). **[No French edition]**

1998 *Jacques Ellul on Religion, Technology, and Politics: Conversations with Patrick Troude-Chastenet.* Translated by Joan Mendès France, Atlanta: Scholars Press. 142 pages. This volume contains some corrections to the original French, renumbers the chapters and adds some explanatory footnotes for non-French audience. An index is also provided (pp137-42). **[Fr: 1994]**

Articles by Jacques Ellul

1937 Le Fascisme, fils du libéralisme. *Esprit* 5 (53), 1 February: 761-797.

1938a Amour de soi. *Le Semeur* 41 (7), May-June: 403-431.
1938b Note sur les impôts municipaux à Montpellier aux XIIIe et XIVe siècles. *Revue Historique de Droit Français et Etranger* 17 <4th series>: 365-403.

1939a Droit. *Foi et Vie* 40 (2-3 <whole nos. 106-107>), March-June: 262-280. Later reprint in *Foi et Vie* (2000).
1939b La politique et nous. *Le Semeur* 42 (3), January: 177-181.

1942 Les communautés naturelles, pp 57-79 in *Communauté*, edited by J. Ellul and L. Joubert. Paris: Editions "Je Sers" S.C.E.L.

1945a Capitalisme et nous. *Réforme*, 20 October, 1, 7.
1945b La guerre inexpiable. *Réforme*, 7 July, 2.
1945c A propos du libéralisme: essai de réponse et de justification. *Réforme*, 7 December, 3.
1945d Signification actuelle de la Réforme, pp 137-165 in *Protestantisme français*, edited by Marc Boegner and Andre Siegfried. Paris: Présences.
1945e Victoire d'Hitler ? *Réforme*, 23 June, 1, 3.

1946a Ça y est. *Réforme*, 12 October, 1, 7.
1946b Chronique des problèmes de civilisation I:En guise d'avertissement. *Foi et Vie* 44 (6), September-October: 678-687. ET in *Sources*, 13-22.
1946c La hiérarchie sociale. *Les Deux Cités: Cahiers des Associations Professionelles Protestantes* 2: 17-21.
1946d L'Eglise et la situation politique actuelle. *Les Deux Cités: Cahiers des Associations Professionelles Protestantes* 2: 23-28.
1946e L'Eglise et la vie économique. *Les Deux Cités: Cahiers des Associations Professionelles Protestantes* 1: 21-34.
1946f Notes sur la formation civique de la jeunesse. *Réforme*, 2 November, 3.
1946g Problèmes de notre société. *Le Semeur* 44 (4-5), February-March: 407-426.
1946h Situation politique actuelle de la France (1er janvier 1946). *Foi et Vie* 44 (3), March-April: 283-300.
1946i Socialisme et communisme. *Réforme*, 26 October, 1, 3.

1947a Indications sur les tâches actuelles des juristes chrétiens. *Le Semeur* 45 (6-7), April-May: 485-493.

1947b   L'économie, maîtresse ou servante de l'homme, pp 43-58 in *Pour une économie à la taille de l'homme*, edited by L. Maire and J. Ellul. Geneva: Roulet.

1947c   Mais où va l'esprit de l'homme ? *Réforme*, 6 September, 1, 3.

1947d   Note sur le procès de Nuremberg. *Verbum Caro* 1 (3), August: 97-112.

1947e   Propositions louches. *Réforme*, 28 June, 1, 2.

1947f   Vers un nouvel humanisme politique, pp 5-21 in *L'homme mesure de toute chose*, edited by J. Ellul, P. Tournier, and Rene Gillouin. Geneva: Publications du Centre Protestant d'Etudes.

1947g   Problèmes de civilisation II: On demande un nouveau Karl Marx. *Foi et Vie* 45 (3), May/June: 360-74. ET in *Sources*, 31-45.

1947h   Problèmes de civilisation III: Le réalisme politique. *Foi et Vie* 45 (7), November/December: 698-734. ET in *Sources*, 51-84.

1948a   Civilisation et croyances. *Réforme*, 10 April, 2.

1948b   Garry, nouveau 'Tulipe'. *Réforme*, 11 December, 4.

1948c   L'Eglise ne suit pas les lois sociologiques du monde mais au contraire le monde suit le plan de Dieu. *Réforme*, 4 December, 2.

1948d   Les assassins vertueux. *Réforme*, 22 May, 2.

1948e   Post-chrétienté. *Réforme*, 25 December, 1, 3.

1948f   The situation in Europe, pp 50-60 in *The church and the disorder of society*, edited by World Council of Churches. London: SCM.

1949a   Conformisme au siècle présent: Le jugement impossible. *Réforme*, 1 October, 1, 3.

1949b   Conformisme au siècle présent: l'immoralisme facile. *Réforme*, 29 October, 1, 3.

1949c   Le fédéralisme pourri. *Réforme*, 17 December, 1, 3.

1949d   Note problématique sur l'histoire de l'église. *Foi et Vie* 47 (4), July-August: 297-324.

1949e   Pour un état laïque. *Réforme*, 30 April, 1, 2.

1950a   Engagement et dégagement. *Réforme*, 21 January, 1, 3.

1950b   J. de Senarclens: le mystère de l'histoire. *Réforme*, 11 March, 2.

1950c   La Bible et la ville. *Foi et Vie* 48 (1), January-February: 4-19.

1950d   La femme et les esprits. *Réforme*, 4 November, 2.

1950e   L'évolution de l'idée de liberté depuis 1936. *Évidences: Revue mensuelle publiée par l'American Jewish Committee* 8 February: 1-5.

1950f   Pourquoi je me suis séparé de Mounier. *Réforme*, 15 April, 6, 7.

1950g   Préface: du problème de l'efficacité, pp 7-17 in *Misère et grandeur de la médicine: Essai sur les conditions d'une médicine efficace*, edited by Ph. Kressmann. Neuchatel: Delachaux & Niestlé.

1950h   Réalisme et révolution. *Réforme*, 7 January, 1, 3.

1950i Réflexion sur le monde de la nécessité. *Vie, art, cité: Revue suisse romande* 14 (1): 37-39.

1950j Urbanisme et théologie biblique. *Dieu Vivant* (16): 109-123.

1951a Alain Sergent: les anarchistes. *Réforme*, 22 December, 7.

1951b Éloge du désordre. *Réforme*, 20 October, 1.

1951c Le sens de la liberté chez St. Paul, pp 64-73 in *Paulus-Hellas-Oikumene: An Ecumenical Symposium.* Athens: Associations Chrétienne d'Étudiants de Grèce. ET in *Sources*, 115-31.

1951d Mobilisation générale. *Le Protestant d'Aquitaine* 3 (29), July: 2-3.

1951e Overture au temps de la paix. *Réforme*, 17 March, 1.

1952a La civilisation à l'épreuve. *Le Monde*, 17 June, 7.

1952b La dogmatique de K.Barth en français. *Christianisme au XXe siècle* (47), 20 November: 416.

1952c L'Homme et l'état. *Le Monde*, 16 December, 9.

1952d Les fondements bibliques de notre responsabilité, pp 11-21 in *Notre responsabilité: Actes et travaux du 3ᵉ congrès médico-social protestant; Bordeaux 1-4 Nov 1951.* Cahors: A. Coueslant.

1953a Concert des maîtres de l'art russe. *Réforme*, 7 November, 8.

1953b Conclusion au débat sur l'article de Jacques Ellul: Goettling et Rosenberg. *Réforme*, 1 August, 4.

1953c Goettling et Rosenberg. *Réforme*, 11 July, 3.

1953d Justice doit être faite. *Sud-Ouest*, 10 January, 1, 7.

1953e Le péril est à l'intérieur. *Le Monde*, 6-7 December, 3.

1953f L'université à Canossa. *Le Monde*, 14 October, 5.

1953g Réflexions 'a posteriori' sur les grèves d'août. *Le Monde*, 9 September, 5.

1953h Responsabilités de la propagande. *Cahiers de la pierre-qui-vivre*: 51-62.

1954a L'État et la vérité: la secte de Montfavet. *Réforme*, 22 May, 1, 8.

1954b L'État et la vérité: La Vérité c'est moi. *Réforme*, 5 June, 1, 2.

1954c L'État et la vérité: une politique de la jeunesse. *Réforme*, 15 May, 1, 5.

1954d Sur le pessimisme chrétien. *Foi et Vie* 52 (2), March-April: 164-180. ET in *Sources*, 94-109.

1955a Avant que l'incendie ne gagne. *Réforme*, 22 October, 1, 3.

1955b Comment les communistes voient la coexistence. *Réforme*, 25 June, 1, 3.

1955c Laïc, mon frère. *Revue de l'évangelisation* 9 <new series> (59), December: 433-438.

1956a Le communisme et la guerre. *Réforme*, 5 May, 6.

1956b Le pessimisme et la présence au monde. *Le Semeur* 55 (2): 51-54.

1957a   De la gauche, de la vertu, du discernment et de la bonne conscience. *Réforme*, 9 March, 3.

1957b   Information et propagande. *Diogène* (18), April: 69-90.

1957c   La vertu est à gauche. *Réforme*, 9 February, 1.

1957d   Le drame algérien: la guerre et la torture. *Réforme*, 4 May, 3.

1957e   L'univers concentrationnaire: le fait est là. *Réforme*, 24 August, 1.

1958a   En pleine morale. *Le Semeur* 56 (1), February: 2-5.

1958b   Les larbins du régime. *Réforme*, 6 September, 4-5.

1958c   Vanité d'un tombeau pour Nagy. *Réforme*, 28 June, 1.

1959a   Actualité de la Réforme. *Foi et Vie* 58 (2), March-April: 39-64. ET in *Sources*, 137-61.

1959b   La Réforme et le pouvoir politique: un citoyen comme les autres. *Réforme*, 23 May, 4.

1959c   The obstacles to communication arising from propaganda habits. *Student World* 52 (4): 401-410.

1959d   Propositions concernant l'attitude chrétienne envers le droit. *Foi et Vie* 58 (1), January-February: 32-43.

1959e   Propositions concerning the Christian attitude toward law. *Oklahoma Law Review* 12 (1), February: 134-146.

1959f   Structures et positions de la droite: une enquête. *Évidences* (76), March: 5-13.

1960a   Christianisme et droit: recherches américaines. *Archives de philosophie du droit* (5): 27-35.

1960b   De la guerre et de la désertion. *Réforme*, 6 August, 1.

1960c   La désertion aujourd'hui. *Réforme*, 13-20 August, 1.

1960d   La nation. *Revue de l'évangélisation* 16 <new series> (89), May-June-July: 206-213.

1960e   La technique et les premiers chapitres de la Genèse. *Foi et Vie* 59 (2), March-April: 97-113. ET in Mitcham & Grote 1984: 123-37.

1960f   L'Armée et la nation. *Réforme*, 6 February, 4.

1960g   Le fonds du problème. *Réforme*, 27 August, 3.

1960h   Les certitudes difficiles. *Réforme*, 3 September, 3.

1960i   Notes en vue d'une éthique du temps et du lieu pour les chrétiens. *Foi et Vie* 59 (5), September-October: 354-374.

1960j   Réflexions sur la 'Dolce Vita'. *Réforme*, 9 July, 6.

1960k   Technique et civilisation. *Free University Quarterly* 7 (2), August: 72-84.

1960l   Foi chrétienne et réalité sociale. *Free University Quarterly* 7 (2), August: 166-177. ET in *Sources*, 168-80.

1961a Essai sur la signification philosophique des réformes actuelles de l'enseignement du droit. *Archives de philosophie du droit* (6): 1-18.

1961b Les sociologues ne prennent pas de risques car la sociologie, c'est de la dynamite ! *Réforme*, 16 July, 12, 6.

1961c Quelle est la signification de la révélation chrétienne pour le droit positif ?, pp 39-49 in *La révélation chrétienne et le droit: colloque de philosophie du droit (24- 25 Nov 1959)*, edited by Jean Bosc. Paris: Dalloz.

1961d Vous y croyez, vous, à la décomposition de l'état ? *Réforme*, 12 August, 2.

1962a Du beurre ou des canons. *Réforme*, 11 August, 2.

1962b Réalité sociale et théologie du droit, pp 36-61 in *Existenz und Ordnung: Festschrift für Erik Wolf*, edited by Thomas Wurtenberger. Frankfurt am Main: V. Klostermann.

1962c The technological order. *Technology and Culture* 3 (4), Fall: 394-421.

1963a Le droit occidental en 1970 à partir de l'expérience française. *Futuribles* (47), 1 January: 3-27.

1963b Le sacré dans le monde moderne. *Le Semeur* (2): 24-36.

1963c L'Homme au pied du mur. *Réforme*, 4 May, 8.

1963d Sur l'artificialité du droit et le droit d'exception. *Archives de philosophie du droit* (8): 21-33.

1964 Max Weber: l'éthique protestante et l'esprit du capitalisme. *Bulletin SEDEIS* 905 (1), 20 December: 4-17.

1965a The biology of technique. *Nation*, 24 May, 567-568.

1965b Law as representation of value. *Natural Law Forum* 10: 54-66.

1965c Réflexions sur l'ambivalence du progrès technique. *La Revue Administrative* 18 July-August: 380-391.

1965d Réflexions sur le droit comme représentation, pp 249-261 in *Philosophy and Christianity: Philosophical Essays dedicated to Herman Dooyeweerd*. Kampen: J.H. Kok.

1965e Sur l'artificialité du droit et le droit d'exception (suite). *Archives de philosophie du droit* 10: 191-207.

1966a The artist in the technological society. *Structurist (University of Saskatchewan)* (6): 35-41.

1966b Genève: Conférence mondiale Église et société: Technique et théologie. *Réforme*, 9 July, 11.

1966c Réponse à M. Merle au sujet de 'L'illusion politique'. *Revue française de* *science politique* 16: 87-100.

1966d Sur 'Église et société': Propos incongrus. *Réforme*, 24 September, 16, 14.

1966e Un professeur et des étudiants. *Le Christianisme au XXe Siècle* 95 (6), 10 February: 65-66.

1967a Faut-il condamner la jeunesse inadaptée ? *Le Christianisme au XXe Siècle* 96 (21), 25 May: 281-282.

1967b Il faut sauver Israël. *Réforme*, 24 June, 5.

1967c Information et vie privée: perspectives. *Foi et Vie* 66 (6), November-December: 52-66.

1967d La technique peut-elle être la mère d'une civilisation ? *Terre entière* (22), March-April: 6-27.

1967e Le droit biblique d'après l'exemple de la royauté et les cultures orientales, pp 253-273 in *Melanges offerts à Jean Brethe de la Gressaye*. Bordeaux: Editions Bière.

1967f Le facteur déterminant des problèmes et de l'évolution de la société contemporaine: la technique. *Sciences* (48), March-April: 28-46.

1967g Mon Dieu mon Dieu pourquoi m'as-tu abandonné ? *Réforme*, 18 March, 5-6.

1967h A propos du drame de Pessac: jeunesse inadaptée. *Le Monde*, 2 September, 10.

1967i Rappels et réflexions sur une théologie de l'état, pp 127-180 in *Les chrétiens et l'état*, edited by Jacques Jullien, Pierre L'Huillier, and Jacques Ellul. Tours: Maisons Mame.

1967j Si Mendès France était élu... *Réforme*, 18 February, 6.

1967k Sur l'université de Bordeaux: Défense du maître. *Réforme*, 4 February, 6.

1967l The technological revolution: its moral and political consequences. *Concilium* 6 (3), June: 47-51.

1967m Y a-t-il une politique chrétienne ? Réponse à l'enquête. *Esprit* 35 <new series> (364), October: 612-659.

1968a La contestation dans l'université. *Sud-Ouest*, 24 July, 2.

1968b Mise en question de l'université. *Sud-Ouest*, 16 May, 1, 4.

1968c Notes innocentes sur la 'question herméneutique', pp 181-190 in *L'évangile hier et aujourd'hui: Mélanges offerts au Professeur Franz J. Leenhardt*. Geneva: Labor et Fides. ET in *Sources*, 186-99.

1968d The psychology of a rebellion - May-June 1968. *Interplay: The Magazine of International Affairs*, December, 23-27.

1968e Que restera-t-il du projet du loi au moment de l'application ? *Sud-Ouest*, 21 September, 2.

1968f Rapports présentés par M. Ellul. *Évangélisation Information* (1 <new series>), January-February: 74-92.

1968g Terrorisme et violence psychologique, pp 43-61 in *Violence dans le* *monde actuel*, edited by Michel Amiot, Jean Dupuy, and Jacques Ellul. Paris: Desclee de Brouwer.

1969a   Cain, the theologian of 1969. *Katallagete: Be Reconciled* 2 (1), Winter: 4-7.

1969b   Can French university reform succeed ? *Interplay: The Magazine of International Affairs*, October, 16-18.

1969c   Comment nommer la société actuelle ? Enquête. *Recherche Sociale* (23-24), May-August: 64-65.

1969d   Initiales pour l'étude de la relation entre les émeutes de mai-juin 1968 et le droit. *Archives de philosophie du droit* (14): 5-19.

1969e   La jeunesse, force révolutionnaire ? *Table Ronde* (251-252), December-January: 150-168.

1969f   A l'écoute du monde...et de Dieu. *Réforme*, 25 October, 3.

1969g   Liminaire. *Foi et Vie* 68 (4), July-August: 1.

1969h   L'inadaptation des jeunes, signe d'une société. *Economie et Humanisme* (185), January-February: 26-34.

1969i   L'information dans la société technicienne. *Revue générale belge* January: 45-62.

1969j   Jean Brun: La société du vertige. Review of Brun's *Le retour de Dionysos*. *Le Monde*, 8 November, VII.

1970a   Drogue et société. *Le Monde*, 20 January, 10.

1970b   Ellul replies on violence. *Christianity and Crisis* 30 (16), 19 October: 221.

1970c   From Jacques Ellul. *Katallagete: Be Reconciled* 2 (3-4), Winter-Spring: 5.

1970d   Israël devant l'appel de Beyrouth. *Réforme*, 30 May, 16.

1970e   La nouvelle nature. *La France Catholique*, 16 October, 20.

1970f   La répression de la jeunesse. *Le Monde*, 14 November, 5.

1970g   Le centenaire de Lénine: révolutionnaire, mais... *Réforme*, 2 May, 8.

1970h   Le phénomène hippy. *Pour, par les parents: Revue de l'École des Parents et des Éducateurs d'Aquitaine* (14): 11-23.

1970i   Les chrétiens et la conférence de Beyrouth. *Le Monde*, 31 May-1 June, 3.

1970j   Mirror of these ten years. *The Christian Century* 87 (7), 18 February: 200-204.

1970k   Nous autres primitifs. *La France Catholique*, 20 November, 20.

1970l   Préface, pp xv-xix in *Le Cantique des Cantiques suivi des Psaumes*, edited by André Chouraqui. Paris: Presses Universitaires de France.

1970m   Proche-Orient: existe-t-il une 'nation' palestinienne ? *Réforme*, 5 September, 5-6.

1970n   Sur une théologie de l'information. *Réforme*, 4 April, 3.

1971a Le néo-romantisme moderne. *Contrepoint* (4), Summer: 45-60.

1971b L'irréductibilité du droit à une théologie de l'histoire. *Rivista Internazionale di Filosofia del Diritto* 48: 220-239.

1971c Théologie dogmatique et spécificité du christianisme. *Foi et Vie* 70 (2-4), April-September: 139-154.

1972a Aliénation par la technique: les dieux masqués. *Réforme*, 2 December, 20.

1972b Conformism and the rationale of technology, pp 89-102 in *Can we survive our future ?*, edited by G. R. Urban and Michael Glenny. New York: St. Martin's Press.

1972c Enseignement de la théologie: la recherche d'un nouveau statut. *Réforme*, 29 April, 7,8.

1972d Le problème de l'éthique sociale d'un point de vue réformé, pp 45-56 in *Une morale chrétienne pour la société ?*, edited by Francais Centre Catholique des Intellectuels. Paris: Desclee de Brouwer.

1972e L'interférence du politique dans le christianisme protestant d'aujourd'hui. *Contrepoint* (6), Spring: 25-37.

1972f Notes préliminaires sur 'église et pouvoirs'. *Foi et Vie* 71 (2-3), March-June: 2-24.

1972g Technique et développement, pp 258-295 in *Development: the western view / La perspective occidentale du développement*, edited by C. A. O. Van Nieuwenhuijze. The Hague: Mouton.

1972h Témoignage et société technicienne. *Archivio di Filosofia (Padua)*: 441-455.

1972i Work and calling. *Katallagete: Be Reconciled* 4 (3-4), Fall-Winter: 8-16.

1973a Droit et histoire, pp 73-82 in *Le droit, les sciences humaines et la philosophie: XXIXe semaine de synthèse; communications et échanges de vues*, edited by Centre International de Synthèse. Paris: Vrin.

1973b Du Chili au Proche-Orient: les tournants de l'histoire. *Réforme*, 3 November, 2-3.

1973c Du texte au sermon: les talents, Matthieu 25:13-30. *Études théologiques et religieuses* 48 (2): 125-138.

1973d Jacques Ellul répond à André Dumas. *Réforme*, 12 May, 10.

1973e Les antinomies de la foi chrétienne et du progrès. *Lumière et Vie (Lyon)* 22 (111), January-March: 69-80.

1973f Mise à mort de l'université. *Le Monde*, 8 September, 9.

1973g Pouquoi voter ? *Réforme*, 3 March, 6.

1973h Réflexions sur la politisation de l'église (Église et politique I). *Conscience et Liberté* (6), Autumn: 51-56.

1973i Réflexions sur la spécificté du droit. *Quaderni Fiorentini per la Storia del Pensiero Giuridico Moderno* 2: 7-35.

1973j Responsabilité d'église. *Réforme*, 13 January, 10.
1973k Violence et non violence. *Réforme*, 18 August, 3.
1973l Un monde clos. *France catholique-ecclesia* 1363 26 January: 20.

1974a Anarchie et christianisme. *Contrepoint* (15): 157-173.
1974b Conflit israélo-arabe: la seule voie. *Réforme*, 7 December, 5-6.
1974c De la mort. *Foi et Vie* 73 (2), March: 1-14.
1974d Interviews with Jacques Ellul: October 20, 24, and 30, 1973, pp 205-224 in *Technique and politics: the political thought of Jacques Ellul*, edited by David Charles Menninger. University of California, unpublished Ph.D.
1974e La blancheur de la liberté. *Réforme*, 8 June, 3.
1974f La liberté dénaturée. *Réforme*, 7 December, 14-15.
1974g Le rapport de l'homme à la création selon la Bible. *Foi et Vie* 73 (5-6), December: 137-155. ET in Mitcham & Grote 1984: 139-55.
1974h Les populations locales sont oubliées. *Sud-Ouest Dimanche*, 17 March, 10.
1974i Loi et sacré, droit et divin: de la loi sacrée au droit divin. *Rivista Internazionale di Filosofia del Diritto (Milan)* 51 <4th series> (2): 195-218.
1974j Réflexions sur le changement des études de théologie. *Études théologiques et religieuses* 49 (4): 489-497.
1974k Remarques au sujet de la Mission Aquitaine. *Sud-Ouest*, 25 June, 22.
1974l Spéculation et bureaucratie: l'Aquitaine victime de ses aménageurs. *Le Monde*, 9 March, 19.
1974m Sur deux livres de Bernard Charbonneau. *Le Monde*, 25 July, 14.
1974n 'The World' in the Gospels. *Katallagete: Be Reconciled* 5 (1), Spring: 16-23.

1975a Aliénation et temporalité dans le droit, pp 191-205 in *Temporalité et aliénation: Actes du colloque organisé par le Centre International d'Étude Humanistes et par l'Institut d'Études Philosophiques de Rome, 3-8 janvier 1975*, edited by Enrico Castelli. Paris: Aubier.
1975b Aménagement, justice et propriété. *Réforme*, 18 October, 3.
1975c Les bonnes intentions. *Le Monde*, 26-27 June, 10.
1975d Review of Jakoby, *Bureaucratisation of the World*. *Journal of Modern History* 47 (3), September: 550-551.
1975e Review of le Guillou, *Le Mystère du Père*. *Contrepoint* (16): 170-175.
1975f Sur la nature et la creation, pp 39-48 in *Mélanges André Neher*, edited by E. Amado Levi-Valensi et.al. Paris: Librairie d'Amérique et d'Orient.
1975g VIIe plan: l'aménagement du territoire et le cadre de vie. Les intentions et les incantations. *Réforme*, 10 May, 3.

1976a Coram (populo...) (suite). *Réforme*, 7 August, 11.

1976b De l'inconséquence, pp 177-190 in *Denis de Rougemont: L'écrivain, l'Européen: Études et témoignages publiés pour le soixante-dixième anniversaire de Denis de Rougemont*, edited by André Reszler and Henri Schwamm. Neuchâtel: A la Baconnière.

1976c Des protestants à Matignon: relation d'une rencontre. *Réforme*, 24 April, 3.

1976d Eros et agape. *Foi et Vie* 75 (2), March-April: 62-81.

1976e Essai sur l'herméneutique de la sécularisation fictive, pp 153-170 in *Herméneutique de la sécularisation: Actes du colloque organisé par le Centre International d'Études Humanistes et par l'Institut d'Études Philosophiques de Rome; Rome 3-8 janvier 1976*, edited by Enrico Castelli. Paris: Aubier.

1976f Le problème de l'émergence du droit. *Annales de la Faculté de Droit..., Centre d'Études et de Recherches d'Histoire Institutionnelle et Régionale* 1: 5-15.

1976g Problems of sociological method. *Social Research* 43 (1), Spring: 6-24.

1976h Réponse de M. Jacques Ellul. *Economie et Humanisme* (230), July-August: 75.

1976i Tolérance et intolérance au Moyen Age. *Conscience et Liberté* (11): 48-55.

1977a Études de théologie et formation permanente. *Le Protestant de l'Ouest*, November, 8-9.

1977b Impressions d'Israël. *Foi et Vie* 76 (4), August: 1-72.

1977c Jacques Ellul en Israël: impressions d'Israël. *Réveil*, December, 2.

1977d La tolérance et l'accusation. *Ouest-France*, 21 June, 1, 6.

1977e Le conflit religieux de la vision et de la parole, pp 143-160 in *La philosophie de la religion: l'herméneutique de la philosophie de la religion; Actes du colloque organisé par le Centre International d'Études Humanistes et par l'Institut d'Études Philosophiques de Rome; Rome 3-8 janvier 1977*, edited by Enrico Castelli. Paris: Aubier.

1977f Le secret et l'exception. *Le Monde*, 26 August, 4.

1977g Réflexions sur 'Foi et Vie'. *Foi et Vie* 76 (6), December: 3-6.

1977h Une non-violence privée de son fondement. *Alternatives Non Violentes* (20-21), January: 15-18.

1978a Aménager où déménager le territoire ? *Ouest-France*, 8 September, 1, 2.

1978b Du réalisme en politique: Éloge de l'autonomisme. *Réforme*, 25 February, 4.

1978c Jacques Ellul: Croire que 'nous sommes tous des assassins' est une source de vengeance collective. *Sud-Ouest Dimanche*, 12 February, 5.

1978d Karl Barth and us. *Sojourners* 7 (12), December: 22-24.

1978e La Cisjordanie palestinienne. *Le Monde*, 5 September, 2.
1978f La politique moderne: lieu du démoniaque, pp 101-122 in *Religion et politique: actes du colloque organisé par le Centre International d'Études Humanistes et par l'Institut d'Études Philosophiques de Rome; Rome, 3-7 juin 1978*, edited by Marco M. Olivetti. Paris: Aubier.
1978g Pour un autre développement. *Sud-Ouest*, 8 June, 2.

1979a An aspect of the role of persuasion in a technical society. *Etc.: A Review of General Semantics* 36 (2), Summer: 147-152.
1979b Droit et morale. *Neue Hefte für Philosophie* (17): 62-76.
1979c Histoire: les trois ages. *Le Monde*, 11-12 March, 2.
1979d Jacques Ellul répond à A. Dumas. *Réforme*, 9 June, 8.
1979e Jean Bosc 10 ans après: dans la lignée des prophètes et des témoins. *Réforme*, 13 October, 6-7.
1979f La douce France. *Ouest-France*, 6 February, 1, 2.
1979g La technique, système bloqué. *Pour* (64), January-February: 13-21.
1979h Le gaspillage et la responsabilité. *Ouest-France*, 11 September, 1, 4.
1979i Messie et messianisme. *Sens: Juifs et Chrétiens dans le Monde Aujourd'hui* (1), January: 1-13.
1979j Préface, pp i-xviii in *Écoute, Kierkegaard: Essai sur la communication de la parole <vol 1>*, edited by Nelly Viallaneix. Paris: Cerf.
1979k Prévision: futurlupinades. *Le Monde*, 23 September, ix.
1979l Remarks on technology and art. *Social Research*, Winter, 805-833.
1979m Review of Roux, *De la désunion vers la communion: un itinéraire pastoral et oecuménique*. *Foi et Vie* 78 (1), January: 116-118.

1980a Aménager ou déménager. *Réforme*, 30 August, 1.
1980b Charbonneau: l'éternel et l'actuel. *Le Monde*, 6 September, 2.
1980c De la Bible à l'histoire du non travail. *Foi et Vie* 79 (4), July: 2-8. ET in *Cross Currents* theme issue on Ellul, 35 (1) (Spring 1985): 43-8.
1980d The ethics of non-power, pp 204-212 in *Ethics in an age of pervasive technology*, edited by Melvin Kranzberg. Boulder, CO: Westview Press.
1980e How I discovered hope. *The Other Side* (102), March: 28-31.
1980f Israël, chance de civilisation. *Cahiers Universitaires Catholiques* (5), May-June: 22-25.
1980g La loi et les faits. *Sud-Ouest Dimanche*, 6 April, 5.
1980h La tour de Babel. *Sud-Ouest Dimanche*, 4 May, 5.
1980i L'Art sauvé par la crise. *Sud-Ouest Dimanche*, 27 April, 34.
1980j Le pouvoir et l'université. *Réforme*, 20 September, 1-2.
1980k Le savant et les humanités. *Sud-Ouest Dimanche*, 15 June, 5.
1980l L'empire du sens, pour moi, c'est la Bible: une interview de Jacques Ellul, recueillie par Gwendoline Jarczyk. *France Catholique-Ecclesia* (1737), 28 March: 10-11.

1980m Les marges de la liberté en Occident. *La Vie Protestante* 43 (8/2), 29 February: 1-2.

1980n L'unique et le tous. *Sud-Ouest Dimanche*, 23 March, 5.

1980o L'université dans la cité. *Sud-Ouest Dimanche*, 19 October, 5.

1980p L'université de l'an 2000. *Ouest-France*, 23 October, 1.

1980q Nature, technique and artificiality. *Research in Philosophy and Technology* 3: 263-283.

1980r The power of technique and the ethics of non-power, pp 242-247 in *The myths of information: technology and postindustrial culture*, edited by Kathleen Woodward. Madison, WI: Coda Press.

1980s Quand l'autre est 'on'. *Sud-Ouest Dimanche*, 27 July, 5.

1980t Thèses sur foi chrétienne et politique. Pp. 35-43 in *HOKHMA: Revue de réflexion théologique (Lausanne)*.

1980u Travail et vocation. *Foi et Vie* 79 (4), July: 9-24. Revision of 1972i.

1980v Une tête politique. *Le Monde*, 27 August, 2.

1980w La violence et la peur. *Réforme*, 23 Feb, 1-2.

1980x Pour qui, pour quoi travaillons-nous ? *Foi et Vie* 79 (4), July: 74-82.

1981a D'une élection à l'autre: rien d'important. *Le Monde*, 27 May, 2.

1981b Encore une fois...christianisme et communisme marxiste. *Conscience et Liberté* (22): 10-22.

1981c The ethics of propaganda: propaganda, innocence and amorality. *Communication* 6 (2): 159-175.

1981d Fédé, encore... *Réforme*, 23 May, 8.

1981e Institution, histoire, psychanalyse. *L'Inter-dit: Revue de psychanalyse institutionnelle* (7): 68-80.

1981f Institution, histoire, psychanalyse: discussion. *L'Inter-dit: Revue de psychanalyse institutionnelle* (7): 82-87.

1981g Jacques Ellul, théologien de l'espérance. *Le Quotidien de Paris*, 27 January, 35.

1981h La crise et l'émerveillement de l'histoire. *Foi et Vie* 80 (2), April: 75-86.

1981i La démocratisation du mal. *Sud-Ouest Dimanche*, 6 September, 5.

1981j La nature et la foi. *Ouest-France*, 7 November, 1, 3.

1981k La trop grande cité. *Le Monde*, 20 October, 42.

1981l L'enflure des mots. *Sud-Ouest Dimanche*, 8 November, 2.

1981m Non-violence quand même. *Réforme*, 17 October, 16.

1981n Professeurs: retrouver le sens. *Sud-Ouest Dimanche*, 22 March, 6, 7.

1981o A qui appartient la Palestine ? *Réforme*, 29 August, 10.

1981p Recherches sur le droit et l'Évangile, pp 115-139 in *Cristianesimo secolarizzazione e diritto moderno: Per la storia del pensiero giuridico moderno*, edited by Luigi Lombardi Vallauri and Gerhard Dilcher.

1981q Réflexions sur les contradictions de la Bible au sujet de la mort. *Archivio di Filosofia (Padua)* (1-3): 315-330.

1981r Un exemple de confrontation: marxisme et christianisme, pp 53-72 in *Les idéologies et la parole*, edited by Gabriel-Ph. Widmer, Jean Brun, and Jacques Ellul. Lausanne: Presses Bibliques Universitaires.

1981s Vivre en Guyenne. *L'Éducation*, 12 March, 47.

1982a Délinquance: vacances et prévention. *Réforme*, 31 July, 4.

1982b Écologie, technique, et société. *Les Cahiers du CPO [Centre Protestant de l'Ouest, Celles-sur-Belle, France]* (26-27), December: 13-20.

1982c Jacques Ellul ou la passion d'un sceptique. *Le Nouvel Observateur*, 17-23 July, 12-16.

1982d Je suis convaincu de la bonne foi de Begin. *Nouvelles Litteraires*, 30 September-6 October, 12.

1982e La lachêté. *Le Monde*, 14 January, 2.

1982f La réforme que personne n'osera jamais faire. *Sud-Ouest Dimanche*, 2 May, 3.

1982g L'An 1: Jacques Ellul...pour en finir avec le 10 mai. *Le Quotidien de Paris*, 15-16 May, 22.

1982h Lech Walesa et le rôle du christianisme. *Esprit* (63), March: 40-47.

1982i Lettre d'un intellectuel de province. *Le Quotidien de Paris*, 13 August, 2.

1982j L'O.L.P. ce n'est pas les Palestiniens. *Sud-Ouest Dimanche*, 15 August, 2.

1982k Police: un seul contrepoids, la morale. *Réforme*, 6 February, 1.

1982l Pour Begin. *Information Juive* 34 <new series> (20), December: 1, 5.

1982m Régionalisme ou nationalisme ? *Sud-Ouest Dimanche*, 19 September, 2.

1982n A theological reflection on nuclear developments: the limits of science, technology and power, pp 114-120 in *Waging peace: a handbook for the struggle to abolish nuclear weapons*, edited by Jim Wallis. San Francisco: Harper and Row.

1983a Chrétien et socialiste ? Christianisme et socialisme sont tout à fait compatibles à condition de s'entendre sur le sens et le contenu de ces mots. *Sud-Ouest Dimanche*, 20 February, 4.

1983b Contre l'oppression étatique. *Le Monde*, 8 December, 2.

1983c Croissance et E.D.F. (Electricité de France). *Le Monde*, 4 August, 2.

1983d Délinquance et société: 'Le Plan de cinq ans': pour en finir avec un malentendu. *Sud-Ouest* <20th ed>, 27 May, 2.

1983e La Corse exemplaire. *Réforme*, 15 January, 1.

1983f Liminaire. *Foi et Vie* 82 (5-6), December: 3-4.

1983g L'impasse: le débat sur l'enseignement supérieur. *Le Monde*, 2 June, 12.

1983h L'université, pour quoi faire ? *Sud-Ouest Dimanche*, 19 June, 3.

1983i New hope for the technological society: an interview with Jacques Ellul. *Etc.: A Review of General Semantics* 40 (2), Summer: 192-206.

1983j Pour un socialisme tout autre. *Réforme*, 12 March, 7.

1983k Rosenzweig et l'Islam. *Foi et Vie* 82 (3), July: 78-96.

1983l Son oeuvre est-elle vraiment scientifique ? *Le Quotidien de Paris*, 13 September,

1983m Non à l'idolatrie du politique. *France catholique-ecclesia*, 14 October, 9.

1984a Jacques Ellul: answers from a man who asks hard questions. *Christianity Today* 28 (7), 20 April: 16-21.

1984b Préface, pp 7-16 in *Le signe et la technique: la philosophie à l'épreuve de la technique*, edited by Gilbert Hottois. Paris: Aubier Montaigne.

1984c Rencontre de printemps avec Jacques Ellul. *L'Inter-dit: Revue de psychanalyse institutionnelle* (11): 57-70.

1985a Preface, pp 25-33 in *The Dhimmi: Jews and Christians under Islam*, edited by Bat Ye'or. London: Associated University Presses.

1985b Rencontre avec Jacques Ellul: le Christianisme, une subversion ? *Signes des Temps*, May, 4-8.

1985c Une introduction à la pensée de Bernard Charbonneau. *Ouvertures: Cahiers du Sud-Ouest* (7), January-March: 39-51.

1986 La faute, le péché, la culpabilité. *Corps écrit* 19: 65-74.

1987 Theological pluralism and the unity of the Spirit. *Church, word and Spirit: historical and theological essays in honour of G.W. Bromiley*: 215-227.

1988a An Interview with Jacques Ellul. *Media Development* 35 (2): 26-30.

1988b Les précurseurs. *Foi et Vie* 87 (3-4), July: 31-41.

1988c Some reflections on the ecumenical movement. *Ecumenical Review* 40: 382-390.

1988d Vers une éthique politique. *Réforme*, 2 July, 12.

1988e The dialectic of theology and sociology in Jacques Ellul: A recent interview (July 19, 1988). Unpublished Chicago AAR Paper.

1989a Afterword: Notes on the current situation, pp 129-132 in *Presence of the Kingdom*, edited by Jacques Ellul. Colorado Springs, CO: Helmers & Howard.

1989b A response to Michael Bauman's review of *Jesus and Marx*. *The Ellul Studies Forum* (3), June: 4.

1989c Un club de prévention. *Foi et Vie* 88 (3-4), July: 75-86.

1990a Petite note complémentaire sur Romains 13,1. *Foi et Vie* 89 (6), December: 81-83.

1990b Review of Giniewski, *L'An prochain ... Jéruslaem: préhistoire de l'État d'Israël. Foi et Vie* 89 (6), December: 106-108.

1994a   Dévoiler l'homme. *Foi et Vie* 93 (5-6), December: 168-171.
1994b   Response to the symposium in his honor at the University of Bordeaux, November 1993. *The Ellul Forum* (13), July: 18.
1994c   The truth will set you free. *The Ellul Forum* 13: 3.

2000   Droit. *Foi et Vie* 99 (2), April: 3-20. Reprint of 1939a.

Unpublished Writings by Jacques Ellul

This part of the bibliography lists unpublished writing by Ellul used in the course of researching the original thesis. Except where another source is given, all the works were kindly provided by the Ellul Archive at Wheaton College, Illinois which Joyce Hanks instituted.

The bibliography is in four parts:
1. Writing from the 1930s.
2. Writing for the Associations Professionnelles Protestantes (A.P.P.).
3. University Lectures.
4. Other Lectures and Writings.

In all sections, except (2), works are listed alphabetically by title because the date of writing is in many cases difficult to ascertain with certainty. Further details about the work are then provided including, where available and relevant, a brief description of such matters as the work's context, date of writing, length, and outline structure.

1. Writing from the 1930s

Directives pour un manifeste personnaliste
Written by Bernard Charbonneau and Jacques Ellul for the personalist movement this is a 15-page typed manifesto in 83 points. It was finally published in 1999 (see Charbonneau & Ellul 1999). The original date has been variously given as 1934 , 1935, 1936 and Winter 1937. Its content is discussed in chapter three of the book. Its basic outline is as follows:

    I - Origine de notre révolte (§1-33).
        A. Naissance de la conscience révolutionnaire (§1-11).
        B. Notre définition de la société (§12-20).
        C. Preuves (§21-26).
        D. Conséquences (§27-33).
    II - Direction pour la construction d'une société personnaliste (§34-83).
        A. Comment devons nous agir (§34-38).
        B. Les membres de cette société (§39-47).
        C. Les institutions:
            1. La société politique (§48-57).
            2. La société économique (§58-72).
            3. La civilisation de la société (culture, art, moeurs) (§73-80).
        D. Une cité ascétique pour que l'homme vive (§81-83).

Les forces morales
A hand-written comment on the Wheaton Archive copy reads 'article de J. Ellul - Esprit 1934'. 'Les forces morales' is a typed piece of 11 pages but the Wheaton copy is clearly an incomplete version of the original.

La formation des villes modernes
A note attached to the Wheaton Archive copy dates this typed 5-page article as from 1935. It is written with the conviction that, in the words of the opening sentence, 'The most decisive trait of contemporary civilization which most sharply differentiates it from all those which preceded it is indisputably the formation of an absolutely new urban civilization'. The article contains both historical/sociological material and theological material addressing the task of the church in this new situation.

Note sur la Normandie
This undated hand-written 2-page piece apparently copied from a notebook was provided by Christian Roy from his personal collection of papers from the 1930s personalist movement and comments on propaganda concerning the wonder of the boat 'Normandie'.

Le personnalisme, révolution immédiate
The 16-page typed article in the Wheaton Archive is headed,
   JOURNAL DU GROUPE DE BORDEAUX DES AMIS D" ESPRIT"
   Revue Internationale, 137, Faubourg St Denis, PARIS - Xème
   Exemplaire: I fr 50.
   LE PERSONNALISME, REVOLUTION IMMEDIATE par Jacques ELLUL.
'Le personnalisme, révolution immédiate' ends on p15. It is followed by a short piece headed, 'Exégèse des lieux communs. IL NOUS FAUT UNE MYSTIQUE par Bernard CHARBONNEAU', and the announcement of a 3-day mountain study camp over Christmas. This piece is referred to at *Season*, 36 and *Conversations*, 10 and 18 (n 44).

Pour un droit vivant
A poorly reproduced, typed 28-page article in the Wheaton Archive which has a hand-written date of '1935' above its title. However, Chastenet (*Conversations*, 9 and 17 (n41)) dates the piece to 1934. The content of this article is discussed in chapter six.

Technique des moyens spirituels
This comprises 16 un-numbered pages in Ellul's handwriting and was kindly provided by Christian Roy. It is undated and its relationship to Mounier's work of the same title is unclear. It attempts to discover what means are appropriate to the personalist groups and stresses their need to be different, to test all means by the group's beliefs, and to reject large-scale spending and propaganda techniques.

2. Writing for A.P.P.

Plan des leçons
A single typed sheet in the Wheaton Archive with the hand-written comment 'APP 1945-47' in the top right-hand corner, this presents the following outline of lessons (a number of which appear below) for A.P.P.

1 - Le chrétien et le monde: le problème central des A.P.P.
2 - L'homme en présence du monde moderne.
3 - Les lieux communs.
4 - L'autorité de la Bible dans la vie concrète.
5-6 - Principes d'interprétation Biblique.
7 - De la vocation.
8 - Méthodes pratiques de travail.
9-10 - Exemples d'études.

Thèmes de réflexion
A single typed sheet in the Wheaton Archive (originally p10 of a larger document) this contains four questions concerning the organisation and task of A.P.P., addressed to those involved in the groups.

Première Leçon - Le Chrétien et le monde
This 10-page, un-dated, typed document concludes with five points for reflection. Its outline structure is as follows:
  I. - Le Monde (pp1-4).
  II. - Le Chrétien dans le monde (pp4-7).
  III. - La Participation au monde (pp7-10).

Troisième Leçon - Les Lieux communs
Another un-dated typed piece, this comprises 12 pages and concludes with five themes for reflection. Its outline structure is as follows:
  I. - Les Lieux communs (pp1-4).
  II. - Remise en question (pp4-9).
  III. - Les Conséquences (pp9-12).

Sixième Leçon - Principes d'interprétation biblique au point de vue éthique (II)
Comprising 10 typed pages, the last of which offers five themes for reflection, this undated piece completes the unavailable fifth lesson by providing two further principles:
  (3) L'analogie de la foi (pp1-5).
  (4) Interprétation christocentrique (pp5-9).

Dixième Leçon - Eglise et A.P.P. - Conclusion et Perspectives
This lengthier, 17-page lesson is also undated and typed but lacks any final questions Its structure is as follows:
  I   *L'Eglise me pose-t-elle une question ? (pp1-2).*
  II   *Que penser de la paroisse ? (pp2-4).*
  III   *Paroisse apparente et Eglise vraie (pp4-6).*
  IV   *Position des A.P.P. dans l'Eglise vraie et devant la paroisse apparente - leur témoignage fidèle (pp6-8).*
  V   *La puissante église du monde: la religion professionnelle (pp8-9).*
  VI   *Les A.P.P. espression professionnelle de la foi ? Ou remise en question de*

l'Eglise ? (pp9-12).
VII   *Et l'Eglise vraie remet en question le travail des A.P.P. par groupes spécialisés, cellules de base (pp12-14).*
VIII *Le groupe local interprofessionel, cellule de base, remet en question la paroisse apparente par sa fidélité de communion dans l'Eglise vraie (pp14-17).*

La hiérarchie sociale
A short, 5-page typed document (headed, 'Associations Professionnelles Protestantes: Journées des 3, 4 et 5 Février') with occasional hand-written headings inserted into the text this appears to be a draft of the article 1946c.

L'Eglise et le problème politique actuelle
This 6-page piece has a number of hand-written annotations and corrections to the text. Its heading includes a year which is, unfortunately, illegible in the reproduced text at Wheaton. It also appears to be related to a published article, 1946d.

3. University Lectures

Droit de l'information
Entitled, 'Droit de l'information: cours de Monsieur le Professeur Ellul' this 109-page document contains the content of a course of lectures examining in some technical detail the structure and control of those agents who disseminate information in the modern world and the administrative and legal controls upon them. Although no date is explicitly given, the fact that there are references to events up to 1966 but no mention of the press in relation to the student troubles of 1968, suggests the lectures may have been given at some point in 1967. This is perhaps confirmed by the timing of Ellul's substantial published articles on the subject which date from the end of 1967.

La pensée de Marx
Lacking any title or further identification ('La pensée de Marx' is my own heading), this comprises a 4-page outline of the course and a 60-page typed document providing the details of what must be one year's edition of the course on Marx which Ellul taught annually at the Institute of Political Studies. Its outline structure is as follows:

Chapitre Premier: Les origines de la pensée Marxiste et la pensée philosophique de Karl Marx (pp1-24).
A. *Les origines de la pensée Marxiste* (1-7).
   §1 - La pensée de Hegel (2-4).
   §2 - La pensée de Feuerbach (4-5).
   §3 - Karl Marx en face de Hegel et Feuerbach (5-7).
B. *Etude de la ligne centrale de la pensée Marx* (8-13).
   §1 - La méthode (8-9).

§1 - La loi de paupérisation (58-59).
§2 - La mystique du prolétaire chez Marx (59-60).

La Propagande

The Wheaton Archive contains a selection of pages headed 'La Propagande Tome 1: Cours professé en 1951/1952'. This is likely part of the work cited as '*Les Techniques de propagande, 1951 (cours polycopié)*' in the bibliography of Ellul's *Propagandes* and now listed at Hanks 2000:15 as published in 1953. The incomplete nature of the document makes close comparison impossible but the material treats the subject matter of the later *Histoire* (1967) and *Propagandes* (1962) although it is structured quite differently.

Les Successeurs de Marx

A 32-page typed document with an additional 2-page 'Plan du cours', this has a hand-written note at the top of the course plan which reads, 'Institut d'Etudes Politiques (1977-78)'. The course structure is as follows:

Introduction: Causes des divergences à partir de la pensée de Marx (pp1-7).
A. *L'oeuvre de Marx n'est pas achevée* (1).
B. *Contradictions dans l'oeuvre de Marx* (1-2).
C. *Problèmes soulevées par Marx et qu'il ne résoud pas* (2).
D. *Présupposés existants dans l'oeuvre de Marx et que Marx n'a pas étudié* (2).
E. *Contradictions entre les auteurs Marxistes* (2-7).
   §1 - Divergences intérieures à la pensée de Marx (2-3).
   §2 - Causes de divergences extérieurs à la pensée de Marx (3-5).
   §3 - Les différents courants que l'on peut reconnaître (5-6).
   §4 - Les limites (6-7).

Le Grand Debat (pp8-32).
A. *Bernstein comme critique de Marx* (8-12).
   §1 - Positions philosophiques de Bernstein (8-9).
   §2 - La pensée économique de Bernstein (9-12).
B. *Kautsky contre Bernstein* (13-15).
   §1 - La critique philosophique de Kautsky (13-14).
   §2 - La critique économique et tactique (de Bernstein par Kautsky) (14-15).
C. *Lénine contre Kautsky* (16-21).
   §1 - De la théorie à l'action (16-17).
   §2 - La discussion doctrinale (17-18).
   §3 - Le disaccord sur les méthodes de la révolution entre Kautsky et Lénine (18-21).
D. *Etude de Lénine par rapport à Marx* (22-28).
   §1 - Généralités (22).
   §2 - Eléments de la doctrine des explications (22-25).
   §3 - La stratégie (25-28).
E. *Rosa Luxembourg contre Bernstein et contre Lénine* (29-32).
   §1 - Rosa Luxembourg comme critique de Bernstein (29-30).
   §2 - Rosa Luxembourg contre Lénine (30-32).

4. Other Unpublished Lectures and Writings

L'Autorité
'L'Autorité: Etudes présentées au colloque des compagnons 1975 à Pomeyrol' is a 22-page, typed document containing a transcript of three addresses (pp1-8, 8-15, 16-22) given by Ellul and also answers to questions from the floor. Its content is discussed in chapters six and seven.

Exposé de M. le Professeur Ellul
A 13-page typed transcript headed 'Exposé de M. le Professeur Ellul de la Faculté de Droit de Bordeaux devant MM les Membres du Corps Enseignement à la Bourse du Travail de Bordeaux, le 9 Novembre 1953' in which Ellul defends strike action by teachers in response to the law of 25 September 1953. He believed that this law threatened the universities' independence by making the French prefect the representative of all government ministries in each *département* (cf 1953f).

GBU Conférence
Entitled simply, 'JACQUES ELLUL - HOSTEVE le 28 AVRIL 198?' (either '1985' or '1983'), this often poorly reproduced 25-page document presents a transcription of addresses given by Ellul to a conference of evangelical students (GBU) along with his answers to their questions. Ellul was asked to address them on the question of 'l'objectif de l'enseignement laïc dans une société laïque, d'un point de vue chrétien' (p1).

Propositions pour des Etats Généraux du protestantisme français
This full version of Ellul's 'Propositions', is an 11-page typed document (discussed in chapter one).

Thèses sur le christianisme et le marxisme
Two typed pages present 11 theses by Ellul on Christianity and Marxism and are headed, 'Rencontre Debat: 7 décembre 1979', with the handwritten annotation 'avec Jean Bauberot' and the address of the 'Centre Protestant d'Etudes et de Documentation'.

Secondary Materials

Agulhon, Maurice. 1993. *The French Republic 1879-1992*. Oxford: Blackwell.

Alison, Michael, and David Edwards (Eds.). 1990. *Christianity and Conservatism*. London: Hodder & Stoughton.

Anonymous. 1972. "Un certain regard: Jacques Ellul." *Sud-Ouest Dimanche*, 19 November, 22

—. 1976 "'Violence Et Mass Media': Une Passionnante Causerie Du Professeur Ellul." *Sud-Ouest 8th edition A (Dordogne)*, 12 April, C

Arendt, Hannah. 1958. *The Human Condition*. Chicago: University of Chicago Press.

—. 1970. *On Violence*. London: Allen Lane.

Aron, Robert, and Arnaud Dandieu. 1993. *La révolution nécessaire <1st Edn, 1933>*. Paris: Jean Michel Place.

Auber, Joel. 1973. "Bordeaux: Le cas de M. Christian Raspiengas." *Le Monde*, 30 November, 25

Augustine of Hippo. 1972. *The City of God*. Harmondsworth, England: Penguin.

Aultman, Mark. 1972. "Technology and the End of Law." *American Journal of Jurisprudence* 17: 46-79.

Badertscher, John. 1978. "George Grant and Jacques Ellul on Freedom in Technological Society." pp 79-89 in *George Grant in Process: Essays and Conversations*, edited by Larry Schmidt. Toronto: Anansi.

Baird, Catherine. 1992. *Russian Personalism: The Influence of Russian Populism on French Personalism, 1930-1938*. M.A. Thesis, McGill University.

Baker, James Wesley. 1991. *The Hope of Intervention: A Rhetorical Analysis of the English Translations of the Writings of Jacques Ellul*. Ph.D. Dissertation, Ohio State University.

Barclay, Oliver R. (Ed.). 1984. *Pacifism and War*. Leicester: IVP.

Barth, Karl. 1935. *The Word of God and the Word of Man*. London: Hodder & Stoughton.

—. 1949. *Dogmatics in Outline*. London: SCM Press.

—. 1960. *Community, State, and Church: Three Essays*. New York: Doubleday.

—. 1961. *Deliverance to the Captives*. London: SCM Press.

—. 1986. *Church Dogmatics Vol I/1-IV/4*. Edinburgh: T. & T. Clark.

Bauman, Michael. 1988. "Review of *Jesus and Marx* by Jacques Ellul." *The Ellul Studies Forum* 2 (November): 4,7.

—. 1989. "Response to Jacques Ellul." *The Ellul Studies Forum* 4 (November): 13.

—. 1992a. "Jesus, Anarchy and Marx: The Theological and Political Contours of Ellulism." *Journal of the Evangelical Theological Society* 35 (2), (June): 199-216.

—. 1992b. *Pilgrim Theology: Taking the Path of Theological Discovery*. Grand Rapids: Zondervan.

Beale, G. K. 1999. *The Book of Revelation :A Commentary on the Greek Text*. Carlisle: Paternoster Press.

Belo, Fernando. 1979. "Réponse à Jacques Ellul." *Foi et Vie* 78 (5-6), (December): 121-127.

Benello, C. George. 1981. "Technology and Power: Technique as a Mode of Understanding Modernity." pp 91-107 in *Jacques Ellul: Interpretive Essays*, edited by Clifford G. Christians and Jay M. Van Hook. Urbana: University of Illinois Press.

Berstein, Serge. 1988. *La France des années 30*. Paris: Armand Colin.

Berthoud, Jean-Marc. 1982. "Jacques Ellul et l'impossible dialectique entre Marx et Calvin." *La Revue Réformée* 33 (4): 176-191.

Bethomeau, Patrick. 1981. "Jacques Ellul: Le crime contre Paris" *Sud-Ouest*, 3 November, 38

Biggar, Nigel (Ed.). 1988. *Reckoning with Barth: Essays in Commemoration of the Centenary of Karl Barth's Birth*. London: Mowbray.

—. 1993. *The Hastening That Waits: Karl Barth's Ethics*. Oxford: Clarendon Press.

Bizeul, Yves. 1991. *L'Identité protestante: étude de la minorité protestante de France*. Paris: Méridiens Klincksieck.

Blanc, Jean-Luc. 1990. "Jacques Ellul et la Dialectique." *La Revue Réformée* 41 (3), (July): 35-45.

Blocher, Henri. 1972. "L'ordre de Dieu et la réponse de l'homme." *Revue Réformée* 23: 119-129.

Bloesch, Donald G. 1992. *A Theology of Word and Spirit: Authority and Method in Theology*. Downers Grove, Illinois: IVP.

—. 1994. *Holy Scripture: Revelation, Inspiration and Interpretation*. Carlisle: The Paternoster Press.

Boli-Bennett, John. 1980. "The Absolute Dialectics of Jacques Ellul." *Research in Philosophy and Technology* 3: 171-201.

Bolle, Pierre. 1982. "L'Influence du Barthisme dans le protestantisme français." pp 59-66 in *Eglises et chrétiens dans la IIe guerre mondiale: La France*, edited by Xavier de Montelos *et. al.* Lyon: Presses Universitaires de Lyon.

—. 1993. "Albert Finet." p 202 in *Les Protestants*, edited by André Encrevé. Paris: Beauchesne.

Bonhoeffer, Dietrich. 1955. *Ethics*. London: SCM Press.

—. 1959. *The Cost of Discipleship*. London: SCM Press.

—. 1971. *Letters and Papers from Prison*. London: SCM Press.

Booker, Christopher, and Richard North. 1994. *The Mad Officials: How the Bureaucrats Are Strangling Britain*. London: Constable.

Brendon, Piers. 2000. *The Dark Valley: A Panorama of the 1930s*. London: Jonathan Cape.

Brethe de la Gressaye, Jean, and Marcel Laborde-Lacoste. 1947. *Introduction générale à l'étude du droit*. Paris: Librairie du Recueil Sirey.

Briselet, Jean. 1967. "La 'bande' est une cellule sociale à la mesure des jeunes." *Le Monde*, 19 September, 10

Bromiley, Geoffrey W. 1981. "Barth's Influence on Jacques Ellul." pp 32-51 in *Jacques Ellul: Interpretive Essays*, edited by Clifford G. Christians and Jay M. Van Hook. Urbana: University of Illinois Press.

Bruce, Brendan. 1992. *Images of Power: How the Image Makers Shape Our Leaders*. London: Kogan Page.

Brueggemann, Walter. 1973. "Review of *The Politics of God and the Politics of Man* by Jacques Ellul." *Journal of Biblical Literature* 92 (September): 470-471.

Brunner, Emil. 1937. *The Divine Imperative: A Study in Christian Ethics*. London: Lutterworth Press.

—. 1945. *Justice and the Social Order*. London: Lutterworth Press.

—. 1949. *Christianity and Civilization (Second Part)*. London: Nisbet & Co.

Bryant, Christopher. 1993. *Reclaiming the Ground: Christianity and Socialism*. London: Hodder & Stoughton.

Burke, David John. 1980. *Jacques Ellul: Theologian and Social Critic*. Ph.D. Dissertation, Washington State University.

Busch, Eberhard. 1976. *Karl Barth: His Life from Letters and Autobiographical Texts*. London: SCM Press.

Caird, G. B. 1966. *A Commentary on the Revelation of St. John the Divine*. London: A & C Black.

Cans, Roger. 1992. "La France 'écolo': l'étrange alchimie des origines." *Le Monde*, 10 June,

Capelle, Jean. 1980. "Réplique à...Jacques Ellul: l'avenir de l'enseignement supérieur." *Le Monde*, 30 September, 2

Carpenter, Stanley R. 1980. "Review of Langdon Winner's *Autonomous Technology*." *Research in Philosophy and Technology* 3: 116-124.

Carrez, M. 1950. "Comment on Ellul's "Notes sur les problèmes éthiques du Rapport Kinsey"." *Bulletin du Centre Protestant d'Etudes et de Documentation*.

Cérézuelle, Daniel. 1979. "Fear and Insight in French Philosophy of Technology." *Research in Philosophy and Technology* 2: 53-75.

—. 1980. "From the Technical Phenomenon to the Technical System." *Research in Philosophy and Technology* 3: 161-170.

—. 1983. "Concerning the Religious Origins of Technological Civilization." *Research in Philosophy and Technology* 6: 175-188.

—. 1993. "Reflections on Social Techniques." *The Ellul Forum* 10 (January): 3-5.

—. 1994. "La critique de la modernité chez Charbonneau: aspects d'un compagnonnage intellectuel." pp 61-74 in *Sur Jacques Ellul*, edited by Patrick Troude-Chastenet. Bordeaux: L'Esprit du Temps.

—. 1996. "From Criticism to Politics: Jacques Ellul, Bernard Charbonneau and the Committee for the Defense of the Aquitaine Coast." *The Ellul Forum* 16

(January): 8-10.

Chan, Sze-chi. 1997. *God in Dialectic with Human Culture: A Critical Examination of the Theology of Culture of Jacques Ellul*. Ph.D. Thesis, King's College, London.

Chappuis, Jean Marc. 1969. *Information du Monde et prédication de l'évangile*. Geneva: Labor et Fides.

Charbonneau, Bernard and Jacques Ellul. 1999 "Directives pour un manifeste personnaliste" (written in 1935). *Revue française d'histoire des idées politiques* 9(1): 159-77.

Charbonneau, Bernard. 1936. Le progrès contre l'homme. *Bulletin du groupe Bordeaux des amis d'Esprit* [Conférence faite à l'Athénée le 15 janvier 1936]

—. 1987. *L'Etat*. Paris: Economica.

—. 1990a. "Le développement scientifique et technique: libération de l'homme ou cataclysme naturel ?" *Vice Versa* 30 (September-October): 10-11.

—. 1990b. *Le système et le chaos*. Paris: Economica.

—. 1991a. *Nuit et jour: science et culture*. Paris: Economica.

—. 1991b. *Sauver nos régions: écologie, régionalisme et sociétés locales*. Paris: Sang de la Terre.

—. 1994. "Unis par une pensée commune." *Foi et Vie* 93 (5-6), (December): 19-28.

—. 1996. *Il court, il court le fric...* Bordeaux: Opales.

—. 2000. *Je fus: essai sur la liberté*. Bordeaux: Opales.

—. n.d. "II - Directions pour la construction d'une Société personnaliste."

—. n.d. "L'esprit personnaliste."

Chastenet, Patrick. 1981. "A 'contre-courant' avec Jacques Ellul: un livre pour mieux connaître la pensée de notre collaborateur." *Sud-Ouest Dimanche*, 9 August, 35

—. 1983. "Le paradoxe Ellul." *Sud-Ouest Dimanche*, 23 October, 34

—. 1992. *Lire Ellul: introduction à l'oeuvre socio-politique de Jacques Ellul*. Bordeaux: Presses Universitaires de Bordeaux.

—. 1994a. "Avant-Propos." pp 7-9 in *Sur Jacques Ellul*, edited by Patrick Troude-Chastenet. Bordeaux: L'Esprit du Temps.

—. 1994b. *Entretiens avec Jacques Ellul*. Paris: La Table Ronde.

—. 1994c. "Jacques Ellul, combattant de la liberté." *Foi et Vie* 93 (5-6), (December): 57-69.

—. 1994d. *Sur Jacques Ellul*. Papers from 'Technique et société dans l'œuvre de Jacques Ellul', Institut d'Etudes Politiques de Bordeaux, 12 & 13 November 1993. Bordeaux: L'Esprit du Temps.

—. 1994e. "Technique et politique dans l'oeuvre de Jacques Ellul." pp 37-59 in *Sur Jacques Ellul*, edited by Patrick Troude-Chastenet. Bordeaux: L'Esprit du Temps.

—. 1999. "Jacques Ellul: une jeunesse personnaliste." *Revue française d'histoire des idées politiques* 9 (1): 55-75.

—. 2000. "Christianisme, personnalisme et fédéralisme dans l'oeuvre de Jacques Ellul." *Europe en formation* 315-316: 239-260.

Christians, Clifford G. 1974. *Jacques Ellul's 'La Technique' in a Communication Context.* Ph.D. Dissertation, University of Illinois.

—. 1977. "Jacques Ellul's Concern with the Amorality of Contemporary Communications." *Communications: International Journal of Communications Research* 3 (January): 62-80.

—. 1981. "Ellul on Solution: An Alternative but No Prophecy." pp 147-173 in *Jacques Ellul: Interpretive Essays,* edited by Clifford G. Christians and Jay M. Van Hook. Urbana: University of Illinois Press.

—. 1988a. *Communications Theory in Ellul's Sociology.* Unpublished AAR paper.

—. 1988b. "Is Ellul Prophetic ?" *Media Development* 35 (2): 6-7.

—. 1992. "Communications Theory in Ellul's Sociology." *The Ellul Studies Forum* 9 (July): 9-11 [1988a revised].

—. 1994. "Ellul's Prophetic Witness to the Academic Community." *The Ellul Forum* 13 (July): 9-10.

Christians, Clifford G., and Michael R. Real. 1979. "Jacques Ellul's Contributions to Critical Media Theory." *Journal of Communication* 29 (1), (Winter): 83-93.

Christians, Clifford G., and Jay M. Van Hook (Eds.). 1981. *Jacques Ellul: Interpretive Essays.* Urbana: University of Illinois Press.

Clark, David L. 1981. "The Mythic Meaning of the City." pp 269-290 in *Jacques Ellul: Interpretive Essays,* edited by Clifford G. Christians and Jay M. Van Hook. Urbana: University of Illinois Press.

Clark, Stephen R. L. 1993. "Review of *Anarchy and Christianity* by Jacques Ellul." *Studies in Christian Ethics* 6 (1): 52-55.

Clendenin, Daniel B. 1985. "Will the Real Ellul Please Stand Up ? A Bibliographic Survey." *Trinity Journal* 6 (2): 167-183.

—. 1987. *Theological Method in Jacques Ellul.* Lanham & London: University Press of America.

—. 1988. "An Interview with Jacques Ellul." *Media Development* 35 (2): 26-30.

—. 1989. "Introduction: Choosing Life and the Possibility of History, An Introduction to the Life and Thought of Jacques Ellul." pp xxi-xlii in Jacques Ellul, *Presence of the Kingdom.* Colorado Springs, CO: Helmers & Howard.

Clouse, R. G. 1981. *War: Four Christian Views.* Downers Grove, Illinois: IVP.

Collot-Guyer, Marie-Thérèse. 1983. *La cité personnaliste D'Emmanuel Mounier.* Nancy: Presses Universitaires de Nancy.

Comte, Gilbert. 1973. "Diagnostic de Jacques Ellul." *Le Monde,* 5 July, 17

Coninck, Pierre de. 1994. "Pour une approche constructive de l'autonomie de la technique." pp 213-239 in *Sur Jacques Ellul,* edited by Patrick Troude-Chastenet. Bordeaux: L'Esprit du Temps.

Courtin, Rene. 1949. "D'une Europe pourrie à une Europe moins pourrie: réponse à J. Ellul par René Courtin." *Réforme,* 17 December, 1, 3

Cox, Harvey. 1965. *The Secular City: Secularization and Urbanization in Theological Perspective*. New York: Macmillan.

—. 1971. "The Ungodly City: A Theological Response to Jacques Ellul." *Commonweal* 94 (15), (9 July): 351-357.

Crick, Bernard. 1971. "Review of *Violence* by Jacques Ellul." *Political Quarterly* 42 (2), (April-June): 229-232.

Cullmann, Oscar. 1963. *The State in the New Testament*. London: SCM Press.

Dawn, Marva. 1988a. "A Second Forum Response to Fasching." *The Ellul Studies Forum* 2 (November): 7.

—. 1988b. "A Visit with Jacques Ellul." *The Ellul Studies Bulletin* 1 (August): 6.

—. 1992. *The Concept of `The Principalities and Powers' in the Works of Jacques Ellul*. Ph.D. Dissertation, University of Notre Dame.

—. 1999. "The Biblical Concept of 'The Principalities and Powers': John Yoder Points to Jacques Ellul." pp 168-86 in *The Wisdom of the Cross: Essays in Honor of John Howard Yoder*, edited by Stanley Hauerwas, et.al. Grand Rapids: Eerdmans.

—. 2001. *Powers, Weakness, and the Tabernacling of God*. Grand Rapids: Eerdmans.

de Montelos, Xavier *et.al.*, (Eds.). 1982. *Églises et chrétiens dans la IIe guerre mondiale: la France*. Lyon: Presses Universitaires de Lyon.

de Senarclens, Pierre. 1974. *Le mouvement 'Esprit' 1932-1941*. Lausanne: Editions L'Age d'Homme.

Dengerink, Jan. 1978. *The Idea of Justice in Christian Perspective*. Ontario: Wedge Publishing Foundation.

Dias, R. W. M. 1976. *Jurisprudence*. London: Butterworths.

Diétrich, Suzanne de. 1939. "Réponse à Jacques Ellul" *Le Semeur* 42 (4), (February): 230-233.

Domenach, J. M. 1972. *Emmanuel Mounier*. Paris: Seuil.

Dravasa, Etienne, Claude Emeri, and Jean-Louis Seurin. 1982. "Une fête pour Jacques Ellul: l'hommage de 60 des siens." *Réforme*, 20 November, 6-7

—. 1983a. "Introduction." pp xi-xiv in *Religion, société et politique: mélanges en hommage à Jacques Ellul*, edited by Etienne Dravasa *et.al.* Paris: Presses Universitaires de France.

— (Eds.). 1983b. *Religion, société et politique: mélanges en hommage à Jacques Ellul*. Paris: Presses Universitaires de France.

Dreyfus, Françoise, and François d'Arcy. 1989. *Les institutions politiques et administratives de la France*. Paris: Economica.

du Pasquier, Claude. 1967. *Introduction à la théorie générale et à la philosophie du droit <1st Edn, 1937>*. Paris: Delachaux & Niestlé.

Duff, Edward S. J. 1956. *The Social Thought of the World Council of Churches*. New York: Association Press.

Duguit, Léon. 1921. *Law in the Modern State*. London: George Allen & Unwin.

Dujancourt, Sylvain. 1989. *Introduction à la pensée juridique de Jacques Ellul*.

Mémoire de Maîtrise en Théologie Protestante, Strasbourg.

——. 1990. "Law and Ethics in Ellul's Theology." *The Ellul Studies Forum* 5 (June): 10-11.

——. 1994. "Technique et éthique selon la pensée de Jacques Ellul." *Foi et Vie* 93 (5-6), (December): 29-41.

——. 1999. "Natural Law or Covenant ?" *The Ellul Forum* 23 (July): 9-14.

Dumas, André. 1967. "Appel à la participation." *Réforme*, 25 February.

——. 1993. "Jacques Ellul." pp 191-192 in *Les Protestants*, edited by André Encrevé. Paris: Beauchesne.

Dunn, James D. G. 1986. "Romans 13.1-7 - a Charter for Political Quietism?" *Ex Auditu* 2: 55-68.

——. 1988. *Romans 9-16*. Dallas, Texas: Word Books.

Dynes, Michael, and David Walker. 1995. *The Times Guide to the New British State: The Government Machine in the 1990s*. London: Times Books.

Eggly, Henri. n.d. "Le groupe Esprit à Pau de 1935 à 1938."

Ehrhardt, Arnold T. 1962. "Christianity and Law: Review of *The Theological Foundation of Law* by Jacques Ellul." *Scottish Journal of Theology* 15 (September): 305-310.

Ehrlich, Eugen. 1936. *Fundamental Principles of the Sociology of Law <1st Edn,1912>*. Cambridge, Massachusetts: Harvard University Press.

Eller, Vernard. 1968. *Kierkegaard and Radical Discipleship: A New Perspective*. Princeton, New Jersey: Princeton University Press.

——. 1971. "Four Who Remember: Kierkegaard, the Blumhardts, Ellul and Muggeridge." *Katallagete: Be Reconciled* 3 (3), (Spring): 6-12.

——. 1972. "How Jacques Ellul Reads the Bible." *Christian Century* 89 (43), (29 November): 1212-1215.

——. 1973. "Jacques Ellul, the Polymath Who Knows Only One Thing." *Brethren Life and Thought* 18 (Spring): 77-84.

——. 1979. "A Voice on Vocation: The Contribution of Jacques Ellul." *Reformed Journal* (May): 16-21.

——. 1981. "Ellul and Kierkegaard: Closer Than Brothers." pp 52-66 in *Jacques Ellul: Interpretive Essays*, edited by Clifford G. Christians and Jay M. Van Hook. Urbana: University of Illinois Press.

——. 1985. "What Ellul Means to Me - in Less Than 3,000 Words ?" *Cross Currents* 35 (1), (Spring): 72-76, 91.

——. 1987. *Christian Anarchy: Jesus' Primacy over the Powers*. Grand Rapids, Michigan: Eerdmans.

——. 1989a. "Christian Anarchy." *The Ellul Studies Forum* 3 (June): 6-7.

——. 1989b. "Eller's Crowning Achievement." *The Ellul Studies Forum* 3 (June): 5-6.

——. 1994. "Merci, Mon Ami." *The Ellul Forum* 13 (July): 8.

Encrevé, André. 1985. *Les protestants en France de 1800 à nos jours: histoire d'une réintégration*. Paris: Editions Stock.

—. 1993a. "Introduction." pp 1-31 in *Les Protestants*, edited by Andre Encreve. Paris: Beauchesne.

— (Ed.). 1993b. *Les Protestants*. Vol 5 of *Dictionnaire du monde religieux dans la France contemporaine* edited by Jean-Marie Mayeur and Yves-Marie Hilaire. Paris: Beauchesne.

Epron, Patrick. 1979. "Jacques César Ellul." in *Ces Bordelais qui font Bordeaux et sa région*, edited by Patrick Epron. Bordeaux: Editions P.P.C.

Fasching, Darrell J. 1978. *The Apocalypse of Freedom: Christian Ethics in the Technological Society: A Defense of the Social Ethics of Jacques Ellul*. Ph.D. Dissertation (2 vols), Syracuse University.

—. 1981. *The Thought of Jacques Ellul: A Systematic Exposition*. New York: Edwin Mellen Press.

—. 1985. "Theologian of Culture." *Cross Currents* 35 (1), (Spring): 9-16.

—. 1988a. "The Ethical Importance of Universal Salvation." *The Ellul Studies Bulletin* 1 (August): 4,5,9.

—. 1988b. "Fasching's Reply to Morris and Dawn." *The Ellul Studies Forum* 2 (November): 7.

—. 1988c. "The Liberating Paradox of the Word." *Media Development* 35 (2): 8-11.

—. 1989. "After Auschwitz and Hiroshima: Judaism and Christianity in a Technological Civilization." *The Ellul Studies Forum* 4 (November): 4-9.

—. 1990. "The Dialectic of Apocalypse and Utopia in the Theological Ethics of Jacques Ellul." *Research in Philosophy and Technology* 10: 149-165.

—. 1991. "Mass Media, Ethical Paradox, and Democratic Freedom: Jacques Ellul's Ethic of the Word." *Research in Philosophy and Technology* 11: 77-103.

—. 1992. *Narrative Theology after Auschwitz: From Alienation to Ethics*. Minneapolis: Fortress Press.

—. 1993. "Ellul and Vahanian: Apocalypse or Utopia ?" *The Ellul Forum* 11 (July): 10,11,14.

—. 1994a. "Jacques Ellul - the Little Giant." *The Ellul Forum* 13 (July): 14-15.

—. 1994b. "Paradoxe éthique et libertés démocratiques: les médias selon l'éthique de la parole chez Jacques Ellul." *Foi et Vie* 93 (5-6), (December): 71-81.

—. 1994c. "Remembering Our Mentor and Friend, Jacques Ellul." *The Ellul Forum* 13 (July): 1.

Faugeron, Claude. 1974. "Recherches sur la violence: Review of *Contre les violents* and *De la révolution aux révoltes* by Jacques Ellul." *L'Année Sociologique* 25: 479-495.

Fesquet, Henri. 1971. "Le synode de l'église réformée de France amorce la refonte des études théologiques." *Le Monde*, 11 May, 35

—. 1972. "Le synode national de l'église réformée de France modifie le régime des études de théologie." *Le Monde*, 3 May, 15

—. 1975. "Le protestantisme français entre le désespoir humain et l'espérance chrétienne." *Le Monde*, 13 November, 15

Finet, Albert. 1982. "Les débuts de `Réforme', hebdomadaire protestant." pp 507-517 in *Églises et chrétiens dans la II* guerre mondiale: la France*, edited by Xavier de Montelos. Lyon: Presses Universitaires de Lyon.

Fouilloux, Etienne. 1993. "Jean Bosc." pp 89-91 in *Les Protestants*, edited by André Encrevé. Paris: Beauchesne.

Fox, Richard W. 1985. *Reinhold Niebuhr: A Biography*. New York: Pantheon Books.

Gaffney, James. 1975. "Jacques Ellul: A Christian Perspective on Revolution." pp 176-191 in *Liberation, Revolution and Freedom: Theological Perspectives*, edited by Thomas McFadden. New York: Seabury.

Gill, David W. 1976a. "Activist and Ethicist, Meet Jacques Ellul." *Christianity Today* 20 (24), (10 September): 22-24.

—. 1976b. "Jacques Ellul: Prophet in the Technological Wilderness." *Catholic Agitator* Oct (October): 3-4.

—. 1976c. "Ours Is Not a Secular Age: Review of *The New Demons* by Jacques Ellul." *Christianity Today* 20 (16), (7 May): 32-33.

—. 1976d. "A Study in Contrasts: Ellul and Bennett." *Radix* 8 (1), (July-August): 6.

—. 1979a. "Biblical Theology of the City." pp 713-715 in *International Standard Bible Encyclopedia Vol 1*. Grand Rapids: Eerdmans.

—. 1979b. *The Word of God in the Ethics of Jacques Ellul*. Ph.D. Dissertation, University of Southern California.

—. 1981a. "Jacques Ellul and Francis Schaeffer: Two Views of Western Civilization." *Fides et Historia* 13 (2), (Spring-Summer): 23-37.

—. 1981b. "Jacques Ellul: The Prophet as Theologian." *Themelios* 7 (1), (September): 4-14.

—. 1982. "Jacques Ellul's View of Scripture." *Journal of the Evangelical Theological Society* 25 (4), (December): 467-478.

—. 1984a. "Jacques Ellul: Answers from a Man Who Asks Hard Questions: An Interview with Jacques Ellul by David W. Gill." *Christianity Today* 28 (7), (20 April): 16-21.

—. 1984b. *The Word of God in the Ethics of Jacques Ellul*. Metuchen, N.J. & London: The Scarecrow Press Inc.

—. 1988. "The Dialectic of Theology and Sociology in Jacques Ellul: A Recent Interview (July 19, 1988)." Unpublished AAR Paper, Chicago.

—. 1994a. "My Journey with Ellul." *The Ellul Forum* 13 (July): 7-8.

—. 1994b. "Obituary: French Theologian Jacques Ellul Dies at 82." *Christianity Today* June 20 (June 20): 67.

—. 1995. "Jacques Ellul." pp 337-338 in *New Dictionary of Christian Ethics and Pastoral Theology*, edited by David J. Atkinson and David H. Field. Leicester: IVP.

Girard, René. 1978. *Things Hidden Since the Foundation of the World*. Stanford,

California: Stanford University Press.

Glover, Jonathan. 1977. *Causing Death and Saving Lives*. London: Penguin Books.

Goddard, Andrew. 1994a. "Christian Soldier of Revolution: Obituary, Jacques Ellul." *The Guardian*, June 9, 2:13

—. 1994b. "Ellul et le réalisme politique du Christ." *Foi et Vie* 93 (5-6), (December): 83-93.

—. 1996. "Obituary: Jacques Ellul." *Studies in Christian Ethics* 9 (1): 140-53.

—. 1998. *The European Union : A Christian Perspective*. Cambridge: Grove.

—. 1999. "Law, Rights and Technology." *The Ellul Forum* 23 (July): 5-8.

—. 2000a. "Jacques Ellul and the Power of the Media." *Studies in Christian Ethics* 13 (1): 66-75.

—. 2000b. "Jacques Ellul: 20th Century Prophet for the 21st Century ?" *The Ellul Forum* 25 (July): 2-7.

Grant, George. 1966. *Philosophy in the Mass Age*. Vancouver: The Copp Clark Publishing Company.

—. 1969a. *Technology and Empire: Perspectives on North America*. Toronto: House of Anansi.

—. 1969b. *Time as History*. Toronto: Canadian Broadcasting Corporation.

—. 1970. *Lament for a Nation: The Defeat of Canadian Nationalism*. Toronto: McClelland and Stewart Ltd.

—. 1985. *English Speaking Justice*. Toronto: House of Anansi Press Ltd.

—. 1986. *Technology and Justice*. Toronto: House of Anansi Press Ltd.

Guisan, François. 1947. "Review of *Le fondement théologique du droit* by Jacques Ellul." *Verbum Caro* 8 (3), (August): 130-136.

Guissard, Lucien. 1962. *Emmanuel Mounier*. Paris: Editions Universitaires.

Gummer, John Selwyn, Eric Heffer, and Alan Beith (Eds.). 1987. *Faith in Politics: Which Way Should Christians Vote ?* London: SPCK.

Gurvitch, Georges. 1973. *Sociology of Law*. London: Routledge & Kegan Paul.

Hanks, Joyce Main. 1984a. *Jacques Ellul: A Comprehensive Bibliography*. Greenwich, Connecticut: JAI Press Inc.

—. 1984b. "A Way Out in a No-Exit Situation ? Jacques Ellul on Technique and the Third World." *Research in Philosophy and Technology* 7: 271-286.

—. 1988a. "Feminism in the Writings of Jacques Ellul." *Media Development* 35 (2): 17-19.

—. 1988b. "Jacques Ellul and the Kingdom." Unpublished AAR Paper, Chicago.

—. 1991. "Jacques Ellul: A Comprehensive Bibliography; Update, 1982-1985." *Research in Philosophy and Technology* 11: 197-299.

—. 1992. "The Politics of God and the Politics of Ellul." *Journal of the Evangelical Theological Society* 35 (2), (June): 217-230.

—. 1993. "Jacques Ellul on Development: Why It Doesn't Work." *The Ellul Forum* 10 (January): 6-8.

—. 1994. "Jacques Ellul, 1912-1994." *The Ellul Forum* 13 (July): 4.

—. 1995. "Jacques Ellul: A Comprehensive Bibliography Update, 1985-1993." *Research in Philosophy and Technology* 15: 287-413.

—. 2000. *Jacques Ellul: An Annotated Bibliography of Primary Works.* Stamford, Connecticut: JAI Press Inc.

—. 2001. "Jacques Ellul and Bernard Charbonneau." *The Ellul Forum* 26 (January): 3-5.

Hanks, Thomas. 1983. *God So Loved the Third World: The Biblical Vocabulary of Oppression.* Maryknoll, New York: Orbis Books.

—. 1984a. "How Ellul Transcends Liberation Theologies." *TSF Bulletin* 8 (1), (September-October): 13-16.

—. 1984b. "Jacques Ellul: The Original 'Liberation Theologian'." *TSF Bulletin* 7 (5), (May-June): 8-11.

—. 1985. "The Original 'Liberation Theologian' ?" *Cross Currents* 35 (1), (Spring): 17-32.

—. 1993. "Liberation Theology after 25 Years: Passé or Mainstream ?" *Anvil* 10 (3): 197-208.

Hart, Trevor A. 1999. *Regarding Karl Barth : Essays toward a Reading of His Theology.* Carlisle: Paternoster.

Hauerwas, Stanley. 1984. *The Peaceable Kingdom: A Primer in Christian Ethics.* London: SCM Press.

—. 1994. "Jacques Ellul, Courage and the Christian Imagination." *The Ellul Forum* 13 (July): 4.

Hays, Richard B. 1996. *The Moral Vision of the New Testament: A Contemporary Introduction to New Testament Ethics.* San Francisco: Harper Collins.

—. 1999. "Victory over Violence: The Significance of N.T. Wright's Jesus for New Testament Ethics." pp 142-58 in *Jesus and the Restoration of Israel,* edited by Carey Newman. Carlisle: Paternoster.

Heddendorf, Russell. 1973. "The Christian World of Jacques Ellul." *Christian Scholar's Review* 2 (4): 291-307.

Heidegger, Martin. 1977. *The Question Concerning Technology and Other Essays.* New York: Harper and Row.

Helgeland, John, Robert J. Daly, and J. Patout Burns. 1985. *Christians and the Military: The Early Experience.* London: SCM Press.

Hellman, John. 1980. "Maritain and Mounier: A Secret Quarrel over the Future of the Church." *Review of Politics* 42 (2), (April): 152-166.

Hendricks, Joseph Millard. 1989. *Technique, the Terror and the Wilderness: Bondage and Freedom in the Thought of Jacques Ellul.* Ph.D. Dissertation, Emory University.

Henry, Carl. 1983. *God Who Stands and Stays. God, Revelation and Authority Vol 6.* Texas: Word Books.

Herron, David Rolfe. 1987. *The Idea of Federalism in Western Europe after World War Two: An Analysis of the Goals and Tactics of the European Union of Federalists (U.E.F.).* Ph.D. Dissertation, Northern Illinois University.

Higginson, Richard. 1988. *Dilemmas: A Christian Approach to Moral Decision-Making.* London: Hodder & Stoughton.

Hoekstra, Harvey T. 1979. *Evangelism in Eclipse: World Mission and the World Council of Churches.* Exeter: The Paternoster Press.

Holland, Sherrill Reid. 1986. *Fear Not: A Study of Jacques Ellul on the Speaking and Silent God.* Ph.D. Dissertation, Union Theological Seminary.

Holloway, James Y. (Ed.). 1970a. *Introducing Jacques Ellul.* Grand Rapids, Michigan: Eerdmans.

—. 1970b. "West of Eden." pp 19-50 in *Introducing Jacques Ellul,* edited by James Y. Holloway. Grand Rapids, Michigan: Eerdmans.

Holmes, Arthur. 1975. "Human Variables and Natural Law." pp 63-79 in *God and the Good,* edited by Clifton Orlebeke and Lewis Smedes. Grand Rapids: Eerdmans.

—. 1981. "A Philosophical Critique of Ellul on Natural Law." pp 229-250 in *Jacques Ellul: Interpretive Essays,* edited by Clifford G. Christians and Jay M. Van Hook. Urbana: University of Illinois Press.

Hornus, Jean-Michel. 1980. *It Is Not Lawful for Me to Fight: Early Christian Attitudes toward, War, Violence and the State.* Scottdale, Pennsylvania: Herald Press.

Horsley, Richard A. 1987. *Jesus and the Spiral of Violence: Popular Jewish Resistance in Roman Palestine.* San Francisco: Harper & Row.

Horsley, Richard A. and John S. Hanson. 1985. *Bandits, Prophets and Messiahs: Popular Movements at the Time of Jesus.* Edinburgh: T & T Clark.

Hottois, Gilbert. 1994a. "L'Impossible symbole ou la question de la `culture technique'." pp 271-298 in *Sur Jacques Ellul,* edited by Patrick Troude-Chastenet. Bordeaux: L'Esprit du Temps.

—. 1994b. "Symbolisation et technoscience." *Foi et Vie* 93 (5-6), (December): 113-124.

Hunt, Alan. 1978. *The Sociological Movement in Law.* London: Macmillan.

Hussey, Andrew. 2001. *The Game of War : The Life and Death of Guy Debord.* London: Jonathan Cape.

Ihara, Randall Homma. 1975. *Redeeming the Time: Theology, Technology and Politics in the Thought of Jacques Ellul.* Ph.D. Dissertation, University of Tennessee.

Illich, Ivan. 1994a. "An Address to `Master Jacques'." *The Ellul Forum* 13 (July): 16-17.

—. 1994b. "Préface." pp 11-17 in *Sur Jacques Ellul,* edited by Patrick Troude-Chastenet. Bordeaux: L'Esprit du Temps.

Johnson, James Turner. 1999. *Morality & Contemporary Warfare.* New Haven, Connecticut: Yale University Press.

Johnson, Kermit D. 1982. "The Nuclear Reality: Beyond Niebuhr and the Just War." *Christian Century* 99 (31), (13 October): 1014-1017.

Jones, Nicholas. 1995. *Soundbites and Spin Doctors : How Politicians Manipulate the Media - and Vice Versa.* London: Cassell.

—. 2000. *Sultans of Spin : The Media and the New Labour Government.* London: Orion.

—. 2001. *The Control Freaks : How New Labour Gets Its Own Way.* London: Politico's.

Kelly, Michael. 1979. *Pioneer of the Catholic Revival: The Ideas and Influence of Emmanuel Mounier.* London: Sheed & Ward.

Kemp, Peter. 1976. "Le postulat poétique de la sécularisation." pp 407-408 in *Herméneutique de la sécularisation*, edited by Enrico Castelli. Paris: Aubier.

Kinsky, Ferdinand. 1979. "Personalism and Federalism." *Publius: The Journal Of Federalism* 9 (4), (Fall): 131-156.

Konyndyk, Kenneth. 1981. "Violence." pp 251-268 in *Jacques Ellul: Interpretive Essays*, edited by Clifford G. Christians and Jay M. Van Hook. Urbana: University of Illinois Press.

Kristensen, Brede. 1976. "Jacques Ellul: A Brief Sketch of His Work." *Christian Graduate* 29 (4), (December): 106-110.

Lacoue-Labarthe, Philippe. 1994. "La protestation." *Foi et Vie* 93 (5-6), (December): 11-17.

Lagarrigue, Georges. 1974. "De la connaissance oubliée à l'espérance vécue: remarques critiques sur la pensée et la spiritualité chrétiennes de Jacques Ellul." *ICHTHUS* 46 (October): 8-12, 21-24.

—. 1975. "Pilotage des églises dans les brumes du politique: sur trois suggestions de Jacques Ellul." *ICHTHUS* 54 (August): 2-5, 21-23.

Larkin, Maurice. 1997. *France Since the Popular Front : Government and People 1936-1996.* Oxford: Clarendon.

Lasch, Christopher. 1970. "The Social Thought of Jacques Ellul." pp 63-90 in *Introducing Jacques Ellul*, edited by James Y. Holloway. Grand Rapids, Michigan: Eerdmans.

Laski, Harold. 1921. "Introduction." pp ix-xxxiv in *Law in the Modern State*, by Léon Duguit. London: George Allen & Unwin.

Latouche, Serge. 1994. "Raison technique, raison économique et raison politique: Ellul face à Marx et Tocqueville." pp 101-113 in *Sur Jacques Ellul*, edited by Patrick Troude-Chastenet. Bordeaux: L'Esprit du Temps.

Lavroff, Dmitri Georges. 1983. "Avant-Propos." pp ix-x in *Religion, société et politique: mélanges en hommage à Jacques Ellul*, edited by Etienne Dravasa, et.al. Paris: Presses Universitaires de France.

Lee, Gary. 1985. "Publishing Ellul." *Cross Currents* 35 (1), (Spring): 92-95.

Léonard, Emile. 1955. *Le Protestant Francais.* Paris: PUF.

Logan, James. 1977. "An Ethics for Modern Noah: Perspective on Jacques Ellul's Writings." *Sojourners* 6 (6), (June): 13-15.

Loubet del Bayle, Jean-Louis. 1969. *Les non-conformistes des années 30: une tentative de renouvellement de la pensée politique française.* Paris: Editions du Seuil.

—. 1983. "Bernanos et l'idée de crise de civilisation." pp 625-641 in *Religion, société et politique: mélanges en hommage à Jacques Ellul*, edited by Etienne Dravasa *et.al*. Paris: Presses Universitaires de France.

—. 1994. "Aux origines de la pensée de Jacques Ellul ? Technique et société dans la réflexion des mouvements personnalistes des années 30." pp 19-35 in *Sur Jacques Ellul*, edited by Patrick Troude-Chastenet. Bordeaux: L'Esprit du Temps.

—. 2001. "Bernard Charbonneau and the Personalist Context in the 1930s and Beyond." *The Ellul Forum* 26: 6-10.

Lovekin, David. 1980. "Technology as the Sacred Order." *Research in Philosophy and Technology* 3: 203-222.

—. 1991. *Technique, Discourse, and Consciousness: An Introduction to the Philosophy of Jacques Ellul*. Bethlehem: Lehigh University Press.

—. 1994. "In Memorium for Jacques Ellul." *The Ellul Forum* 13 (July): 10.

—. 1995. "Response to Casey's Review of *Technique, Discourse and Consciousness*." *The Ellul Forum* 14 (January): 11-13.

Macfarlane, Leslie. 1974. *Violence and the State*. London: Thomas Nelson and Sons.

Macquarrie, John. 1982. "Review of *The Ethics of Freedom* by Jacques Ellul." *Religious Studies* 18 (1), (March): 109-111.

Maillot, Alphonse. 1994. "L'homme et l'église." *Foi et Vie* 93 (5-6), (December): 43-46.

Mandrou, Robert. 1977. "Jacques Ellul." pp 397-398 in *Histoire des protestants en France*, edited by Robert Mandrou. Paris: Privat.

Margolis, Joseph. 1984. "Three Conceptions of Technology: Satanic, Titanic, Human." *Research in Philosophy and Technology* 7: 145-158.

Maritain, Jacques. 1954. *Man and the State*. London: Hollis & Carter.

Markovitch, Milan P. 1933. *La doctrine sociale de Duguit - ses idées sur le syndicalisme et la représentation professionnelle*. Paris: Editions Pierre Bossuet.

Marlin, Randal. 1982. "Translator's Introduction." pp 1-12 in Ellul, *F.L.N. Propaganda in France During the Algerian War*. Ottawa: By Books.

Marshall, Paul. 1984. *Thine Is the Kingdom: A Biblical Perspective on the Nature of Government and Politics Today*. Basingstoke: Marshall Morgan & Scott.

Marshall, Peter. 1993. *Demanding the Impossible: A History of Anarchism*. London: Fontana Press.

Marty, Martin E. 1981. "Creative Misuses of Jacques Ellul." pp 3-13 in *Jacques Ellul: Interpretive Essays*, edited by Clifford G. Christians and Jay M. Van Hook. Urbana: University of Illinois Press.

Matheke, David G. 1972. *To Will and to Do God's Word: An Examination of the Christian Meaning of the Works of Jacques Ellul*. Doctor of Divinity Dissertation, Vanderbilt Divinity University.

Mazower, Mark. 1999. *Dark Continent: Europe's Twentieth Century*. London: Penguin.

Mehl, Roger. 1948. "Review of *Présence au monde moderne* by Jacques Ellul." *Revue d'Histoire et de Philosophie Religieuses* 28-29 (2): 161-164.

Menninger, David C. 1974. *Technique and Politics: The Political Thought of Jacques Ellul*. Ph.D. Dissertation, University of California-Riverside.

—. 1975. "Jacques Ellul: A Tempered Profile." *Review of Politics* 37 (2), (April): 235-246.

—. 1980. "Political Dislocation in a Technical Universe." *Review of Politics* 42 (1), (January): 73-91.

—. 1981a. "Marx in the Social Thought of Jacques Ellul." pp 17-31 in *Jacques Ellul: Interpretive Essays*, edited by Clifford G. Christians and Jay M. Van Hook. Urbana: University of Illinois Press.

—. 1981b. "Politics or Technique: A Defense of Jacques Ellul." *Polity* 14 (1), (Fall): 110-127.

Merle, Marcel. 1965. "Sur un livre de Jacques Ellul: *L'Illusion politique*." *Revue Française de Science Politique* 15: 767-779.

Mesthene, Emmanuel G. 1984. "Technology as Evil: Fear or Lamentation?" *Research in Philosophy and Technology* 7: 59-74.

Metzger, Pierre. 1992. "Qu'est-ce que la liberté? La position de Jacques Ellul." *La Revue Réformée* 175 (5), (November): 39-55.

Meury, André. 1975. "Un colloque 'interministériel' à Marly-Le-Roy sur la prévention de la délinquance: Educateurs incompris et fonctionnaires soupçonnés." *Le Monde*, 31 January, 32

Michel, A. 1965. "Review of *L'Illusion politique* by Jacques Ellul." *Revue Française de Sociologie* 6 (4), (October-December): 535-536.

Miller, Duane R. 1970. *The Effect of Technology Upon Humanization in the Thought of Lewis Mumford and Jacques Ellul*. Ph.D. Dissertation, Boston University.

—. 1973. "Watergate and the Thought of Jacques Ellul." *Christian Century* 90 (34), (26 September): 943-946.

Minnema, Theodore. 1973. "Evil in the Thought of Jacques Ellul." *Reformed Journal* 23 (5), (May-June): 17-20.

Mitcham, Carl. 1969. *From Sociology to Philosophy: On the Nature of Criticisms of the Tech- Nological Society*. M.A. Thesis, University of Colorado.

—. 1985a. "About Ellul." *Cross Currents* 35 (1), (Spring): 105-107.

—. 1985b. "Jacques Ellul and His Contribution to Theology." *Cross Currents* 35 (1), (Spring): 1-8.

Mitcham, Carl, and J. Grote (Eds.). 1984. *Theology and Technology: Essays in Christian Analysis and Exegesis*. New York: University Press of America.

Mitcham, Carl, and Robert Mackey. 1971. "Jacques Ellul and the Technological Society." *Philosophy Today* 15 (2), (Summer): 102-121.

—. 1972. "Introduction: Technology as Philosophical Problem." pp 1-30 in

Philosophy and Technology: Readings in the Philosophical Problems of Technology, edited by Carl Mitcham and Robert Mackey. New York: Free Press.

Moltmann, Jürgen. 1974. *The Crucified God: The Cross of Christ as the Foundation and Criticism of Christian Theology*. New York: Harper and Row.

Monsma, Stephen V. 1986. *Responsible Technology: A Christian Perspective*. Grand Rapids, Michigan: Eerdmans.

Morgan, Bruce. 1971. "Review of *Violence* by Jacques Ellul." *Union Seminary Quarterly Review* 26 (4), (Summer): 407-413.

Morris, Ken. 1988. "The Importance of Eschatology to Ellul's Ethics and Soteriology: A Response to Darrell Fasching." *The Ellul Studies Forum* 2 (November): 5-6.

Mounier, Emmanuel. 1952. *Personalism*. Notre Dame & London: University of Notre Dame Press.

—. 1966. *Communisme, anarchie et personnalisme*. Paris: Edition du Seuil.

Mulkey, Robert Cranford. 1973. *The Theology of Politics in the Writings of Jacques Ellul*. Th.D. Dissertation, Southern Baptist Theological Seminary.

Muller, Jean-Marie. 1977. "Réponse à Jacques Ellul." *Alternatives Non Violentes* 24-25 (August-October): 61-66.

Munby, Denys. 1955. "Review of *L'Homme et l'argent*." *The Ecumenical Review* VII (April), (April): 291.

Nanos, Mark D. 1996. *The Mystery of Romans: The Jewish Context of Paul's Letter*. Minneapolis: Fortress Press.

Newman, Carey. 1999. *Jesus and the Restoration of Israel: A Critical Assessment of N.T. Wright's Jesus and the Victory of God*. Downers Grove, Illinois.: IVP.

Nicholls, David. 1989. *Deity and Domination: Images of God and the State in the Nineteenth and Twentieth Centuries*. London: Routledge.

Nisbet, Robert A. 1970. "The Grand Illusion: An Appreciation of Jacques Ellul." *Commentary* 50 (2), (August): 40-44.

Norton-Taylor, Richard. 1995. *Truth Is a Difficult Concept: Inside the Scott Inquiry*. London: Fourth Estate Limited.

Nygren, Anders. 1932-9. *Agape and Eros*. London: SPCK.

O'Donovan, Joan E. 1984. *George Grant and the Twilight of Justice*. Toronto: University of Toronto Press.

—. 1985. "The Battleground of Liberalism: Politics of Eternity and Politics of Time." *The Chesterton Review* 11 (2), (May): 131-154.

O'Donovan, Joan Lockwood, and Oliver O'Donovan. 1999. *From Irenaeus to Grotius: A Sourcebook in Christian Political Thought 100-1625*. Grand Rapids: Eerdmans.

O'Donovan, Oliver. 1972. "Justified War in Recent American Theology." *The Churchman* 86 (3), (Autumn): 184-197.

—. 1977. *In Pursuit of a Christian View of War*: Grove Books.

—. 1984. *Begotten or Made ?* Oxford: Clarendon Press.

—. 1986a. "The Political Thought of the Book of Revelation." *Tyndale Bulletin* 37: 61-94.

—. 1986b. *Resurrection and Moral Order: An Outline for Evangelical Ethics.* Leicester: IVP.

—. 1987. "Augustine's City of God XIX and Western Political Thought." *Dionysius* XI (December): 89-110.

—. 1989. *Peace and Certainty: A Theological Essay on Deterrence.* Oxford: OUP.

—. 1993. "War and Peace." pp 652-7 in *The Blackwell Encyclopedia of Modern Christian Thought,* edited by Alister E. McGrath. Oxford: Blackwells.

—. 1996. *The Desire of the Nations: Rediscovering the Roots of Political Theology.* Cambridge: Cambridge University Press.

Orsy, Ladislas. 1961. "Review of *The Theological Foundation of Law* by Jacques Ellul." *Heythrop Journal* 2 (3), (July): 282-284.

Outka, Gene. 1981. "Discontinuity in the Ethics of Jacques Ellul." pp 177-228 in *Jacques Ellul: Interpretive Essays,* edited by Clifford G. Christians and Jay M. Van Hook. Urbana: University of Illinois Press.

Pannenberg, Wolfhart. 1981. *Ethics.* Philadelphia: Westminster Press.

Pascal, Jacques. 1948. "Review of *Le fondement théologique du droit* by Jacques Ellul." *Foi et Vie* 46 (3), (April-May): 306-309.

Paton, George Whitecross. 1972. *A Textbook of Jurisprudence.* Oxford: Oxford University Press.

Philip, André. 1960. "Pas d'accord." *Réforme,* 17 September, 3

Pilgrim, Walter E. 1999. *Uneasy Neighbors: Church and State in the New Testament.* Minneapolis: Fortress Press.

Prades, Jacques (Ed.). 1997. *Bernard Charbonneau: une vie entière à dénoncer la grande imposture.* Toulouse: Éditions Érès.

Preston, Ronald. 1977. "Review of *The Ethics of Freedom* by Jacques Ellul." *Theology* 80 (676), (July): 306-308.

Punzo, Vincent C. 1980. "Jacques Ellul on the Presence of the Kingdom in a Technological Society." *Logos (University of Santa Clara, CA)* 1: 125-137.

R.J. 1977. "Environnement: M. Jacques Ellul fait le procès de la M.I.A.C.A." *Sud-Ouest,* 20 January, A

Raban, Jonathan. 1989. *God, Man & Mrs Thatcher: A Critique of Mrs Thatcher's Address to the General Assembly of the Church of Scotland.* London: Chatto & Windus.

Ramsey, Paul. 1950. *Basic Christian Ethics.* New York: Scribners.

—. 1961. *War and the Christian Conscience: How Shall Modern War Be Conducted Justly ?* Durham, N.C.: Duke University Press.

—. 1968. *The Just War: Force and Political Responsibility.* New York: Scribners.

—. 1988. *Speak up for Just War or Pacifism: A Critique of the United Methodist Bishops' Pastoral Letter 'In Defense of Creation'.* University Park & London:

The Pennsylvania State University Press.

Rapp, Friedrich. 1982. "Philosophy of Technology." pp 361-412 in *Contemporary Philosophy: A New Survey Vol 2: Philosophy of Science*, edited by Guttorm Fløistad. The Hague: Martinus Nijhoff.

—. 1994. "Il faut analyser le tout pour mieux le comprendre." pp 115-132 in *Sur Jacques Ellul*, edited by Patrick Troude-Chastenet. Bordeaux: L'Esprit du Temps.

Rawnsley, Andrew. 2001. *Servants of the People: The Inside Story of New Labour*. London: Penguin.

Ray, Ronald R. 1973. *A Critical Examination of Jacques Ellul's Christian Ethic*. Ph.D. Dissertation, St. Andrew's University.

—. 1977. "Letter About Ellul." *Sojourners* 6 (2), (February): 6.

—. 1979. "Jacques Ellul's Innocent Notes on Hermeneutics." *Interpretation: A Journal of Bible and Theology* 33 (3), (July): 262-282.

Rees, Laurence. 1992. *Selling Politics*. London: BBC Books.

Reid, J. K. S. 1952. "Review of *The Presence of the Kingdom* by Jacques Ellul." *Scottish Journal of Theology* 5: 321-324.

Reymond, Bernard. 1985. *Théologien ou prophète ? Les francophones et Karl Barth avant 1945*. Lausanne: Age D'Homme.

Riddell, Peter. 1993. *Honest Opportunism: The Rise of the Career Politician*. London: Hamilton.

Rooum, Donald. 1993. *What Is Anarchism ?: An Introduction*. London: Freedom Press.

Rose, Stephen. 1970a. "Bethge's Monument." *Christianity and Crisis* 30 (13), (20 July): 154-155.

—. 1970b. "Whither Ethics, Jacques Ellul?" pp 123-134 in *Introducing Jacques Ellul*, edited by James Y. Holloway. Grand Rapids, Michigan: William B. Eerdmans.

Roux, Hebert. 1982. "Les relations entre protestants et catholiques à Bordeaux 1943-1946." pp 519-524 in *Églises et chrétiens dans la IIe guerre mondiale: la France*, edited by Xavier de Montelos. Lyon: Presses Universitaires de Lyon.

Roy, Christian. 1990. "Nature et liberté: le combat solitaire De Bernard Charbonneau." *Vice Versa* 30 (September-October): 12-14.

—. 1991. "Transmission de la culture ou bluff technologique ? Propos de Jacques Ellul." *Vice Versa* 33 (May-June): 21-22.

—. 1992. "Aux sources de l'écologie politique: le personnalisme 'gascon' de Bernard Charbonneau et Jacques Ellul." *Canadian Journal of History* 27 (April): 67-100.

—. 1995. "Le Personnalisme français 1930-1950: origines, mutations et permutations d'un discours anti-Libéral."

Rumpf, Louis. 1976. "Le seul chemin de l'espérance." *Réforme*, 7 February, 7-8

Schmidt, Larry (Ed.). 1978. *George Grant in Process: Essays and Conversations*. Toronto: Anansi.

Schram, Stuart R. 1954. *Protestantism and Politics in France*. Alençon, France: Imprimerie Corbière & Jugain.

Schrey, Heinz Horst. 1952. "Review of *Le fondement théologique du droit* by Jacques Ellul." *Ecumenical Review* 4 (September): 446-448.

Schuller, Bruno S. J. 1963. *Die Herrschaft Christi und das Weltliche Recht: Die Christologische Rechtsbegründung in der Neueren Protestantischen Theologie* Rome: Päpstlichen Gregorianische Universität.

Schuurman, Egbert. 1980. *Technology and the Future: A Philosophical Challenge*. Toronto: Wedge Publishing Foundation.

—. 1984. "A Christian Philosophical Perspective on Technology." pp 107-119 in *Theology and Technology*, edited by Carl Mitcham and Jim Grote. Lanham, MD: University Press of America.

Scott, Gregory Mahlon. 1989. *A Comparison of the Political Thought of Jacques Ellul and Jurgen Moltmann*. Ph.D. Dissertation, University of Virginia.

Seurin, Jean-Louis. 1994a. "Jacques Ellul: L'Interprétation de la politique à la lumière de la Bible." pp 321-355 in *Sur Jacques Ellul*, edited by Patrick Troude-Chastenet. Bordeaux: L'Esprit du Temps.

—. 1994b. "Religion et politique à la lumière de la Bible selon Jacques Ellul." *Foi et Vie* 93 (5-6), (December): 95-109.

Sider, Ronald. 1979. *Christ and Violence*. Tring, Herts.: Lion.

Siedentop, Larry. 2001. *Democracy in Europe*. London: Penguin Books.

Skillen, James W. 1982. *Prophecy, Critique, Action: Political Philosophy in the Light of Biblical Revelation*. Association for Calvinistic Philosophy 2nd International Symposium.

Spirlet, Jean-Pierre. 1976. "Le Professeur Ellul: 'on veut transformer l'université en petites écoles techniques en négligeant son rôle critique'." *Sud-Ouest*, 22 April, 2

Stanley, John L. 1981. "The Uncertain Hobbesian: Ellul's Dialogue with the Sovereign and the Tradition of French Politics." pp 69-90 in *Jacques Ellul: Interpretive Essays*, edited by Clifford G. Christians and Jay M. Van Hook. Urbana: University of Illinois Press.

Strauss, Leo. 1953. *Natural Right and History*. Chicago: University of Chicago Press.

Stringfellow, William. 1967. "Introduction." pp 1-6 in *The Presence of the Kingdom*, edited by Jacques Ellul. New York: Seabury.

—. 1970. "The American Importance of Jacques Ellul." pp 135-138 in *Introducing Jacques Ellul*, edited by James Holloway. Grand Rapids, Michigan: Eerdmans.

—. 1971. "Meet Jacques Ellul." *Christian Advocate* 24 June (24 June): 15.

—. 1977. "Kindred Mind and Brother." *Sojourners* 6 (6), (June): 12.

Sturm, Douglas. 1984. "Jacques Ellul." pp p561-582 in *A Handbook of Christian Theologians*, edited by Marty E. Martin and Dean G. Peerman. Cambridge: Lutterworth Press.

Sullivan, Robert R., and Alfred J. DiMaio. 1982. "Jacques Ellul: Toward Understanding His Political Thinking." *Journal of Church and State* 24 (1), (Winter): 13-28.

Swartley, Willard M. 1983. *Slavery, Sabbath, War and Women: Case Issues in Biblical Interpretation.* Scottsdale, Pennsylvania: Herald Press.

—. 1988. *Essays on Peace Theology and Witness.* Elkhart, Indiana: Institute of Mennonite Studies.

Taylor, Charles. 1989. *Sources of the Self: The Making of Modern Identity.* Cambridge: CUP.

Temple, Katharine. 1976. *The Task of Jacques Ellul: A Proclamation of Biblical Faith as Requisite for Understanding the Modern Project.* Ph.D. Dissertation, McMaster University.

—. 1977. "Ellul as Sociologist." *Sojourners* 6 (8), (August): 38.

—. 1980. "The Sociology of Jacques Ellul." *Research in Philosophy and Technology* 3: 223-261.

—. 1983. "Doubts Concerning the Religious Origins of Technological Civilization." *Research in Philosophy and Technology* 6:189-97.

—. 1985. "A Consistent Distinction." *Cross Currents* 35 (1), (Spring): 33-42, 48.

—. 1988. "Jacques Ellul: A Consistent Distinction." *Media Development* 35 (2): 19-22.

—. 1989a. "On Christians, Jews and the Law." *The Ellul Studies Forum* 4 (November): 10-11.

—. 1989b. "Review of *Anarchie et christianisme* by Jacques Ellul and Eller, *Christian Anarchy*." *The Ellul Studies Forum* 3 (June): 8.

—. 1991. "Jacques Ellul: A Catholic Worker Vision of the Culture." *The Ellul Studies Forum* 7 (July): 6-7.

Tenzer, Nicolas. 1993. "Préface." pp i-xxxiii in *La révolution nécessaire*, by Robert Aron and Arnaud Dandieu. Paris: Jean Michel Place.

Tomlin, Graham. 2002. *The Provocative Church.* London: SPCK.

Thorson, Thomas Landon. 1968. "Review of *The Political Illusion* by Jacques Ellul." *Political Science Quarterly* 83 (1), (March): 117-119.

Vahanian, Gabriel. 1970. "Technology, Politics, and the Christian Faith." pp 51-62 in *Introducing Jacques Ellul*, edited by James Holloway. Grand Rapids, Michigan: Eerdmans.

—. 1981. "Jacques Ellul and the Religious Illusion." pp xv-xxxviii in *The Thought of Jacques Ellul: A Systematic Exposition*, edited by Darrell J. Fasching. New York: Edwin Mellen Press.

—. 1983a. "Dieu et le Christ: la conception Christique de Dieu." *Foi et Vie* 82 (1), (January): 54-67.

—. 1983b. "Espérer, faute de foi ?" pp 153-167 in *Religion, société et politique: mélanges en hommage à Jacques Ellul*, edited by Etienne Dravasa et.al., Paris: Presses Universitaires de France.

—. 1988. "Review of *Présence au monde moderne* by Jacques Ellul and

Clendenin, *Theological Method in Jacques Ellul.*" *Foi et Vie* 87 (3-4), (July): 188-190.

—. 1993. "Back to Ellul by Way of Weyembergh." *The Ellul Forum* (11), (July): 8-9.

—. 1994a. "Anarchie et saintété ou l'illusion du sacré." *Foi et Vie* 93 (5-6), (December): 153-167.

—. 1994b. "Anarchy and Holiness." *The Ellul Forum* 13 (July): 11-13,15.

—. 1994c. "Jacques Ellul, un homme d'amitié." *Foi et Vie* 93 (5-6), (December): 1-8.

—. 1994d. "Sacré, technique et société." pp 299-320 in *Sur Jacques Ellul*, edited by Patrick Troude-Chastenet. Bordeaux: L'Esprit du Temps.

—. 1999. "Human Rights and the Natural Flaw." *The Ellul Forum* 23 (July): 3-4.

Van Elderen, Marlin. 1990. *Introducing the World Council of Churches.* Geneva: WCC.

Van Hook, Jay. 1976. "The Burden of Jacques Ellul." *Reformed Journal* 26 (10), (December): 13-17.

—. 1981. "The Politics of Man, the Politics of God, and the Politics of Freedom." pp 128-146 in *Jacques Ellul: Interpretive Essays*, edited by Clifford G. Christians and Jay M. Van Hook. Urbana: University of Illinois Press.

—. 1983. "The Prophet of Bordeaux." *Reformed Journal* 33 (12), (December): 26-27.

Vanderburg, Willem H. 1985. "What an Engineer Found in Ellul." *Cross Currents* 35 (1), (Spring): 88-91.

—. 1987. "Technique and Responsibility: Think Globally, Act Locally, According to Jacques Ellul." pp 115-132 in *Technology and Responsibility*, edited by Paul T. Durbin. D. Reidel Publishing Company.

—. 1988. "Idolatry in a Technical Society: Gaining the World but Losing the Soul." *Media Development* 35 (2): 23-26.

—. 1994. "Thinking Globally, Acting Locally: In Memory of Jacques Ellul." *The Ellul Forum* 13 (July): 5-6.

Verene, Donald Phillip. 1984. "Technological Desire." *Research in Philosophy and Technology* 7: 99-112.

Viallaneix, Nelly. 1974. *Kierkegaard: l'unique devant Dieu.* Paris: Les Editions du Cerf.

Vitalis, André. 1994. "Informatisation et autonomie de la technique." pp 151-164 in *Sur Jacques Ellul*, edited by Patrick Troude-Chastenet. Bordeaux: L'Esprit du Temps.

Voegelin, Eric. 1952. *The New Science of Politics: An Introduction.* Chicago: University of Chicago Press.

Wacks, Raymond. 1987. *Jurisprudence.* London: Blackstone Press.

Walzer, Michael. 1977. *Just and Unjust Wars: A Moral Argument with Historical Illustrations.* New York: Basic.

Ward, Colin. 1988. *Anarchy in Action.* London: Freedom Press.

Weber, Eugen. 1995. *The Hollow Years: France in the 1930s.* London: Sinclair-Stevenson.

Webster, John. 2000. *Barth.* London: Continuum.

Weinstein, Jay. 1981. "Feeling Helpless: The Idea of Autonomous Technology in Social Science." *Theory and Society* 10 (4), (July): 567-578.

Wennemann, D. J. 1991a. "Freedom and Dialectic in Ellul's Thought." *Research in Philosophy and Technology* 11: 67-75.

——. 1991b. *The Meaning of Subjectivity in a Technological Society: Jacques Ellul's View of Man as Dialogic Agent.* Ph.D. Dissertation, Marquette University.

Westermann, Claus. 1984. *Genesis 1-11: A Commentary.* Minneapolis: Augsburg Publishing House.

Weyembergh, Maurice. 1989. "La critique de l'utopie et de la technique chez J.Ellul et H.Jonas." *Tijdschrift Voor de Studie Van de Verlichting en Van Het Vrije Denken* 17 (1-2): 63-136.

——. 1993. "Ellul and Vahanian on Technology and Utopianism." *The Ellul Forum* 11 (July): 4-7.

——. 1994a. "J. Ellul et M. Heidegger: le prophète et le penseur." pp 75-100 in *Sur Jacques Ellul*, edited by Patrick Troude-Chastenet. Bordeaux: L'Esprit du Temps.

——. 1994b. "La technique et l'utopisme selon Ellul et Vahanian." *Foi et Vie* 93 (5-6), (December): 137-151.

Wilkinson, John. 1970. "The Divine Persuasion." pp 161-183 in *Introducing Jacques Ellul*, edited by James Holloway. Grand Rapids, Michigan: Eerdmans.

Williams, Roger. 1971. *Politics and Technology.* London: Macmillan.

——. 1972. "The Technological Society and British Politics." *Government and Opposition* 7 (1), (Winter): 56-84.

Wilson, H. T. 1975. "The Sociology of Apocalypse: Jacques Ellul's Reformation of Reformation Thought." *Human Context* 7 (3): 479-494.

——. 1985. "Technology and/as/or the Future." *Philosophy of the Social Sciences* 15: 349-358.

Wink, Walter. 1984. *Naming the Powers: The Language of Power in the New Testament.* Philadelphia: Fortress Press.

——. 1986. *Unmasking the Powers: The Invisible Forces That Determine Human Existence.* Philadelphia: Fortress Press.

——. 1992. *Engaging the Powers: Discernment and Resistance in a World of Domination.* Minneapolis: Fortress Press.

Winner, Langdon. 1977. *Autonomous Technology: Technics-out-of-Control as a Theme in Political Thought.* Cambridge, MA: MIT Press.

Winock, Michel. 1975. *Histoire politique de la revue 'Esprit' 1930-1950.* Paris: Seuil.

Wolterstorff, Nicholas. 1983. *Until Justice and Peace Embrace.* Grand Rapids, Michigan: Eerdmans.

Wren, Gary Paul. 1977. *Technique, Society and Politics: A Critical Study of the Works of Jacques Ellul*. Ph.D. Dissertation, Claremont Graduate School.

Wright, Christopher J. 1983. *Living as the People of God: The Relevance of Old Testament Ethics*. Leicester: IVP.

—. 1990. *The People of God and the State: An Old Testament Perspective*. Bramcote, Nottingham: Grove Books.

Wright, N. T. 1990. "The New Testament and the "State"." *Themelios* 16 (1), (October/November): 11-17.

—. 1992. *The New Testament and the People of God*. London: SPCK.

—. 1996. *Jesus and the Victory of God*. London: SPCK.

Yoder, John Howard. 1984. *The Priestly Kingdom: Social Ethics as Gospel*. Notre Dame, Indiana: University of Notre Dame Press.

—. 1992. *Nevertheless: Varieties of Religious Pacifism*. Scottdale, Pennsylvania: Herald Press.

—. 1994. *The Politics of Jesus (2nd, Revd Edn)*. Carlisle: Paternoster.

Ziesler, John. 1989. *Paul's Letter to the Romans*. London: SCM Press.

Zorn, Jean-Francois. 1971. *Deus ex machina (le Dieu machine): présentation et interprétation de la pensée sociologique et théologique de Monsieur Jacques Ellul*. License en Théologie Thesis, Faculté de Théologie Protestante de Montepellier.

Index

Paternoster Biblical and Theological Monographs

Joseph Abraham
Eve: Accused or Acquitted?
A Reconsideration of Feminist Readings
of the Creation Narrative Texts in Genesis 1–3
Two contrary views dominate contemporary feminist biblical scholarship. One finds in the Bible an unequivocal equality between the sexes from the very creation of humanity, whilst the other sees the biblical text as irredeemably patriarchal and androcentric. Dr. Abraham enters into dialogue with both camps as well as introducing his own method of approach. An invaluable tool for any one who is interested in this contemporary debate.
2002/ 0-85364-971-5 /

Emil Bartos
Deification in Eastern Orthodox Theology
An Evaluation and Critique of the Theology of Dumitru Staniloae
Bartos studies a fundamental yet neglected aspect of Orthodox theology: deification. By examining the doctrines of anthropology, christology, soteriology and ecclesiology as they relate to deification, he provides an important contribution to contemporary dialogue between Eastern and Western theologians.
1999 / 0-85364-956-1 / xi + 370pp

Jonathan F. Bayes
The Weakness of the Law
God's Law and the Christian in New Testament Perspective
A study of the four New Testament books which refer to the law as weak (Acts, Romans, Galatians, Hebrews) leads to a defence of the third use in the Reformed debate about the law in the life of the believer.
2000 / 0-85364-957-X / xi + 243pp

Mark Bonnington
The Antioch Episode of Galatians 2:11–14
in Historical and Cultural Context
The Galatians 2 'incident' in Antioch over table-fellowship suggests significant disagreement between the leading apostles. This book analyses the background to the disagreement by locating the incident within the dynamics of social interaction between Jews and Gentiles. It proposes a new way of understanding the relationship between the individuals and issues involved.
2002 / 1-84227-050-8 /

Mark Bredin
Jesus as a Non-Violent Revolutionary
A Study in the Functional Christology of the Book of Revelation
2003 / 1-84227-153-9 /

Colin J. Bulley
The Priesthood of Some Believers
Developments in the Christian Literature of
the First Three Centuries
The first in-depth treatment of early Christian texts on the priesthood of all believers shows that the developing priesthood of the ordained related closely to the division between laity and clergy and had deleterious effects on the practice of the general priesthood.
2000 / 1-84227-034-6 / xii + 336pp

Daniel J-S Chae
Paul as Apostle to the Gentiles
His Apostolic Self-awareness and its Influence on
the Soteriological Argument in Romans
Opposing 'the post-Holocaust interpretation of Romans', Daniel Chae competently demonstrates that Paul argues for the equality of Jew and Gentile in Romans. Chae's fresh exegetical interpretation is academically outstanding and spiritually encouraging.
1997 / 0-85364-829-8 / xiv + 378pp

Luke L. Cheung
The Genre, Composition and Hermeneutics of
the Epistle of James
The present work examines the employment of wisdom genre with
a certain compositional structure and the interpretation of the law
through the Jesus' tradition of the double love command by the
author of the Epistle of James to serve his purpose in promoting
perfection and warning against doubleness among the
eschatologically renewed people of God in the Diaspora.
2002 / 1-84227-062-1 /

Andrew C. Clark
Parallel Lives
The Relation of Paul to the Apostles in the Lucan Perspective
This study of the Peter–Paul parallels in Acts argues that their
purpose was to emphasize the themes of continuity in salvation
history and the unity of the Jewish and Gentile missions. New light
is shed on Luke's literary techniques, partly through a comparison
with Plutarch.
2001 / 1-84227-035-4 / xviii + 384pp

Sylvia I. Collinson
Discipling as an Educational Strategy
An Enquiry into the Congruence of Discipling with the Objectives
of Christian Faith Communities
This study examines the biblical practice of discipling, formulates a
definition, and makes comparisons with modern models of
education. A recommendation is made for greater attention to its
practice today.
2002 / 1-84227-116-4 /

Stephen M. Dunning
The Crisis and the Quest
A Kierkegaardian Reading of Charles Williams
Employing Kierkegaardian categories and analysis, this study
investigates both the central crisis in Charles Williams's authorship
between hermetism and Christianity (Kierkegaard's Religions A
and B), and the quest to resolve this crisis, a quest that ultimately
presses the bounds of orthodoxy.
2000 / 0-85364-985-5 / xxiv + 254pp

Keith Ferdinando
The Triumph of Christ in African Perspective
A Study of Demonology and Redemption in the African Context
The book explores the implications of the gospel for traditional
African fears of occult aggression. It analyses such traditional
approaches to suffering and biblical responses to fears of demonic
evil, concluding with an evaluation of African beliefs from the
perspective of the gospel.
1999 / 0-85364-830-1 / xvii + 450pp

Andrew Goddard
Living the Word, Resisting the World (Provisional title)
The Life and Thought of Jacques Ellul
This work offers a definitive study of both the life and thought of
the French Reformed thinker Jacques Ellul (1912–1994). It will
prove an indispensable resource for those interested in this
influential theologian and sociologist and for Christian ethics and
political thought generally.
2002 / 1-84227-053-2 /

Scott J. Hafemann
Suffering and Ministry in the Spirit
Paul's Defence of His Ministry in 2 Corinthians 2:14 – 3:3
Shedding new light on the way Paul defended his apostleship, the
author offers a careful, detailed study of 2 Corinthians 2:14 – 3:3
linked with other key passages throughout 1 and 2 Corinthians.
Demonstrating the unity and coherence of Paul's argument in this
passage, the author shows that Paul's suffering served as the
vehicle for revealing God's power and glory through the Spirit.
2000 / 0-85364-967-7 / xiv + 261pp

John G. Kelly
One God, One People
*The Differentiated Unity of the People of God
in the Theology of Jürgen Moltmann*
The author expounds and critiques Moltmann's doctrine of God
and highlights the systematic connections between it and
Moltmann's influential discussion of Israel. He then proposes a
fresh approach to Jewish–Christian relations building on
Moltmann's work using insights from Habermas and Rawls.
2003 / 0-85346-969-3 /

Mark Lovatt
Confronting the Will-to-Power
A Reconsideration of the Theology of Reinhold Neibuhr
Confronting the Will-to-Power is an analysis of the theology of
Reinhold Niebuhr, arguing that his work is an attempt to identify,
and provide a practical theological answer to, the existence and
nature of human evil.
2001 / 1-84227-054-0 / xvii + 217pp

Neil B. MacDonald
Karl Barth and the Strange New World within the Bible
Barth, Wittgenstein, and the Metadilemmas of the Enlightenment
Barth's discovery of the strange new world within the Bible is
examined in the context of Kant, Hume, Overbeck, and, most
importantly, Wittgenstein. Covers some fundamental issues in
theology today; epistemology, the final form of the text and biblical
truth-claims.
2000 / 0-85364-970-7 / xxvi + 373pp

Gillian McCulloch
The Deconstruction of Dualism in Theology
with Special Reference to Ecofeminist Theology
and New Age Spirituality
This book challenges eco-theological anti-dualism in Christian
theology, arguing that dualism has a twofold function in Christian
religious discourse. Firstly, it enables us to express the discontinuities and divisions that are part of the process of reality. Secondly,
dualistic language allows us to express the mysteries of divine
transcendence/immanence and the survival of the soul without
collapsing into monism and materialism, both of which are
problematic for Christian epistemology.
2002 / 1-84227-044-3 / xii + 281pp

Leslie McCurdy
Attributes and Atonement
The Holy Love of God in the Theology of P.T. Forsyth
Attributes and Atonement is an intriguing full-length study of P.T.
Forsyth's doctrine of the cross as it relates particularly to God's
holy love. It includes an unparalleled bibliography of both primary
and secondary material relating to Forsyth.
1999 / 0-85364-833-6 / xii + 327pp

Nozomu Miyahira
Towards a Theology of the Concord of God
A Japanese Perspective on the Trinity
This book introduces a new Japanese theology and a unique
Trinitarian formula based on the Japanese intellectual climate: three
betweennesses and one concord. It also presents a new interpretation of the Trinity, a co-subordinationism, which is in line with
orthodox Trinitarianism; each single person of the Trinity is
eternally and equally subordinate (or serviceable) to the other
persons, so that they retain the mutual dynamic equality.
2000 / 0-85364-863-8 / xiv + 256pp

Stephen Motyer
Your Father the Devil?
A New Approach to John and 'The Jews'
Who are 'the Jews' in John's Gospel? Defending John against the
charge of antisemitism, Motyer argues that, far from demonising
the Jews, the Gospel seeks to present Jesus as 'Good News for
Jews' in a late first-century setting.
1997 / 0-85364-832-8 / xiii + 260pp

Eddy José Muskus
**Origins and Early Development of Liberation Theology in
Latin America**
With Particular Reference to Gustavo Gutiérrez
This work challenges the fundamental premise of Liberation
Theology, 'opting for the poor', and its claim that Christ is found in
them. It also argues that Liberation Theology emerged as a direct
result of the failure of the Roman Catholic Church in Latin
America.
2002 / 0-85364-974-X /

Esther Ng
Reconstructing Christian Origins?
*The Feminist Theology of Elizabeth Schüssler Fiorenza:
An Evaluation*
In a detailed evaluation, the author challenges Elizabeth Schüssler
Fiorenza's reconstruction of early Christian origins and her
underlying presuppositions. The author also presents her own views
on women's role both then and now.
2002 / 1-84227-055-9 /

Ian Paul
Power to See the World Anew
The Value of Paul Ricoeur's Hermeneutic of Metaphor
in Interpreting the Symbolism of Revelation 12 and 13
This book is a study of the hermeneutics of metaphor of Paul
Ricoeur, one of the most important writers on hermeneutics and
metaphor of the last century. It sets out the key points of his theory,
important criticisms of his work, and how his approach, modified in
the light of these criticisms, offers a methodological framework for
reading apocalyptic texts.
2002 / 1-84227-056-7 /

David Powys
'Hell': A Hard Look at a Hard Question
The Fate of the Unrighteous in New Testament Thought
This comprehensive treatment seeks to unlock the original meaning
of terms and phrases long thought to support the traditional doctrine
of hell. It concludes that there is an alternative – one which is more
biblical, and which can positively revive the rationale for Christian
mission.
1999 / 0-85364-831-X / xxii + 478pp

Ed Rybarczyk
Beyond Salvation
An Analysis of the Doctrine of Christian Transformation
Comparing Eastern Orthodoxy and Classical Pentecostalism
2003 / 1-84227-144-X /

Signe Sandsmark
Is World View Neutral Education Possible and Desirable?
A Christian Response to Liberal Arguments
(Published jointly with The Stapleford Centre)
This thesis discusses reasons for belief in world view neutrality,
and argues that 'neutral' education will have a hidden, but strong
world view influence. It discusses the place for Christian education
in the common school.
2000 / 0-85364-973-1 / xiv + 181pp

Andrew Sloane
On Being a Christian in the Academy
Nicholas Wolterstorff and the Practice of Christian Scholarship
An exposition and critical appraisal of Nicholas Wolterstorff's
epistemology in the light of the philosophy of science, and an
application of his thought to the practice of Christian scholarship.
2002 / 1-84227-058-3 /

Daniel Strange
The Possibility of Salvation Among the Unevangelised
An Analysis of Inclusivism in Recent Evangelical Theology
For evangelical theologians, the 'fate of the unevangelised'
impinges upon fundamental tenets of evangelical identity. The
position known as 'inclusivism', defined by the belief that the
unevangelised can be ontologically saved by Christ whilst being
epistemologically unaware of him, has been defended most
vigorously by the Canadian evangelical Clark H. Pinnock. Through
a detailed analysis and critique of Pinnock's work, this book
examines a cluster of issues surrounding the unevangelised and its
implication for Christology, soteriology and the doctrine of
revelation.
2001 / 1-84227-047-8 / xviii + 362pp

G. Michael Thomas
The Extent of the Atonement
A Dilemma for Reformed Theology from Calvin to the Consensus
A study of the way Reformed theology addressed the question, 'Did
Christ die for all, or for the elect only?', commencing with John
Calvin, and including debates with Lutheranism, the Synod of Dort
and the teaching of Moïse Amyraut.
1997 / 0-85364-828-X / ix + 277pp

Mark Thompson
A Sure Ground on Which to Stand
*The Relation of Authority and Interpretative Method
of Luther's Approach to Scripture
2003 / 1-84227-145-8 /*

Graham Tomlin
The Power of the Cross
Theology and the Death of Christ in Paul, Luther and Pascal
This book explores the theology of the cross in St Paul, Luther and
Pascal. It offers new perspectives on the theology of each, and
some implications for the nature of power, apologetics, theology
and church life in a postmodern context.
1999 / 0-85364-984-7 / xiv + 343pp

Kevin Walton
Thou Traveller Unknown
The Presence and Absence of God in the Jacob Narrative
The author offers a fresh reading of the story of Jacob in the book
of Genesis through the paradox of divine presence and absence.
The work also seeks to make a contribution to Pentateuchal studies
by bringing together a close reading of the final text with
historicalcritical insights, doing justice to the text's historical depth,
final form and canonical status.
2002 / 1-84227-059-1 /

Graham J. Watts
Revelation and the Spirit
*A Comparative Study of the Relationship between
the Doctrine of Revelation and Pneumatology in the Theology of
Eberhard Jüngel and of Wolfhart Pannenberg*
The relationship between revelation and pneumatology is relatively
unexplored. This approach offers a fresh angle on two important
twentieth-century theologians and raises pneumatological questions
which are theologically crucial and relevant to mission in a post
modern culture.
2002 / 1-84227-104-0 /

Alistair Wilson
**Matthew's Portrait of Jesus the Judge, with Special Reference
to Matthew 21–25**
2003 / 1-84227-146-6 /

Nigel G. Wright
Disavowing Constantine
*Mission, Church and the Social Order in the Theologies of John
Howard Yoder and Jürgen Moltmann*
This book is a timely restatement of a radical theology of church
and state in the Anabaptist and Baptist tradition. Dr. Wright
constructs his argument in dialogue and debate with Yoder and
Moltmann, major contributors to a free church perspective.
2000 / 0-85364-978-2 / xv + 251pp

Stephen Wright
The Voice of Jesus
Studies in the Interpretation of Six Gospel Parables
This literary study considers how the 'voice' of Jesus has been
heard in different periods of parable interpretation, and how the
categories of figure and trope may help us towards a sensitive
reading of the parables today.
2000 / 0-85364-975-8 / xiv + 280pp

The Paternoster Press
P.O. Box 300
Carlisle, Cumbria,
CA3 0QS
United Kingdom

Web: www.paternoster-publishing.com